Advanced

Ruth Gairns and Stuart Redman

Oxford
Word Skills

OXFORD
UNIVERSITY PRESS

OXFORD
UNIVERSITY PRESS

Great Clarendon Street, Oxford OX2 6DP

Oxford University Press is a department of the University of Oxford.
It furthers the University's objective of excellence in research, scholarship,
and education by publishing worldwide in

Oxford New York

Auckland Cape Town Dar es Salaam Hong Kong Karachi
Kuala Lumpur Madrid Melbourne Mexico City Nairobi
New Delhi Shanghai Taipei Toronto

With offices in

Argentina Austria Brazil Chile Czech Republic France Greece
Guatemala Hungary Italy Japan Poland Portugal Singapore
South Korea Switzerland Thailand Turkey Ukraine Vietnam

OXFORD and OXFORD ENGLISH are registered trade marks of
Oxford University Press in the UK and in certain other countries

© Oxford University Press 2009

ACKNOWLEDGEMENTS

*The authors and publisher are grateful to those who have given permission to
reproduce the following extracts and adaptations of copyright material*:
p 86 adapted from 'A Revolutionary Era in Medicine',
www.fiftyyears.healthcare.ucla.edu. Reproduced by permission.
p 98 from 'Organised Crime', www.soca.gov.uk © Copyright SOCA
Serious Organised Crime Agency. All rights reserved 2006. Reproduced
under the terms specified on the website.

Sources: www.holisticonline.com, www.raisingkids.co.uk,
www.uk.tickle.com, www.acornhouserestaurant.com,
www.bbc.co.uk, www.npr.org, http://en.wikipedia.org

Illustrations by: Mark Duffin p 145; Andy Hammond pp 134, 138, 162,
166; Gavin Reece p 29; Willie Ryan pp 102, 125, 159
Cover illustration by Carol Verbyst

*The authors and publisher would also like to thank the following for permission
to reproduce the following photographs*: Alamy pp 7 (leak/David Wasserman/
Jupiterimages/ Brand X), 7 (microscope/IS-200601/Image Source Black),
14 (drawing pins/Indigo Photo Agency), 14 (paper clips/Barrie Watts),
14 (barbed wire/colinspics), 14 (nail polish/Jupiterimages/ Pixland), 17
(firefighters /John Powell Photographer), 30 (IS669/Image Source Black),
31 (clenched fist/Vincent Abbey), 31 (leaning towards/Mel Yates/Cultura),
31 (fiddling with hair /Radius Images), 31 (stroking earlobe/Dorota
Szpil), 33 (stretching/paul postle), 33 (press-ups/paul postle), 35 (growl/
F1online digitale Bildagentur GmbH), 35 (buzz/CJPhotography), 35
(crow/Tony Fagan), 35 (hoot/Bob Elsdale/Eureka), 40 (leg showing
muscle/Nucleus Medical Art, Inc/PHOTOTAKE Inc.), 45 (axel leschinski),
51 (Rafal Strzechowski/PhotoAlto), 61 (pomegranate/D. Hurst), 61
(passion fruit/Arco Images/imagebroker), 61 (papaya/blickwinkel/
fotototo), 61 (beetroot/Nigel Cattlin), 61 (bean sprouts/Purestock), 61
(squash/Krys Bailey), 61 (fennel/Tim Hill), 61 (almonds/Geoffrey Kidd),
61 (cashews/Nikreates), 61 (lentils/foodfolio), 61 (cinnamon/Teubner
Foodfoto/Bon Appetit), 61 (sage/foodfolio), 61 (sultanas/Wolfgang
Heidasch), 61 (raisins/William Nicklin), 62 (wok/Arras, Klaus/Bon Appetit),
62 (whisk/foodfolio), 62 (grater/Joe Tree), 62 (kitchen scales/foodfolio),
64 (Algarve/Alan Copson/Jon Arnold Images Ltd), 64 (Great Wall of
China/Jon Arnold Images Ltd), 70 (plant/Cleuna (Medicinal Plants)),
71 (digging/David Noton Photography), 71 (mowing/aberystwyth), 82
(light bulb/Clynt Garnham), 82 (battery charger/Jeff Lam), 86 (stethoscope/
Judith Collins), 113 (Alessandra Sarti/imagebroker), 131 (Tom Grill/
Corbis Premium RF), 140 (Collection24/Glow Images), 144 (dilapidated
house/Coston Stock), 144 (ruined tower/Brian Gibbs (Oxfordshire)/
PBPA/PBPA Paul Beard Photo Agency), 145 (guidebook/Jon Bower),
145 (Egyptian ornament/Pink Sun Media), 145 (grandfather clock/
Adrian Sherratt), 145 (exercise bike/IS326/Image Source Black), 178
(The Print Collector), 184 (winking/Dimitri Vervits), 193 (magnet/D.
Hurst), 200 (Philip Wolmuth); Corbis pp 34 (house with lightning/Craig
Aurness), 34 (woman screaming/John Springer Collection), 35 (howl/
Daniel J. Cox), 38 (Goodshoot), 97 (Richard Bryant/Arcaid), 193 (bullet-
proof vest/Reuters); Dorling Kindersley pp 62 (deep fat fryer/David
Murray and Jules Selmes), 71 (pruning/Peter Anderson); Getty Images
pp 7 (flood/Daniel Berehulak), 12 (Marc Romanelli/The Image Bank), 28
(sister/Bambu Productions/Iconica), 28 (uncle/Leland Bobbe/Stone), 28
(Gran/Chris Windsor/Riser), 35 (bark/Dorling Kindersley), 35 (squeak/
Konrad Wothe/Minden Pictures), 37 (Richard Packwood/Photolibrary),
46 (William Edward King/Stone), 62 (food processor/Dave King/Dorling
Kindersley), 62 (peeler/Lew Robertson/StockFood Creative), 62 (corkscrew/
Steve Gorton/Dorling Kindersley), 64 (Prague/Peter Adams/Riser), 70
(butterfly/Pete Turner/The Image Bank), 71 (planting/Johner/Johner
Images), 83 (Joerg Lehmann/StockFood Creative), 85 (Gerry Ellis/
Minden Pictures), 86 (scanner/Dana Neely/Taxi), 102 (DON EMMERT/
AFP), 182 (Mark Horn/Photonica), 183 (footings/Zubin Shroff/Stone+),
183 (crane/Johannes Kroemer/Photonica), 184 (mobile phone/Erik Von
Weber/Taxi); PA Photos pp 17 (flames/Nikolas Giakoumidis/AP), 68
(Alvaro Barrientos/AP); Punchstock pp 10 (Dougal Waters/Digital Vision),
28 (Keira/PhotoAlto/Laurence Mouton), 28 (Tom/Image Source), 28
(Jessica/Plush Studios/Photodisc), 31 (folded arms/Marcy Maloy/Photodisc),
35 (roar/Tom Brakefield/Digital Vision), 40 (scratching head/George
Doyle/Stockbyte), 50 (Nancy R Cohen/Photodisc), 56 (Foodcollection),
61 (ginger/Stockdisc/Photodisc), 61 (coriander/Brand X/Burke Triolo),
62 (casserole/Stockbyte), 62 (colander/Stockbyte), 62 (garlic crusher/
Creativ Studio Heinemann/Westend61), 62 (lemon squeezer/Image
Source), 91 (George Doyle & Ciaran Griffin/Stockbyte), 114 (Digital
Vision), 145 (mobile phone/George Diebold/Digital Vision), 183 (glass
building/Frederic Cirou/PhotoAlto Agency RF Collections), 198 (Peter
Dazeley/Photographer's Choice RF); Royalty-free pp 61 (radishes), 61
(artichoke/Ingram), 62 (steamer/Photodisc), 62 (sieve/Stockbyte), 62
(ladle/simple stock shots); Courtesy of The Woman in Black. Adapted by
Stephen Mallatratt from the novel by Susan Hill. Production photos/
Pascal Molliere p 66

Images sourced by: Suzanne Williams/Pictureresearch.co.uk

*The authors and publishers would like to thank teachers and students from the
following schools who helped with the development of this book*: International
House, Business English Centre, Madrid, Spain; Shamrock School of
English, Getxo, Bizkaia, Spain; English Language Institute, Macarena,
Seville, Spain; English Centre, Valencia, Spain; Tti School of English,
London, UK; Bell International, London, UK; Mark Appleton, Mark
Lloyd, and the students at International House, Bath, UK; Małgorzata
Salomądry, Dorota Brach, Anna Wnuk, and Iza Algermissen in Poland

They would also like to thank: Rachel Godfrey, Carol Tabor, Michael Terry,
and Scott Thornbury for their valuable comments on early drafts of the
text; the actors Nigel Greaves and Joanna Hall and The Soundhouse Ltd
for the listening material; Suzanne Williams for picture research.

The authors would like to acknowledge their use of the following dictionaries:
Oxford Advanced Learner's Dictionary, Longman Dictionary of
Contemporary English, Macmillan English Dictionary for Advanced
Learners.

Contents

Introduction 5

Starter: vocabulary at advanced level 7

Abbreviations 9

Expanding your vocabulary

1 I can talk about meaning and style 10
2 I can use familiar words in a new way 12
3 I can use compounds 14
4 I can use a range of collocations 17
5 I can use a dictionary productively 20
6 I can build word families 22

   Review 25

The body

7 I can describe the human body 28
8 I can talk about body language 30
9 I can describe physical movement 32
10 I can describe sounds 34
11 I can describe sight 36
12 I can describe touch, smell, and taste 38
13 I can describe illness and injuries 40

   Review 42

You and other people

14 I can discuss aspects of character 45
15 I can talk about feelings 48
16 I can talk about relationships 50
17 I can talk about people I admire
   and loathe 52
18 I can talk about behaviour 54
19 I can talk about manners 56

   Review 58

Leisure and lifestyle

20 I can talk about food 61
21 I can talk about holidays 64
22 I can talk about plays and films 66
23 I can talk about competitive sport 68
24 I can talk about gardens and nature 70
25 I can talk about shopping habits 72
26 I can talk about socializing 74

   Review 76

A changing world

27 I can talk about change 80
28 I can talk about energy conservation 82
29 I can discuss wildlife under threat 84
30 I can describe medical advances 86
31 I can talk about communication
   technology 88
32 I can talk about migration 90

   Review 92

Institutions

33 I can discuss health services 94
34 I can talk about local government 96
35 I can talk about crime and the police 98
36 I can discuss prisons 100
37 I can talk about the armed forces 102

   Review 105

News and current affairs

38   I can understand news headlines   108
39   I can understand news journalism   110
40   I can read human interest stories   112
41   I can talk about celebrity   114
42   I can discuss political beliefs   116
43   I can talk about areas of conflict   118

Review   119

Work and finance

44   I can explain job benefits   121
45   I can describe ways of working   122
46   I can talk about the business world   124
47   I can talk about money markets   126
48   I can talk about personal finance   128
49   I can discuss time management   130
50   I can discuss workplace disputes   132
51   I can talk about office problems   134

Review   135

Concepts

52   I can describe cause and effect   138
53   I can talk about truth and lies   140
54   I can discuss problems and solutions   142
55   I can describe old and new   144
56   I can talk about success and failure   146
57   I can describe the past, present,
     and future   148

Review   150

Spoken English

58   I can use everyday language   152
59   I can use idioms and set phrases (1)   154
60   I can use idioms and set phrases (2)   156
61   I can use set phrases with two key words 158
62   I can use similes   159
63   I can use a range of phrasal verbs   160
64   I can use discourse markers   162
65   I can use vague language   164
66   I can use sayings and proverbs   165

Review   168

Written English

67   I can write a formal letter   172
68   I can use formal link words   175
69   I can use academic English   176
70   I can talk about literature   178
71   I can use scientific English   180
72   I can use technical English   182
73   I can use abbreviations   184

Review   187

Aspects of language

74   I can use prefixes   190
75   I can use suffixes   192
76   I can use words with prepositions   194
77   I can use prepositional phrases   196
78   I can use a range of adjectives   198
79   I can use different types of adverb   200
80   I can use euphemisms   203

Review   204

Vocabulary building   207
Answer key   209
Answer key to review units   227
List of spotlight boxes   235
Word list / Index   236

Introduction

What is Oxford Word Skills?

Oxford Word Skills is a series of three books for students to learn, practise, and revise new vocabulary.

Basic:	elementary and pre-intermediate (CEF levels A1 and A2)
Intermediate:	intermediate and upper-intermediate (CEF levels B1 and B2)
Advanced:	advanced (CEF levels C1 and C2)

There are over 2,000 new words or phrases in each level, and all of the material can be used in the classroom or for self-study.

How are the books organized?

Each book contains 80 units of vocabulary presentation and practice. Units are between one and three pages long, depending on the topic. New vocabulary is presented in manageable quantities for learners, with practice exercises following immediately, usually on the same page. The units are grouped together thematically in modules of five to ten units. At the end of each module there are further practice exercises in the review units, so that learners can revise and test themselves on the vocabulary learned.

At the back of each book you will find:

- vocabulary building tables
- an answer key for all the exercises (other than personalized exercises)
- a list of all the vocabulary taught, with a phonetic pronunciation guide and a unit reference to where the item appears

There is a CD-ROM at each level with oral pronunciation models for all the vocabulary taught, and further practice exercises, including listening activities.

What vocabulary is included?

At advanced level, the vocabulary includes:

- a wide range of topics, e.g. behaviour, competitive sport, medical advances
- a range of concepts, e.g. problems and solutions, truth and lies, old and new
- different fields of academic English, e.g. literature, science, technical English
- an increased focus on different styles of English, e.g. informal English, newspaper journalism, formal letters
- a wide range of idiomatic expressions, with a particular focus on figurative uses of language
- various aspects of language, e.g. compounds, discourse markers, prepositional phrases

The series includes almost all of the words in the Oxford 3000™, which lists the 3,000 words teachers and students should prioritize in their teaching and learning. The list is based on frequency and usefulness to learners, and was developed by Oxford University Press using corpus evidence and information supplied by a panel of over 70 experts in the fields of teaching and language study. In addition, we have included a wide range of high frequency phrases, e.g. *at the last minute, for the time being*, as well as items which are extremely useful in a particular context, e.g. *in danger of extinction* when discussing wildlife conservation, or *remanded in custody* when discussing the law.

We have taken great care to ensure that learners will be able to understand the meaning of all the new words and phrases as used in the particular contexts by supplying a clear illustration or glossary definition. Learners should be aware that many English words have more than one meaning, and they should refer to an appropriate learner's dictionary for information on other meanings.

How can teachers use the material in the classroom?

New vocabulary at this level is presented primarily through different types of text, but also through tables, and where appropriate, through visuals. The meaning of new vocabulary is explained in an accompanying glossary unless it is illustrated in visuals or diagrams. Important items, or those that require additional information, are highlighted by means of 'spotlight' boxes.

Here is a procedure you could follow:

- Students study the presentation for 5–10 minutes (longer if necessary).
- You answer any queries the students may have about the items, and provide a pronunciation model of the items for your students where necessary.
- Students do the first exercise, which they can check for themselves using the answer key, or you can go over the answers with the whole class.
- When you are satisfied, you can ask students to go on to further exercises, while you monitor them as they work individually or in pairs, and assist where necessary.
- When they have completed the written exercises, students can often test themselves on the new vocabulary using the cover card enclosed with the book. The material has been designed so that students can usually cover the glossary definitions while they look at the target items, and test themselves; or cover the items and look at the definitions. This is a simple, quick, and easy way for learners to test themselves over and over again, so there is no pressure on you to keep searching for different exercises.
- After a period of time has elapsed, perhaps a couple of days or a week, you can use the review exercises for further consolidation and testing.
- You will often notice the headings 'About you' or 'About your country'. These indicate personalized exercises which give learners an opportunity to use the new vocabulary within the context of their own lives. Students can write answers to these, but they make ideal pair work activities for learners to practise their spoken English while using the new vocabulary. If you use these as speaking activities, students could then write their answers (or their partner's answers) as follow-up.

How can students use the material on their own?

The material has been designed so that it can be used effectively both in the classroom or by learners working alone. If working alone, learners should look at the Starter unit first. For self-study, we recommend that learners use the book alongside the CD-ROM, as it gives them a pronunciation model for every item of vocabulary, as well as further practice exercises. They can check their own answers and use the cover card to test themselves. One advantage of self-study learning is that students can select the topics that interest them, or the topics where they most need to expand their knowledge.

Starter: vocabulary at advanced level

Six steps to a wider vocabulary

Here are six ways to help you achieve a wider vocabulary, and become a more effective learner. Each one illustrates a feature of vocabulary learning which is given particular emphasis at the advanced level of *Oxford Word Skills*.

1 Adding new meanings to familiar words

An important part of vocabulary expansion is learning new meanings for familiar words.

What are the different meanings of *still* in these sentences?
(Go to Units 11, 28, and 64 to find or check the answers.)

Come over here and stand **still**. _____

These apples are very nice, but the others are better **still**. _____

My arm's very sore after the accident. **Still**, *it feels better than it did yesterday.* _____

2 Understanding the figurative meaning of vocabulary items

Many words have a literal meaning and a figurative meaning. For example, the literal meaning of *crawl* is to move forwards on your hands and knees, but we can also describe traffic as *crawling along the road*, which means that it is moving very slowly.

What is the figurative meaning of the words in bold in these sentences?
(Go to Units 39 and 42 to find or check the answers.)

The contents of the report have already been **leaked** *to the press.*
_____

Thousands of refugees are now **flooding** *across the border.*
_____

The Trade Secretary could find herself under the **microscope**.
_____

3 Expanding your knowledge of collocation

These are common examples of collocation.

She's an **old friend**.   (= a friend I have known a long time)
I **missed** *the* **bus**.   (= I wasn't able to catch the bus)
It's **highly unlikely** *he'll come.*   (= it's very unlikely he'll come)

In English, we choose to combine certain words in order to express particular meanings. Other languages might choose different words to express the same ideas; for example, many languages would say *I lost the bus* where we say *I missed the bus*. Common collocations appear in all three levels of *Oxford Word Skills*, but in the Advanced there is an even greater emphasis on this aspect of vocabulary learning.

Can you complete the collocations in these sentences?
(Go to Units 4, 9, 45, and 50 to find or check the answers.)

Last night we had **torrential** _____.

His mother is very elderly and needs **constant** _____.

If we work together on this, we'll be able to _____ *our* **resources**.

Do you think they'll be able to _____ *the* **deadlock**?

4 Using a wider range of idiomatic expressions

At an advanced level you should be able to use a wider range of idiomatic expressions.

Can you complete these idioms? (Go to Units 39, 59, and 61 to find or check the answers.)

It may seem a lot of money, but really it's just **a drop in the** _____.

They're bound to win; it's **a foregone** _____.

She might as well apply for the job; she's **got nothing to** _____.

First and _____ *we must decide what to do.*

5 Vocabulary building

At the end of a glossary entry for a particular word, we often include related word forms. Here is an example from Unit 53.

Glossary	
deteriorate	become worse. **deterioration** N.
interrogation	the process of asking sb a lot of questions, especially in an aggressive way. **interrogate sb** V.
catch sb out	make sb make a mistake which shows they have been lying.
humiliated	feeling ashamed because you have lost the respect of other people. **humiliate sb** V. **humiliation** N.
needless to say	obviously.

We also provide vocabulary building tables at the back of the book. Building word families is an easy way to expand your vocabulary and increase your range of expression.

Can you complete these sentences with the correct form of the word in capital letters? (Go to Units 36 and 71, and the vocabulary building tables on pages 207–8, to find or check the answers.)

Most people find the treatment very _____. THERAPY

His behaviour was very _____. PROVOKE

They are sure to _____ *the results carefully.* SCRUTINY

Some people prefer to maintain their _____. ANONYMOUS

6 Vocabulary expansion beyond the book

At this level, we have introduced a new feature called **more words**. After you have completed a unit and the review section for that unit, **more words** gives you an opportunity to expand your vocabulary further within the same topic or linguistic area. Here is an example, from Unit 9.

7   On a long walk, why might you alternate between walking and running? _____

8   What should you do if you feel stiff? _____

A Z   more words: *stumble, trudge, shuffle, meander, get a* **move** *on, stampede*

Unit 10

Suggested procedure with more words

- Look up the words and phrases listed in **more words** in a good monolingual dictionary. In the *Oxford Advanced Learner's Dictionary*, you will find that the meanings of the phrases are explained at the entry for the word in **bold**, although it may be different in some other dictionaries.

- Write the word or phrase in your notebook, then leave a small gap before adding the meaning of the item. Below the meaning, write an example sentence using the target word or phrase; take one from the dictionary, or write your own. For example:

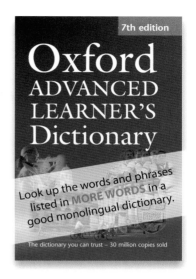

predicament a difficult or unpleasant situation, especially one where it is difficult to know what to do:
Without any money, he was in quite a predicament.

The CD-ROM and cover card

A Walking and running

Word	Example

 You can use the **CD-ROM** to listen to the texts and dialogues, or to hear the words, and then practise the pronunciation. Or you can look at the **word list** (pages 236–56) to find out how to say the words.

Remember to test yourself

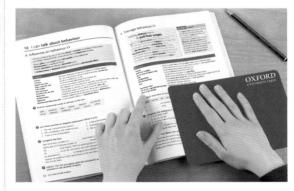

Use the **cover card** to test yourself when you have completed the exercises.

Abbreviations

N	noun	C	countable
V	verb	U	uncountable
ADJ	adjective	PP	past participle
ADV	adverb	AmE	American English
OPP	opposite	BrE	British English
SYN	synonym	sth	something (used in glossaries and tables)
INF	informal	sb	somebody (used in glossaries and tables)
FML	formal	etc.	You use 'etc.' at the end of a list to show there are other things, but you aren't going to say them all.
PL	plural		
SING	singular	i.e.	that is
USU	usually	e.g.	for example

1 I can **talk about meaning and style**

A Asking about meaning 🎧

A Are the words *phase* and *stage* **synonymous**?
B In one **sense**, they're **interchangeable**. They both
  mean a particular point in a process.

A It's a bit **ambiguous** to say 'She's a good student', isn't it?
B Yes, you can **interpret** it in different ways. *Good* can
  mean well behaved or hard-working.

A The meaning of *wrapping paper* is **transparent**,
  isn't it?
B Yes, it's **self-explanatory** – just paper for
  wrapping presents and stuff.

A Can you give me a more **precise** definition of *soul*?
B Well, it's **virtually** the same as *spirit* – the part of
  you that is believed to exist after you die. But it can
  also mean your inner character.

Glossary

synonymous	having the same, or nearly the same, meaning. **synonym** N.
sense	the meaning of a word or phrase.
interchangeable	if two things are **interchangeable** you can use one instead of the other and the effect will be the same.
ambiguous	not clear; able to be explained in different ways. **ambiguity** N.
interpret sth	decide that sth has a particular meaning. **interpretation** N.
transparent	(of language) easy to understand. OPP **opaque**.
self-explanatory	easy to understand and not needing more explanation.
precise	clear and accurate. SYN **exact**. **precision** N.
virtually	almost; very nearly (**virtually the same/ impossible/certain**).

❶ Is the meaning the same or different? Write S or D.

1	The meaning's virtually the same.	The meaning's opaque.	
2	This is the final phase of the project.	This is the final stage of the project.	
3	These two words are synonymous.	These two words mean the same.	
4	These phrases are self-explanatory.	These phrases are interchangeable.	
5	The meaning is ambiguous.	The meaning is exactly the same.	
6	What she said was quite transparent.	What she said was quite precise.	
7	The soul lives on after the body dies.	The spirit lives on after the body dies.	
8	The word *leg* has several senses.	The word *leg* has several meanings.	

❷ Complete the sentences with the correct form of the word in capitals at the end.

1 If you want to make something clear, it's better to avoid _____ . AMBIGUOUS
2 She always expresses herself with accuracy and _____ . PRECISE
3 *Hide* and *conceal* are very similar, but not completely _____ . SYNONYM
4 In most contexts, *get better* and *improve* are _____ . CHANGE
5 I think this sentence is open to _____ . INTERPRET
6 The instructions were _____ ; a child could understand them. EXPLAIN

 Remember to test yourself

B Explaining meaning and style 🎧

Word	Example	Meaning
irony N **ironic** ADJ	*'Thank you, Sam,' she said, with **heavy irony**. In fact, Sam had hardly helped at all.*	the use of words to say the opposite of what you mean, often humorously (**a trace/hint of irony** = a little irony).
sarcasm N **sarcastic** ADJ	*'I've broken your CD.'* *'Oh, that's just great,' was her **sarcastic** reply.*	the use of words to say the opposite of what you mean in order to be unpleasant to sb or **make fun of** sb.
figurative	*Slim is used **figuratively** in the sentence Many firms are slimmer than they were.*	(of words) not used with their **literal** (= usual) meaning.
literary	*Heart can be used in a **literary** way, e.g. She put her hand on her heart.*	used of the kind of language you find in stories and poems.
disapproving	*The dictionary marks stupid as '**disapproving**'.*	(often used in dictionaries) showing that sth is bad or wrong.
old-fashioned	*Spiffing means 'great', but it's very **old-fashioned**.*	no longer modern or fashionable. SYN **dated**. OPP **in current use**.
slang	*In **slang**, wicked means 'very good'.*	very informal words which are not suitable in formal situations.
pejorative	*His **pejorative** comments about my essay upset me.*	FML expressing disapproval or criticism. SYN **derogatory**.
insulting **insult sb** V	*He called Mark an 'old woman': how **insulting**!*	rude or offensive (**deliberately/highly insulting**).

---

spotlight *make fun of someone*

If you **make fun of** or **poke fun at** someone or something, you make jokes about them in an unkind way. To **mock** someone means to make fun of them, often by copying what they say or do.
*Stop **making fun of** her!   He's always **mocking** her country accent.*

---

❸ Circle the correct word(s). Sometimes both words are correct.

1 The literal / literary meaning of curtain is 'a piece of cloth which covers a window'.
2 The curtain fell on her career is figurative / dated, meaning 'her career ended'.
3 I hate people making / poking fun of my pronunciation.
4 She told him his acting was brilliant without a hint / trace of irony.
5 He uses sarcasm / old-fashioned language as a way of insulting people.
6 I got upset when my teacher mocked / insulted the way I pronounced 'castle'.
7 He was being ironic / sarcastic – he didn't mean any harm.
8 Telling me I was a second-rate journalist was highly / deliberately insulting.

❹ Complete the sentences with a suitable word.

1 The word *racist* has a negative meaning and is marked '_____' in the dictionary.
2 Her written work is very _____ : it's a bit like reading a novel by Charles Dickens!
3 The children _____ fun of Josie because of her red hair; it was very cruel of them.
4 My brother's lived abroad for years. He tends to use a lot of informal language and _____ which is not in _____ use, so some of his speech sounds rather _____ .
5 Does this phrase have a positive meaning, or is it _____ ?
6 I know the literal meaning of *flood*, but what does it mean when it's used _____ ?

📖 Remember to test yourself

2 I can use familiar words in a new way

A Phrases and figurative meaning 🎧

Familiar words may appear with an unfamiliar meaning (often a figurative meaning), or surrounded by other words that form an idiom or set phrase.

As I **crawled** along the motorway, I was **having second thoughts** about staying with Marcus. I**'d been in two minds about** going in the first place, but it was **sweet of** him to invite me, and I **wasn't tied up**, so I said, 'Yes'. But now it **dawned on** me that he may have had an **ulterior motive**: he wanted to go out with me! How could I be so **thick**? Marcus was very nice, but a romantic relationship **was the last thing on my mind**. How can I **get out of** this, I wondered? Just as the traffic started to speed up, something went into the back of me and **sent** the car **flying** off the road. Dazed but OK, I pulled my mobile out of my bag. 'Is that you, Marcus? Listen, **you're not gonna believe this**, but . . .'

Glossary

crawl	(of a vehicle) move very slowly.
have second thoughts	start having doubts about a decision you have made.
be in two minds about sth	be unable to decide what to do about sth.
sweet (of sb)	kind (of sb).
be tied up	be busy and unable to do other things.
dawn on sb	If sth **dawns on** you, you begin to realize it for the first time.
ulterior motive	a reason for doing sth that you keep hidden.
thick	INF stupid.
be the last thing on sb's mind	be the thing that sb is least likely to be thinking about.
get out of sth	avoid doing sth.
send sth/sb flying	make sth/sb move quickly and without control.
you're not gonna believe this	used to introduce surprising and often unwelcome news (**gonna** INF = going to).

1 Complete the dialogues with a word or phrase.

1 Do you still want to go? ~ Actually, I'm having ....
2 Are you thinking of getting married? ~ That's the last thing .... !
3 Do you want to go to the wedding? ~ No, but I can't .... it.
4 You're not gonna .... , but . . . ~ You've lost my keys again! How could you?
5 Did he bump into you? ~ Yes, he sent me .... across the room.
6 Are you going or not? ~ I'm afraid I'm still in .... about it.
7 I'm sure it's just an innocent request. ~ Mm. I think he has an .... motive.
8 Could we talk about it this morning? ~ I'm afraid I'm .... this morning.

2 Complete the sentences using words from the glossary with their more common meanings.

1 She's only eight months old, so she's still .... across the living room floor.
2 It's a very .... book: almost 1,000 pages.
3 These oranges are lovely; they're very ....
4 The men were .... , with both hands behind their backs.
5 The morning .... with a clear blue sky after the storm.

Remember to test yourself

B Common verbs with less familiar meanings 🎧

Verb	Example	Meaning
get sth/sb to do sth	*I finally **got** the car to start.* *I couldn't **get** him to leave the party.*	make or persuade sb/sth to do sth.
keep **keep sb going**	*We must eat the grapes – they won't **keep**.* *I'll have a sandwich. That will **keep me going** until lunchtime.*	remain fresh. be enough for sb until a later time.
put sth	*It's hard to **put** your feelings **into words**.* *I think he **put** it very well in his essay.*	say or write sth in a particular way.
push sb	*Some parents **push** their kids really hard.* *I need to **push myself** more at work.*	make sb work harder.
leave sth to/ with sb	*We need to book a table. **I'll leave that to you**.* ***Leave it to/with me** – I'll do it.*	allow sb to take care of sth.
make sth sth	*My watch says 10.20. What time do you **make it**?* *He bought ten more; I **make that** 25 now.*	think or calculate sth to be a particular time or number.
bring sb somewhere	*It was the war that **brought** him to power.* *What **brings** you here? ~ I've got a meeting.*	cause sb to reach a particular condition or place.
come with **come in**	*I'm sure the radio **comes with** batteries.* *The chairs **come in** four different colours.*	be sold or produced with a particular feature.
do (for sb/ sth)	*I peeled six potatoes. Will that **do**?* *Will these shoes **do for** the wedding?*	be enough or be acceptable in a particular situation.

3 One word is missing in each sentence. What is it, and where does it go?

1 How did you him to do it? ~ I offered him money. _____
2 Take this apple to keep you until lunchtime. _____
3 If we can find another ten chairs, that will it 90 altogether. _____
4 It was the fishing that people to this part of the coast. _____
5 We'd better finish the cream – it won't after tomorrow. _____
6 He has great ideas but finds it difficult to them into words. _____
7 I've got a packet of noodles – do you think that will for six people? _____

4 Complete the dialogues with suitable verbs.

A Hello. What (1) _____ you to this part of the building?
B I can't (2) _____ this new clock to work, and it didn't (3) _____ with instructions.
A OK, (4) _____ it with me.
B Thanks. Oh, one other thing, we've run out of paper for the photocopier.
A Er, there's some over there. Will that (5) _____ ?
B Yeah, that'll (6) _____ us going for now.

C What are the bookings like for this evening?
D We had two more this morning, so I (7) _____ that 36 now.
C OK. We'll need more tables, then. Can I (8) _____ that with you?
D I'll see how things go, but I may have to (9) _____ Mario to do it.
C OK, but don't (10) _____ him too hard; he's had a very tough week.

5 ABOUT YOUR LANGUAGE Translate the meanings in the table into your own language.

Remember to test yourself

3 I can **use compounds**

A Nouns 🎧

drawing pins

paper clips

barbed wire

nail polish

Cover the compounds below and read the meanings. Do you know the compounds, or can you guess them?

Meaning	Compound noun
an official document that shows you are qualified to drive	**driving licence**
an official document showing when and where you were born	**birth certificate**
a part for a car or machine to replace an old or broken part	**spare part**
a person walking past a place by chance	**passer-by**
a short holiday from Friday to Sunday, or Saturday to Monday	**long weekend**
the number of years that a person is likely to live	**life expectancy**
a path or route that is quicker than the normal way	**short cut / shortcut**
clothes that you wear to a party to make you appear a different character	**fancy dress**
a short and usually very old song or poem for young children	**nursery rhyme**
a machine into which you put money in the hope of winning more back	**fruit/slot machine**
your closest living relative (often used on official documents)	**next of kin**

❶ Replace the crossed-out word with a more appropriate word that forms a compound.

1 Do you know a short ~~way~~ to the school from here? ....
2 I ripped my shirt on the ~~twisted~~ wire around the field. ....
3 What's the average life ~~length~~ for men in your country? ....
4 I stepped on a drawing ~~nail~~; it really hurt. ....
5 I need some paper ~~staples~~ to put these notes together. ....
6 Have you got any nail ~~paint~~? ....
7 Is it easy to get ~~new~~ parts for your car? ....
8 I stopped and asked a ~~walker~~-by where the park was. ....

❷ Complete the compound in each sentence.

ABOUT YOU

1 Have you got a driving .... ? How long have you had it? ....
2 Have you written your next of .... in your passport? Who is yours? ....
3 Have you been to a .... dress party? If so, who did you go as? ....
4 Do you remember any nursery .... ? If so, which ones? ....
5 When did you last go away for a long .... ? Where did you go? ....
6 Do you know where your birth .... is? If so, where is it? ....
7 Do you ever play on .... machines? If so, do you often win? ....

❸ ABOUT YOU Write answers to the questions in Exercise 2, or ask another student.

 Remember to test yourself

B Adjectives 🎧

It was a **last-minute** decision, but we managed to get a cheap holiday in Spain. The area's quite **built-up**, but the beach is lovely.

Most compound adjectives are hyphenated.

These boots are **worn out** now, but they've been incredibly **hard-wearing**.

My cousin is very **absent-minded**. He leaves things lying around and then gets **panic-stricken** when he can't find them.

My uncle's very **narrow-minded**: whenever I visit him, the rows seem to be **never-ending**. It makes me very **bad-tempered**.

My brother's pretty **thick-skinned**, whereas I'm more sensitive. He often criticizes me in front of other people; I find this very **off-putting** and it makes me a bit **tongue-tied**.

Glossary

last-minute	happening at the last possible moment.
built-up	A **built-up** area has a lot of houses and not many open spaces.
panic-stricken	extremely anxious about sth.
thick-skinned	not easily upset by unkind or critical comments.
off-putting	(of behaviour) irritating or unattractive.
tongue-tied	unable to speak easily because of nerves or shyness.
worn out	1 (of a thing) no longer useful because it has been used so much. 2 (of a person) exhausted from work or exercise.
hard-wearing	(of a product) remaining in good condition for a long time.
never-ending	(especially of sth unpleasant) seeming to last for ever.
bad-tempered	often angry and easily annoyed.

spotlight — **Adjectives with -minded**

narrow-minded = not willing to listen to the ideas and opinions of others, SYN **bigoted**. OPPS **broad-minded**, **open-minded**.
absent-minded = forgetful.
single-minded = thinking in a concentrated way about sth and determined to achieve it.

4 Find six compound adjectives using words from the box.

built	worn	thick	panic	narrow	bad	minded
	tempered	up	skinned	stricken	out	

_____   _____   _____

_____   _____   _____

5 Complete the sentences with a suitable compound adjective.

1 He's very bigoted, isn't he? ~ Yes, he's very _____ .
2 Had you planned to go? ~ No, it was a _____ decision.
3 Were you unable to speak? ~ Yes, I got completely _____ .
4 He's very determined, isn't he? ~ Yes, he's extremely _____ .
5 It's rather irritating behaviour. ~ Yes, very _____ .
6 They aren't bigoted, are they? ~ Quite the opposite. They're very _____ .

Remember to test yourself

C Phrasal verb to compound noun 🎧

A number of compound nouns are created from one particular meaning of a related phrasal verb.
This gives you an opportunity to learn two words instead of one.

> The course has been a real **let-down**. Some people have **dropped out** already, and last night the **turnout** was awful. There could be quite a **shake-up** at the end of the year.

> A car **broke down** on the side of the road and a lorry crashed into it; we were **held up** in the ensuing **tailback**. Fortunately no one was injured, but the car was a **write-off**.

> The **break-up** of their marriage was a real **setback** for Paula . . .

Glossary

let-down	a disappointment. **let sb down** v.
drop out (of sth)	leave school, college, a course, etc. without finishing your studies. **dropout** n.
turnout	the number of people who attend an event. **turn out** v.
shake-up	large changes made in an organization to improve it. **shake sth up** v.
break down	(of a vehicle or machine) stop working. **breakdown** n.
hold sth/sb up	delay sth/sb. **hold-up** n.
tailback	a long line of traffic, moving very slowly. **tail back** v.
write-off	a vehicle that is so badly damaged that it is not worth repairing. **write sth off** v.
break-up	the ending of a relationship or association. **break up** v.
setback	a problem that delays or prevents progress, or makes a situation worse for sb. **set sth/sb back** v.

spotlight — outbreak, outlay, etc.

A few compounds based on phrasal verbs change the position of the particle.
*When did war **break out**?*
(= start)
*The **outbreak** of war followed.*
*Did he **lay out** much money?*
(INF = spend)
*What was the initial **outlay**?*

6 Rewrite the sentences using the phrasal verbs as compound nouns.

▶ How much did they lay out for the wedding?   *What was the outlay for the wedding?*
1 Did many people drop out?
2 The traffic tailed back for five miles.
3 It set him back when he failed the exam.
4 We were held up for two hours.
5 A car broke down on the motorway.
6 It was awful after they broke up.
7 How many people turned out?
8 It was inevitable that war broke out.

7 Complete the sentences with a compound.

1 There was a really good _____ at the annual food festival: over 3,000 people.
2 My brother had an accident last week. He's all right, but the car is a _____ .
3 I thought the concert was a real _____ . I was very disappointed.
4 It wasn't a happy marriage, but I don't know exactly what caused the _____ .
5 Long _____ are expected on the motorway after the violent storms.
6 I spent over £50,000 in the end, but the initial _____ was about £10,000.

Remember to test yourself

4 I can **use a range of collocations**

A Collocations relating to fire 🎧

Collocation is the common combination of particular words with each other. These are some common collocations with **fire** and **flames**.

Two boys **set fire to** the school.	= made it start burning.
These buildings **catch fire** easily.	= start to burn.
The **fire broke out** in the kitchen.	= the fire started.
The building is **on fire**.	= burning.
The **fire spread** to the first floor.	= the fire moved and covered a larger area.
The plane **burst into flames**.	= suddenly began burning strongly.
The cottage **went up in flames**.	= was destroyed by fire.
The **fire/flames** soon **died down**.	= the fire/flames became weak.
They managed to **put out the fire**.	= stop the fire burning. SYN **extinguish the fire** FML.
We get a lot of **forest fires** here.	= fires that occur in forests during hot summer months.
I **lit a fire** this morning.	= started a fire for a purpose (e.g. in a fireplace or garden).
The **fire went out** last night.	= the fire stopped burning.

1 Complete the sentences in different ways.

1 A fire can ▶ break   out   / .... / .... / .... / ....

2 A person can .... / .... a fire.

3 A building can .... fire / be on .... / .... into flames / .... in flames.

2 Complete the text.

A large warehouse near the river (1) .... fire early this morning. The fire brigade was called when a fire (2) .... out on the ground floor, but the fire quickly (3) .... to the upper floors, and the timber roof just (4) .... into flames. Within minutes, the whole building was (5) .... fire. By this afternoon firemen had managed to (6) .... it ...., but the damage has been considerable. The exact cause has not been established, but several boys were seen (7) .... fire to some wooden boxes near the warehouse entrance.

3 Complete the sentences.

1 We lit the fire last night but unfortunately it had .... by this morning.

2 I shall wait for the noise to .... before I start speaking.

3 There was a loud bang and all the lights ....

4 How can you ask a smoker to .... their cigarette .... without being rude?

5 The fight .... after the football match.

6 She .... tears when I told her about the accident.

7 They get awful .... fires in the south of France during the summer.

8 The government has taken measures to stop the disease from ....

4 ABOUT YOUR LANGUAGE Translate the sentences about fire into your own language. How similar are they?

Remember to test yourself

B Adjective + noun 🎧

Example	Meaning
We had **torrential rain** last night.	very heavy rain.
They are predicting **gale-force winds** tonight.	very strong winds.
I had **considerable difficulty** getting here.	a lot of difficulty. SYN **great difficulty**.
The storms caused **extensive damage**.	a lot of damage. SYN **widespread damage**.
He speaks with a **strong accent**.	a very noticeable accent. OPP **slight accent**.
It was a **great honour** to meet the president.	an action or occasion that creates a feeling of pride.
We made a **real effort** to finish it on time.	a big effort. SYNS **special/concerted effort**.
My **main concern** is the effect of the drugs.	biggest worry. SYN **principal concern** (also **growing concern** = an increasing concern).
It's nice to see a **familiar face**.	a person who you recognize and know.
Could you give us a **brief summary**?	a short statement giving the main points of sth.
It was a **classic example** of his stupidity.	a very typical example of sth. SYN **perfect example**.
I had to face **strong criticism** over this issue.	a lot of disapproval from others. SYN **fierce criticism** (also **widespread criticism**).
The place was in **utter chaos** when I arrived.	a state of complete confusion. SYN **total chaos**.
The children had a **narrow escape**.	= they were lucky to get away safely.

5 Replace the underlined adjective with a different adjective which keeps the same meaning.

1 I had <u>great</u> difficulty with it. .... 4 Why is there <u>strong</u> criticism? ....
2 What's your <u>main</u> concern? .... 5 It'll be <u>total</u> chaos. ....
3 Was there <u>extensive</u> damage? .... 6 It's a <u>perfect</u> example of his writing. ....

6 Complete the dialogues.

1 Were you proud to meet her? ~ Yes, it was a great ....
2 Did you know anyone at the event? ~ Yes, there were one or two familiar ....
3 Can you give us the details? ~ No, but I'll give you a brief ....
4 Did you try hard enough? ~ Yes, everyone made a real ....
5 Many people disapprove of it. ~ Yes, there's been widespread ....
6 Did they know what to do? ~ No, it was utter ....
7 Does she still sound very foreign? ~ Yes, she has quite a strong ....
8 The car missed me by inches. ~ So, you had a very narrow ....

7 Complete the text.

(1) .... rain and (2) .... winds have caused (3) .... chaos on many roads. The emergency services have had (4) .... difficulty clearing some of the roads, and have been out all night in a (5) .... effort to help stranded motorists. The Highways Agency has said their (6) .... concern now is to clear the roads of abandoned cars. It is feared that local villages will also have suffered (7) .... damage, and there is already (8) .... criticism of the authorities.

Remember to test yourself

C Collocation in text 🎧

Notice how collocation (verb + noun, verb + adjective, adjective + noun, etc.) forms such an important part of a typical passage of English.

Neighbours refuse to mend fences

WHEN BARRY HUNT put a three-metre wire fence round his garden, neighbour Adam Clark thought it was **a real eyesore**, and asked him to remove it. Mr Hunt **took offence** and **made it clear that** he would **do no such thing**. One year on, the two men still haven't **reached agreement**, and now **face the prospect** of having to **settle their dispute** in court. 'It's absurd,' said Mr Clark. 'He **holds me entirely responsible** and refuses to **take** any of **the blame**. The sad truth is, we've **reached the point** where neither of us will **back down**.'

spotlight   *entirely*

Entirely means 'completely' and is often used with these words: *entirely different*; *entirely responsible*; *agree entirely*. **Not entirely** is used to soften what you are saying and is often used with these words: I'm *not entirely sure/happy/satisfied*.

Glossary

a real eyesore	a building or object that is very unpleasant to look at.
take offence (at sth)	show you are angry or upset about sth, or feeling insulted by it.
make it clear (that)	say sth to make sb understand a situation.
do no such thing	refuse to do the thing you have been asked to do.
reach (an) agreement	successfully arrive at an agreement (**reach a conclusion/compromise/verdict**).
face the prospect (of/that . . .)	recognize the possibility that sth may happen.
settle a dispute	end an argument between people (**settle an argument**).
hold sb responsible (for sth)	think that sb should be blamed for sth.
take the blame (for sth)	accept responsibility for sth.
reach the point (where/when)	arrive at a time or stage at which sth happens.
back down	stop asking for sth, or stop saying you will do sth.

8 Cross out the word that doesn't follow the underlined word.

1 You can <u>reach</u>: a) an agreement b) a compromise c) a conversation
2 You can <u>settle</u>: a) a discussion b) an argument c) a dispute
3 You can <u>take</u>: a) offence b) the blame c) enjoyment
4 <u>Entirely</u>: a) different b) similar c) responsible
5 <u>Not entirely</u>: a) sad b) satisfied c) sure

9 Complete the sentences with a suitable word in each space.

1 Stella thinks the new cinema is a real _____ and I _____ agree; it's very ugly.
2 He _____ me completely responsible, but I refuse to _____ all the blame.
3 It wasn't my fault and I _____ that very clear to my boss.
4 How are you going to _____ this dispute if no one is prepared to _____ down?
5 We've tried to get him to agree to it, but he'll do no _____ .
6 He feels we've _____ the point where we must decide, but I'm not _____ sure.
7 If we lose our first few opening games, we face the _____ of a difficult season.
8 I'm afraid he took _____ at something I said, so now we'll never _____ agreement.

5 I can **use a dictionary productively** 🎧

Dictionaries include a wide range of information that will help you to expand your vocabulary, and use words more effectively when you speak and write.

Dictionary entries*	Important information
reflect O⟶ /rɪˈflekt/ *verb* **1** [VN] [usually passive] ~ **sb/sth** (**in sth**) to show the image of sb/sth on the surface of sth such as a mirror, water or glass: *His face was reflected in the mirror.* **4** ~ (**on/upon sth**) to think carefully and deeply about sth: [V] *Before I decide I need time to reflect.* ◇ *She was left to reflect on the implications of her decision.*	• The key (O⟶) tells you that **reflect** is in the Oxford 3000 and is an important word. • The numbers tell you that **reflect** has different meanings. • The information in bold tells you that **reflect** can be followed by different prepositions.
count O⟶ /kaʊnt/ *verb* ▸ SAY NUMBERS **1** [V] ~ (**from sth**) (**to/up to sth**) to say numbers in the correct order: *Billy can't count yet.* ◇ *She can count up to 10 in Italian.* ▸ FIND TOTAL **2** ~ (**sth**)(**up**) to calculate the total number of people, things, etc. in a particular group: [VN] *The diet is based on counting calories.* ◇ [V wh-] *She began to count up how many guests they had to invite.* ▸ INCLUDE **3** [VN] to include sb/sth when you calculate a total: *We have invited 50 people, **not counting** the children.*	• The words in blue give a general idea of the different meanings of **count**.
absorb O⟶ /əbˈsɔːb/ *verb* [VN] ▸ LIQUID/GAS **1** to take in a liquid, gas or other substance from the surface or space around: *Plants absorb oxygen.* ◇ *This cream is easily **absorbed into** the skin.* ▸ INFORMATION **3** to take sth into the mind and learn or understand it ⒮ⓎⓃ TAKE IN: *It's a lot of information to absorb all at once.*	• Dictionaries often provide synonyms (**take in** is a synonym for one meaning of **absorb**) and opposites: these help you expand your vocabulary.
favour O⟶ /ˈfeɪvə(r)/ *noun* ▸ HELP **1** [C] a thing that you do to help sb: *Could you **do me a favour** and pick up Sam from school today?* ◇ *Can I **ask a favour**?* ◇ *I'm going **as a favour** to Ann, not because I want to.* ◇ *I'll ask Steve to take it.* **He owes me a favour.**	• The phrases in bold show common phrasal structures and/or collocations; they will help you to use **favour** naturally in different contexts.
propose O⟶ /prəˈpəʊz/ *verb* ▸ SUGGEST PLAN **1** (*formal*) to suggest a plan, an idea, etc. for people to think about and decide on: [VN] *The government proposed changes to the voting system.* ◇ [VN that] ***It was proposed that** the president be elected for a period of two years.* ◇ [V -ing] *He proposed changing the name of the company.*	• **propose** is a *formal* word and more common in written English. • It is followed by a noun, a ***that*** clause, or an ***-ing*** form, so you cannot say: *He proposed us to go.*
circumstance O⟶ /ˈsɜːkəmstəns/ *noun* **1** [C, usually pl.] the conditions and facts that are connected with and affect a situation, an event or an action: *The company reserves the right to cancel this agreement in certain circumstances.* ◇ *changing social and political circumstances*	• **circumstance** is usually used in the plural (**circumstances**).

VOCABULARY BUILDING **actions expressing emotions**	• The *Oxford Advanced Learner's Dictionary* has a number of features to increase your vocabulary or help you choose the right word in different situations. This list of actions is included beside the entry for *body*.

action	part of the body	you are . . .
hang	head	ashamed
lick	lips	anticipating sth good, nervous
nod	head	agreeing
raise	eyebrows	inquiring, surprised
shrug	shoulders	doubtful, indifferent
stamp	foot	angry

* These are adapted extracts from the *Oxford Advanced Learner's Dictionary*.

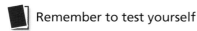 Remember to test yourself

1 Complete the sentences with the correct verb, and use the numbers in the dictionary entries to say which meaning is being used.

▶ There were about twelve on the bus, not ___counting (3)___ the teachers.

1 I think she'll have to go away and _____ on what we've said to her.

2 There's no liquid at the bottom because the sponge _____ all the juice.

3 From the list, I _____ fifteen who still haven't replied to the invitation.

4 There was too much information to _____ in one session; I couldn't take it all in.

5 In this game, you close your eyes and _____ up to 50, while we all hide.

6 He was standing behind me, but I could see his face _____ in the water.

2 Complete the collocations.

1 She just looked at me and _____ her shoulders.

2 I'm sure Bob will do it. He _____ me a favour.

3 When I told him, he just _____ an eyebrow in mild surprise.

4 I only went to the party as a _____ to Anne.

5 He _____ his head, so I assume he agreed.

6 You can change the date in certain _____ .

7 The little boy_____ his foot in anger.

3 Cross out the grammar mistake in each sentence and write the correction at the end.

1 We could see our faces reflected on the water.   ....

2 She proposed to leave the children behind.   ....

3 You can take dogs into shops in certain circumstance.   ....

4 There were ten people there, no counting the two of us.   ....

5 He proposed us to take the car.   ....

6 I'll need to reflect in what he said.   ....

4 Use the *Oxford Advanced Learner's Dictionary* to complete these sentences. You will find the answers in the full dictionary entries for the words shown on page 20.

1 Complete the collocation in this sentence with a word that can also mean 'consider':

I _____ *myself* lucky to have a job that I really enjoy.

2 Complete the idiom in this sentence with the correct prepositions:

I'm _____ *favour* _____ equal pay.

3 Complete the idiom in this sentence:

Under the _____ , I would prefer not to say anything.

4 Complete the idiom in this sentence:

The whole incident _____ *badly on everyone* involved.

5 ABOUT YOUR DICTIONARY Look up the meaning of these adjectives and the preposition which normally follows each one. Then, write a sentence example for each.

conducive _____   example: _____

fraught _____   example: _____

devoid _____   example: _____

immune _____   example: _____

Remember to test yourself

6 I can build word families

A Making one word from another 🎧

By learning words that are part of the same word family, you can often increase your vocabulary quickly and easily. For example, you will already know the words in the left-hand column below, but do you know the related forms with similar meanings?

Word	Example of related word	Meaning of related word
mistake N	I **mistook her for** a friend.	**mistake sb/sth for sb/sth** wrongly think that sb/sth is sb/sth else.
excellent ADJ	The university **excels at/in** sciences.	be very good at sth.
final ADJ	I haven't **finalized** my plans.	complete the last part of a plan/an arrangement.
point N	The exercise was completely **pointless**.	having no purpose.
follow V	Chelsea have a large **following** in Asia.	a group of supporters.
house N	We need more family **housing**.	buildings for people to live in.
heart N	It was a **heartless** thing to say.	showing no kindness or consideration. SYN **cruel**.
handle V	The situation needs careful **handling**.	the way sb deals with sth/sb.
emotion N	Cancer is a very **emotive** subject.	causing people to have strong emotions.
apologize V	It's his fault and he's very **apologetic**.	showing you are sorry.
forgive V	His behaviour was **unforgivable**.	so bad it cannot be forgiven. SYN **inexcusable**.
describe V	The pain in my arm was **indescribable**.	so extreme it is impossible to describe.
notice V	The scar on his face is quite **noticeable**.	easily noticed.
include V	Bed and breakfast is £80, **fully inclusive**.	(of a price or cost) including everything.
compare V	This year's figures look good. Are there **comparable** figures for last year?	similar; able to be compared.
reputation N	It's a very **reputable** company, so you should be OK.	having a good reputation; known to be good.
furniture N	Are they going to **furnish** the flats? ~ One is **fully furnished** already; the other will be **unfurnished**.	**furnish sth** put furniture in a place. **furnished** containing furniture. OPP **unfurnished**.
event N	I hear you had a very **eventful** trip in China.	full of interesting or important things that happen. OPP **uneventful**.
explain V	His behaviour was **inexplicable**.	that cannot be explained.
recognize V	There is a growing **recognition** that we can't go on polluting the atmosphere.	acceptance that sth is true or legal.

---

spotlight **Different related forms**

There may be several related forms with different meanings.
*I thought the meeting was very **worthwhile*** (= important, interesting, etc.)
*The necklace is **worthless**.* (= without value)   *He's a **worthy** champion.* (= one who deserved to win)

Remember to test yourself

1 Circle the correct word.

1 The company is very *reputative / reputable*, so I'm sure you can rely on it.
2 You get flights, accommodation, and food; it's fully *included / inclusive*.
3 I don't know why the brakes failed; it's *unexplainable / inexplicable*.
4 We're amateurs and they're professionals, so we're not *comparable / comparative*.
5 The way he treated Jan was *inexcusable / unexcusable*.
6 Nothing much happened; it was rather an *eventless / uneventful* evening.
7 The delay was his fault, but he wasn't very *apologizing / apologetic* about it.
8 The whole thing was *undescribable / indescribable*.

2 Rewrite the sentences using the correct form of the word in capitals. The meaning must stay the same.

1 They have a great reputation for sport. EXCEL ....
2 I think he deserved to win. WORTHY ....
3 Nothing much happened at the party. EVENT ....
4 The flat hasn't got any furniture. FURNISH ....
5 The trip was a waste of time. POINT ....
6 It's an interesting vase but it has no value. WORTH ....
7 A lot of people support the movement. FOLLOWING ....
8 People are increasingly aware of its value. RECOGNIZE ....

3 Complete the dialogues with a suitable word.

1 Are there enough homes?   ~ No, we need more ....
2 Can you still see the marks?   ~ Yes, they're quite ....
3 Was she sorry?   ~ Yes, she was very ....
4 Is that £65 for everything?   ~ Yes, it's fully ....
5 Her behaviour was dreadful.   ~ Yes, absolutely ....
6 Was there any reason to do that? ~ No, it was completely ....
7 Do they have a lot of support here? ~ Oh yes, a massive ....
8 Do you need to buy furniture?   ~ No, it's fully ....

4 Complete the sentences with a suitable word.

1 Jan and Brad still have to .... the arrangements for the wedding reception.
2 It's a very good school and they .... at languages.
3 Capital punishment is a very .... issue; people have strong feelings about it.
4 I was impressed with the police; their .... of the situation was just right.
5 He never listens to anyone, so it's .... giving him advice.
6 I walked off with someone else's coat; I .... it for my own.
7 Flats in big cities are expensive in England. A .... flat in Spain would cost less.
8 Stephen's remarks were very cruel. How could he be so .... ?

5 ABOUT YOUR COUNTRY. Write answers to the questions or ask another student.

1 If you rent a flat, is it usually furnished or unfurnished? ....
2 Which football team has the largest following? ....
3 Do hotels usually give a fully inclusive price for a room and breakfast? ....
4 Is housing a particular problem in any part of the country? ....
5 Are prices generally comparable with other countries nearby, or are they very different?
....

B Saying things another way 🎧

If you know different parts of a word family, you can express ideas in different ways.
Notice the words in bold which go together, e.g. **keep yourself occupied**.

How does she **occupy** her time?	~ She **keeps herself occupied** with work.
Did he **confess to** the robbery?	~ Yes, he eventually **made a confession**.
He won't **commit himself**, will he?	~ No, he just can't **make a commitment**.
What's the **origin of** the disease?	~ Nobody knows where it **originated**.
Did he **assure** you it would be OK?	~ Yes, he **gave** us his full **assurance**.
Should we try to **simplify** things?	~ Yes, we need a **simplification of** the rules.
Was he **abused** when he was young?	~ Yes, he **suffered** physical **abuse** as a child.
Couldn't you **defend yourself**?	~ No, I was completely **defenceless**.
Are the injuries **severe**?	~ We don't know the **severity of** them yet.
What does the report **indicate**?	~ Well, it **gives** some **indication of** progress.

Glossary

occupy sth	fill or use a space, area, or amount of time. **occupied** ADJ.
confess (to sth)	admit formally that you have done sth wrong or illegal. **confession** N.
commit yourself	promise to do sth that requires time and loyalty. **commitment** N.
origin	the cause of sth, or the place where it starts to exist. **originate** V.
assure sb (that / of sth)	tell sb that sth is definitely true or definitely going to happen. **assurance** N.
simplify sth	make sth easier to do or understand. **simplification** N.
abuse sb	treat sb in a cruel or violent way, often sexually. **abuse** N.
defend sb/yourself	protect sb or yourself. **defenceless** ADJ.
severe	extremely bad or serious. **severity** N.
indicate sth	show that sth exists or is likely to be true. **indication** N.

6 Find the missing word in each sentence and show where it goes.

▶ It was a simplification ⟋ the facts. _of_
1 He needs something to himself occupied. _____
2 When he attacked me, I couldn't defend. _____
3 What's the origin this idea? _____
4 When did he the confession? _____
5 She assured it would be fine. _____
6 He just wasn't able to commit. _____

7 Rewrite the sentences using a related form of the underlined word.
1 What's the <u>origin</u> of this? _____
2 I want a <u>simplification</u> of the procedure. _____
3 A lot of people <u>abuse</u> alcohol. _____
4 Does the research <u>indicate</u> a link? _____
5 He's got to <u>commit</u> himself. _____
6 Did she <u>confess</u>? _____
7 The boy was racially <u>abused</u>. _____
8 I was surprised at how <u>severe</u> the conditions were. _____

8 Test yourself. Cover the answers at the top of the page and look at the questions. Can you ask the questions using a related word form?

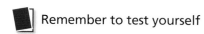 Remember to test yourself

Review: Expanding your vocabulary

Unit 1

1 Complete the dialogues using a suitable word that isn't used in the question.

1 You can explain this in different ways, can't you? ~ Yes, it's a bit _____ .
2 Is the meaning obvious? ~ Yes, it's completely _____ .
3 Is this word rather dated now? ~ Yes, it's quite _____ .
4 She gets upset when he mocks her. ~ I know; he shouldn't _____ _____ at her.
5 Is this word quite negative? ~ Yes, dictionaries mark it as _____ .
6 Is that the exact meaning? ~ To be honest, I can't give you a _____ definition.
7 Can I use 'miserable' instead of 'sad'? ~ Yes. In this context, they're _____ .
8 Do they mean the same? ~ Not exactly, but _____ the same. (Don't use *almost* or *nearly*!)

A Z **more words**: *derivative, taboo, dialect, satirical, pun, archaic, overtones*

Unit 2

1 Rewrite the sentences using the words in capitals. Make any necessary changes, but the meaning must remain the same.

1 I suddenly realized who had stolen my mobile. DAWN _____
2 I can't decide what to do about the job. TWO MINDS _____
3 In his haste, he knocked the vase over. FLYING _____
4 She ate some chocolate, which was enough until she was rescued. KEEP _____
5 The laptop's a bargain and includes free software. COME _____
6 Do many people try to avoid paying tax? GET _____
7 You were so kind to do that for me. SWEET _____
8 Changing his job is his least likely option. MIND _____

A Z **more words**: look up these words in a dictionary and see if you can find at least one new meaning for each one, or a new idiom containing the word: *break, settle, pull, stick, hold*

Unit 3

1 Tick the word(s) in italics that are possible. One or two may be possible.

1 He had a panic-stricken *look* ☐ *occasion* ☐ .
2 Look at his worn out *shoes* ☐ *equipment* ☐ .
3 It was an *off-putting* ☐ *single-minded* ☐ remark.
4 We had a long *hold-up* ☐ *dropout* ☐ .
5 The police spoke to the *passer-by* ☐ *next of kin* ☐ .
6 The *car* ☐ *exercise* ☐ was a write-off.
7 It was a terrible *setback* ☐ *break-up* ☐ .
8 Use that *drawing pin* ☐ *paper clip* ☐ in the wall.

2 Make compounds using a word on the left with a word on the right. Then use them to complete the sentences below.

barbed break last	part out down
nursery open shake	cut minded minded
turn short absent spare	minute wire rhymes up

1 You need to be more _____ and listen to new ideas.
2 We made a _____ booking on the internet and flew out the following day.
3 She thinks she's too old to listen to _____ .
4 We were a bit late, so I decided to take a _____ . What a silly idea that was!
5 There was an impressive _____ for the meeting – over 100, in fact.
6 I'm a bit worried about my grandmother – she's getting rather _____ .
7 We need a _____ for the coffee machine – I'll order one on the internet.
8 There's been a management _____ so I think things will start looking up soon.
9 If you have car _____ insurance, you can get help very quickly on the road.
10 The _____ is designed to keep the animals in and people out.

A Z more words: use your dictionary to find more compound nouns and adjectives starting with these items: *birth* (e.g. *birthplace*), *paper, public, life, short,* and *nail*

Unit 4

1 One word is missing in each line. What is it, and where does it go?

TAUNTON HOTEL GOES ⟨ IN FLAMES   UP

Firefighters were called out last night to a Taunton hotel which fire	1 _____
at around midnight. It appeared that the fire had broken on the first	2 _____
floor and rapidly throughout the building. Unfortunately it coincided	3 _____
with gale winds which fuelled the flames. Although they had no	4 _____
advance, the guests were able to get out and the hotel manager felt	5 _____
they had had a escape. Firefighters fought the blaze for several	6 _____
hours but eventually put it. This fire comes at a time when	7 _____
there is growing about the health and safety regulations in holiday	8 _____
accommodation; the hotel owners now face the of an enquiry into	9 _____
the causes of the fire, and if they are held, they could face prosecution.	10 _____

2 Complete the speech with a suitable word.

'Over the years, our city has had (1) _____ difficulty in raising the finance to pull down the ugly bus station which is a (2) _____ eyesore, and replace it with something far more attractive and practical. At last, it seems, we have managed to (3) _____ an agreement with the banks, and we are now reaching the (4) _____ where we can start to work on the design in more detail. We know there has been (5) _____ criticism of the initial plans, but I would like to (6) _____ it absolutely clear that our main (7) _____ has always been to find a design which will be acceptable to everyone; to that end we hope we can reach a (8) _____ with all parties involved. It is therefore an (9) _____ that the distinguished architect, A. C. Rally, who also happens to be a (10) _____ face in the city, has agreed to give us a (11) _____ summary of his proposed plans. Mr Rally, over to you.'

A Z more collocations: *extensive* research, sounds *familiar*, *widespread* support, *settle* the bill, face the *consequences*, *catch* sb by surprise

Unit 5

Complete the crossword. The letters in the grey squares spell a word. What is it?

A Z more words: look at the dictionary entry for a very common word such as *face*, *head*, or *take*.

Note down five or six new collocations, phrases, or phrasal verbs that include your target word.

1 You _____ your lips when you are nervous or expect something good to happen.
2 There are fifteen of us, though I didn't _____ the babies as they travel free.
3 I need time to _____ on this before I make a decision.
4 There was far too much information for me to _____ on the spot.
5 You don't seem to care – don't just _____ your shoulders and walk away!
6 Children sometimes _____ their feet when they're angry or frustrated.
7 I'll ask Sue to give me a lift home; she owes me a _____ anyway.
8 You are only allowed to take dictionaries into the exam under certain _____ .
9 If you _____ your eyebrows like that, you look surprised.
10 We _____ these changes in the belief that they will be beneficial to everyone.
11 She _____ her head in shame.

Unit 6

1 Complete the tables.

Verb	Adjective
apologize	
occupy	
forgive	
defend	
	final
	excellent

Adjective	Noun
	point
	emotion
	heart
severe	

A Z more words: you will know the following words in bold, but do you know the related forms in brackets? *authority* (authoritarian. authoritative, unauthorized); *escape* (escapism, inescapable); *man* (manly, mankind, unmanned); *standard* (substandard, standardize)

7 I can describe the human body

A Physical features 🎧

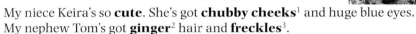

My niece Keira's so **cute**. She's got **chubby cheeks**[1] and huge blue eyes.
My nephew Tom's got **ginger**[2] hair and **freckles**[3].
My cousin Jessica's wearing a **brace**[4] to **straighten** her teeth.
My sister has a **gorgeous** figure – and she **shows** it **off** at every opportunity.
My uncle's got a **paunch**[5] which really **sticks out**. He needs to lose weight.
Gran**'s getting on for** 80. She's got lots of **wrinkles**[6] and looks a bit **frail**.

Glossary

cute	(of babies, puppies, etc.) pretty and attractive.
chubby	slightly fat, but in an attractive way (**chubby cheeks/fingers**).
gorgeous	INF very beautiful and attractive. SYN **lovely**.
show sth off	show sth you are proud of.
paunch	a fat stomach on a man.
stick out	1 be or push out further than sth else. 2 be noticeable.
be getting on for sth	be nearly a particular age, time, or number.
frail	(especially of an old person) physically weak and thin. **frailty** N. (A person who is **doddery** walks slowly and shakily because they are frail.)

spotlight   Suffix -*en*

We add **-en** to some adjectives to form verbs: *straighten, loosen, tighten, weaken*; and occasionally to some nouns: *lengthen, strengthen*.

1 Find six more pairs of words in the box and explain the connection.

babies ✓	frail	paunch	doddery	freckles	stomach	hair
chubby	brace	cute ✓	skin	ginger	teeth	fat

▶ *Babies are often described as* **cute**.

....
....
....

2 Complete the sentences.

1 My daughter wants to go out and .... her new clothes to her friends.
2 My mum's .... 50, but still has a .... figure.
3 Most babies seem to have a round face and chubby ....
4 I don't like my hair curly: I want to .... it.
5 He's got big ears that .... and make him look rather funny.
6 There's a picture of the two kittens asleep on a chair. They look very ....

Remember to test yourself

B The body and clothes 🎧

Dress FOR YOUR shape

The key to dressing for your body shape is to **enhance** your best **features** and **discreetly conceal** the not-so-good ones.

Here are a few **guidelines**.

- Wearing dark colours or vertical **stripes**[1] will **create the illusion** of being slimmer.
- For women, high heels are **flattering** because they **exaggerate** the length of the legs.
- If you are pear-shaped (narrow shoulders and broad **hips**[2]), jeans that sit below the waist are flattering, as they **draw attention to** the waistline and make the bottom look smaller.
- For women with broad shoulders and narrow hips, a V-neck dress **draws attention** down and in, and away from the shoulders and arms.

Glossary

the key to sth	the thing that makes you able to understand or achieve sth. SYN **the secret of sth**.
enhance sth	increase or improve the quality, value, or status of sth.
feature	a part of sb's face or body.
discreetly	in a way that others will not notice. **discreet** ADJ. OPP **indiscreet**.
conceal sth	FML hide sth.
guidelines	information that can help you, e.g. to make a decision.
create an illusion	make sth which is false appear true.
flattering	making sb look more attractive. OPP **unflattering**.
exaggerate sth	make sth seem bigger, better, worse, or more important than it really is. **exaggeration** N.

spotlight — Expressions with *attention*

He **drew** my **attention to** the mistakes. = He made me see the mistakes.
Attract the waiter's **attention**. = Do sth to make the waiter notice you.
He never **pays attention to** me. = He never listens to or considers what I say.

---

❸ Circle the correct word(s).

1 If you create an illusion, you make something appear true / false.
2 Guidelines usually stop you doing something / help you.
3 If you enhance something, it's positive / negative.
4 If you attract someone's attention, they like / notice you.
5 If you exaggerate something, you make it seem more / less important than it really is.
6 If you do things in a discreet way, people usually notice / don't notice.
7 If you wear something that is flattering, it makes you look worse / better.
8 If you conceal something, others can / can't see it.

❹ Complete the sentences with a suitable word from above.

1 If you don't _____ attention, you won't learn anything.
2 Those trousers are very _____ : they make her look fat.
3 The right clothes can show off your best _____ , e.g. long legs or a slim waist.
4 I don't look good in jeans: my waist is quite small but I've got broad _____ .
5 Clothes with vertical _____ tend to make you look slimmer.
6 The _____ to her success is good looks, not talent!
7 He wears a hat because he doesn't want to _____ attention to the fact he's bald.
8 To say he's the best-looking man in the world is a bit of an _____ !

📓 Remember to test yourself

8 I can **talk about body language**

A Reading the signs 🎧

BODY LANGUAGE can be very informative, but if you **jump to conclusions** when you interpret a particular **gesture**, you may **misinterpret** what it means. For example, people who look away to avoid **eye contact** may **not necessarily** be lying: they could just be very shy. To understand body language, therefore, we need to **observe** a **combination** of behaviour that a person **displays**. With lying, for example, **look out** for any or all of these:

- 💗 avoidance of eye contact
- 💗 **going red**
- 💗 **biting fingernails**[1]
- 💗 **sweating** a lot
- 💗 **excessive** hand gestures.

Glossary

jump to conclusions	make a decision about sth too quickly, before you have thought about all the facts. SYN **leap to conclusions**.
gesture	a body movement you make to show a particular meaning.
misinterpret sth	If you **misinterpret sth**, you understand it wrongly.
eye contact	the action or moment of looking into another person's eyes.
not necessarily	used to say that sth is possibly true but is not always true.
observe sth	FML see or notice sth; an **observant** person is good at noticing things. **observation** N.
combination	a mix of two or more things. **combine** V.
display sth	show signs of sth, often a quality or a feeling. **display** N.
look out for sth/sb	look and try to see or find sth/sb.
go red	become red in the face, often when you're angry or embarrassed.
sweat	If you **sweat**, water appears on the surface of your skin because you are hot. SYN **perspire** FML. (The related nouns are **sweat** and **perspiration**.)
excessive	more than is reasonable or necessary. **excess** N. **exceed** V.

❶ Good or bad? Write G or B.

1 He sweats a great deal. _____
2 She goes red all the time. _____
3 She has strong powers of observation. _____
4 She never bites her fingernails. _____
5 She's covered in perspiration. _____
6 He always leaps to conclusions. _____
7 He can't make eye contact with me. _____
8 The cost didn't exceed his ability to pay. _____

❷ Complete the sentences with a suitable word.

1 You should stop and think before _____ to conclusions.
2 The teacher said she'd _____ for more articles on body language.
3 My brother is very _____ : he always notices people's body language.
4 Even when he's very angry, he doesn't _____ any sign of emotion.
5 It's easy to _____ someone's body language if you don't know them very well.
6 If you *go red*, does it mean you're angry? ~ No, _____ .
7 I use hand _____ a lot, but I hope they're not _____ .
8 The increase in the number of students is the result of a _____ of different factors.

Remember to test yourself

B Interpreting gestures 🎧

Here are some common interpretations of gestures, although **bear in mind** the danger of **making generalizations about** body language (as stated on the previous page).

A **clenched fist**[1] shows anger; **folded arms**[2] may **imply stubbornness**.

People who **lean towards**[3] each other are displaying an interest in each other.

Women who **fancy** someone often **fiddle with** their hair; men **stroke** an earlobe. Women lift their heads to show more of their neck when they're **flirting**.

Glossary

bear sth in mind	remember to consider sth.
make generalizations about sth	make general statements about sth that may only be based on a few examples. **generalize** v.
imply sth	suggest that you feel or think sth without saying so directly. **implication** N.
stubbornness	a determination not to change your opinion or attitude. SYN **obstinacy**. (The related adjectives are **stubborn** and **obstinate**.)
fancy sb	INF be attracted to sb.
fiddle with sth	keep moving or touching sth with your hands.
stroke sth	move your hand or fingers gently over the surface of sth.
flirt (with sb)	behave towards sb as if you find them sexually attractive, but not in a serious way.

3 Cross out the wrong word.

1 make / do generalizations
2 a clenched hand / fist
3 stroke / fancy someone's arm
4 fold your arms / legs
5 fiddle with / on something
6 flirt with someone / something

4 Complete the words in each sentence.

1 He didn't actually say I was being rude, but that was the i_____ .
2 Both girls like Conrad, and they're always f_____ with him.
3 She l_____ towards him and whispered in his ear. I think she f_____ him.
4 If my dad decides something, he won't change his mind; he's very s_____ /o_____ .
5 When a man talks to a woman and strokes his ear, it i_____ that he fancies her. But bear in m_____ that it is very dangerous to g_____ about body language.
6 Girls often f_____ with their hair when they fancy someone, or they're bored.

5 ABOUT YOU Write your answers or ask another student.

Do you do any of these things? If so, what do you think they often mean?

- stroke your ear, chin, or the back of your head? _____
- fiddle with your hair, jewellery, or watch strap? _____
- fold your arms or cross your legs? _____
- clench your fist or bite your nails? _____

Remember to test yourself

9 I can describe physical movement

A Walking and running 🎧

Word	Example	Meaning
creep	*I **crept** up the stairs, so that I wouldn't wake anyone.*	move slowly and quietly so you are not seen or heard (also **tiptoe** = walk on your toes so you are not heard).
stroll	*We **strolled** along the beach.*	walk casually for pleasure.
limp	*He **limped** quite badly after his accident.*	walk slowly and with difficulty because one leg or foot is injured.
stagger	*Despite his injury, he **staggered** to the nearest house and phoned for help.*	walk with difficulty, being almost unable to stand up.
hike	*They **hiked** across the countryside.*	walk long distances in the country.
march	*The soldiers **marched** for over 20 kms.*	walk with stiff regular steps.
chase sb/sth	*Police **chased** the man for miles.*	run, drive, etc. after sb/sth to catch them.
dash	*I **dashed** across the road for the bus.*	run quickly and suddenly.
gallop	*The horse **galloped** across the field.*	(of a horse or rider) run quickly.
charge	*An angry section of the crowd **charged** towards the security men.*	move quickly in a particular direction, often to attack sb/sth.

1 Correct the underlined verb in the sentences.

1 He obviously had a bad leg; he was <u>hiking</u>. _____
2 The man was clearly drunk, but managed to <u>gallop</u> home after the party. _____
3 The car appeared suddenly, so I had to <u>stroll</u> across the road. _____
4 I got nervous as the horse <u>crept</u> towards me. _____
5 My dog loves to <u>charge</u> rabbits. _____
6 The victorious army <u>tiptoed</u> into town. _____
7 I <u>limped</u> to the door when the alarm went off. _____
8 I <u>marched</u> upstairs, so he wouldn't know I was there. _____

> **spotlight** | **Verbs and nouns**
>
> Many of the verbs above are also used as nouns. The words in bold below are often used with them.
> *We decided to **go for a stroll**.*
> *He had a **pronounced limp**.*
> *I **went for** a ten-mile **hike**.*
> *He **made a dash for** the door.*
> *The horse **broke into** a **gallop**.*
> *Who **led the charge**?*
> *The film has a high-speed **car chase**.*

2 Rewrite the sentences using the underlined verbs as nouns. Make any other changes that are necessary.

▶ We <u>hiked</u> across the valley. / We went for a hike across the valley.
1 He <u>limped</u> badly. / He _____ .
2 It was raining, so we <u>dashed</u> for cover. / It was raining, so we _____ .
3 They <u>strolled</u> along the beach. / They _____ .
4 The horses soon started <u>galloping</u>. / The horses soon _____ .
5 Who was at the front when they <u>charged</u>? / Who _____ ?
6 Did you see the car <u>chasing</u> the other one? / Did you see _____ ?

Remember to test yourself

B Physical exercise 🎧

My 20-minute **workout**

❝ I'm not as **supple** or **agile** as I used to be, and I was beginning to feel quite **stiff** and **sluggish** first thing in the morning, so I asked a friend to **devise** a workout routine for me. First I **loosen up** with some **stretching**[1] and **bending**, then I go on to something more **strenuous**. I don't like **press-ups**[2] – I find them **relentless**, and I also have a **recurrent** elbow problem. I prefer to **alternate between** jogging and **sprinting** because I enjoy the **constant** change of activity. ❞

Glossary

workout	a period of physical exercise you do to keep fit. **work out** v.
supple	able to bend and move parts of your body easily.
agile	able to move quickly and easily. **agility** N.
stiff	feeling some pain and unable to move easily. **stiffness** N.
sluggish	moving slowly, below your normal activity level. **sluggishness** N.
devise sth	invent a method or plan of doing sth. SYN **think sth up**.
loosen up	do physical activities to prepare the muscles for exercise. SYN **warm up.**
bend	lean over at the waist (also **bend** your **knee**, **elbow**, etc.).
strenuous	needing effort and energy. SYN **arduous**.
relentless	A thing that is **relentless** never seems to stop or get any easier.
recurrent	happening or appearing again and again. **recur** V.
alternate between A and B	do A, then B, then do A again, and so on.
sprint	run a short distance very fast.

❸ Circle the correct word(s). Sometimes both are correct.

1 I slept badly, so I feel a bit stiff / sluggish today.
2 Stretch / Bend your knees and touch your toes.
3 Gymnasts always look so supple / agile.
4 I recur / alternate between swimming and cycling.
5 My brother thought up / devised this new training method last year.
6 The garage is in relentless / constant use.
7 Lifting weights is quite strenuous / arduous.
8 I have this recurrent / constant back problem, but I'm fine at the moment.

spotlight **Expressions with *constant***

Constant means happening all the time or a lot of the time. It is commonly used with particular nouns.
*There were **constant interruptions**.*
*The phone is in **constant use**.*
*His wife needs **constant attention**.*
*They live in **constant fear**.*

❹ Complete the sentences with a suitable word or phrase.

1 I couldn't do any work because of the .... interruptions.
2 For breakfast I usually .... between cereal and toast.
3 It's important to .... first before you do any strenuous exercise.
4 My brother used to do 50 ....-............... every day.
5 I could .... when I was younger but I can't run very fast now.
6 They've been burgled three times and now live in constant ....

📓 Remember to test yourself

10 I can describe sounds

A A sound story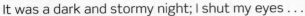

It was a dark and stormy night; I shut my eyes . . .

The windows **rattled** in the wind and there was a distant **rumble** of thunder. Trees **rustled** and big raindrops **splashed onto** the windows.

Then someone **beeped** their horn and a car stopped with a **screech** of brakes. Someone **slammed** the car door **shut** . . . footsteps **squelched** through the mud . . . a floorboard on the stairs **creaked** . . . and there was a **high-pitched** scream – from me!

Glossary

rattle	make or cause sth to make short, loud sounds. **rattle** N.
rumble	a long, deep sound or series of sounds. **rumble** V.
rustle	make or cause sth to make a noise like paper, leaves, etc. rubbing together. **rustle** N.
splash on/ onto sth	(of a liquid) fall onto sth in large drops and make it wet. **splash** N.
beep	If a car horn **beeps** it makes a short high or loud sound. **beep** N.
screech	a loud, high, unpleasant sound. **screech** V.
slam sth (shut)	shut sth with a lot of force so that it makes a loud noise.
squelch	make a wet, sucking sound, e.g. when you walk through mud.
creak	make the sound that an old door or floor makes. **creak** N.
high-pitched	(of sounds) very high in the register of sound. OPP **low-pitched**.

spotlight Ergative verbs

Ergative verbs, e.g. *slam, splash, rattle, rustle, beep,* can be used in a transitive and intransitive way, with the object in the transitive structure (e.g. *the door*) being the subject in the intransitive structure.
*Marta **slammed** the door.*
*The door **slammed**.*

❶ Complete the sentences with a word describing the sound you might hear.

► A badly played violin, tyres, and brakes can all make a screeching noise.

1 Computers, reversing lorries, and cameras all make a ＿＿＿＿＿ sound.

2 Bottles in a bag, stones in a box, and old cars can make a ＿＿＿＿＿ noise.

3 Feet walking through muddy fields make a ＿＿＿＿＿ noise.

4 You can ＿＿＿＿＿ the lid of a box, a fridge door, or a gate.

5 An old staircase and a bedroom door may ＿＿＿＿＿ .

6 A mobile phone ring tone, a whistle, and a child screaming make a high-＿＿＿＿＿ sound.

7 Newspapers or autumn leaves make a ＿＿＿＿＿ noise.

8 Distant traffic, gunfire, or thunder can make a ＿＿＿＿＿ noise.

❷ Complete the text with a suitable word.

I share an office with two colleagues and it's really hard to work with the constant noise. One of them sits on a wooden chair that (1) ＿＿＿＿＿ every time he moves; the other is constantly (2) ＿＿＿＿＿ bits of paper as he works. Plus he has a mobile phone which is always (3) ＿＿＿＿＿ . Across the corridor, there's a man who has a very (4) ＿＿＿＿＿ -pitched voice and he always seems to be (5) ＿＿＿＿＿ at his secretary, poor woman. He's extremely bad-tempered and can't even leave his office without (6) ＿＿＿＿＿ the door. It drives me mad. To make matters worse, there's a constant low (7) ＿＿＿＿＿ of traffic outside, and as our windows don't fit properly, they (8) ＿＿＿＿＿ when it's windy. I think I'm in the wrong job.

Remember to test yourself

B Animal sounds, human behaviour 🎧

Words describing animal sounds are often used figuratively to describe human behaviour.

Animal + sound		Meaning	Human behaviour
dogs **bark**		make a short loud sound.	*My boss's **bark is worse than his bite**.* INF = He's not really as angry or aggressive as he sounds.
wolves howl		make a long loud cry.	*He was **howling in pain**.* = crying loudly with pain. *The audience **howled with laughter**.* = laughed loudly.
dogs **growl**		make a deep, angry sound.	*'What are you doing here?' he **growled**.* = said in a low, angry voice. SYN **snarl**.
bees buzz		make a continuous low sound.	*After the meeting, my head was **buzzing** for hours.* = I was thinking about it continuously. *I was **buzzing about** all day.* = moving around continuously from place to place.
lions **roar**		make a very loud deep sound.	*There was **a** huge **roar** when Drogba scored.* = a huge noise from the crowd. *We **roared with laughter**.* = laughed loudly.
mice **squeak**		make a short high but not loud sound.	*'I've won the cup!' she **squeaked** down the phone.* = spoke in a high-pitched, excited voice. **squeaky** ADJ.
cocks crow		make repeated loud sounds especially in the morning.	*He was **crowing about** his victory all night.* = talking too proudly about. SYN **boast** (**about sth**).
owls hoot		make a long 'oo' sound.	*She **hooted** at me.* = sounded her car horn. *There were **hoots of derision** from the audience.* = loud cries suggesting sb is stupid.

3 Write the correct animal for each noise.

▶ ~~dogs~~ roar *lions roar*   3 mice bark _____   6 dogs crow _____
1 cats squeak _____   4 bees howl _____   7 wolves buzz _____
2 lions hoot _____   5 owls growl _____

4 Positive or negative? Write P or N.

1 We were howling with laughter. _____   5 She roared with laughter. _____
2 There were hoots of derision. _____   6 She growled at me. _____
3 He boasts a lot. _____   7 His head's buzzing with ideas. _____
4 She was crowing about her results. _____   8 He snarled at me. _____

5 Complete the sentences.

1 We were a long way away, but we could hear the _____ from the stadium.
2 The tiger was lying there, _____ in pain, but we couldn't get nearer to help.
3 Don't worry about Mrs Clarkson – her _____ is worse than her _____ .
4 The speaker had a high-pitched, _____ voice which was a bit annoying to listen to.
5 The driver behind _____ at me but I just sat waiting for the children to cross the road.
6 Ella was _____ about, passing drinks and handing out snacks to the party guests.

11 I can **describe sight**

A Are computers bad for your eyesight? 🎧

👁 **eye**SIGHT

Many of us spend hours every day working at a computer. As a result, **eye strain**, **discomfort**, and **blurred vision** are common complaints. Most people also **blink** less frequently when they are concentrating, resulting in poor **tear** production and dry, **irritated** eyes. Here's how you can change your computer use and **ease** your discomfort:

▸ **adjust** your computer screen so that it is 50–65 cm from your eyes, just below eye level

▸ adjust lighting to **eliminate glare**

▸ take frequent breaks, blink often to keep your eyes **moist**, and let your eye muscles relax by looking into the distance every 15 minutes.

Glossary	
eyesight	the ability to see. SYN **sight**. (You may **have good/poor eyesight**.)
eye strain	a slight pain in your eyes, e.g. from reading a lot.
discomfort	a feeling of slight pain.
blurred vision	If your **vision** is **blurred** you cannot see clearly.
blink	shut and open your eyes quickly.
tear	a drop of liquid that comes out of your eye when you cry.
irritated	painful, red, or swollen. **irritation** N.
ease sth	make sth less unpleasant or painful. SYN **alleviate sth**.
adjust sth	change sth slightly to make it more suitable. **adjustment** N.
eliminate sth	remove or get rid of sth. **elimination** N.
glare	a bright, unpleasant light. (To **glare at sb** is to look at sb in an angry way.)
moist	slightly wet, often in a way that is useful or pleasant. (**Damp** means slightly wet, often in a way that is unpleasant.)

spotlight   *-sighted*

If you are **short-sighted**, you are only able to see things if they are near you. OPP **long-sighted**. A **partially sighted** person can see very little.

❶ Circle the correct word(s). Sometimes both words are correct.

1 Did you know that pigs often have really poor sight / eyesight?
2 If you suffer from discomfort / irritation, try to get a better office chair.
3 His eyes are irritated so he keeps blinking / glaring.
4 We are currently trying to eliminate / adjust theft from our offices.
5 These sunglasses are great because they reduce glare / tears.
6 I'm seeing my optician tomorrow because I'm suffering from moist / blurred vision.

❷ One word is missing in each line. What is it, and where does it go?

▸ The wood feels ⎰ so you won't be able to burn it. _damp_
1 Sore, tired, or burning eyes are classic symptoms of eye. ....
2 If your eyes are dry and try using eye drops. ....
3 He must be very because he can't read the dictionary definitions. ....
4 You should get up and walk about to the problem of back pain. ....
5 Make a conscious effort to more often to prevent dry eyes. ....
6 Whenever I make too much noise in the office, my colleague glares me. ....

Remember to test yourself

B A peaceful sight 🎧

We stood at the top of the hill for ages, **gazing at** the **breathtaking** view below. In the distance, the port was **barely visible** through the early morning **haze**, but we could just **make out** the island. As we drove back down, I **caught a glimpse of** a waterfall and asked Marcello to stop. Suddenly, a deer **came into view**, and then we **spotted** two of her young. They **stood** completely **still**, **eyeing us warily**, then ran off and **vanished into thin air**.

Glossary	
gaze at sth	look at sth for a long time because you are interested in it or are thinking about sth else. **gaze** N.
breathtaking	very impressive. SYN **spectacular**.
barely	only with great difficulty or effort. SYN **only just**.
visible	A thing that is **visible** can be seen. OPP **invisible**.
haze	smoke, dust, or mist in the air which is hard to see through. **hazy** ADJ.
make sth/sb out	see, hear, or understand sth/sb with difficulty.
come into view/sight	appear. OPP **disappear from view/sight**.
stand still	stand without moving (also **keep/stay/sit still**).
eye sb/sth	look at sb/sth carefully or because you are suspicious of them/it.
warily	carefully, because you think there may be danger or a problem.
vanish into thin air	disappear suddenly or in a way you cannot explain.

spotlight   Ways of seeing

To **catch a glimpse of sth/sb** or **glimpse sth** means to see them for a very short time and not clearly or completely. To **catch sight of sb/sth** means to see them suddenly, often when you have been hoping to see them. To **spot sb/sth** means to see them suddenly, especially when they are hard to see.
*We **caught a glimpse of** the actress as she left the theatre.*
*She **caught sight of** her cousin in the crowd.*
*I **spotted** several mistakes in my work before I handed it in.*

3 Tick the words which are possible. More than one word may be possible.

1 She spotted him through the *haze* ☐ *hazy* ☐ *gaze* ☐ of cigarette smoke.
2 The scenery was absolutely *visible* ☐ *spectacular* ☐ *breathtaking* ☐.
3 After an hour's wait, we finally *caught sight of* ☐ *spotted* ☐ *eyed* ☐ the rare bird.
4 Could you please *stand* ☐ *wait* ☐ *keep* ☐ still?
5 We could *warily* ☐ *only just* ☐ *barely* ☐ see the church in the distance.
6 The Grand Palace finally *came into* ☐ *disappeared from* ☐ *caught* ☐ sight.

4 Rewrite the sentences using the word in capitals. The meaning must stay the same.

▶ He sat without moving while I drew him. STILL   *He sat still while I drew him.*
1 I was only just able to see the boat on the horizon. MAKE _____
2 As I turned the corner, I suddenly saw the house. CAME _____
3 Those stars can't be seen without a telescope.   INVISIBLE _____
4 We could barely see the trees through the fog. ONLY _____
5 She looked at me very suspiciously. EYE _____
6 The thief left the building and disappeared from view. AIR _____
7 I saw the thief as he ran out of the building. GLIMPSE _____
8 We watched the boat until eventually it vanished. SIGHT _____

Remember to test yourself

12 I can **describe touch, smell, and taste**

A Touching 🎧

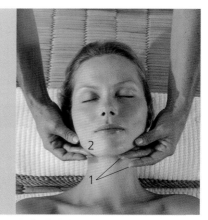

A Simple Face **Massage**

1 Start by **gently stroking** the whole face. With both hands, work up the neck, across the cheeks, **sliding steadily** up and over the forehead. **Apply** gentle **pressure** to the temples.
2 **Stimulate** the skin by gently **patting** the cheeks, neck, and under the chin.
3 Use your **fingertips**[1] to **lightly pinch** the skin along the line of the **jaw**[2] and under the chin.
4 To **release tension** around the eyes, **firmly squeeze** the eyebrows with your fingertips.
5 Massage the scalp **vigorously** as if shampooing the hair. This involves no risk of harm.

Glossary

massage	*see picture.* **have a massage**, **massage sb** v.
stroke sth	move your hand over the skin, hair, etc. gently and slowly.
slide	move or make sth move easily over a smooth or wet surface.
apply pressure to sth	press on sth hard with your hand, foot, etc.
stimulate sth	make a part of the body or skin more active.
pat sth	touch sth lightly several times with your hand flat.
pinch sth	hold sth tightly between the thumb and finger.
tension	the feeling you have if your muscles are tight and not relaxed (**release** the tension = allow or cause the muscles to relax).
squeeze sth	press sth firmly with your fingers.

spotlight   Adverbs of manner

Gently and **lightly** describe soft, relaxed movements; **firmly** is much stronger. If you move your hands **steadily** you make regular, controlled movements. **Vigorously** means in a very energetic and active way. SYN **energetically**.

1 Are these movements pleasant or unpleasant? Write P or U.

1 She stroked the child's face. _____
2 She rubbed my nose energetically. _____
3 She massaged my scalp gently. _____
4 She applied pressure firmly to my neck. _____
5 She pinched my skin vigorously. _____
6 She released the tension in my back. _____
7 She patted my face lightly. _____
8 She slid her fingertips across my back. _____

2 Complete the sentences.

1 Don't _____ that tube too firmly – the toothpaste will come out all over you.
2 You can use certain products when showering to _____ your skin.
3 She sat staring into the distance, gently _____ the cat.
4 He _____ his hand over the magnificent marble statue.
5 He was nervous, but he concentrated on breathing _____, which calmed him down.
6 My horrible brother used to _____ my arms and legs when our mum wasn't looking.
7 The doctor _____ pressure to the wound to stop the bleeding.
8 Don't use the whole of your fingers for massage, just the _____ .

Remember to test yourself

B Smelling and tasting 🎧

Pleasant smells/flavours	Meaning
*What a **delicate** flavour/ **fragrance**.*	**delicate** light and pleasant. SYN **subtle**. **fragrance** 1 a pleasant smell. **fragrant** ADJ. 2 a perfume.
*It has a **faint** smell of pear.*	**faint** just possible to smell, see, or hear.
*The book has lots of **appetizing** recipes.*	**appetizing** making you feel hungry. OPP **unappetizing**. (**Lose** your **appetite** = lose your desire for food.)
*The smells from the kitchen were **making my mouth water**.*	**water** If your mouth **waters**, you produce **saliva** (= the liquid produced in the mouth) and you want to eat. **mouth-watering** ADJ.
*The **aroma** of fresh coffee.*	**aroma** a pleasant, distinctive smell.
Less pleasant smells/flavours	
*This soup is **insipid**.*	**insipid** not having much taste. SYN **bland**.
*Garlic has a **pungent** smell.*	**pungent** very strong smelling.
*The house has a **musty odour**.*	**musty** smelling unpleasant or damp; without freshness. SYN **dank**. **odour** a smell, especially an unpleasant one.
*This fish smells **revolting**. I think it's **gone off**.*	**revolting** very unpleasant. SYN **disgusting**. **go off** (of food and drink) go bad and be unfit to eat or drink.
*There was a **nauseating stench** in the basement.*	**nauseating** making you feel you want to vomit. **stench** a strong, very unpleasant smell.

❸ Circle the correct word.

1 a nutty fragrance / flavour
2 an appetizing / unappetizing odour
3 a pungent / bland smell of burning rubber
4 the musty / salty smell of old books
5 a delicate aroma / stench
6 it makes your mouth saliva / water
7 a fragrant / nauseating smell of old fish
8 meat without salt is revolting / insipid

> **spotlight** **Adjectives ending in -y**
>
> **Lemony, fishy, woody, nutty, peppery, salty, fruity** are often used to describe smells and flavours. The *-y* suffix can mean 'full of something', e.g. *This soup's very **salty***; or it means 'having a flavour/smell similar to sth', e.g. *a **lemony** perfume; cheese with a **nutty** flavour.*

❹ Complete the text.

We found a table by the window and looked at the menu. It all looked very (1) a_____ and the smells coming from the kitchen were (2) m_____ . I chose the steamed fish with herbs, which I expected to have quite a (3) d_____ flavour, but when it arrived, it had an unpleasant, almost (4) p_____ smell. I took a mouthful and realized that the fish had actually (5) g_____ _____ ; it tasted absolutely (6) d_____ . The waiter was extremely apologetic, but by this time I had lost my (7) a_____ . I couldn't get the (8) s_____ of that horrid fish out of my mind. My brother's meal, however, was more successful: he had a chicken soup which was delicious, with delicate, (9) s_____ flavours.

❺ ABOUT YOU Write your answers, or ask another student.

What makes *your* mouth water? _____
What's your favourite smell? _____
What food do you find bland or insipid? _____
What odour do you find nauseating or revolting? _____
Is there a dank or musty smell in any buildings you know? _____

Remember to test yourself

13 I can describe illness and injuries

A Problems from head to toe 🎧

Example	Meaning
I had an **itchy scalp** until I started using this special shampoo.	**scalp** the skin covering the part of the head where your hair is. If it **itches** (or is **itchy**), you want to **scratch** it (*see picture*).
I've got a **splitting headache**.	a very bad headache.
I suffer from **hay fever** in the summer.	an allergy affecting the nose, eyes, and throat, caused by pollen from plants.
Why does he get **mouth ulcers**?	small sore areas inside the mouth, usually lasting a few days.
He **dislocated** his shoulder.	put a bone out of its normal position.
That's a **nasty rash** on your arm.	**rash** an area of red spots on the skin, caused by an illness or a reaction to sth; **nasty** = unpleasant (also a **nasty accident**).
I had an **upset stomach** this morning. (or I had a **stomach upset** . . .)	a stomach problem causing sickness or **diarrhoea** (= passing waste from the body too often and in liquid form).
I often get **constipated** on holiday.	unable to move waste material from the body. **constipation** N.
My mother's got **high blood pressure**.	**blood pressure** the pressure of the blood as it moves round the body. (**High** and **low blood pressure** are problem conditions.)
I **sprained** my **ankle**[1] running. He **pulled a muscle**[2] in training.	**sprain sth** injure a part of the body (usually the wrist or ankle) by turning it suddenly. SYN **twist sth**. **pull a muscle** injure a muscle by stretching it too much.
I've got a **blister** on my **heel** from wearing those new shoes.	a sore swelling on the surface of the skin (here on the back of the foot) often caused by rubbing or burning.

1 Combine words in the box to form nine common illnesses or injuries.

sprain	high	hay	upset	nasty	dislocated	splitting	itchy
stomach	scalp	blood pressure	mouth	shoulder	fever	headache	
your ankle	rash	ulcer					

....

....

2 Complete the sentences with a single word.

1 I've got .... on my hands from working so hard in the garden.
2 I sometimes get a .... on my face if I eat seafood.
3 The .... was caused by something I ate last night.
4 I've got a few mosquito bites and they really ....
5 I took tablets for diarrhoea, then I had the opposite problem. I was ....
6 He .... a muscle in training yesterday.

3 ABOUT YOU Which problems do you think are serious, and how many of them would require a visit to the doctor? Write your answers or ask another student.

Remember to test yourself

B Medicine labels 🎧

Tablets must be **dissolved** in water.

Please read the **enclosed leaflet** before taking these tablets.

This product can cause **lethargy** or **drowsiness**.

Possible **side effects** may include stomach **disorders**.

For **short-term** use only.

Discard any remaining solution 60 days after opening the bottle.

WARNING
DO NOT **EXCEED**
THE STATED **DOSE**

If symptoms **persist**, consult your doctor.

Do not use after **expiry date**.

spotlight	*exceed* and related forms

1 do more of sth than is stated in an order or a law.
*Do not **exceed** the **stated dose**.*
*You shouldn't **exceed** the **speed limit**.*
2 be greater than a number, amount, or quality.
*The cost won't **exceed** $5,000.* OR *The cost won't be **in excess of** $5,000.*
*The film **exceeded my expectations**.*
(= it was better than I had expected)

Glossary

dissolve sth (in sth)	mix a solid with a liquid until it becomes part of it. (If sth is **soluble** it can be dissolved, e.g. **soluble aspirin**.)
lethargy	the state of not having any energy to do things. **lethargic** ADJ.
drowsiness	the state of feeling tired and almost asleep. **drowsy** ADJ.
short-term	lasting only a short period, e.g. **a short-term solution**. OPP **long-term**, e.g. **a long-term contract**.
dose (or dosage)	the amount of a medicine that you take at any one time.
enclosed	included inside sth else, usually inside a letter or packet.
leaflet	one or several pages of information about sth.
side effect	an extra and usually bad effect that a drug has on you.
disorder	an illness in a part of the body.
discard sth	get rid of sth you no longer want or need.
persist	continue to exist (used especially about sth unpleasant). **persistent** ADJ.
expiry date	the date after which sth should not be used. **expire** V.

4 True or false? Write T or F.

1 Drugs can have side effects. _____
2 Drowsiness means dying under water. _____
3 You can read a leaflet. _____
4 Lethargy means a lack of energy. _____
5 If something persists, it stops. _____
6 'In excess of 50' is more than 50. _____
7 You can dissolve sugar in water. _____
8 If you feel drowsy, you want to sleep. _____

5 Add a word to complete a common phrase.

1 Don't exceed the stated _____
2 a long-_____ solution
3 the expiry _____
4 soluble _____
5 exceed the speed _____
6 common side _____

6 Rewrite the sentences but keep the meaning the same. You only need one word.

1 I don't have any energy.
I feel _____ .
2 He's got something wrong with his stomach.
He's got a stomach _____ .
3 The information is included with this letter.
The information is _____ .
4 It was better than I thought it would be.
It exceeded my _____ .
5 I keep getting headaches.
I've had _____ headaches.
6 They threw away the old newspapers.
They _____ the old newspapers.

Remember to test yourself

Review: The body

Unit 7

1 Match the sentence halves.

1	The baby had chubby	a	attention.
2	His stomach sticks	b	hips.
3	He wouldn't pay	c	paunch.
4	When she walks she swings her	d	beard.
5	He's got freckles all over his	e	guidelines.
6	He eats far too much; he's got a	f	out.
7	I followed the	g	face.
8	He's got a ginger	h	cheeks.

2 One word is incorrect in each sentence. Cross it out and write the correct word at the end.

▶ Fashion experts always recommend that you ~~pull~~ off your best features.   _show_

1 The teacher attracted my attention to several errors in my essay.   ....

2 Light-coloured walls in a room make an illusion of space.   ....

3 As a child, I had to wear a brace for a year to loosen my teeth.   ....

4 Unfortunately, tight shirts only enhance the size of his paunch.   ....

5 I'm not sure of her exact age but she must be going on for ninety.   ....

6 Vertical stripes can be unflattering, making you look slimmer.   ....

7 I wish I knew the key for success in life.   ....

8 Vertical stripes on sleeves can cover the fact that you have plump arms.   ....

A Z **more words:** *stocky, lanky, gaunt, stooped, rugged features, ruddy cheeks*

Unit 8

1 Complete the dialogue.

A   I had an embarrassing time last night; I was in a bar and this guy thought I was
    (1) f_____ with him.

B   And why was that?

A   Well, he must have thought I (2) f_____ him for some reason.

B   Why? Were you staring at him or (3) f_____ with your hair, or something?

A   Well I was actually looking at the people behind him, but I guess he thought I was trying to make
    eye (4) c_____ with him. Basically he just jumped to the wrong (5) c_____ .
    Anyway, he came over and started chatting, and he was (6) l_____ towards me, a bit
    too close, actually. And I realized I was being quite defensive because I noticed that my arms were
    (7) f_____ across my chest, and I was just (8) g_____ redder and redder with
    embarrassment.

B   Well, maybe he just (9) m_____ the signals you were giving off. Did you get rid of him?

A   Well, no … in the end we got talking and I realized he was really nice, so I think I might see him again.

A Z **more words:** *wink, frown, twitch, pout, grimace, wriggle*

Unit 9

1 Write a logical answer.

1 Why might someone have a pronounced limp? _____
2 What would make a horse gallop? _____
3 Why might you go for a stroll? _____
4 Why might you creep downstairs? _____
5 Is it good to have constant interruptions at work? _____
6 If work is relentless, is it enjoyable? _____
7 On a long walk, why might you alternate between walking and running? _____
8 What should you do if you feel stiff? _____

A Z **more words:** *stumble, trudge, shuffle, meander, get a **move** on, stampede*

Unit 10

1 Complete the sound story from the unit.

It was a dark and stormy night; I shut my eyes . . .

1 the wind r_____ the windows
2 thunder r_____ in the distance
3 the trees r_____ in the wind
4 I heard the rain s_____ on to the windows
5 a horn b_____
6 there was a s_____ of brakes
7 a car door was s_____ shut
8 footsteps s_____ through the mud
9 there was a c_____ noise on the stairs
10 there was a high-p_____ scream – from me!

2 Match the things/animals with the correct noise in the box.

1 lions _____
2 floorboards _____
3 wolves _____
4 windows _____
5 car brakes _____
6 dogs _____
7 bees _____
8 doors _____

slam	howl
rattle	buzz
roar	bark
creak	screech

A Z **more words:** *hiss, grunt, whine, squeal, shriek, yap, purr*

Unit 11

1 There is one spelling mistake in each sentence. Find the mistake and correct it.

1 It was so dark when we left that I could barily see. _____
2 You get breathmaking views from the top of the hill. _____
3 I think she's been suffering from blured vision. _____
4 They were eyeing us wearily, so they obviously didn't trust us. _____
5 There were teals running down her cheeks. _____
6 I noticed that she was blinting a lot; perhaps she was nervous. _____
7 We stood and gazed at the view; it was spectactular. _____
8 I've got some drops to allariate the pain. _____

A Z **more words:** *squint, peer, scan, conspicuous, bleary-eyed, distinct*

Unit 12

1 Put these words into the correct columns below.

tap   stench   fragrance   vigorous   bland   squeeze   aroma   insipid
musty   stroke   slide   pungent   pinch   peppery

TOUCH	SMELL	TASTE

A Z more words: *slap, nudge, feel around for sth, poke, tickle, flick, scrape*

Unit 13

1 Complete the crossword. The letters in the grey squares spell out a phrase. What is it?

1 Some drugs can give you side .... you don't expect.
2 We guarantee that the rise will not be in .... of 3 per cent.
3 I had a terrible headache and an .... stomach yesterday.
4 He .... his ankle walking in the mountains.
5 Go and see your doctor if the symptoms .... for more than two days.
6 If your skin feels ...., avoid scratching it if possible.
7 Take care not to exceed the .... stated on the packet.
8 Some medicine can make you feel drowsy or ....
9 Her skin is very soft, so she easily gets .... on her fingers when playing tennis.
10 I have a mouth .... – it's really sore.

2 Cross out any words which are not possible.

1 The *long-term / short-term / soluble* answer to this problem is to have an operation.
2 I had a *persistent / twisted / splitting* headache this morning.
3 What is the correct *dose / dosage / side effect* for this medicine?
4 She exceeded *the speed limit / the expiry date / all my expectations*.
5 I have *constipated / an itchy scalp / a nasty rash*.
6 *A rash / Drowsiness / Lethargy* indicates a lack of energy.

A Z more words: *dandruff, bowels, gums, runny nose, lump, cramp*

14 I can **discuss aspects of character**

A Personal qualities 🎧

Online dating: find your dream partner

Katarina's profile:
....

I'm a **spontaneous**, **happy-go-lucky** sort of person, but I'm pretty **down-to-earth** too. My friends say I'm a real **chatterbox** but maybe that's because I'm truly **passionate** about people, ideas, life, etc. I'll **give** anything **a go**, **within reason**!

Katarina describes her ideal match:
....

I'**m drawn to** men who are **considerate** and happy to show **affection**. A guy with **integrity**, and NOT **pretentious**. As you can imagine, I think **spontaneity** is a positive **attribute** – I love things to be a bit unpredictable.

Glossary

spontaneous	acting in an open and natural way, without worrying about what you say or do. **spontaneity** N.
happy-go-lucky	not caring or worrying about the future.
down-to-earth	sensible and realistic in things you say or think.
chatterbox	INF a person who talks a lot. **chatty** ADJ.
passionate	very enthusiastic or interested in sth. **passion (for sth)** N.
give sth a go	be prepared to try sth. SYN **have a go**, **give sth a try**.
within reason	according to what is practical, possible, or sensible.
be drawn to sth/sb	be attracted to sb/sth.
considerate	always thinking about other people's wishes and feelings. SYN **thoughtful**. OPP **inconsiderate**.
affection	the feeling of liking or caring about sth/sb. **affectionate** ADJ.
integrity	the quality of being honest and having strong moral principles.
pretentious	trying to appear important, intelligent, etc. to impress others.
attribute	a quality or feature of sb/sth.

❶ Correct the mistakes.

▶ I've never been drawn ~~by~~ people just because they're affectionate.
   to

1 My cousin's a very lucky-go-happy person.

2 You can wear what you like to school, with reason.

3 I'd love to have a go for skydiving.

4 She's very kind and inconsiderate; she's always helping people.

5 My father had a lifelong passionate for classical music.

6 She's good fun but she's a real chatty!

7 He's a great boss – really down-the-earth.

❷ Complete the sentences.

1 Integrity is usually considered to be a positive _____ .

2 Marisa was very cold and strict with her children and showed them little _____ .

3 If you want to try skiing, why don't you just give it a _____ ?

4 She's always using foreign words when she speaks – I just find that very _____ .

5 He loves to do things without any planning – he's very _____ .

6 I've never trusted Morgan; he's got no principles. He lacks _____ .

B Character in a work context

A **What did you make of** the two candidates for the job?

B I thought Joe Pascoe was **a real character** – **quick-witted**, and **shrewd**.

A Shrewd, yes, and I'd say pretty **ruthless** too. But I didn't **take to** him personally. I thought he **came across as** rather **pushy** and a bit **conceited**. Catherine actually **struck me as** being more suitable for this job.

B She certainly seemed very **conscientious** and **trustworthy**, but I wonder whether she's got the necessary **charisma**, or whether she's **assertive** enough for this role.

A Maybe not. But she's not the kind of person who'd **get up people's noses**, which Joe might.

Glossary

What do you make of sb/sth?	= What's your impression of sb/sth?	**conceited**	DISAPPROVING thinking you are very important, clever, etc.
character	INF An interesting or unusual person can be called **a character** (or **a real character**).	**strike sb (as sth)**	give sb a particular impression.
		conscientious	taking care to do things carefully and correctly.
quick-witted	able to think quickly; intelligent.	**trustworthy**	able to be relied on as good, honest, etc.
shrewd	good at judging people and situations. SYN **astute**.	**charisma**	a quality that makes other people like you and be attracted to you. **charismatic** ADJ.
ruthless	determined to get what you want and not caring about others.		
take to sb/sth	start liking sb/sth.	**assertive**	behaving confidently so that people take notice of what you say.
come across (as)	make a particular impression.		
pushy	INF trying hard to get what you want, especially in a rude manner.	**get up sb's nose**	INF annoy sb very much.

3 Positive or negative? Write P or N.

1 She gets up my nose. _____
2 He's pretty trustworthy. _____
3 She strikes me as shrewd. _____
4 He's very quick-witted. _____
5 He comes across as quite pushy. _____

6 She's pretty ruthless. _____
7 He's a real character. _____
8 He's not very astute. _____
9 I'd say she was conscientious. _____
10 She's very charismatic. _____

4 Complete the text.

There's a new guy living next door to us and I didn't know what to (1) m_____ of him at first. He wasn't very friendly and he walked about as if he was 'Mr-Know-It-All', so he (2) s_____ me as rather (3) c_____ . I just didn't (4) t_____ to him at all. He took my parking space several times, which really got up my (5) n_____ . So, last night, I decided to be (6) a_____ and challenge him about it. He was fine and apologized! I was really quite surprised.

5 ABOUT YOU Complete the questions, then write your answers or ask another student.

1 Do you consider yourself to be c___nsc___nt___s? _____
2 How ___ss___rt___v___ are you if things don't go your way? _____
3 Do you think you're shr_____d with money? _____
4 Do you have the capacity to be r___thl___ss if necessary? _____
5 How tr___stw___rthy do you consider yourself to be? _____

Remember to test yourself

C Judging character 🎧

HOW SOMEONE appears **on the surface** may not be a true picture of what they're really like. A person who seems **aloof** and **stand-offish** may just be shy and **diffident**. As they say: **don't judge a book by its cover**. Other personality **traits** can be **misleading**; a bad quality in one context may be a **virtue** in another, e.g. being **cunning**, or **impulsive**, or **naive**. Then there are qualities considered to be negative, but is it always wrong to be cruel or **cynical**? Remember the saying: sometimes you have to **be cruel to be kind**.

Don't judge a book by its cover

Glossary

on the surface	when not looked at or thought about carefully.	**virtue**	a good or desirable quality. OPP **vice**. **virtuous** ADJ.
aloof	not friendly towards others. SYNS **distant**, **stand-offish** INF.	**cunning**	able to do things by being clever, but not always honest. SYN **crafty**.
diffident	not confident; not wanting to talk about yourself. SYN **shy**.	**impulsive**	doing things quickly, without thinking about the results. SYNS **impetuous**, **rash**.
don't judge a book by its cover	SAYING don't form an opinion of sth/sb by their appearance only.	**naive**	lacking experience of life, and trusting others too easily. **naivety** N.
trait	a feature of sb's character.		
misleading	giving the wrong idea or impression. SYN **deceptive**. **mislead sb** V. SYN **deceive sb**.	**be cruel to be kind**	SAYING make sb suffer because it will be good for them later.

spotlight *cynical, sceptical*

If you are **cynical**, you believe people do things for themselves rather than for unselfish reasons. **cynicism** N.
If you are **sceptical about sth**, you are not confident that it is true or will happen. **scepticism** N.
*My brother is very **cynical** about politicians and their motives.*   *I'm very **sceptical about** the results of this survey.*

6 Replace the underlined word with another word that has a similar meaning.

1 Don't be <u>deceived</u> by her sweet smile; she's really tough. _____
2 I don't know why he's so <u>aloof</u>, but he certainly isn't very friendly. _____
3 Simon is usually rather <u>shy</u> in company. _____
4 Jumping off that wall was such an <u>impetuous</u> thing to do. _____
5 You have to keep an eye on Will because he's very <u>crafty</u>. _____
6 His charm is <u>misleading</u> because he can be ruthless if necessary. _____

7 Complete the sentences with a suitable word.

1 Most people believe that honesty is a _____ and jealousy is a _____ .
2 He told me he'd win the race but I'm a bit _____ . I don't think he's good enough.
3 He says he loves her. I'm a bit _____ ; I think he just wants her money.
4 I felt bad not giving my dog any food when he was ill, but you have to be _____ to be kind.
5 On the _____ she seemed quite cold, but you can't judge a book by its _____ .
6 Cynicism is one of his less appealing character _____ .
7 Ella's problem is _____ ; she trusts people too easily and then gets hurt.

📓 Remember to test yourself

15 I can **talk about feelings**

A Strong feelings and reactions 🎧

Word/Phrase	Example	Meaning
ecstatic	I was **ecstatic** about my new job.	very happy. SYNS **euphoric**, **elated**, **over the moon** INF.
jubilant	The **jubilant** fans were cheering as they left the stadium.	feeling extremely happy because of a success.
in tears	She was **in tears** by the time we got to the hospital.	crying (**close to tears** = nearly crying).
devastated	I was **devastated** when she left me.	very upset. SYN **heartbroken**.
lose your temper **hit the roof** INF	He completely **lost his temper**. He'll **hit the roof** when he sees it.	become very angry. SYN **go mad** INF.
gutted INF	I was **gutted** when we lost the match.	very disappointed.
hysterical	When the little girl collapsed, her mother became **hysterical**. The kids at the party were **hysterical**.	being in a state of extreme distress or excitement and crying, laughing, or shouting, etc.
stunned	I was **stunned** when they gave me the prize.	shocked and surprised. SYN **gobsmacked** INF.
appalled	I was **appalled** by the conditions they had to live in.	shocked because sth is very unpleasant. SYN **horrified**.

1 Are these positive or negative? Write P or N.

1 ecstatic ....
2 gutted ....
3 horrified ....
4 jubilant ....
5 euphoric ....
6 appalled ....
7 elated ....
8 desperate ....

> **spotlight** *desperate and related forms*
>
> **Desperate** means extremely anxious. *Without food or money, Karen was **desperate**. Jumping into the freezing water was an act of **sheer** (= absolute) **desperation** N. He was **desperately unhappy** ADV (= extremely unhappy).*

2 Find six phrases in the box.

lose	over	desperately	close	unhappy	hit	your temper	mad
go	to tears	the roof	the moon				

....

....

3 Complete the dialogues by repeating what the speaker says in a different way.

1 I should think she was gobsmacked.~ She was – absolutely ....
2 Did he get very angry?~ Yes, I'm afraid he lost ....
3 Had he given up hope of being rescued?~ Yes. It was an act of ....
4 Was he terribly upset?~ Yes, he was absolutely ....
5 He must've gone mad.~ He did. He hit ....
6 I bet they were over the moon.~ Yes, they were absolutely ....
7 She was really emotional, wasn't she?~ Yes, she was in ....
8 Were the children overexcited?~ Yes, they were ....

Remember to test yourself

B Expressing your emotions 🎧

ARE YOU the kind of person who **bottles up their emotions**? Or do you **wear your heart on your sleeve**? As a journalist, I'm aware that if you **disclose** too much about yourself, you could make yourself rather **vulnerable**. And if I'm honest, as a man I feel a bit **uneasy** when people **pour out** their **innermost thoughts** to me. My own **instinct** is to be quite **guarded** and not **give away** too much about how I feel. On the other hand, psychologists say it's unhealthy to **suppress your feelings**. It can lead to severe anxiety and depression if you don't learn how to release your **pent-up** emotions. ●

spotlight	Other expressions with *heart*

*I started a business degree, but **my heart wasn't** really **in it**.* (= I wasn't interested in or enthusiastic about it.)
I didn't have the heart to *tell her she'd failed.* (= I was unable to tell her that she'd failed, because I knew she'd be upset.)
My heart told me *to help him.* (= Emotionally, I felt I should help him.)

Glossary

bottle sth up	stop yourself showing negative emotions or feelings, especially over a long time (**bottle up your emotions**).
wear your heart on your sleeve	make your feelings obvious to others.
disclose sth (to sb)	give sb information about sth, especially sth that has been secret. SYN **reveal sth**. (Related nouns are **disclosure** and **revelation**.)
vulnerable	weak and easily hurt, physically or emotionally.
uneasy	slightly nervous, embarrassed, or worried. SYN **uncomfortable**.
pour sth out	express all your feelings, often because you are unhappy.
innermost thoughts	the thoughts which are most personal and private.
instinct	a way of behaving that results from responses you were born with rather than responses you have learned. **instinctive** ADJ.
guarded	careful not to give too much information. SYN **cautious**.
give sth away	tell people secret information.
suppress your feelings	stop yourself from having or expressing feelings.
pent-up	(of emotions, energy, etc.) held back; not shown or expressed.

4 Replace the underlined word(s) with a word that has a similar meaning.

1 I felt <u>uncomfortable</u> when he talked about his marriage problems. ....
2 He wouldn't <u>disclose</u> information if he thought it was secret. ....
3 I think it's dangerous to <u>bottle up</u> your feelings. ....
4 It's a difficult time for him and he's very <u>weak and easily hurt</u>. ....
5 She's a bit <u>cautious </u>if you ask about her private life. ....
6 He's happy to tell anyone his <u>most personal and private</u> thoughts. ....

5 Complete the sentences.

1 I knew he would be upset and I'm afraid I didn't have the .... to tell him.
2 She took part in the dancing competition, but you could tell her heart ....
3 The wedding date was meant to be a secret, but I'm afraid he .... it ....
4 Maxine's problem is that she wears her heart .... , whereas Gavin's the opposite: he has all these .... emotions which he can't express.
5 I should consider this more carefully, but my .... says it's the right thing to do.

Remember to test yourself

16 I can **talk about relationships**

A Difficult relationships 🎧

When I married Vince, he already had two daughters from his first marriage, and they **took an instant dislike to** me. They **resented** me being in their home, and either ignored me or were openly **hostile**. The neighbours didn't help either – nice enough **to my face** but not so c**omplimentary behind my back**. It was a **tough** time, and **inevitably** it **put a strain on** my relationship with Vince. Fortunately, he **stuck up for me** when the kids were difficult, and **as time went by**, things **settled down** a bit. Now, two years on . . .

Glossary

take an instant dislike to sb dislike sb as soon as you meet them.

resent sth feel anger about sth, often when it seems unfair. **resentment** N.

hostile unfriendly and aggressive. **hostility** N.

to sb's face If you say sth **to sb's face**, you say it to them directly.

complimentary (about sb) saying nice things about sb. (You can also **compliment sb on sth** or **pay sb a compliment**.)

behind sb's back If you say or do sth **behind sb's back**, you say or do it without their knowledge, and usually it is bad or unkind.

inevitably used for saying that sth is certain to happen. **inevitable** ADJ.

put a strain on sb/sth create pressure and anxiety for sb; create tension in a relationship.

stick up for sb support and defend sb if they are criticized.

as time went by over a period of time.

settle down become calmer and more relaxed.

1 Positive or negative? Write P or N.

1 She was full of resentment. _____
2 He was very complimentary. _____
3 She did it behind my back. _____
4 She can stick up for herself. _____
5 He was hostile. _____
6 Things have settled down. _____

2 Complete the words in the text.

Martin had been a top designer, and his boss had always been very (1) c_____ about his work. It was, therefore, a nasty shock when he was made redundant. Martin (2) r_____ the fact that he was chosen because he was the youngest, but he was even more shocked by his wife's (3) h_____. She blamed Martin for not (4) s_____ up for himself, and this fact, on top of the loss of his income, (5) i_____ put a big (6) s_____ on their relationship. They would need to make some (7) t_____ decisions about the future.

spotlight   tough

Tough has different meanings.
1 difficult: *It's a* **tough** *decision. He had a* **tough** *childhood.*
2 strict: **tough** *new driving laws.*
3 able to deal with difficult situations: *She'll be OK – she's* **tough**.

3 Complete the sentences.

1 Have you ever taken an _____ dislike to someone? Why?
2 When did you last have to stick _____ for yourself? Why?
3 When did you last pay someone a _____ ? What for?
4 Do you find it difficult to criticize people to their _____ ?
5 Do you think your life is getting better as time _____ by?

ABOUT YOU

_____
_____
_____
_____
_____

4 ABOUT YOU Write your answers to Exercise 3, or ask another student.

Remember to test yourself

B Successful relationships 🎧

Now, two years on, **things** are **looking up. Initially** the kids were **reluctant** to **accept** me and **made things difficult,** but I gave up work to spend more time with them, and that's helped to create a closer **bond.** I've **gained** their **respect** in other ways, too – they're prepared to **confide in** me now, especially the younger one. Vince and I still have our **ups and downs** – who doesn't? – but I know he **appreciates** the **sacrifices** I've **made,** and **the way things are** now, I'm feeling optimistic.

Glossary

things USU. PL used to talk about a situation or life in general (e.g. **the way things are; make things difficult; how are things?**).

look up INF (used about sb's situation or business) start to become better.

initially in the beginning. **initial** ADJ.

reluctant not wanting to do sth. SYN **unwilling. reluctance** N.

bond a connection between people based on shared feelings or experiences.

respect (for sb) a feeling of admiration for sb because of their qualities. (You can **gain, earn,** or **win sb's respect.**) **respect** V.

confide in sb tell sb personal information because you trust them.

ups and downs a mixture of good and bad things in life or a relationship.

appreciate sth recognize sth and welcome it. **appreciation** N.

make a sacrifice give up sth important or valuable in order to do sth that seems more important. **sacrifice sth** V.

spotlight   *accept*

Accept has other meanings apart from saying 'yes' to an offer.

1 allow sb to be part of a group:
   *They **accepted me** as one of the family.*
2 agree to sth:
   *The council has **accepted** the latest proposal.*
3 believe that sth is true:
   *He won't **accept that** nothing can be changed.*
4 admit you did sth wrong:
   *He **accepts responsibility** for the accident.*

5 Correct the mistake in each sentence.

1 He's fully accepted to our decision. ....
2 She feels she can confide with me. ....
3 I think they all respect for him. ....
4 The initially problem was money. ....
5 I regret his reluctant to go. ....
6 It took time to hold their respect. ....

6 Replace the underlined word/phrase with another word/phrase that has the same meaning.

1 How's <u>life</u>? ....
2 They were very <u>unwilling</u> to leave. ....
3 She <u>recognizes and is grateful for</u> everything you've done. ....
4 <u>In the beginning</u> it was a difficult relationship. ....
5 He <u>is prepared to take</u> responsibility for what happened. ....
6 There is widespread <u>admiration</u> for what he has achieved. ....
7 We've had <u>good times and bad times</u> in our relationship. ....
8 I had a tough time last year but things are <u>improving</u> now. ....
9 I like the <u>situation as it is</u>. ....
10 Because of the special <u>connection</u> parents have with their children, they often <u>give up many important things</u> for them. .... , ...

Remember to test yourself

17 I can **talk about people I admire and loathe**

A Qualities of personal heroes 🎧

My **heroine** was Mother Theresa. I admired her **courage**, her **dignity**, and her **humility**. More than anyone, she **inspired** me to devote my life to looking after people.

I used to **idolize** David Beckham. I admired him for his **dedication**, and the fact that when the press **had a go at** him, he never reacted in a negative way.

I really **looked up to** my grandfather. He was a lifeboat captain for 20 years, and showed remarkable **bravery** on many occasions. One day I hope to **follow in his footsteps.**

Glossary	
heroine	Your **heroine** is a woman you admire for her ability or personal qualities (**hero** for a man). SYN **idol**.
courage	the ability to do sth, even though it is dangerous, frightening, or very difficult. **courageous** ADJ. SYNS **bravery** N, **brave** ADJ.
dignity	a calm, controlled manner in a difficult situatioN. **dignified** ADJ.
humility	the quality of not believing you are better or more important than others. **humble** ADJ.
inspire sb	give sb the enthusiasm and desire to do sth. **inspiration** N. **inspirational** ADJ.
idolize sb	admire or love sb very much. SYN **worship sb**.
dedication	the hard work and effort that sb puts into an activity because they care about it. **dedicate sth/ yourself to sth/sb** V. **dedicated** ADJ.
have a go at sb	INF say unkind things or complain about sb. SYN **criticize sb**.
look up to sb	admire and respect sb, often sb who is older or in a higher position.
follow in sb's footsteps	do the same work or be as successful as sb before you.

1 Complete the sentences with the correct form of the word in CAPITALS.

1 He was so _____ . COURAGE
2 He's a very _____ man. HUMILITY
3 She showed great _____ . BRAVE
4 He's an _____ leader. INSPIRATION
5 She has such _____ . DIGNIFIED
6 I _____ him. IDOL

2 Rewrite the sentences starting with the words given. The meaning must stay the same.

1 I admired my father.   I looked _____ .
2 I want to do the same work as him.   I want to follow _____ .
3 Why did she criticize him?   Why did she have _____ ?
4 He was dedicated to helping the poor.   He dedicated _____ .
5 She inspired me.   She was _____ .
6 Paula worshipped him.   He was _____ .

3 ABOUT YOU Write your answers or ask another student.

Who do you idolize or look up to? Why? _____
Would you like to follow in anyone's footsteps? _____
Do you know anyone who you would describe as:
courageous or dignified or humble or dedicated? _____

Remember to test yourself

B People we loathe and why we hate them 🎧

Pop stars who start off as **rebels** or **idealists** with strong moral **principles**. Then, as soon as they become rich and famous, their **values** change completely. What **hypocrites**!

Snobs. You know, people who **look down on** others, and think they're **vulgar**.

I **was bullied** at school, and since then I've always **despised bullies**.

People who spread **malicious gossip** are just **despicable** in my opinion.

Glossary	
rebel	a person who opposes people in authority. **rebel** V. **rebellious** ADJ.
idealist	a person who believes the world can be perfect. **idealistic** ADJ.
hypocrite	a person who says they have strong principles but does not act according to these principles. **hypocrisy** N. **hypocritical** ADJ.
snob	a person who thinks they are better than people in lower social classes.
look down on sb	think that you are better than sb.
vulgar	not polite, elegant, or having good taste. SYNS **coarse**, **crude**.
be bullied	be hurt or frightened by sb who is bigger and stronger (the person who does the **bullying** is a **bully**).
despise sb/sth	hate and have no respect for sb/ sth. **despicable** ADJ.
malicious	showing hatred and the desire to hurt people's feelings. **malice** N. SYNS **spiteful** ADJ, **spite** N (e.g. *He did it out of malice/spite*.).
gossip	stories about other people's private lives, which may be unkind or untrue. **gossip** V (also **spread gossip**; the person who does this is **a gossip**).

---

spotlight	*principles* and *values*

Principles (USU. PL) are strong beliefs that influence how you behave; **values** are beliefs about what is right and important in life. The words are almost synonymous but are used in different expressions. *Eating meat is* ***against my principles***. *I won't go there* ***on principle***. *She has a different* ***set of values***.

4 Write the related adjective.

1 hypocrite ....
2 rebel ....
3 idealist ....
4 malice ....
5 spite ....
6 despise ....

5 Write a word at the end of the line to describe each of these people.

1 He looks down on other people. He's a ....
2 She's always talking about others behind their back. She's a ....
3 She's against anyone in a position of power or authority. She's a ....
4 He's horrible to anyone he sees as smaller or weaker. He's a ....
5 She believes everything in the world can be perfect. She's an ....
6 He tells us it's wrong to swear, then he uses bad language. He's a ....
7 I'm afraid he's got bad manners and he's very rude. He's ....

6 ABOUT YOU Write your answers or ask another student.

Being a snob or being a hypocrite – which is worse? ....
Is bullying worse than either of the above? Why/why not? ....
How do you feel about people who spread gossip? ....
Is there anything or anyone that you despise? Why? ....

Remember to test yourself

18 I can **talk about behaviour**

A Influences on behaviour 🎧

Why do we behave the way we do? Is it **nature** or **nurture**? According to behavioural psychologist Michael Woods, various factors have an **impact on** our lives.

Parents **play** a crucial **part**; other **role models** are less influential.
Peer pressure is a significant factor.
Positive **incentives** are effective; **deterrents** aren't.
A **broken home** or **deprived** childhood needn't have a **detrimental effect**.

Glossary

nature	the basic character of a person: *Violence isn't in his nature.*
nurture	the care and attention given to help sb develop. **nurture sb** v.
impact (on sth)	an effect or influence on sth.
play a part (in sth)	be involved and influential in developing sth.
role model	a person you admire and learn from.
peer pressure	the influence on your behaviour of people around you of the same age.
incentive (to do sth)	a thing that encourages you to work harder, do sth, etc.
deterrent	a thing that makes you less likely to do sth. **deter sb** v.
broken home	a family in which the parents are divorced or separated.
deprived	without sufficient food, education, or money. **deprivation** N.
detrimental effect (on sth)	a very negative effect. OPP **beneficial effect**.

1 Find six compound words or phrases in the box.

peer	nature or	play	broken	deprived	a beneficial
home	pressure	childhood	a part	nurture?	effect

....

....

2 Are these positive or negative statements? Write P or N.

1 She was nurtured by her parents. ....   4 It had a detrimental effect on me. ....
2 He's considered a role model for boys. ....   5 It proved to be a real incentive. ....
3 There is a lot of deprivation. ....   6 It was a deterrent to helping others. ....

3 Complete the text.

Dan came from a broken (1) .... , had a fairly (2) .... childhood, and was stealing by the age of 13 because of peer (3) .... He also got into fights, although it wasn't in his (4) .... to be violent. Then he joined a boxing club, which had a real (5) .... on his life. The owner was Dan's first positive role (6) .... , and he played an important (7) .... in changing Dan's attitude to life. Dan is now dedicated to boxing. He could be in the England team at the next Olympics, and that is a real (8) .... for him to train hard.

4 ABOUT YOU Do you agree with the statements at the top of the page? Write your answers or ask another student.

Remember to test yourself

B Teenage behaviour 🎧

Getting **messy** teens to **pull their weight**

YOU CAN **go on and on** about the state of your teenager's bedroom, but **nagging** doesn't work. Their room may be untidy and **unappealing**, but it's not **life-threatening**, so why **make a fuss**? Instead, **lay down rules** for the rest of the home which you all share. Explain what you **expect** your teenagers to do, and get them to agree to it. **Set an example** by being tidy yourself, but don't **give in** and clear up their **mess**. ⊠

Glossary

messy	dirty or untidy. **mess** N (sb can **make a mess**; sth can **be in a mess**).
pull your weight	work as hard as everyone else in a job or activity. SYN **do your fair share**.
go on and on (about sth, at sb)	keep talking (about sth or to sb) in a boring way.
nag	keep complaining about sb's behaviour.
unappealing	not pleasant or attractive. OPP **appealing**.
life-threatening	likely to cause death (here it is being used humorously).
fuss	If you **make a fuss about sth**, you become angry and complain about sth which probably isn't important. SYN **kick up a fuss** INF.
lay down rules	say officially what the rules are.
set an (or a good/bad) example	behave in a way that others may copy.
give in (to sb/sth)	agree to do sth that you don't want to do. SYN **capitulate** (**to sb/sth**) FML.

5 Use each verb once to complete the expressions.

> pull   kick up   set   lay down   do   make

1 .... an example   3 .... a mess   5 .... your fair share
2 .... a fuss   4 .... your weight   6 .... rules

6 Complete the dialogues in a suitable way.
1 A Is he likely to die?
   B No, it's not life-............... .
2 A Do they make a fuss about things?
   B Yes, they go ....
3 A Did you tidy up your room?
   B Yes, because Mum kept ....
4 A Is the room untidy?
   B Yes, it's in ....
5 A Did you agree to do it?
   B Not at first, then I .... / ....
6 A It's not an attractive colour.
   B No, it's very ....

7 ABOUT YOU Write your answers or ask another student.

What do/did your parents expect you to do around the home? ....
Do/Did they set a good example around the home? ....
Do you think you do/did your fair share of the work? ....
Is/Was your bedroom in a mess most of the time? ....

Remember to test yourself

19 I can **talk about manners**

A Table manners 🎧

Dining **etiquette**

1

In the Philippines, it's **considered good manners** to eat all the food on your plate.

In Afghanistan, wasting food is **frowned upon**, and talking with your mouth full is **viewed as** being **discourteous**.

In China, it's **customary** and **respectful** to pass food to the elderly first. You should never stab **chopsticks**[1] into a bowl of rice and leave them pointing **upwards**: this is **regarded as** extremely **disrespectful**. It can also be **offensive** to remove rice from a bowl with a spoon.

Glossary

etiquette	the formal rules of correct or polite behaviour in society.
manners	(PL) behaviour that is considered polite in a particular society or culture.
frown on/upon sth/sb	(often passive) disapprove of sth/sb.
discourteous	FML having bad manners and not showing respect. OPP **courteous. courtesy** N.
customary	usually done in a particular place or situation. **custom** N.
respectful	showing polite behaviour towards sb/sth. OPP **disrespectful**.
upwards	moving or pointing towards a higher position. OPP **downwards**.
offensive	rude in a way that makes sb upset or annoyed. OPP **inoffensive**.

> **spotlight** *consider, regard, view, perceive* FML
>
> These verbs all mean to think about something in a particular way. They are commonly used in passive constructions like this:
> *It is **considered** (**to be**) the correct thing to do.*
> *It is **regarded**/**viewed**/**perceived as** the correct thing to do.*

❶ Correct the spelling mistakes.

1 inoffencive ....
2 curteous ....
3 etikette ....
4 percieve ....
5 downwords ....
6 chopstiks ....

❷ Complete the sentences.   ABOUT YOUR COUNTRY

1 It is c................ to eat chicken with your fingers when you're at the table. ....
2 Talking with your mouth full is usually f................ upon. ....
3 Parents think it's important for children to have good table m................ . ...
4 Not eating food you are given is generally v................ as discourteous. ....
5 It is c................ very bad manners to eat everything you are given. ....
6 C................ related to the serving of food are the same all over the country. ....
7 It is r................ as r................ to offer food to the elderly first. ....
8 As a guest, it would be o................ to say the host's food was badly cooked. ....
9 It is d................ to start eating before others have been served. ....
10 It is normal e................ to put your knife and fork / chopsticks by the side of your plate/bowl when you have finished eating. ....

❸ ABOUT YOUR COUNTRY Are the sentences in Exercise 2 true or false, or does it depend on different factors? Write your answers, or ask another student.

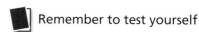 Remember to test yourself

B Polite or impolite? 🎧

DAN   Felicity's manners are **impeccable**, aren't they?
BETH   Yes, **exemplary**, but that brother of hers is a bit **cheeky**.
DAN   I'd call him **insolent**, actually, or even **downright** rude.

JO   I don't think Julian will **be put out** if you leave the party early.
JIM   I just don't want to **put my foot in it**, you know. His family are very **upper class**.
JO   Well, you'll just have to **be on your best behaviour**, then!

KAZ   I really **took exception to** Arnold's **remarks**; I thought they were **disgraceful**.
BEN   Yes, I couldn't agree more. They really were **in poor taste**.

Glossary

impeccable	perfect (**impeccable manners/behaviour/service**).
exemplary	FML excellent, and done in a way that others should copy.
cheeky	INF rude, often in an amusing way (often used by adults about children). **cheek** N (**What a cheek!** = How rude!).
insolent	extremely rude and disrespectful. **insolence** N.
downright	used to emphasize sth negative (**downright rude/offensive**).
be put out	be upset or offended. SYN **take offence**.
put your foot in it	INF say sth that offends or upsets sb.
upper class	considered to have the highest social status (also **middle class**, **lower class**, **working class**).
be on your best behaviour	behave in the most polite way you can.
take exception to sth	object strongly to sth and be angry about it.
remark	a few words that give your opinion about sth. SYN **comment**.
disgraceful	very bad or unacceptable. **disgrace** N (**What a disgrace!**).
be in poor/bad taste	be offensive and not at all appropriate.

4 Cross out any words in italics which are not possible. All three may be possible.

1 He was *put out / put his foot in it / on his best behaviour*.
2 She made *a rude / an insolent / a cheeky* remark.
3 What she said was in *poor / bad / cheek* taste.
4 Unfortunately she took *exception / offence / her foot in it*.
5 His behaviour is *impeccable / disgraceful / exemplary*.
6 I thought they were downright *rude / comments / disgrace*.
7 Is he *upper / working / middle* class?
8 What *a cheek / a disgrace / an insolence*!

5 Complete the texts.

I have a very unusual friend called Erwin who considers himself to be very upper (1) _____ .
He is incredibly polite and has exemplary (2) _____ , and I always feel rather uncomfortable
with him, because I feel I have to be on my best (3) _____ all the time. I'm very nervous
about putting my (4) _____ in it, especially if I go to his place for dinner. If I get there even
five minutes late, he seems to be quite (5) _____ out.

I've taken a strong dislike to one of the guys who work for me. He's quite insolent; in fact, I'd say he's
(6) _____ rude, actually. The other day he made an offensive (7) _____ about my
appearance, which frankly is none of his business, and I really took (8) _____ to it. Calling me
'carrot top' because of my red hair was in very poor (9) _____ , I felt.

Review: You and other people

Unit 14

1 Complete the table.

NOUN	ADJECTIVE
	cynical
	sceptical
affection	
	charismatic

NOUN	ADJECTIVE
	naive
	spontaneous
passion	
virtue	

2 Rewrite the sentences using the word or a form of the word in capitals. Keep the meaning the same.

1   What was your impression of him? MAKE _____
2   I think you ought to have a try. GIVE _____
3   I'll do anything if it's practical and sensible. REASON _____
4   He doesn't believe the figures. SCEPTICAL _____
5   I started liking him after a while. TAKE _____
6   I think he's very bright. STRIKE _____
7   He really annoyed me. NOSE _____
8   He's interesting and rather unusual. CHARACTER _____
9   I haven't thought about it much but it seemed sensible. SURFACE _____
10   Don't base your opinion only on appearance. BOOK _____

A Z   **more words:** *bubbly, gullible, taciturn, gregarious, sly, two-faced*

Unit 15

1 Complete each sentence with <u>two</u> words or phrases from the word pool with a similar meaning.

> devastated   stunned ✓   suppress   ecstatic   hit the roof   uneasy
> cautious   gobsmacked ✓   disclose   went mad   over the moon   guarded
> uncomfortable   reveal   bottle up   heartbroken

▶ We were ___stunned___ / ___gobsmacked___ when he suddenly appeared after ten years.
1   The police refused to _____ / _____ the identity of the man arrested.
2   I always feel _____ / _____ in his company; he's just a bit strange.
3   I was _____ / _____ when my boyfriend left me for another woman. It took me months to get over it.
4   Marisa was _____ / _____ about becoming a mother; in fact we were all delighted.
5   Andrea was late for work again and her boss just _____ / _____ . She'd better watch out or she might get the sack.
6   It's never a good idea to _____ / _____ your feelings for too long.

7   The sales figures looked promising, but the boss's response was quite _____ /
_____ . He never wants to appear too positive.

A Z more words: *distraught, grief-stricken, **beside** yourself (with sth), go **bananas**, dumbfounded, on **top** of the world*

Unit 16

1 One word is missing in each line. Where does it go? Write it at the end of the line.

Starting a new job isn't easy, and you're always going to have some ⟋ and   ups
downs. Unfortunately one colleague took an instant to me, which made me   1 _____
very upset. I was sure he was talking about me my back, and even though   2 _____
I did everything to his respect, nevertheless it was a stressful period, and   3 _____
it really put a strain me. After a while, I thought the best thing was to try   4 _____
and in my boss, who explained that the colleague was hostile because   5 _____
he the fact that I had got the position that he had wanted. I had a   6 _____
really decision – whether to talk to him about it directly or not – and   7 _____
in the end I decided to stick for myself and talk to him. Initially he was a   8 _____
bit surprised, but as time has gone, our relationship has improved a lot,   9 _____
and I definitely feel that are looking up. I feel happy to carry on now.   10 _____

A Z more words: *love-hate relationship, inseparable, animosity, incompatible, irreconcilable (differences), cut (all ties with sb)*

Unit 17

1 Complete the crossword. The letters in the grey squares spell another word. What is it?

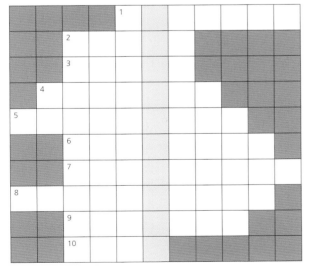

1   admire someone very much.
2   fight against or refuse to obey an authority.
3   vulgar; coarse.
4   give someone the enthusiasm and desire to do something.
5   have a go at someone.
6   a person who believes that the world can be perfect.
7   If you follow in someone's _____ , you want to be as successful as they are.
8   If something is against your _____ , it is against your very strong beliefs.
9   a woman you admire very much for her qualities or ability.
10 If you look _____ on someone, you think you are better than they are.

A Z more words: ***think** the world of sb / think **highly** of sb, sycophantic, repulsive, creepy, foul-mouthed*

Unit 18

1 Tick the words that are possible. More than one word may be correct.

1   The children often make *a mess* ☐ *a fuss* ☐ *an example* ☐.
2   He was from a *broken* ☐ *detrimental* ☐ *deprived* ☐ home.
3   Does money have a *messy* ☐ *beneficial* ☐ *detrimental* ☐ effect on people?
4   She's great, and she always *pulls her weight* ☐ *sets a good example* ☐ *does her fair share* ☐.
5   Nagging is *an unappealing* ☐ *an appealing* ☐ *a life-threatening* ☐ habit.
6   He *goes on and on at* ☐ *gives in to* ☐ *nags* ☐ the children about doing their homework.

A Z **more words:** *anti-social behaviour, truancy, reckless (behaviour), reprimand sb, ringleader, lead sb **astray***

Unit 19

1 Are these positive or negative remarks? Write P or N.

1   His manners were exemplary. ....
2   I took exception to his comments. ....
3   She was very insolent. ....
4   The service was impeccable. ....
5   Taking photos is frowned upon. ....
6   What a cheek! ....
7   She put her foot in it. ....
8   They're always courteous. ....

2 Complete the sentences in a suitable way.

ABOUT YOU AND
YOUR COUNTRY

1   If you invited someone to your house for a meal at 7 o'clock, and they arrived at 8 o'clock, would you be .... out?
2   Do you often say the wrong thing and put your .... in it?
3   If someone made a cheeky remark which you took .... to, would you normally say something or keep quiet?
4   Is it .... in your country for most people to .... themselves to be .... class or .... class, or working class? Do you .... yourself as coming from a particular class?
5   Do people .... upon people, especially women, who smoke in the street?
6   If you are invited to someone's house for a meal, what is the normal ....? Do you take flowers or chocolates, or something like that?

3 ABOUT YOU AND YOUR COUNTRY Write your answers to Exercise 2, or ask another student.

A Z **more words:** *(invade sb's) **personal space**, **uncivil** behaviour, churlish, protocol, (have the) **decency** to do sth, indiscretion*

20 I can **talk about food**

A Fruit, vegetables, nuts, herbs, and spices 🎧

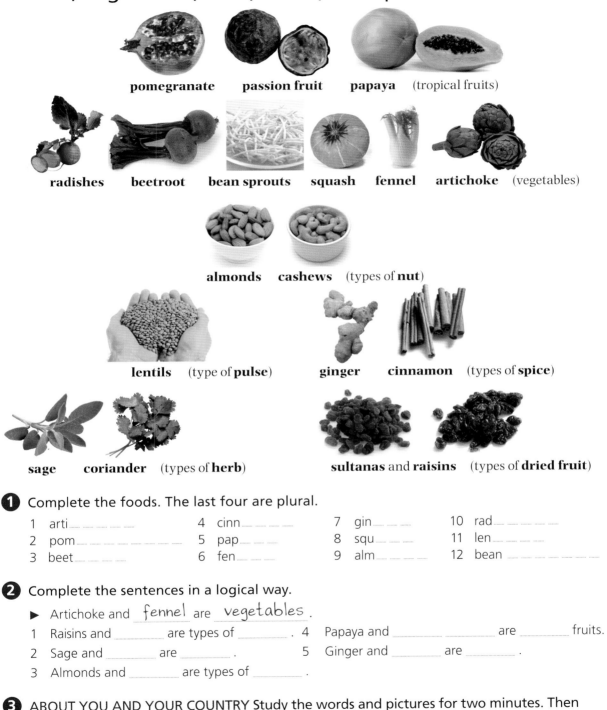

pomegranate   **passion fruit**   **papaya**   (tropical fruits)

radishes   **beetroot**   **bean sprouts**   **squash**   **fennel**   **artichoke**   (vegetables)

almonds   **cashews**   (types of **nut**)

lentils   (type of **pulse**)   **ginger**   **cinnamon**   (types of **spice**)

sage   **coriander**   (types of **herb**)   **sultanas** and **raisins**   (types of **dried fruit**)

1 Complete the foods. The last four are plural.

1 arti...........	4 cinn...........	7 gin...........	10 rad...........
2 pom...........	5 pap...........	8 squ...........	11 len...........
3 beet...........	6 fen...........	9 alm...........	12 bean...........

2 Complete the sentences in a logical way.

▶ Artichoke and _fennel_ are _vegetables_ .

1 Raisins and .... are types of ....   4 Papaya and .... are .... fruits.

2 Sage and .... are ....   5 Ginger and .... are ....

3 Almonds and .... are types of ....

3 ABOUT YOU AND YOUR COUNTRY Study the words and pictures for two minutes. Then shut your book and write down the items that you grow in your own country, and a list of the ones you have eaten.

📓 Remember to test yourself

B Kitchen equipment 🎧

Equipment	used to ...	what? e.g.:	Equipment	used to ...	what? e.g.:
wok	**stir-fry**	vegetables, meat, fish	**garlic crusher**	**crush**	garlic
steamer	**steam**	fish, rice, vegetables	**sieve**	**sieve** (separate solids from liquid or larger solids from smaller ones)	flour, tomatoes
deep fat fryer	**deep-fry**	fish, potatoes			
casserole	**braise/stew** (cook meat slowly in liquid in a closed container)	meat, vegetables	**peeler**	**peel**	vegetables
food processor	**chop**, **slice**, and **mix**	meat, vegetables, etc.	**lemon squeezer**	**squeeze**	lemons, limes
whisk	**beat**	eggs, cream	**corkscrew**	open	wine bottles
colander	**drain**	vegetables that have been washed or cooked in water	**ladle**	serve	soup
grater	**grate**	cheese, e.g. parmesan	**kitchen scales**	weigh	all types of food

4 Find six compound words or word combinations in the box.

cheese	lemon	kitchen	food	garlic	deep fat
processor	fryer	grater	crusher	squeezer	scales

....

....

5 Write down the equipment you would need to:

1 drain vegetables cooked in water ....
2 stir-fry vegetables ....
3 open a bottle of wine ....

4 serve soup ....
5 remove lumps in flour ....
6 beat eggs ....

6 Write down a type of food you can:

1 squeeze ....
2 grate ....

3 sieve ....
4 steam ....

5 slice ....
6 braise ....

 Remember to test yourself

C Food words, different meanings 🎧

Many food words form part of an idiomatic expression, or are used informally in spoken English with a different meaning.

> I said the plan would work, but it all **went pear-shaped**, so I had to **eat my words**.

> The trouble with Tanya is she always wants to **have her cake and eat it**.

> Since Jamie lost his job, Marcia has been the main **breadwinner**.

> Eric was very angry when he didn't get the job, but it was just **sour grapes**. To be honest, if he had worked here, he would've been **a fish out of water**.

> He managed to fix the door, but he really **made a meal of it**.

> You should get the job, but **don't count your chickens**.

> The whole thing sounded a bit **fishy** to me.

> Ali's calm and sensible; his brother's a complete **nutcase**. They're **like chalk and cheese**.

Glossary

go pear-shaped	INF go badly wrong and be very unsuccessful.
eat your words	admit that sth you said was wrong.
sour grapes	a negative response to sth because you're angry you can't have it.
a fish out of water	a person who feels uneasy and out of place in their surroundings.
have your cake and eat it	have the advantages of sth without the disadvantages.
make a meal of sth	INF spend more time doing sth than is necessary.
fishy	INF suspicious, and probably involving dishonesty.
breadwinner	a person who supports their family with money they earn.
don't count your chickens (before they're hatched)	SAYING don't be too confident that sth will be successful, because it may go wrong.
nutcase	INF a crazy person.
like chalk and cheese	used for saying that two people are very different.

7 Complete the missing food word in each expression.

1 sour _____
2 don't count your _____
3 a _____ out of water
4 _____ winner
5 like chalk and _____
6 go _____ -shaped
7 want to have your _____ and eat it
8 a _____ case

8 Finish the sentences with an expression which summarizes the situation.

▶ He was only rude about the party because he wasn't invited. It was just ___sour grapes___ .
1 It took two men three days to build that little wall. They really _____ .
2 Axel wants to use his father's car all the time, but still expects his father to pay all the bills. His problem is that he wants _____ .
3 Maggie spends all her time working; her sister doesn't do a thing and is out with her friends every night. They're like _____ .
4 I told Freddie he wasn't good enough to get in the football team. Then, last week, they picked him, so I had to _____ .
5 Everyone at the party except me had a good job, a big house, and a wife and two children. Frankly, I felt like _____ .
6 A man knocked on the door and said that if I gave him £100, he could invest it and make me £1,000 in less than two years. It sounded _____ .

Remember to test yourself

21 I can **talk about holidays** 🎧

City breaks in PRAGUE

Prague is a **stunning** city, and this **thriving** capital of the Czech Republic makes a romantic and **vibrant** city-break destination. A stroll through Prague's **cobbled streets** is wonderfully exciting: its architecture is **remarkably diverse**, and amazingly untouched by the Second World War, although Charles Bridge and the Astronomical Clock have recently been **undergoing restoration**.

Unwind on the ALGARVE

If you need to **unwind**, try the Algarve in southern Portugal. **Laze around** on the golden, sandy beaches, **soak up** the atmosphere of traditional fishing villages like Alvor, or just **go for a wander around** Albufeira's old town, which still **retains** its wonderful **charm**.

Off the beaten track on the great wall of CHINA

Our China **trek** offers a **unique** experience for the adventurous traveller who wants to **get away from it all**. Apart from the spectacular scenery, you will have the rare opportunity to camp in a **remote** part of rural China and experience local life in its most **unspoilt** state.

Glossary

stunning	extremely attractive or impressive. SYN **beautiful**.
thriving	growing and developing, and very successful. SYN **flourishing**.
vibrant	full of life and energy.
cobbled streets	streets with a surface of old round stones.
remarkably	in an unusual or surprising way. **remarkable** ADJ.
diverse	of many different kinds.
undergo sth	experience a process of change.
restoration	the work of repairing old buildings, paintings, etc. **restore** V.
laze around	relax and do very little.
soak sth up	absorb or take sth into your senses, body, or mind.
go for a wander (around/in)	walk slowly without a real purpose or direction. **wander (around/in)** V.
retain sth	FML keep sth. **retention** N.
charm	a pleasant or attractive quality or feature. **charming** ADJ.
off the beaten track	far away from other people and houses.
trek	a long hard walk, often in the mountains. **trek** V.
unique	being the only one of its kind.
get away from it all	go somewhere different to have a rest or holiday.
remote	far from places where other people live. SYN **isolated**.
unspoilt	(of a place) beautiful because it has not been changed or built on.

spotlight *relax*

There are different ways of saying **relax**. You can **unwind**, **take it easy** INF, or **chill out** INF. And if you take a break or holiday to get your energy back, you **recharge your batteries** (IDIOM).

 Remember to test yourself

1 Complete the phrases with words from the box.

| track | easy | wander | atmosphere | batteries | it all | around | streets |

1 cobbled _____
2 go for a _____
3 take it _____
4 get away from _____
5 off the beaten _____
6 soak up the _____
7 laze _____
8 recharge your _____

2 Complete the words in the dialogues.

1 Is the town centre different now? ~ Yes, it has u_____ major changes.
2 Is it still a thriving holiday resort? ~ Yes, it's really f_____ .
3 Is the restaurant cheap?   ~ Yes, it's r_____ good value.
4 There's nowhere like Cuenca.   ~ Absolutely true. It's completely u_____ .
5 The village hasn't changed at all. ~ No, it's completely u_____ .
6 The villa's miles from anywhere. ~ Yes, it's very r_____ .

3 Replace the underlined word(s) with a word or phrase with a similar meaning.

▶ The village has many <u>pleasant and attractive qualities</u>.   charms
1 He's running a <u>flourishing</u> new business. _____
2 Just look at that <u>beautiful</u> view of the mountains. _____
3 My son's interests are very <u>varied</u>. _____
4 The villa was quite <u>remote</u>. _____
5 We're going on a <u>long walk</u> across the desert. _____
6 Our preference is to <u>keep</u> the original design for the garden. _____
7 We just want to <u>relax and do very little</u>. _____
8 The old buildings in the centre need to be <u>repaired</u>. _____

4 Complete the text.

Great Expectations …

I'd been having a terrible time at work, so I was really looking forward to taking it
(1) _____ for a couple of weeks on a Greek island, staying miles from anywhere in a
(2) _____ villa by the sea. At least, that's what I had hoped. The reality was somewhat
different. The villa was undergoing (3) _____ , so I had to stay in a nearby beach
resort, where most people were trying to do the same as me: (4) _____ around on the
beach during the day, and then (5) _____ around the pretty (6) _____ streets in
the evening. Unfortunately, the place turned out to be very noisy and unpleasant, so my idea of
getting (7) _____ ` _____ all just didn't happen.

5 ABOUT YOU Write your answers, or ask another student.

What do you want from a holiday? Do you want to …   Yes, usually / Occasionally / No, never
… go somewhere vibrant and exciting? _____
… laze around on a beach and unwind? _____
… go somewhere remote and get away from it all? _____
… go on an adventurous holiday? _____
… wander around interesting towns and villages? _____

Remember to test yourself

22 I can **talk about plays and films**

A A fabulous play 🎧

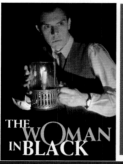

THE WOMAN IN BLACK

'The Woman in Black' is a **spine-tingling ghost story** that will have you **on the edge of your seat** throughout the production. With just a minimal **set** and few **sound effects**, this drama will **scare you out of your wits**!

A **nail-biting adaptation** of Susan Hill's novel. The plot **twists** are brilliant, and the **cast** of two are **sensational!** The **applause** went on and on.

Phenomenally successful, and **unanimously acclaimed** by the critics. A must-see thriller!

Glossary

spine-tingling	very frightening or exciting in a way that you enjoy.
ghost story	a story about the spirit of a dead person that sb hears or sees.
on the edge of your seat	very excited and interested in sth.
set	the scenery and furniture used in a play, film, etc.
sound effects	sounds that are made artificially in a play, film, etc. to make it more realistic, e.g. wind, thunder.
scare sb out of their wits	frighten sb very much.
nail-biting	making you very excited or worried. SYN **gripping**.
adaptation	a book or play that has been made into a film, TV programme, etc.
twist	an unexpected change or development in a story or situation.
cast	(+ SING OR PL V) all the people who act in a play or film.
sensational	INF extremely good; wonderful. SYNS **fabulous, brilliant**.
applause	the sound of an **audience** (people watching a play, etc.) showing approval by hitting their hands together. **applaud** V. SYN **clap**.
phenomenally	in a very great or impressive way. SYN **extraordinarily**.
unanimously	in a way that is agreed by everyone. **unanimous** ADJ.
acclaimed	publicly talked or written about in an admiring way. **acclaim** N.

1 Cover the texts and glossary. Circle the correct word.

1 I was on the end / edge of my seat.
2 There were great sound affects / effects.
3 The race had a nail-eating / -biting finish.
4 We were scared out / out of our wits.
5 There's a great twist / cast in the story.
6 We agreed phenomenally / unanimously.
7 It's an adaption / adaptation of a book.
8 The music was spine-tingling / -tingly.
9 Are you keen on ghost / spirit stories?
10 Did they applause / applaud at the end?

2 Replace the underlined word or phrase with a word or phrase with a similar meaning.

1 The people watching the play loved it. ....
2 The play was absolutely fabulous. ....
3 There has been considerable public praise for the play. ....
4 The actors in the play were very good indeed. ....
5 What did you think of the scenery and furniture? ....
6 The musical was extraordinarily good. ....
7 It was a really tense and exciting story. ....
8 Someone started applauding and then everyone joined in. ....

Remember to test yourself

B A terrible movie 🎧

A   I had to sit through some **atrocious**, **sentimental** movie that Frankie wanted to see on TV last night, called 'Love in Summer'.

B   Oh, I saw that – yes, it was **tedious**, wasn't it? Full of **clichés** – you know, all men are **shallow**, dishonesty is bad . . .

A   Yes, it was all terrible – **feeble** jokes, **wooden** dialogue, and the acting was very **mediocre**. And Jack Burns was totally **miscast** as the romantic lead, wasn't he?

B   Yeah, he was **dire**, and Maggie Lovett was pretty **unconvincing** too. I don't know why I watched it all the way through – it was **utter rubbish.**

Glossary

atrocious	very bad and unpleasant. SYN **dire** INF.
sentimental	OFTEN DISAPPROVING making people experience feelings of sadness, sympathy, etc. in a deliberate and obvious way.
cliché	a phrase or idea that has been used so often it no longer has much meaning and is not interesting. **clichéd** ADJ.
shallow	not showing serious thought, feelings, etc. SYN **superficial**.
feeble	very weak.
wooden	not showing enough natural expression, emotion, or movement.
mediocre	of only average quality.
miscast	(of an actor) not suitable for the role they have been given.
unconvincing	not seeming true or real. OPP **convincing**.
utter	complete (used to emphasize sth, usually sth bad) (**an utter waste of time, utter rubbish/nonsense**).
rubbish	INF We say sth is **rubbish** if we think it is of poor quality.

spotlight   Boredom

Tedious is a synonym for **boring**, and **deadly dull** is 'very boring'. These idioms mean 'very bored': **bored to tears**, **bored to death**, **bored stiff**, or **bored out of your mind**.

❸ Is the meaning the same or different? Write S or D.

1	It's a very romantic film.	It's a very sentimental film.	
2	The acting was quite wooden.	The acting didn't seem natural.	
3	I was bored to tears.	I found it very tedious.	
4	The female characters were shallow.	The female characters were superficial.	
5	The leading actor was miscast.	The leading actor was convincing.	
6	We were bored stiff.	We were bored out of our minds.	
7	The movie was dire.	The movie was atrocious.	
8	The film was mediocre.	The film was utter rubbish.	

❹ Complete the words in the sentences.

1   If a film is d_____ dull, or you are bored s_____ , you should leave before the end.

2   Many movies are c_____ : they're just boring and lacking in original themes.

3   If the director is poor, the actors may give a w_____ performance as well.

4   There's nothing worse than a comedy film with f_____ jokes.

5   If the plot of a film is hard to believe, the acting may be u_____ too.

6   Most films made in Hollywood are utter r_____ .

7   People are bored to d_____ by all the m_____ romantic comedies around.

8   I hate musicals. Every single one I've seen has been absolutely d_____ .

❺ ABOUT YOU Think of some atrocious films you've seen. Why were they dire? Write your answer, or ask a partner.

Remember to test yourself

23 I can **talk about competitive sport**

A A cup competition 🎧

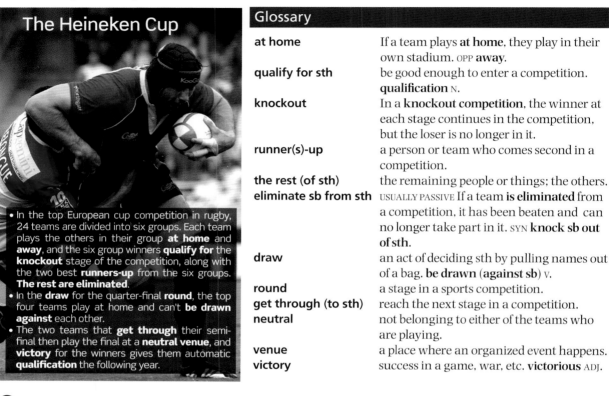

The Heineken Cup

- In the top European cup competition in rugby, 24 teams are divided into six groups. Each team plays the others in their group **at home** and **away**, and the six group winners **qualify for** the **knockout** stage of the competition, along with the two best **runners-up** from the six groups. **The rest are eliminated**.
- In the **draw** for the quarter-final **round**, the top four teams play at home and can't **be drawn against** each other.
- The two teams that **get through** their semi-final then play the final at a **neutral venue**, and **victory** for the winners gives them automatic **qualification** the following year.

Glossary

at home	If a team plays **at home**, they play in their own stadium. OPP **away**.
qualify for sth	be good enough to enter a competition. **qualification** N.
knockout	In a **knockout competition**, the winner at each stage continues in the competition, but the loser is no longer in it.
runner(s)-up	a person or team who comes second in a competition.
the rest (of sth)	the remaining people or things; the others.
eliminate sb from sth	USUALLY PASSIVE If a team **is eliminated** from a competition, it has been beaten and can no longer take part in it. SYN **knock sb out of sth**.
draw	an act of deciding sth by pulling names out of a bag. **be drawn (against sb)** V.
round	a stage in a sports competition.
get through (to sth)	reach the next stage in a competition.
neutral	not belonging to either of the teams who are playing.
venue	a place where an organized event happens.
victory	success in a game, war, etc. **victorious** ADJ.

1 True or false? Write T or F.

1 If you qualify for a competition, you will win it. _____
2 A venue is the last game in a competition. _____
3 The runner-up comes second in a competition. _____
4 In the knockout stage of a competition, every team plays more than one game. _____
5 If you are eliminated, that is the end of your competition. _____
6 If you are victorious, it is a good result. _____
7 If you play away, you're at a neutral venue. _____
8 The draw is a way of deciding which teams play against each other. _____

2 Complete the words in the text.

We did well in the cup this year. We played ▶ _____*away*_____ in the first (1) r_____ but managed to win, then we were (2) d_____ at home in the next two rounds and had fairly easy (3) v_____ . In the (4) d_____ for the quarter-final, we had to play the (5) r_____-_____ from last year, but we played really well and (6) g_____ t_____ to the semi-final. Unfortunately, we then lost because one or two of our best players were injured in training, and that seemed to affect (7) t_____ r_____ of the team. However, at least we were (8) k_____ o_____ by the team that went on to win the competition.

📖 Remember to test yourself

B Playing well and playing badly 🎧

At the beginning of the season our **form** in the **league** was poor, but we've had **a good run** lately, and we're **unbeaten** now in five games.

We had an **outside chance of promotion** before Christmas, but now we've got **no chance**.

Carter was **in great form** for us last season, but recently he's **let us down**.

When the opposition put us **under pressure**, we just **went to pieces**.

We **dominated** the game and were **on the verge of** winning, then we **gave away** a silly penalty.

<table>
<tr><td>spotlight</td><td>chance</td></tr>
</table>

Chance is used in many phrases as it can mean a *possibility* (a fact that sth might happen) or an *opportunity* (a situation which makes sth possible):
*We've got an **outside chance of** promotion.* (= a small chance) OPP *a **great chance**.*
*This season could be my **big chance**.* (= opportunity for success)
*He's retiring soon, so this is his **last chance**.* (= final opportunity)

Glossary

form	the way in which sb is performing (sb **in** or **on good/great form** is performing well; sb who is **off form** is performing badly).
league	a set of teams who play each other over a season to find the best team.
a (good/bad) run	a period of performing well or badly.
unbeaten	not having lost.
promotion	the action of moving a team up to a higher league. **be promoted** V. OPP **relegation** N, **be relegated** V.
let sb down	fail to give sb the help and support they need.
under pressure	in a stressful situation, often because sb is forcing you to do sth in a certain way.
go to pieces	INF become very nervous or upset and unable to perform.
dominate	(in sport) play better than sb and be in control of the game. SYN **be on top**. **dominant** ADJ.
on the verge of sth	near to the moment of doing or achieving sth.
give sth away	lose a game, point, or competition through a bad mistake.

❸ One word is missing in each line of the text. What is it and where does it go?

We've been ⟨ good form recently, and last Saturday we
started the match really well, and we the first half.
Then, at the start of the second half, they put us a lot of
pressure, and we gave a silly goal. After that, I'm afraid,
we completely went pieces. I thought our goalkeeper, in
particular, really let us. And after losing that game, we have
no of promotion this year. In fact, if we go on playing badly,
we could be at the end of the season.

▶ in
1
2
3
4
5
6
7

❹ Rewrite the sentences on the left without changing the meaning.

1 They've done well recently.   They've had a good _____.
2 She could win at the Olympics.   The Olympics could be her big _____.
3 We could go up to the next league.   We could be _____.
4 We're close to victory.   We're on the _____.
5 We haven't lost this season.   We are _____.
6 Recently he's been playing badly.   Recently he's been off _____.
7 We dominated most of the game.   For most of the game we were _____.

📓 Remember to test yourself

24 I can **talk about gardens and nature**

A A natural garden 🎧

I've always been excited by the idea of a garden which **imitates** the best of **nature**, so, having **acquired** a **cottage** in the country, I'm now **in the process of** creating my own **wildlife** garden. The **site** is ideal – a gentle **slope** going down to a pond, plus there's a **shed** – and there are already **plants** to **attract** wildlife such as bees and **butterflies**[1]. I've **scattered seeds** to create a wild-flower **meadow**, and I hope birds will soon build **nests**.

stem

flower

plant

leaf

roots

Glossary

imitate sth/sb	SYN **copy sth/sb. imitation** N. **copy** N.
acquire sth	obtain sth by buying it or being given it.
cottage	a small house, especially in the country.
in the process of doing sth	doing things that are necessary to achieve sth.
wildlife	animals, birds, and insects that live in a natural state.
site	an area of land that is used for sth (**camping site/building site**).
slope	an area of land that is higher at one end than the other. **slope** V.
shed	a small simple building, made of wood, and often found in gardens.
attract sth/sb	make sth/sb come towards you.
scatter sth	throw or drop things in different directions over a wide area.
seed	the small hard part of a plant from which new plants grow.
meadow	a field covered in grass, and often wild flowers.
nest	a place where birds lay their eggs and live with their young. **nest** V.

spotlight *nature*

We can say someone is interested in **nature** (= the physical world and everything that lives in it). We don't talk about being *in the nature*. We say *I like being* **in the countryside**, or *I looked at the* **beautiful scenery**.

❶ Circle the correct word(s). Both words may be correct.

1 We grow potatoes in that field / meadow.
2 He works on a building land / site.
3 This plant will attract / scatter butterflies.
4 I copied / imitated my neighbour's garden.
5 How did you obtain / acquire that land?
6 There's a camping / camping site nearby.
7 We need to protect wildlife / wildliving.
8 Look at the scenery / nature!

❷ Complete the sentences.

1 I'm in the _____ of building a new wall round the garden.
2 There are two blackbirds building a _____ under the roof of the garden _____ .
3 For the _____ to grow, the water has to go up the _____ from the _____ .
4 I love being in the _____ surrounded by the beauties of nature.
5 I've bought lots of packets of _____ to grow different flowers and vegetables.
6 From the kitchen of our _____ , the garden _____ down quite steeply to the river.

Remember to test yourself

B Gardening chores 🎧

SPRING: Add **compost** to **enrich** the **soil**.
Prune certain **bushes**[1] and plants.
Dig[2] the ground if it's not too **muddy**.

SUMMER: **Mow the lawn**[3] once a week.
Do regular **weeding**.
Put your feet up and enjoy the garden.

AUTUMN: Tidy **hedges** and fallen leaves.
Plant bulbs[4] for the following spring.

spade

lawnmower

Glossary

chore	a small job that you have to do regularly, often around the home.
compost	a mixture of decaying plants and food that is added to soil to help things grow (**compost** makes soil more **fertile**; **fertility** N).
enrich sth	improve the quality of sth by adding sth to it.
soil	the top part of the earth in which trees and plants grow.
prune sth	remove some of a plant's stems or branches to improve future growth. SYN **cut sth back**.
muddy	(of the earth) wet from too much rain. **mud** N.
do the weeding	remove the **weeds** (= wild plants growing where they are not wanted in a garden).
put your feet up	IDIOM sit down and relax.
hedge	a line of bushes growing close together around a garden or field.
plant sth	put flowers and other plants into the soil.

3 Good news or bad news? Write G or B.

1 The ground is muddy. ....
2 We've got lots of compost. ....
3 I've got lots of chores. ....
4 The lawn is full of weeds. ....
5 There's loads of digging to do. ....
6 The bulbs are coming up. ....

4 Rewrite the sentences without using the underlined words. Keep the meaning the same.

1 Have you got <u>something I can use for digging</u>?   Have you got a .... ?
2 I'm going to <u>sit down and relax</u>.   I'm going to put ....
3 He's going to <u>cut</u> the <u>grass</u>.   He's going to ....
4 You'll need to <u>prune</u> this bush.   You'll need to ....
5 I'm going to <u>improve</u> the soil.   I'm going to add ....
6 I want to <u>put</u> some roses <u>in the ground</u>.   I want to ....
7 There's a <u>line of bushes</u> round the field.   There's a ....
8 I need to <u>take out the weeds</u>.   I need to do ....
9 We need to <u>enrich</u> the soil.   We need to make the soil ....

Remember to test yourself

25 I can **talk about shopping habits**

A Different kinds of shopper 🎧

What kind of shopper are you?

Impulse shopper: You might go to the shops **in search of** sandals and come back with a winter coat. You may also have things in your wardrobe with the **price tag** still on them.

Situational shopper: **Shop till you drop?** Not you. You're not there for **browsing** – you're **after** a particular buy. And **the minute** you've got it, you're **off**.

Bargain buyer: You **have an eye for** a bargain, and you'll **shop around** until you find it.

Serious shopper: You're incredibly **focused** and won't **be distracted by** cheap offers.

Glossary

impulse (to do sth)	a sudden desire to do sth without thinking about the results (**buy sth on impulse**).
in search of sth	looking for sth.
price tag	a label on sth which shows how much you must pay.
shop till you drop	MODERN IDIOM spend a long time shopping because you don't want to stop (**till** = until).
browse	casually look at things in a shop, or look through the pages of a book.
after sth	looking for and trying to obtain sth (**after a jacket / after a job**).
the minute	as soon as. SYN **the moment**.
be off	go; leave.
have an eye for sth	have a natural ability to see or find sth (to **have your eye on sth** is to have seen sth and want to have it or buy it).
shop around	go to different shops until you find what you want.
focused	having a very clear aim; knowing what you want to do.
be distracted by sth	be looking at or thinking about sth so that you are unable to pay attention to other things. **distract sb from sth** v.

❶ Circle the correct word.

1 If I don't find something immediately, I'm happy to shop around / away .
2 He's got an / his eye on a small vase, which he might buy.
3 He's very distracted / focused at work and just keeps going till the job's finished.
4 She really has an / her eye for detail.
5 You're distracting me from / by my work. Go away!
6 I just stopped to page / browse through this magazine.

❷ Complete the text with suitable words and phrases.

I went into town with Patsy. I was in (1) _____ some shoes, Patsy was
(2) _____ a top and a skirt. I saw some lovely shoes in 'Shoon', but then I looked at the price
(3) _____ and decided I'd (4) _____ for something a bit cheaper. Patsy then
pointed out some boots in the shop opposite. The (5) _____ I saw them I knew I had to have
them. I just bought them (6) _____ – I couldn't stop myself. The trouble is, after
that I was bored and wanted to go home. I'm not the kind of person who shops till they
(7) _____ , so I told Patsy that I had to be (8) _____ in order to get home and finish an
essay. She didn't mind. I left her (9) _____ in a very expensive boutique that opened last month.

📓 Remember to test yourself

B Shopping habits 🎧

SHOPPING is the UK's fourth favourite leisure **pursuit**. Whether it's a **spending spree**, **bargain hunting**, or just browsing, millions of us **head for** the shops every weekend. And it's not just women who **indulge in** this popular **pastime**. Men over 50 now **outspend** women of the same age, because of their love of **gadgets**, and it's estimated that two to eight per cent of all UK adults are **shopaholics**. A small number, though, may become **compulsive** shoppers: they become **addicted to** it and end up with **crippling** financial debts.

Glossary

pursuit	SYNS **hobby, pastime** (**leisure/outdoor pursuits**).
spree	a short period of time doing one activity, often in an uncontrolled way (**spending/shopping spree**).
bargain hunting	looking for sth at a good price and cheaper than usual.
head for/towards	go in the direction of.
indulge in sth	do sth you like, especially sth that is bad for you.
gadget	a small tool or piece of equipment that does sth useful.
shopaholic	INF sb who enjoys shopping and spends a lot of time doing it (also **workaholic/chocoholic**; see **alcoholic** below).
compulsive	a **compulsive** person finds it difficult to control their actions (a **compulsive shopper/gambler/liar**).
addicted to sth	unable to stop doing sth which is usually harmful (**addicted to drugs/alcohol**; a person is a **drug addict** or an **alcoholic**).
crippling	very serious (**crippling debts/disease**).

spotlight · Prefix *out-*

Used as a prefix with verbs, **out-** means more/greater/longer, etc.
*Men over 50 **outspend** women.*
*He **outlived** his wife by five years.*
*The women **outnumbered** the men 3 to 1.*
*The advantages **outweigh** the disadvantages.* (= are greater than)

3 Find six compound words or common phrases in the box.

bargain	drug	compulsive	crippling	shopping	leisure
debts	gambler	spree	hunting	pursuit	addict

....

....

4 Complete the sentences.

1 When I saw Sue she was .... for the supermarket.
2 I don't have time to .... in too many leisure pursuits. I'm too busy at work.
3 Steve loves any kind of .... , so I gave him an alarm clock which changes colour.
4 It's not perfect, but the advantages .... the disadvantages.
5 The men .... the women 5 to 1 in that company.
6 It's easy to get .... things such as drugs or alcohol.

5 ABOUT YOU Write your answers or ask another student.

How often do you go on a spending spree? ....
What's your attitude to bargain hunting? ....
What kind of gadgets do you buy, if any? ....
Would you describe yourself as a shopaholic? ....

Remember to test yourself

26 I can **talk about socializing**

A Parties 🎧

Organizing a party

- The **host** is expected to **lay on** food and drink, which can be expensive and **time-consuming**. Consider asking others to **make a contribution** and bring something.
- A lot of food means a lot of **clearing up**. Think about **disposable** plates and cutlery.
- Don't advertise it on the internet **beforehand**. You don't want **gatecrashers**.
- Parties take a while to **warm up**. Consider music (not so **deafening** that it **drowns out** the conversation) or party games to **liven** things **up**.
- Finally, don't **get carried away**. You're planning a party, not a theme park.

Glossary

socialize	spend time with other people in a friendly way. **sociable** ADJ.
host	a person who is giving a meal or a party (**hostess** can be used for a woman).
lay sth on	INF provide sth for sb, especially food, drink, or transport.
time-consuming	needing a lot of time (a **time-consuming process**).
contribution	a thing that you give or do to help sth be successful (**make a valuable/significant contribution**). **contribute** v.
clear (sth) up	leave everything clean and tidy.
disposable	intended to be used once or twice then thrown away.
beforehand	before sth else happens or is done.
gatecrasher	a person who tries to get into a party without an invitation.
warm up	(of a party or event) start to become interesting and enjoyable.
deafening	very loud.
drown sth out	be louder than other sounds, so they can't be heard.
liven sth up	make sth more exciting (**liven up** = become more exciting).
get/be carried away	become very excited or lose control of your feelings.

❶ Complete the dialogues with a suitable word.

1   Whose party is it? ~ Paula and Simon are the ....
2   Can we throw these plates away? ~ Yes, they're ....
3   Can we do anything we like? ~ Yes, but don't get carried .... !
4   Did this take long? ~ Yes, it was very ....-........... .
5   She's always out with people. ~ Yes, she .... a lot.
6   Why did you turn up the music? ~ To .... the noise from next door.
7   Did people help out at the party? ~ Yes, everyone made a ....

❷ Complete the words in the text.

... and the party was great! Carol (1) l................... o................... a lot of hot food, but I think she prepared most of it (2) b................... . And most of the people who were invited (3) c................... by bringing a bottle. She also put a couple of big guys near the door to stop (4) g................... , which was sensible. It (5) w................... u................... after a while, and by 11 o'clock things had really (6) l................... u................... , and it was great. A neighbour complained that the music was (7) d................... but that's all. I bet Carol had a lot of (8) c................... u................... the next day, but it was worth it.

Remember to test yourself

B In other people's company 🎧

A   Shall we **pop round** and see Glynnis?
B   Yes – she may **fancy** a bit of **company**.

A   They'll have fun tonight, **no doubt**.
B   Yes, but I'm sure they won't **get drunk**.

A   Jim's quite **awkward** when he's **in company**.
B   Yeah. I think he's a bit of a **loner**.

A   We're having a **get-together** tonight.
B   Oh, can I **join in**?

A   You never get a **warm welcome** at Laura's.
B   No. And her friends are all a bit **cliquey** as well.

spotlight	*company*

I like **company**.
(= being with other people)
She's **good company**.
(= enjoyable to be with)
He enjoys his **own company**.
(= being by himself)
He's not very good **in company**.
(= with other people)
I'll **accompany** *you*.
(FML = go with you)

Glossary

pop round/over/in	INF go somewhere quickly or for a fairly short time.
fancy sth	INF want sth or want to do sth.
no doubt	used to say you expect sth will happen.
drunk	having drunk too much alcohol (**get/be drunk**).
awkward	not relaxed or comfortable with other people.
loner	a person who is often alone and usually prefers to be alone.
get-together	a friendly informal meeting or party. SYN **do** N, INF.
join in	take part in an activity with other people.
warm welcome	If sb gives you a **warm welcome** you feel relaxed in their home. **welcome** ADJ (**make sb feel welcome**).
cliquey	INF, DISAPPROVING forming a small group and not letting others join in. **clique** N.

3 Rewrite the sentences without using the underlined words. Keep the meaning the same.

1 She's not very good <u>with other people</u>.
   She's not very good _____ .
2 He <u>had too much to drink</u>.
   He _____ .
3 He <u>prefers his own company</u>.
   He's a _____ .
4 Come to the <u>get-together</u> tonight.
   Come to the _____ .
5 He's very <u>uncomfortable</u> with people.
   He's very _____ .
6 She <u>made me feel relaxed in her home</u>.
   She gave me a very _____ .
7 They're <u>unfriendly to outsiders</u>.
   They're a bit _____ .
8 Someone will <u>go with</u> you.
   Someone will _____ .

4 Complete the dialogues in a suitable way.

1 Did you go with them?
   Yes, I asked if I could _____ .
2 Do we know when she's arriving?
   No, but no _____ she'll ring us.
3 Are you staying in?
   Yes. Do you want to _____ round?
4 He's a bit of a loner, isn't he?
   Yes, he prefers his _____ .
5 Are you going out?
   No, we're having a big family _____ .
6 Are they having a _____ at the club?
   Yeah. Do you _____ going?
7 She's great to be with.
   Yeah, she's good _____ .
8 They're not very nice to other classmates.
   No, they're a very tight little _____ .

Remember to test yourself

Review: Leisure and lifestyle

Unit 20

1 Match the sentence halves.

1	My brother and I are like	a	meal of it.
2	You can't have your	b	chickens.
3	It was a small repair, but he made a	c	fish out of water.
4	That deal sounds a bit	d	chalk and cheese.
5	You might get the money but don't count your	e	cake and eat it.
6	Bad news: the plans have gone	f	fishy to me.
7	I felt like a	g	words.
8	I was wrong and in the end I had to eat my	h	pear-shaped.

2 Use a word from the left and a word from the right, and write a sentence explaining the connection between them.

cinnamon ✓	braise
corkscrew	herb
whisk	pulse
raisin	beat
colander	nut
lentils	soup
casserole	spice ✓
ladle	wine
cashew	dried fruit
wok	drain
sage	stir-fry

▶ *Cinnamon is a type of spice.*

 more words: ***butter** sb up, **egg** sb on, have **egg** on your face, be full of **bean**s, **rub** salt into the wound, sell like **hot** cakes*

Unit 21

1 Replace words in the text with words from the box so that the meaning stays the same. You may have to change the form of the verbs in the box.

unwind	thriving	diverse	vibrant	recharge your batteries	stunning ✓
restore	remarkable	wander	retain	soak up	

Lisbon is surrounded by seven hills, and from most of them you have ▶ beautiful stunning views of this unusual city, which has managed to keep so much of its varied architecture and cultural heritage. But it is also a modern, flourishing European capital, and in recent years many of the old buildings have been repaired. For tourists, one of the most popular parts is the Alfama, where you can casually walk around and absorb the charms of the old town. The Chiado district is famous for shops and restaurants, but for really exciting night life, head for the Bairro Alto. Then after all that, you can relax on the nearby beaches of Cascais and Estoril: wonderful places to get your energy back.

2 Complete the definitions with a suitable word.

1 *unique*: the _____ one of its kind.
2 *off the beaten track*: _____ away from other people and houses.
3 *unspoilt*: beautiful because it hasn't _____ .
4 *cobbled streets*: streets with a surface of old round _____ .
5 *take it easy*: _____ and do very little.
6 *trek*: a long hard _____ .
7 *undergo something*: experience a process of _____ .
8 *charms*: very _____ qualities or features.

A Z more words: *heritage, exotic, renowned, long-haul (flight/destination), tranquil*

Unit 22

1 Complete the review with suitable words.

The Last Servant is advertised as a (1) nail-_____ ghost story that will have theatre (2) _____ on the (3) _____ of their seats. Well, not me, I'm afraid. Giles Harrison (looking all of his 25 years) was completely (4) _____ as the 14-year-old son of the mad doctor, and the plot borrowed all the same old (5) _____ that we've seen a hundred times before; even the sound (6) _____ were pathetic. After the first twenty minutes I was, frankly, bored to (7) _____ , and while it may please some people, I thought it was utter (8) _____ .

2 Put the words in the correct column below.

sensational   dire   tedious   fabulous   mediocre   phenomenal   brilliant
feeble   unconvincing   extraordinary   atrocious   sentimental

Negative	Positive

A Z more words: *witty, rave about sth, bitter-sweet, tear jerker, grim, harrowing*

Unit 23

1 Tick the words in italics which are possible. More than one word may be correct.

1 I think the team will be *promoted* ☐ *relegated* ☐ *qualified* ☐ next season.
2 They're playing badly because they're *on top* ☐ *under pressure* ☐ *off form* ☐.
3 They now have *a last* ☐ *a great* ☐ *an outside* ☐ chance of victory.
4 The team are playing at *home* ☐ *away* ☐ *a neutral venue* ☐ this weekend.
5 There's a chance they'll get *through* ☐ *knocked out* ☐ *drawn* ☐.
6 They didn't win, but at least they were *victorious* ☐ *eliminated* ☐ *runners-up* ☐.

2 Complete the words in the dialogues.

1 A Do you know who we've been d_____ against in the next round of the cup?

   B Well, it can't be Oxford because they've already been e_____ : they lost in the last round.

2 A Federer really deserved his v_____ in the final.

   B Yes, he did. And I think it was probably his l_____ chance, because he'll be retiring soon.

3 A How are Leeds doing this season?

   B Really well. They've had a very good r_____ since the beginning of the year; in fact, they're u_____ in six matches.

   A So they're on really good f_____ , then.

4 A What on earth happened to us in the second half?

   B I don't know. We were well on t_____ , then we g_____ a_____ a penalty. It was a disaster.

A Z more words: *fixture*, **sign** *a player*, *thrash sb*, *transfer sb*, *seed*, *make your* **debut**

Unit 24

1 Find 15 more words related to gardening in the word square.

M	C	O	M	P	O	S	T	S	T
E	L	R	Y	R	M	I	S	P	O
A	A	B	B	U	S	H	H	A	W
D	W	U	S	N	I	E	E	D	I
O	N	L	Y	E	G	S	D	E	L
W	M	B	H	E	D	G	E	S	D
W	O	F	E	R	T	I	L	E	L
E	W	A	F	F	E	D	I	E	I
E	E	N	R	I	C	H	N	D	F
D	R	O	O	T	S	A	G	S	E

2 Use the words from the word square in the sentences.

▶ I added *compost* to improve the soil.

1 The _____ take up the water into the plant.

2 All gardeners want to attract _____ such as bees and butterflies into their gardens.

3 You just scatter the _____ over the soil and then cover them.

4 I want a more informal garden, with wild flowers and grass – a _____ , in fact.

5 Some flowers grow from a _____ which you plant in the soil.

6 Look – there's a big _____ growing next to the door. Take it out.

7 It's important to _____ the soil with compost before planting.

8 Compost makes the soil more _____ .

9 You can plant a row of bushes to make a beautiful _____ along your garden.

10 If the bushes get too big, you'll have to _____ them a bit.

11 The grass needs cutting – you'll find the _____ in the garden _____ .

12 I need to do some digging but I can't find the _____ .

A Z more words: *rake*, *saw*, *stake*, *slug*, *sow*, *germinate*, *cultivate*, *pests*

Unit 25

1 Complete the phrases with words from the box.

spree	tag	around	pursuit	gambler	impulse	hunting	debts	addict

1 buy something on ....
2 an outdoor ....
3 a drug ....
4 shop ....
5 a spending ....

6 bargain ....
7 a compulsive ....
8 crippling ....
9 a price ....

2 Correct the error in each sentence.

▶ Something ~~destructed~~ me from what I was saying. *distracted*

1 I'm just off to the shops – I'm before a new sweater. ....
2 I knew she would be a difficult customer the minutes I saw her. ....
3 I've had my eye for that coat for ages. ....
4 When she's feeling low she tends to induct in a bit of bargain hunting. ....
5 What time are you out to Paris in the morning? ....
6 Do you know anyone who's addict to internet shopping? ....
7 He left the bank and headed to the railway station. ....
8 We went to Crete this summer in searching of the sun. ....

A Z more words: *retail* therapy, **charity** shop, haggle, merchandise, designer **label**, get a **buzz**/ rush from / out of sth

Unit 26

1 Complete the text with words from the box.

drowns	get-together	make	lay	awkward	away	pop
host	join	socialize	loner	liven	company	

Do you want to make new friends? Yes?

Well, follow our suggestions; they will help you to (1) .... more effectively!

★ If you're a bit of a (2) .... and prefer your own (3) ...., make a special effort to (4) .... in with any social events at work. At least you'll know a few people so you should feel less (5) ....

★ Start by inviting one or two people to (6) .... round and have a drink one evening. Try to (7) .... on a bit of food and drink that you think they will enjoy. Put some music on to help (8) .... things up a bit, but don't have it so loud that it (9) .... out the conversation. It's important to (10) .... your guests feel welcome.

★ When you have a little experience of being the (11) ...., have a small (12) .... for a few neighbours – not more than about half a dozen. Don't get carried (13) .... and start inviting loads of people – take things step-by-step, and in no time you'll start to feel more confident.

A Z more words: break the **ice**, throw a **party**, **housewarming** party, **hen** party, **stag** night/party, cater/catering

27 I can **talk about change**

A Words describing change 🎧

Word	Example	Meaning
transform sth	*Computers have **transformed** our lives.*	completely change the appearance or character of sth, often to make it better. **transformation** N.
amend sth	*Civil servants are now **amending** the document.*	make changes to correct a mistake or improve a law, statement, document, etc. **amendment** N.
adapt to sth	*We must **adapt to** a changing world.*	change your behaviour in order to be more successful in a new situation. SYN **adjust (to sth)**.
assimilate sth	*It takes time to **assimilate** new ideas.*	learn and get used to sth which is new and different. **assimilation** N.
evolve	*Democracy has **evolved** over hundreds of years.*	change gradually, often from something simple to something more complicated. **evolution** N.
transition FML	*We hope for a smooth **transition**.*	a process or period of change from one state to another (a society **in transition** is changing).
revert (back) to sth	*After weeks of unrest, life has **reverted to normal**.*	change back to a state or situation that existed in the past. SYN **go back**.
restore sth	*Some people want to **restore** the monarchy.*	return sth to its former state or condition. **restoration** N.
reverse sth	*They were going to let him go, but they **reversed** their decision.*	change sth so it is the opposite of what it was before (**reverse a decision/trend/policy**, etc.). **reversal** N. **reversible** ADJ. OPP **irreversible**.
reform sth	*There are new proposals to **reform** the prison system.*	improve a system, an organization, a law, etc. by making changes to it. **reform** N.

❶ Organize these words into the categories below.

> evolve   restore   amend   assimilate   adapt
> transition   revert   reform   reverse   transform

1   a word that describes complete change: _____
2   words that describe a change to improve something: _____
3   words that describe changing back: _____
4   words that describe a gradual change: _____

❷ Complete the sentences with a suitable word.

1   There will be a period of _____ when the new government takes over.
2   The building was badly damaged, but they are planning to _____ it.
3   As a company we believe in _____ , not revolution.
4   They've changed their minds completely: this is a _____ of the previous policy.
5   After years of civil war, the country will find it difficult to _____ back to normal.
6   We will all have to _____ to climate change, or it will be a disaster for the planet.
7   Once the ice caps melt at the poles, the change is completely _____ .
8   We'll need time to _____ all the new ideas in their proposed plan.

Remember to test yourself

B Change management 🎧

Managing change

Most employees **resist** change that is **enforced** and **imposed upon** them. So, if a company wants to **pursue** a policy that aims to **bring about sweeping**, or even **subtle**, **changes**, managers need to remember that their role is to **facilitate** change and not impose it. This requires an **ongoing consultation** process with the staff, so that any changes have their support before they are **implemented**.

Glossary

resist sth	refuse to accept sth and try to stop it happening. **resistance** N.
enforce sth	make people obey sth (**enforce the law**). enforcement N.
impose sth on/upon sb	make sb accept sth against their wishes.
pursue sth	follow or try to achieve sth over a period of time (**pursue a policy/goal**).
bring sth about	make sth happen. SYNS **create sth, cause sth**.
sweeping change	a big change that will have an important effect.
subtle	not easy to notice or understand (**subtle difference**). OPP **obvious**.
facilitate sth	make an act or process easier to achieve.
ongoing	continuing to develop (an **ongoing process/investigation**).
consultation	the act of discussing sth with sb before making a decision. **consult sb** V. **consultative** ADJ.
implement sth	make sth that has been decided start to happen. SYNS **carry out sth, put sth into practice. implementation** N.

3 Positive or negative? Write P or N.

1 They've enforced the change. _____
2 They've resisted any change. _____
3 They've been very consultative. _____
4 They've imposed change. _____
5 They've introduced refreshing changes. _____
6 They want to facilitate change. _____

> **spotlight** Adjective + *change*
>
> A number of adjectives are commonly used with the noun ***change***: ***sweeping*/*radical*/*major*/*wholesale*** *changes* (= big changes) *a **refreshing**/**welcome*** *change* (= a change that is pleasantly new or different)

4 Replace the underlined words with different words that give a similar meaning.

1 It's only a <u>small</u> difference but we believe it will have an effect. _____
2 He wants to introduce <u>radical</u> changes. _____
3 The new furniture is a <u>welcome</u> change. _____
4 They have the power to <u>make people obey</u> the law. _____
5 They plan to <u>carry out</u> a number of changes. _____
6 The new measures will <u>create</u> further change. _____

5 Complete the words in the text.

When the new head teacher arrived, it was rumoured that she planned to (1) p_____ a policy of (2) s_____ changes to the way the school was organized, and that she wouldn't be very sympathetic to staff who showed any real (3) r_____ . However, unlike the former head who never talked to anyone, Mrs Palmer has (4) c_____ members of staff, and that has been a (5) w_____ change. She set up a staff committee, and we have been involved in an (6) o_____ process of (7) c_____ for about two months. We have also (8) i_____ a few changes which have already made an (9) o_____ difference.

28 I can **talk about energy conservation**

A Saving energy in the home 🎧

Three easy ways to **conserve** energy in the home

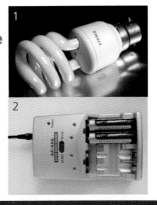

- **Switch to energy-saving eco** light bulbs[1]. They **emit** less heat and last far longer. They may be more expensive, but you can greatly reduce your energy **consumption**.

- Never leave electrical **appliances** such as TVs **on standby**, or leave your mobile phone **charging** unnecessarily. Get rid of your **tumble dryer**: they **consume** masses of energy.

- Every year we throw away thousands of batteries, making **landfill** sites even more toxic. Use **rechargeable batteries**[2], or **better still**, solar **chargers**.

Glossary

conserve sth	avoid wasting sth. **conservation** N.
switch to sth	change from using one thing to using another.
energy-saving	not wasting much energy (**water-saving, labour-saving**).
eco(-)	(short for **ecology**) relating to the environment (**eco-home, eco-disaster**).
emit sth	send out sth such as light, heat, sounds, gas, etc. **emission** N.
consumption	the act of using energy, food, or materials. **consume** v (a person is a **consumer**).
appliance	a machine you use at home e.g. fridge, washing machine.
on standby	If a TV is **on standby**, it is connected to the power supply but is not in use.
charge sth (up)	pass electricity through sth to store it there, using a **charger** (N).
tumble dryer	a machine that uses hot air to dry clothes.
landfill (site)	an area of land where large amounts of rubbish are buried.
toxic	poisonous (**toxic chemicals/gases/substances**).
better still	even better (**still** is used to make a comparison stronger).

1 Good or bad, in terms of energy-saving? Write G or B.

1 I left the TV on standby overnight. _____
2 We don't use eco light bulbs. _____
3 I switched to rechargeable batteries. _____
4 Our energy consumption increased. _____
5 The machine emits toxic substances. _____
6 We took energy conservation measures. _____
7 He left the phone charger on all day. _____
8 Our energy emissions are high. _____
9 We avoided sending it to landfill. _____
10 I threw away a water-saving device. _____

2 Complete the sentences.   ABOUT YOU

1 Have you got a tumble - _____ ? If so, could you manage without it?
2 When you _____ your mobile phone, do you leave it plugged in overnight?
3 Do you know how much electricity you _____ in an average week?
4 How many electrical _____ in your kitchen do you use regularly?
5 Do you always turn off lights in rooms you aren't using to _____ energy?
6 Do you use rechargeable _____ , or better _____ , a solar _____ ?
7 Which energy- _____ steps in the article above do you actually take?
8 Are you an above-average or below-average _____ of electricity?

3 ABOUT YOU Answer the questions in Exercise 2, or ask another student.

Remember to test yourself

B Saving energy in a restaurant 🎧

ACORN HOUSE RESTAURANT is London's first truly **environmentally-friendly** restaurant. It's a training restaurant which aims to turn out **green** chefs, making it a **groundbreaking enterprise**. The principles are clear: use local produce which is **in season** to reduce **food miles**; avoid **disposable** products; and **recycle** at least 80 per cent of all waste. Even the building itself has been designed to **maximize** natural light and to **minimize** energy use. In the most **sustainable** restaurant in the capital, everything is done to reduce each customer's **carbon footprint**. Is this the restaurant of the future?

Glossary

green	concerned with or supporting the protection of the environment.
groundbreaking	using new methods or making new discoveries.
enterprise	a large, new project. SYN **venture**.
in season	(of fruit and vegetables) ready for eating now and available in large numbers. OPP **out of season**.
food miles	the distance food travels from where it is grown or produced to where it is consumed.
disposable	made to be thrown away after use. **dispose of sth** v.
recycle sth	treat sth so that it can be used again. **recycling** N.
maximize sth	1 make the best use of sth. 2 increase sth as much as possible. OPP **minimize sth**.
sustainable	using methods which do not harm the environment (**sustainable agriculture/energy**). **sustainability** N.
carbon footprint	Your **carbon footprint** shows how much CO_2 is emitted from your personal energy use (**reduce your carbon footprint**).

spotlight   *-friendly*

-friendly is often used with nouns, adjectives, and adverbs to mean 'helping a person or thing; not harming them'.
*an **eco-friendly** light bulb*
***environmentally-friendly** cleaning products*
***user-friendly** instructions*
(= easy to use or understand)

4 Tick the word(s) which are possible. One, two, or three may be possible.

1   Using natural materials such as cotton or wool is more *environmentally-friendly* ☐ *eco-friendly* ☐ *user-friendly* ☐ than using man-made fabrics.
2   We should try to eat food which is *in season* ☐ *out of season* ☐ *disposable* ☐.
3   We should try to reduce *food miles* ☐ *our carbon footprint* ☐ *sustainability* ☐.
4   In new buildings, it's important to *minimize* ☐ *maximize* ☐ *dispose of* ☐ natural light.
5   The restaurant is an exciting new *enterprise* ☐ *carbon footprint* ☐ *venture* ☐.
6   We are interested in *groundbreaking* ☐ *sustainable* ☐ *green* ☐ projects.

5 Complete the texts.

Two university scientists have been given an award for their (1) g_____ research into ways of (2) r_____ used computers. Their unusual (3) v_____ aims to (4) r_____ 95 per cent of all computer parts, and ensure that the remaining 5 per cent will be (5) d_____ of in a way which (6) m_____ the impact on the environment.

Food (7) m_____ (or food kilometres) are the distance food travels from the farm to your plate. Here at The Good Food Forum we aim to educate communities on this issue, and to encourage consumers to buy locally produced food which is in (8) s_____ .

Remember to test yourself

29 I can **discuss wildlife under threat**

A Threats to wildlife in general 🎧

Word	Example	Meaning
habitat	*Some birds are in danger of losing their **habitat**.*	the place where a plant or animal is usually found (**natural habitat**).
deforestation	***Deforestation** is a real threat.*	the act of **clearing** forests (= removing trees).
endangered species	*The African elephant is an **endangered species**.*	**endangered** in danger because numbers are falling. **species** a group of animals, plants, etc. whose members are similar and can breed with each other.
under threat (of sth)	*Many wild animals are **under threat**.*	likely to be harmed or damaged; also **threatened with sth**.
reserve	*We can protect certain species by creating **reserves**.*	a protected area for plants, animals, etc. (a **wildlife/nature reserve**).
in the wild	***In the wild**, giant pandas eat bamboo exclusively.*	in a natural environment not controlled by people.
in captivity	*The bear was born **in captivity**.*	kept in a zoo or park, etc.
in decline	*Snow leopard populations are **in decline**.*	continuously decreasing in number, quantity, etc. (**gradual/steady decline**).
breed v	*Eagles **breed**[1] in spring. We **breed**[2] eagles in captivity.*	1 (of animals) have sex and produce young. 2 keep animals in order for them to produce young.
wipe sb/sth out	*Deforestation is **wiping out** certain species.*	destroy or get rid of sth completely.
die out	*This species of cat is **dying out**.*	become less common and eventually disappear.

---

spotlight   *extinct, extinction*

If a plant or animal is **extinct**, it no longer exists.   *Are sharks **becoming extinct**?*
The species is **in danger of extinction**.   It is **on the verge of extinction**. (= very close to extinction)

---

1 Is the meaning of the sentences the same or different? Write S or D.

1 The tiger population is in decline.	There are fewer tigers than there were.	
2 We are destroying their natural habitat.	We are destroying the nature reserves.	
3 It is on the verge of extinction.	It is almost extinct.	
4 They breed better in the wild.	They feed better in the wild.	
5 This species is endangered.	This species is under threat.	
6 I've seen widespread deforestation.	I've seen many forests cleared.	
7 In time, it will die out.	In time it will gradually disappear.	

2 Complete the dialogues with a single word in each space.

1 Has the dodo been wiped _____? ~ Yes, it's _____.
2 They're in steady _____, aren't they? ~ Yes, it's just a _____ process.
3 These birds are in _____ of extinction. ~ That's awful. Can they _____ more?
4 Did you see them _____ captivity? ~ No, I was lucky – I saw them in the _____.
5 I went to a nature _____ last year. ~ It's great to see animals in their natural _____.
6 There's far too much fishing of cod.~ Yes, many _____ of fish are _____ extinct.

Remember to test yourself

B Threats to an endangered species 🎧

Under threat:
the rhino[1]

- **Poaching**: This **poses** the greatest **threat to** this species, despite the ban on trade in **rhino horn**[2], which is particularly **sought after** for medical or decorative use.
- **Civil disturbance**: War **diverts funds** from conservation, and the high levels of **poverty** in affected areas increase the **likelihood** that people will turn to poaching. In some African countries, civil disturbance has **taken a heavy toll** on rhino populations.
- **Habitat loss**: If people **encroach on** the rhinos' **territory** through deforestation, the consequences are a lack of food and a limited **gene pool** for breeding.

Glossary

poaching	the illegal hunting of animals, birds, etc. (the person is a **poacher**).
pose a threat to sb/sth	create a threat (also **pose a risk/danger to sb/sth**).
sought after	wanted by many people but not easy to get.
divert sth (from sth)	use sth for a purpose that is different from its original purpose.
funds	PL money available to be spent (**raise funds** = collect money).
poverty	the state of being poor.
likelihood	SYN **probability**.
take a heavy toll on sth/sb	have a bad effect on sth.
encroach on/upon sth	FML gradually cover more and more of an area.
territory	an area an animal regards as its own and defends against others. **territorial** ADJ.
gene	a unit of information inside a cell which controls what the living thing will be like (the **gene pool** is the total of all the genes in a species).

❸ Cross out the error in each sentence. Write the correct word(s) at the end.

1 Cash will need to be divested from one project to another. ....
2 Pollution is putting a heavy toll on the seabird population. ....
3 The factory puts a substantial danger to wildlife in the area. ....
4 You hear people talk about the genes pool all the time. ....
5 I'm worried that the new developments are encroaching in the countryside. ....
6 The horn of the animal is sought over by poachers. ....
7 It's important to raise fund to support conservation. ....
8 This poses a threaten to both humans and wildlife. ....

❹ Write a word at the end of the sentence with the same meaning as the underlined words.

1 There is little <u>probability</u> of things improving soon. ....
2 You should avoid going into the animals' <u>land</u>. ....
3 He was sent to prison for <u>illegal hunting of</u> birds' eggs. ....
4 I saw a <u>large heavy animal with a horn on its nose</u> at the zoo. ....
5 The animal is extremely <u>protective of its land</u>. ....
6 Living in <u>a situation with very little money</u> is common in Africa. ....

 Remember to test yourself

30 I can **describe medical advances** 🎧

A revolutionary **era** in medical **advances**

In recent **decades**, we have witnessed radical changes in **conventional** medicine:

- Fifty years ago, **scanners**[1] did not exist. **Diagnostic** tools were **restricted** to **stethoscopes**[2] and basic x-ray machines.
- Until recent years, children were **prone to** certain infectious diseases, for which there was no effective **cure**. **Vaccines** have almost **eradicated** some of these **conditions**.
- In the past, if you needed a major operation, you would be **confined to bed** for weeks. Today many operations use less **invasive procedures**, requiring day surgery only.
- In the past, the **mortality rate** for patients with **organ** failure, such as heart, lung, or kidney failure, was 100 per cent. Today, **transplants** can allow patients to **resume** a normal life.
- The **survival rate** for many cancers has improved considerably over recent decades, due to the development of **chemotherapy** to treat the condition.

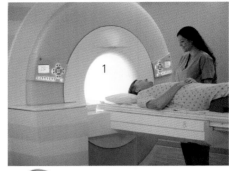

Glossary

era	a period of time that has a particular quality or character.
advance(s) (in sth)	progress made in science, medicine, technology, etc.
decade	a period of ten years.
conventional	usual or traditional; not new or different. **convention** N.
diagnostic	used for finding out what physical or mental problem sb has. **diagnose** V. **diagnosis** N.
restrict sth (to sth)	limit the size, number, or amount of sth. **restriction** N.
prone to sth	likely to suffer from sth (also **accident-prone**).
cure	a medical treatment that makes a sick person well again. **cure** V. **curable** ADJ. OPP **incurable**.
vaccine	a substance which is put into the blood and protects the body from disease (the process of giving **vaccine** is **vaccination** N). **vaccinate** V.
eradicate sth	destroy or get rid of sth (bad) completely. SYN **wipe sth out**.
condition	a long-term illness or medical problem.
be confined to bed / a wheelchair	have to stay in bed / a wheelchair.
invasive	(of medical treatment) involving cutting of the body. **invasion** N. **invade** V.
procedure	a medical operation or investigation (**carry out / perform a procedure**).
organ	a part of the body that has a particular purpose, such as the heart or brain.
transplant	an operation in which a damaged organ is replaced with one from a **donor** (= sb who gives part of their body, blood, etc.). **transplant** V.
resume sth	FML begin sth again after an interruption. **resumption** N.
chemotherapy	the treatment of diseases, especially cancer, by drugs.

---

spotlight *rate*

A **rate** is a measurement of the number of times something happens within a period, e.g. the **mortality/death rate** is the number of people dying; the **survival rate** is the number of people continuing to live despite a serious illness.
*The **birth rate rocketed**.* = The number of babies born rose sharply.
*The **accident rate plummeted**.* = The number of accidents fell sharply.

 Remember to test yourself

1 Complete the table.

Noun	Verb	Adjective
	invade	
	cure	
	resume	xxxxxx
convention	xxxxxx	

Noun	Verb	Adjective
vaccine,		xxxxxx
diagnosis		
	transplant	xxxxxx

2 Write *yes* or *no*.

1 If a disease is wiped out, does it mean it has been restricted? ....
2 Does an organ donor receive an organ from someone else? ....
3 If you're prone to injury, are you more likely to be injured than most people? ....
4 If you have a disease which is diagnosed, does it mean you are better? ....
5 Is flu usually described as a medical condition? ....
6 Are we living in a technological era? ....
7 If your dentist takes your tooth out, is it usually an invasive procedure? ....
8 Has heart disease been eradicated in the world? ....
9 If something plummets, does it go down? ....
10 If the accident rate rockets, is that a good thing? ....

3 Match 1–10 with a–j.

1 They have been doing research on the disease for a
2 There's a prize for the most important technological
3 After the operation, she was confined
4 My sister is prone
5 I needed to know the current survival
6 The surgeons had to perform a delicate medical
7 His life was saved thanks to an organ
8 Cancer treatment is often in the form of
9 It's her third cycling injury; she's really accident-
10 Sadly, this disease is thought to be

a chemotherapy.
b decade.
c transplant.
d incurable.
e to depression.
f prone.
g rate.
h to bed.
i advance.
j procedure.

4 Complete the dialogues.

1 A The brain disease meningitis C has been .... , I believe.
   B Yes, it's been almost completely .... That's brilliant news.
2 A In some areas, lung cancer treatment is .... to non-smoking patients only.
   B Yes, I think that may be true for patients needing an organ .... as well.
3 A The government has a policy to .... the elderly against flu.
   B I know, but there's often a shortage of the appropriate .... when it's needed.
4 A I'm not in favour of drug treatments; I just don't trust .... medicine.
   B Really? But there have been some fantastic .... in drugs in the last few years.
5 A The mortality .... in the UK has been falling since the 19th century.
   B That's true. .... rates have improved particularly among the very young.
6 A The surgeons had to .... a highly invasive procedure on Jason.
   B Yes, he was .... to bed for ages, but he's recovering well, thank goodness.

Remember to test yourself

31 I can **talk about communication technology**

A Computer jargon 🎧

Word	Example	Meaning
jargon	*She used a lot of technical **jargon** in her explanation.*	OFTEN DISAPPROVING special words and phrases used by people who do the same kind of work.
password	*Never tell anyone your **password**.*	the secret numbers or letters you have to put into a computer in order to use it.
username	*My **username** is LuluG.*	the name you use to operate a computer or program.
log on/in OPP **log off/out**	*When you **log on**, **enter** a username or password.*	perform the actions that let you start to use a computer system.
scroll (up/ down)	***Scroll up** and **down** the page using the **scroll bar**.*	move text on a screen up or down so that you can read different parts.
google sb/sth SYN **do a search (on sth/sb)**	*I found him by **googling** him / **doing a** web **search on** him.*	type words into a search engine to find information about sb/sth.
link	*Click on the **link** at the bottom of this page.*	a connection between one file or document and another on the web.
spam **spamming**	*I hate **spam**; I spend ages deleting it from my inbox.*	unwanted email advertisements; you **block spam** (= prevent it) with **anti-spam filters**.
virus N.	*Have you got **anti-virus protection**?*	a program that enters your computer and destroys or damages your data.
hack into sth	*They **hacked into** the bank and stole thousands.*	use a computer to connect secretly to sb else's computer and find or change information on it.

1 Correct the errors.

1 stroll up a document ....
2 enter your passport ....
3 use computer jargot ....
4 hack onto someone's computer ....
5 anti-viro protection ....
6 cyber-learning ....
7 make a web search ....
8 black spam from your inbox ....

> **spotlight** | **e-** and **cyber-**
>
> **e-** and **cyber-** are used with nouns to mean 'related to the internet':
> an **e-business** (a web-based company)
> **e-learning** (learning that takes place on computers or the internet)
> a **cyber-café** (a café where people pay to use the internet. SYN **internet café**)
> **cyberspace** (the imaginary place where emails exist when being sent between computers).

2 Complete the text.

I spend a lot of time on the internet for my work (I'm a TV researcher), but I have to say I'm not very good at it. For a start, when I go to a website, I often forget my (1) p................ or (2) u................ , and of course, I can't (3) l................ in until I find it. I spend a lot of time trying to find information about TV personalities; I (4) g................ their names and go to various websites, and sometimes I find (5) l................ to other sites with more information. I often forget to save these sites, which means each time I have to start again and do another (6) s................ .
Still, my brother is brilliant with computers, so he looks after various things like protecting me against computer (7) v................ or providing anti-spam (8) f................ . One of these days, I'll do a course and learn how to use my computer properly.

Remember to test yourself

B Video sharing

YouTube, the **phenomenally** successful video-sharing website, was **dreamt up** over dinner by three Americans in 2004. They produced a simple routine for taking videos in any **format** and making them play in any **web browser** on any computer. They built a **virtual** video village where **registered users** could **upload** their own **videoblogs** and **clips**, and watch and **rate** other people's. The rise of such websites **coincided** with the availability of cheap **camcorders**, and **alongside** that, the development of easy-to-use **software**.

Glossary

phenomenally	in a very great or impressive way. **phenomenal** ADJ.
dream sth up	INF have an idea, especially an unusual one. SYN **think sth up**.
format	(in computing) the way data is organized in a computer file or program.
(web) browser	a program that lets you look at files on the internet.
virtual	(in computing) created by computers or appearing on computers or the internet (a **virtual community**, a **virtual office**, **virtual reality**).
registered user	a person whose username and password are recorded on a website, so they can enter it.
upload sth	send a file, video, etc. from your computer to a larger system using the internet. OPP **download sth**.
videoblog	a personal video made by sb on sth they are interested in.
(video) clip	a short part of a video or film.
rate sth	say how good you think sth is, e.g. good, acceptable, or bad.
coincide with sth	happen at the same time as sth else. **coincidence** N.
camcorder	a video camera that can be carried around.
alongside sth/sb	together or at the same time as sth/sb.
software	the programs used to operate a computer (**install/run** a piece of **software**).

3 True or false? Write T or F.

1 You make a videoblog on a camcorder. _____
2 If you rate a clip as phenomenal, you think it's terrible. _____
3 If you are a registered user of a website, the site knows your name. _____
4 You need a browser to look at documents. _____
5 If two events coincide, one happens before the other. _____
6 If one event happens alongside another, they happen at the same time. _____

4 Complete the sentences with a suitable word.

Have you ever …   ABOUT YOU

1 _____ a piece of software onto your computer and had problems? _____
2 become a _____ user of a website and then received a lot of spam? _____
3 watched a _____ on YouTube, and _____ it as good? _____
4 _____ a video clip onto a website yourself? _____
5 been part of a _____ community on the internet? _____
6 _____ up a brilliant idea for a website? _____
7 _____ free software from the internet onto your computer? _____
8 converted a video file from any _____ to any other one? _____

5 ABOUT YOU Answer the questions in Exercise 4, or ask another student.

Remember to test yourself

32 I can **talk about migration**

A People on the move 🎧

Word	Example	Meaning
flee (from) sth/ sb	*We saw long queues of people* **fleeing** *the war.*	escape from a dangerous situation, place, or person very quickly.
refugee	*Many* **refugees** *have crossed the border to escape the war.*	a person who is forced to leave their country for political/religious reasons.
seek/take refuge (from sth/sb)	*The men had to* **take refuge** *in the French embassy.*	find shelter or protection from trouble or danger.
(political) asylum	*The numbers seeking* **asylum** *have increased recently.*	the protection a country gives to a refugee (**seek asylum**, **apply for asylum**).
ethnic minority ethnic group	***Ethnic minorities*** *make up almost 10 per cent of the town's population.*	a group of people with the same culture or race living in a place where most people are of a different culture/race.
be uprooted	*Following the flooding, many villagers* **were uprooted**.	be made to leave the place where you live and go somewhere else.
discrimination discriminate v	*He had become a victim of racial* **discrimination**.	the practice of treating a person or group in society less fairly than others.
deport sb deportation N	*Foreigners may be* **deported** *if they enter the country illegally.*	force sb to leave a country, often because they have no right to be there.
prejudice (against sb/sth) prejudiced ADJ	*There is no* **prejudice against** *people from the ethnic community.*	an opinion about sb/sth that is not based on reason or experience, especially a dislike based on race, religion, etc.

1 Circle the correct word(s). Both words may be correct.

1 In 2001, over 250,000 people deported / emigrated to Canada.
2 Most refugees who seek / apply asylum do so in a country neighbouring their own.
3 The villagers took refugee / refuge in the nearby towns.
4 The council are seeking the opinions of members of the economic / ethnic minority.
5 People fled / flew in terror to escape the flood.
6 Ignorance is often behind the prejudice / prejudiced against the incoming economic migrants / emigration.
7 Women and children were forced to seek / take refuge in the local church.

> **spotlight** *migration*
>
> **Migration** is the movement of people or animals from one place to another. More specifically, **immigration** is the process of coming to live in a country that is not your own (people are **immigrants**). The opposite process of going to live in another country is **emigration** (**emigrate** v; people are **emigrants**). People who move abroad to find a better job are often called **economic migrants**.

2 One word is missing in each line. What is it, and where does it go?

1 There's no limit on the number of people granted political in this country. ....
2 Racial and sexual is against the law in matters of employment. ....
3 Economic to richer countries has existed for centuries. ....
4 There's been a rise in the of illegal workers back to their home countries. ....
5 Nearly half a million people were forced to their homes during the civil war, ... and many of them refuge in the mountains, away from the fighting. ....
6 Many families uprooted against their will to make way for the new road. ....

Remember to test yourself

B Migration: a personal experience 🎧

Moving from my **native** country was a huge **culture shock**. There was a lot I had to **get accustomed** to – not least the food! But I didn't suffer the prejudice or **animosity** that some migrants complain of. People have accepted me for what I am, including my religious **faith**; they've seen beyond the **stereotype**. And for my part, I recognize the need for **integration** in order to be able to **live at peace with** my neighbours. I still have feelings of **nostalgia** for the place where I grew up, but this is home now, and I have no **desire** to go back.

Glossary

native	connected with the place where you were born and lived for the first years of your life (**native country/land/city**).
culture shock	a feeling of confusion and anxiety often felt by people staying in another country.
animosity (towards sb)	a feeling of anger or hatred. sᴇɴ **hostility**.
faith	a strong belief in sth (this is often a **religious faith**).
stereotype	a fixed idea of what a particular type of person or thing is like, but which is often not true in reality. **stereotypical** ᴀᴅᴊ.
integration	the process of becoming a full member of a group or society. **integrate (into sth)**.
live at peace with sb	live without quarrelling with others.
nostalgia	a feeling of sadness mixed with pleasure when you think of happy times in the past. **nostalgic** ᴀᴅᴊ.
desire	a strong wish (**have no desire to do sth**).

spotlight Getting used to things

If you **get accustomed to (doing) sth**, or **get used to (doing)** it, you become familiar with it and accept it as normal. If you **get acclimatized (to sth)**, you become familiar with a new climate or situation. If you **get the hang of sth** ɪɴꜰ, you learn how to do, use, or understand something.

3 Cross out the word which is wrong. Write the correct word at the end.

1 Why is there so much animosity for politicians here? ....
2 I couldn't stop sweating at first, but now I'm starting to get acclimated. ....
3 Do you have feelings of nostalgic about your childhood? ....
4 He doesn't fit the stereoscope of a typical 30-year-old businessman. ....
5 The government policy is to aid newcomers' integrity into society. ....
6 I'm a natural New Yorker; in fact, I've never lived anywhere else. ....

4 Complete the dialogue.

A Amy, when you first emigrated, what kinds of things did you have to get (1)........................ to?

B The main thing was the climate! But seriously, in my (2)........................ country, many people no longer have a strong religious (3)........................ , whereas here, religion is at the heart of people's lives, so that added to my sense of culture (4)........................ . I discovered that people had a (5)........................ view of how Western women behave, as they seemed surprised when they got to know me. I dressed appropriately and behaved sensitively, as I had no (6)........................ to alienate people. Ultimately I was keen to (7)........................ into society as best I could. And to be truthful, I've never felt any (8)........................ towards me. People here just want to live at (9)........................ with each other, as I do. Actually, the worst thing was the transport system – it took me ages to get the (10)........................ of it!

Remember to test yourself

Review: A changing world

Unit 27

1 Complete the words in the dialogues.

1 Can we stop the decline? ~ No, it's i_____ .
2 Were the changes obvious? ~ No, they were quite s_____ , actually.
3 Has the consultation stage ended? ~ No, it's o_____ .
4 Were the changes very noticeable? ~ Oh, yes, they were s_____ changes.
5 Has the firm reverted to its old name? ~ Yes, it's g_____ b_____ to calling itself AGD.
6 Will the plan be carried out? ~ Yes, he's putting it into p_____ at once.

A Z more words: *change* hands, *instigate*, *revoke*, *turn the* **corner**, *tweak*, **change** *of heart*, **go** *back on sth*

Unit 28

1 Complete the chart with one word in each space.

How to be _____ : dos and don'ts
😊 Eat locally produced fruit and vegetables to reduce food _____ .
😊 Try to eat fruit and vegetables that are in _____ .
😊 _____ most of your waste rather than throwing it away.
😊 Use energy-_____ light bulbs, which _____ less CO_2.
😊 Use _____ batteries.
☹ Don't use a tumble _____ : it _____ masses of energy.
😊 Maximize natural light in order to _____ the use of electric lights.
☹ Don't leave electrical appliances such as TVs on _____ .
☹ Avoid things which are _____ and designed to be thrown away after use.

A Z more words: *carbon emission*, **renewable** *energy source*, *thermostat*, *insulation*, **draught** *excluder*, **solar** *panel*

Unit 29

1 Complete the sentences on the right with a <u>single</u> word that keeps the same meaning.

1 It is because they're cutting down trees.   It is because of _____ .
2 Some species no longer exist.   Some species have been _____ out.
3 Rhinos could disappear altogether.   Rhinos are in danger of _____ .
4 It's where the animals normally live.   It's the animals' natural _____ .
5 Can they breed them in zoos?   Can they breed them in _____ ?
6 You see them in their natural environment.   You see them in the _____ .
7 They are mostly in protected areas.   They are mostly in nature _____ .
8 It's having a very bad effect.   It's taking a very heavy _____ .

A Z more words: *put in* **jeopardy**, **adverse** *effect*, *biodiversity*, *deplete*, **indigenous** *species*

Unit 30

1 Circle the words that are possible. One, two, or three may be possible.

1   Modern medicine has transplanted / eradicated / wiped out many diseases.
2   The doctors had to perform a very evasive / invasive / persuasive procedure.
3   He was confined to bed / a sofa / a wheelchair .
4   It was a significant era / decade / period in medical science.
5   The doctors have managed to limit / restrain / restrict the spread of the disease.
6   It's a serious medical condition / illness / situation .
7   After an operation it can take time to presume / perform / resume a normal life.
8   The heart is one of the vital aspects / parts / organs of the body.

A Z   more words: *heart **bypass**, radiotherapy, **alternative** medicine, hip/knee/shoulder* ***replacement**, general/local **anaesthetic**, **administer** drugs/medicine*

Unit 31

1 Finish each word or phrase in two different ways.

1   log _____ OR log _____   4   e- _____ OR e- _____
2   cyber _____ OR cyber _____   5   virtual _____ OR virtual _____
3   scroll _____ OR scroll _____ 6   _____ OR _____ load something

2 Complete the words in each sentence.   ABOUT YOU

1   Have you ever made your own personal **video**_____ ?
2   Do you ever forget your **pass**_____ ?
3   Do you ever use a **cam**_____ ?
4   Do you **up**_____ many files or videos?
5   Do you find it easy to **in**_____ software on your computer?

3 ABOUT YOU Write your answers to Exercise 2, or ask another student.

A Z   more words: *screensaver, computer **geek**, firewall, netiquette, **zip/compress** a file, bug*

Unit 32

1 Complete the text with suitable words.

Kamil was forced to (1)_____ from his (2)_____ Somalia after three members of his family were killed, and his life was also endangered. He took (3)_____ in Uganda for several months before seeking political (4)_____ in Britain. When he arrived, he obviously experienced a huge culture (5)_____ , although he did not suffer any racial (6)_____ . He says his religious (7)_____ is still strong despite what he has been through, and he is just happy to be able to live at (8)_____ with his neighbours, despite his obvious feelings of (9)_____ for his own country.

A Z   more words: ***brain** drain, feel alienated, outsider, displacement, hardship, **dual** nationality*

33 I can **discuss health services**

A Healthcare services 🎧

> ### Healthcare services: frequently asked questions
> - ► How do I **register with** a GP?
> - ► How do I get a **referral** to a specialist?
> - ► Can I request a **second opinion**?
> - ► Are medical records strictly **confidential**?
> - ► What if I suspect medical **negligence**?
>
> - ► How do I **access out of hours** care in my area?
> - ► Can I get **cosmetic surgery free of charge**?
> - ► How can I **get hold of** data about **clinical trials**?
> - ► Is **complementary medicine** freely available?

Glossary

register (at/for/with sth)	put your name on an official list (**enrol** = register to join a course, school, etc.).
referral	the act of sending sb to get professional help (**be referred to sb**).
second opinion	advice from another person (i.e. not the original doctor).
confidential	meant to be kept secret (**strictly confidential**). **confidentiality** N (**protect patient/ client confidentiality**).
negligence	fml failure to give proper care or attention. **negligent** ADJ.
access sth	fml reach, enter, or use sth (**gain/have access to sth**).
out of hours	when a surgery, office, etc. is closed.
cosmetic surgery	medical treatment intended to improve sb's appearance (surgical repair after accidents, burns, etc. is called **plastic surgery**).
free of charge	If sth is **free of charge** it costs you nothing.
get hold of sth	find or obtain sth (**get hold of sb** = find or contact sb).
clinical trial	a piece or period of research on the effectiveness or safety of drugs or treatment.
complementary medicine	treatments that are not part of traditional Western medicine, e.g. acupuncture.

❶ Make six phrases from the box.

protect someone's	get hold	clinical	enrol	strictly	cosmetic
on a course	surgery	of something	confidential	confidentiality	trial

....

....

❷ Complete the text.

When you move to a new area, you need to (1) .... with a doctor. With most surgeries, if you need out of (2) .... care and your doctor is not available, there will be an answerphone message, and you will be (3) .... to another doctor. If you have a serious problem which involves seeing a specialist, you can get a (4) .... by asking your GP to write to the hospital. If you aren't happy with the specialist's diagnosis, ask for a second (5) .... You can gain (6) .... to your medical records at your GP's surgery. All health care is free of (7) .... , even plastic (8) .... if it is for medical reasons, and some surgeries also make use of complementary (9) .... If you are unhappy with your treatment and suspect medical (10) .... , you should speak to the medical staff first before taking any further action.

❸ ABOUT YOU Answer the questions at the top of the page about your health service.

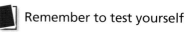 Remember to test yourself

B In hospital: patients' experiences 🎧

> The nursing staff immediately **put me at my ease** and I was **kept informed** at all times.

> I had **keyhole surgery** on my knee; apart from a **mix-up** over my notes, the treatment was **second to none**.

> Sister Ann's ward was **spotless**, and everything was done with **meticulous** care. **Nothing was too much trouble**.

> I know staff were **rushed off their feet**, but no one **took any notice of** my calls for help.

> I was **admitted** to the ward, seen by a **junior** doctor, then nothing happened for two days!

spotlight	A stay in hospital

If you need medical care, you may be **admitted to hospital** (= taken there and treated). After treatment, you are **discharged** (= given permission to leave). Then you may go home to **convalesce** (= spend time recovering). **convalescence** N. SYN **recuperate. recuperation** N.

Glossary

put sb at (their) ease	make sb feel relaxed and not nervous.
keep sb informed	continue to give sb information about sth.
spotless	perfectly clean (also **spotlessly clean**). SYN **immaculate**.
meticulous	paying careful attention to every detail. SYN **fastidious**.
nothing is too much trouble	= sb is always ready to help.
keyhole surgery	a medical operation in which only a very small cut is made in the body.
mix-up	INF a situation full of confusion due to a mistake. SYN **muddle**.
second to none	If a treatment is **second to none**, it is the best.
rushed off your feet	extremely busy, with too many things to do.
take (no) notice of sb/sth	pay (no) attention to sth/sb.
junior	having a low rank in an organization or profession. OPP **senior**.

4 Is the meaning the same or different? Write S or D.

1 There was a bit of a mix-up.	There was a bit of a muddle.	
2 The doctor ignored me.	The doctor took no notice of me.	
3 The treatment was second to none.	The treatment was inferior.	
4 She convalesced at home.	She recuperated at home.	
5 Nothing was too much trouble.	The care was too much trouble.	
6 The rooms were spotless.	The rooms were immaculate.	
7 When were you discharged?	When were you admitted?	
8 Did they put you at your ease?	Did they make it look easy?	
9 She's meticulous about cleaning.	She's fastidious about cleaning.	

5 Complete the sentences with a suitable word.   ABOUT YOUR COUNTRY

1 In hospital, patients are always _____ informed about their treatment. _____
2 Keyhole _____ is increasingly common these days. _____
3 Staff in hospitals are _____ off their feet all the time. _____
4 There are more senior doctors than _____ doctors. _____
5 All the wards in our local hospital are _____ clean. _____
6 Recuperation (or _____) always takes place at home. _____

6 ABOUT YOUR COUNTRY Are the statements in Exercise 5 true about your country? Write your answers or ask another student.

 Remember to test yourself

34 I can **talk about local government**

A Local election manifesto 🎧

Independent Party **manifesto** for the local **council** elections. We will:
- **Stand up for** the community and speak **on behalf of residents** on green issues.
- **Take** complaints **seriously**, and **give** neighbourhoods **a say** in local decisions.
- **Allocate** better funding for youth projects and **ensure** they are properly managed.
- Provide **grants** for **voluntary** organizations helping with the elderly and disabled.

Glossary

manifesto	a written statement by a political party saying what they believe in and what they intend to do.
council	the organization that provides local government in a city or area. A **councillor** is an elected member of the council.
stand up for sth/sb	support or defend sth/sb. SYN **stick up for sb** INF.
on behalf of sb / on sb's behalf	as the representative of sb.
resident	a person who lives in a particular place. (This is also a meaning of **citizen**, although **citizen** can also mean a person with legal rights in a country.)
take sth/sb seriously	think that sth/sb is important and deserves respect.
say	the right to take part in deciding sth (**give sb a say / have a say in sth**).
allocate sth	give sth officially to sb/sth for a particular purpose.
ensure sth	make sure that sth happens or is definite.
grant	a sum of money given, often by the government, for a purpose.
voluntary	(of work) done by people (**volunteers**) who choose to do it without being paid (the **voluntary sector** includes organizations called **charities / charity organizations**, which help people in need).

❶ Complete the words.

1 r___s___d___nt
2 ___ns___re
3 v___l___nt___ry
4 co___n_____l
5 ch___r___ty
6 ___ll___c___te
7 m___n___f___st___
8 co___n_____ll___r

❷ One word is incorrect in each sentence. Cross it out and write the correct word at the end.

1 I've read the manifests and they all say the same thing. _____
2 They should give us a say to what happens in our city. _____
3 Do you think the councillors will make our ideas seriously? _____
4 My sister's done a lot of work for the volunteer sector. _____
5 She spoke movingly on behalf for all of us. _____
6 They should stand out for people who don't have a say. _____

❸ Complete the sentences.

1 There are no local _____ in my town who speak on my _____ .
2 How much do local _____ help _____ organizations such as 'Help the Aged'?
3 I don't really feel I _____ a say in local politics.
4 Local politicians should _____ up for people and _____ their ideas seriously.
5 Do you think you can get a _____ from the council to improve your home?
6 There are thousands of British _____ living in other parts of Europe.

Remember to test yourself

B The role of the mayor 🎧

The **Mayor** of London is elected by any Londoners **eligible** to vote, and has quite a **high profile**. The mayor is the capital's **spokesperson**; he has a range of powers and duties, such as **promoting** economic development. He **sets** the annual **budget** for the Greater London Authority (the **strategic city-wide** government for London). He heads the Metropolitan Police Authority (which provides **policing** in the capital), the Fire Service, the London Development **Agency**, and finally, Transport for London (which controls the transport **network**). He also **chairs** meetings of the board of Transport for London.

Glossary

mayor	the most important chosen or elected official in a town or city.	**city-wide**	happening or existing across the whole of a city (also **nationwide**, **worldwide**)
eligible	allowed by rules or laws to do or receive sth. OPP **ineligible**.	**policing**	the activity of keeping order in a place, using the police. **police** v.
high profile	A person or thing with a **high profile** gets attention and is easily noticed (*a high-profile job*).	**agency**	a business or government department that provides a particular service (**employment/advertising/travel agency**).
spokesperson	a person who speaks on behalf of a group or an organization.	**network**	a system of roads, lines, wires, etc. that are connected to each other (**rail/road/underground/network**).
promote sth	help sth to happen or develop. **promotion** N.		
budget	the amount of money a person or organization has to spend on sth (**set a budget** = decide a budget).	**chair (a meeting)**	be in charge of (a meeting) (*see spotlight*).
strategic	carefully planned in order to achieve a particular goal. **strategy** N.		

spotlight Gender

Some people are offended by job titles which refer only to men.
Neutral: **spokesperson chair/chairperson mayor**   Men only: **spokesman chairman**
Women only: **spokeswoman chairwoman mayoress** (= female mayor or mayor's wife)

4 Tick the words which are possible. One, two, or three words may be possible.

1 The robbery has produced a *nationwide* ☐ *city-wide* ☐ *worldwide* ☐ police investigation.
2 Our department is responsible for the *transport* ☐ *budget* ☐ *road* ☐ network.
3 The job has a high *profile* ☐ *policing* ☐ *promotion* ☐.
4 My uncle is the *chairman* ☐ *chairperson* ☐ *chairwoman* ☐ of the transport committee.
5 We heard the *chair* ☐ *spokesperson* ☐ *spokesman* ☐ making a statement to the press.
6 People under 21 may be *eligible* ☐ *ineligible* ☐ *strategic* ☐ to vote in the election.

5 Complete the sentences with a suitable word.

1 We need a large force to .... the city.
2 He .... the city around the world.
3 Mrs Bryant will .... the meeting.
4 He runs an employment ....
5 She sets the annual ....
6 The rail .... is very complicated.
7 If you're over 18, you're .... to vote.
8 We have an elected .... in our city.

35 I can **talk about crime and the police**

A Organized crime 🎧

The Serious **Organized Crime** Agency tackles a range of illegal activities including:

➔ **drug-trafficking**, which is considered to pose the greatest threat to the UK in terms of organized criminal involvement, the illegal **proceeds** obtained, and the overall harm caused.

➔ immigration crime, which includes both people-**smuggling** and **human-trafficking**, that is, trafficking people for criminal **exploitation**, such as **forced labour**.

➔ **fraud** committed against individuals or companies often by organized **gangs**, for example investment fraud, when people are **enticed** to pay money against false promises of returns.

Other threats include **forgery** of official documents and the use of **firearms**.

Glossary

organized crime	crime committed by professional criminals working in large groups.	**forced labour**	hard physical work that sb is forced to do.
trafficking	the buying and selling of sth illegally. **drug-/human-trafficking**.	**fraud**	the crime of obtaining money from sb by tricking them. **defraud sb** v.
proceeds (of sth)	the money you receive when you sell or organize sth.	**gang**	a group of criminals working together.
smuggling	the crime of moving goods or people illegally into or out of a country. **smuggle sth/sb** v.	**entice sb to do sth**	persuade sb to do sth, usually by offering them sth.
exploitation	DISAPPROVING a situation in which sb treats sb else unfairly in order to make money from their work. **exploit sb** v.	**forgery**	the crime of making an exact copy of documents or works of art in order to make money by selling them. **forge sth** v.
		firearm	FML a gun that can be carried.

❶ Tick the words which describe an illegal activity.

1 smuggling _____
2 gang _____
3 entice someone _____

4 fraud _____
5 forgery _____
6 firearm _____

7 forced labour _____
8 drug-trafficking _____

❷ Complete the words in the sentences.

1 The gang were accused of d_____ the company of $300,000.
2 Six boys were rescued at the border, and the men were charged with human-t_____ .
3 In the developing world, large companies e_____ young children in order to make goods cheaply.
4 A man was arrested for attempting to s_____ illegal weapons through customs.
5 Most o_____ crime is financially motivated, while some is politically motivated.
6 The police believe the men are responsible for the f_____ of hundreds of passports.
7 In internet fraud schemes, victims may be e_____ to give their bank account details with the false promise of financial returns. Criminals use the p_____ to finance further schemes.

❸ ABOUT YOU AND YOUR COUNTRY Which crimes in the text are people in your country most concerned about? Which are the most difficult to solve, and why? Write your ideas, or discuss them with another student.

📓 Remember to test yourself

B An arrest 🎧

An arrest is when a police **constable** lawfully **detains** someone suspected of an offence. In the UK, the police can arrest you if they have a valid arrest **warrant** (**issued** by a **magistrate**), or if they have reasonable **grounds** for suspecting you have committed or **are about to** commit an offence. You are **cautioned** and then taken to a police station as soon as possible. Once you are **in custody**, you have the right to legal advice from a **solicitor**. If there is sufficient evidence, the police will charge you; you will then appear in court where a magistrate will decide whether you should be **remanded in custody** or **released on bail**.

Glossary

detain sb	keep sb in an official place, e.g. a police station, and prevent them from leaving (**be detained in custody**).	**caution sb**	FML warn sb officially that anything they say may be used against them as evidence in court.
warrant	a legal document signed by a judge that allows the police to do sth; a judge **issues a warrant**.	**custody**	the state of being in prison while awaiting trial (**in custody**).
		solicitor	a lawyer who gives legal advice and prepares documents.
magistrate	an official who acts as a judge in trials involving minor offences.	**remand sb**	send sb away from court until their trial (**remanded in custody** = sent to prison until the trial).
grounds (for sth)	PL, FML good or true reasons for saying or doing sth (**reasonable grounds for sth**, **on the grounds that ...**).	**bail**	money left with a court to ensure that a prisoner will return for their trial (a judge **releases sb on bail / grants bail** or **refuses bail**).
be about to (do sth)	be going to do sth very soon.		

4 Write your answers.

1 Who has a lower rank than a sergeant? ....
2 Who is above a sergeant? ....
3 Who is the head of a regional force? ....
4 Who issues an arrest warrant? ....
5 Who detains someone? ....
6 Who offers legal advice? ....
7 Who is able to grant bail? ....
8 Who is remanded in custody? ....
9 Who may be refused bail? ....

spotlight **The police**

A **police officer** is any member of the **police force**. In the UK, a (**police**) **constable** (**PC**) is an officer of the lowest **rank** (= position in an organization). Above the rank of constable is the **sergeant**, the **inspector**, and so on. The **chief constable** is the head of each regional police force.

5 Complete the text.

ARRESTED IN ROAD RAGE INCIDENT

An 82-year-old man is facing prison after a road rage incident in which he allegedly pointed a gun at another driver and was, allegedly, (1) a............... to use it. A young (2) p............... constable (3) d............... the man at the scene of the crime on the (4) g............... that he was in possession of an illegal firearm. He was (5) c............... at the roadside, and then taken to the police station. Once in (6) c..............., the suspect refused to say anything and also refused his right to speak to a (7) s................ The police later charged him, and the man will now appear before a (8) m............... tomorrow morning, when he hopes to be (9) r............... on bail.

Remember to test yourself

36 | I can **discuss prisons**

A The prison system 🎧

Since the **abolition** of **capital punishment** in the UK, time in prison is the most serious punishment allowed by law. It satisfies our need for **retribution**, and longer sentences are meant to be a **deterrent**. Furthermore, criminals who are **locked up** are no threat to society, and **rehabilitation** programmes in prison give criminals a chance to **turn over a new leaf**. However, the current system is **in crisis**. More people are being **imprisoned**, over 60 per cent **reoffend**, and for some criminals, prison is simply **regarded** as an **occupational hazard**. Is it just our way of **taking revenge**? If so, can we **justify** its continued existence?

Glossary

abolition	the official ending of a law, system, or institution. **abolish sth** v.	**turn over a new leaf**	change your behaviour and become a better person.
capital punishment	punishment by death.	**in crisis**	in a period of great difficulty and uncertainty.
retribution	FML severe punishment for sth serious that sb has done.	**reoffend**	FML commit a crime again (a person is a **reoffender**).
deterrent	a thing that makes sb less likely to do sth. **deter sb** v.	**regard sth/sb as sth**	think about sth/sb in a particular way.
lock sb up	INF put sb in prison. SYN **imprison sb. imprisonment** N.	**occupational hazard**	a risk or danger (= hazard) that is part of a job.
rehabilitation	the process of helping people to live a normal life after they have been ill or in prison. **rehabilitate sb** v.	**take revenge**	take action to punish sb because they made you suffer.
		justify sth	show that sth is right or fair. **justification** N. **justifiable** ADJ.

1 Rewrite the sentences on the left, using the sentence beginnings on the right.

1	He's been imprisoned.	He's been locked ....
2	She thinks of me as a friend.	She regards ....
3	He wants to change and become better.	He wants to turn ....
4	Can we justify the prison system?	Is the prison system .... ?
5	He was imprisoned for life.	He got life ....
6	It changed after they abolished the law.	It changed after the ....
7	It's one of the risks of the job.	It's an ....
8	Do many people commit a crime again?	Are there many .... ?

2 Complete the words in the sentences, then write your own answers, or ask another student.

ABOUT YOU

1 Do you believe you can r............... most criminals?

2 Do you think prison is an effective d............... ?

3 Do you believe in c............... punishment?

4 Would you like to a............... anything in your prison system?

5 Is there ever any justification for taking r............... ?

6 Is the prison system in c............... in your country?

Remember to test yourself

B A different system 🎧

GRENDON is not a typical prison. It is constructed **exclusively** on the principles of group **therapy**, and operates as a 'therapeutic community' for offenders. The **inmates** are all serving long sentences, and a high **proportion** are guilty of violent crime. Yet the prison **deviates from** the normal system in almost every way, with an absence of physical force and **segregation**. The prison is divided into five **self-contained** communities, the inmates are not **confined** in **cells**, and decisions are only taken with their **consent**.

Glossary

exclusively	only, and with nothing else (e.g. *We rely **exclusively** on aid.*).
therapy	treatment of a physical or mental problem or illness (**group therapy** involves discussing each other's problems). **therapeutic** ADJ.
inmate	a person living in a prison.
proportion	a part or share of the whole amount or number.
deviate from sth	be different from what is normal. **deviation** N.
segregation	the policy of separating people of different sex, race, religion, etc. **segregate** V.
confine sb/ sth in sth	keep sb/sth within an enclosed area. **confinement** N.
cell	a lockable room for prisoners in a prison or police station.
consent	agreement about sth (**by common consent** = with everyone's agreement; **by mutual consent** = with the agreement of both parties involved). **consent** V.

spotlight   *self-*

Before nouns and adjectives, **self-** means of, to, or by yourself.
Self-contained communities exist without outside help.
With a *self-catering* holiday, you cook for yourself.
Self-assessment is when you judge your own progress and achievements.

❸ Circle the correct word(s). Sometimes both words are correct.

1 The men were both confined / contained in a small cell.
2 The plane had to segregate / deviate from the normal route.
3 Many of the prisoners / inmates are serving long sentences.
4 The management course is based on self- catering / self-assessment.
5 I think it requires the parents' agreement / consent.
6 The club is exclusively / inclusively for men; women aren't allowed in.

❹ Complete the dialogues with a single word.

1 Do they discuss each other's problems? ~ Yes, it's a type of group _____.
2 Do they separate men from women? ~ Yes, there's a policy of _____.
3 They're locked up every night. ~ Yes, and the _____ are very small.
4 Did everyone agree? ~ Yes, it was by common _____.
5 Are many of the men violent? ~ Yes, quite a high _____.
6 Did you both agree to the deal? ~ Yes, it was by _____ consent.
7 Did the massage help your back pain? ~ Yes, it was very _____.
8 Are the couple very independent? ~ Yes, they're quite self-_____.

❺ ABOUT YOU What do you think of this prison? Is it likely to be more successful than a normal prison? Write your answers or ask another student.

Remember to test yourself

37 I can **talk about the armed forces**

A Organization

The US **military comprises** five **branches** in its field of **operations**: army, navy, air force, marine corps, and coast **guard**, all under **civilian authority**. More than 1.4 million people **serve** in the professional full-time military, with a further 1.2 million in **the reserve** army (**the draft** has not been enforced since 1986). The US military **distinguishes between enlisted** personnel, who **make up** 85 per cent of the armed forces and carry out **fundamental** operations such as **combat** and administration, and officers, who manage and supervise operations. The range of jobs is **vast**, and **encompasses** such **diverse** activities as running a hospital, **commanding** a **tank**, programming computers, operating a **nuclear reactor**, and maintaining **weapons** systems.

tank

helicopter

parachutes

missile

Glossary

the military	a country's **army**, **navy**, and **air force**. SYN **the armed forces**. military ADJ.
branch	a part of a large organization (**branch** of a **bank**).
operation	a planned military or police action (**military operation**).
guard	a person or group of people who protect sth/sb. **guard sth/sb** v.
civilian	not belonging to the armed forces. **civilian** N.
authority	the power to give orders to other people.
serve	do useful work (**serve your country** / **in the army** / etc.).
the reserve(s)	an extra force that performs part-time duties and is available if needed (we also talk about having people **in reserve**).
the draft	AmE the practice of ordering people to serve in the armed forces (called **military service** in many countries). SYN **conscription** (BrE).
distinguish between people or things	recognize a difference between people or things. SYNS **differentiate**, **make a distinction** N.
enlisted	ESPECIALLY AmE relating to members of the armed forces below officer rank (to **enlist** is to join the armed forces).
fundamental	central, and forming the necessary basis of sth.
combat	fighting between forces (**armed/unarmed combat** = fighting with/without guns, bombs, etc.).
vast	extremely large (**vast majority/numbers/amount**). SYN **huge**.
encompass sth	FML include sth within an area or area of activity.
diverse	different from each other and of various kinds. **diversity** N.
command sb/sth	(in the forces) be in charge of people (a person is **in command**).
nuclear reactor	a structure which produces nuclear energy (a country with **nuclear weapons** is said to have a **nuclear capability**).
weapon	an object such as a knife, gun, or bomb that is used for fighting (**nuclear/chemical weapons**; a **deadly/lethal weapon** can kill sb).

---

spotlight *comprise, make up, consist of, compose*

These verbs describe the way in which something is formed:
*A group **comprises** / **is composed of** / **consists of** / **is made up of** 30 people.*
When you mention the parts first, use **make up** or **comprise**:
*Men **make up** / **comprise** the majority of the group.*

Remember to test yourself

1 Correct the spelling mistakes.

1 civilan _____
2 wepon _____
3 nucleur _____

4 ennlisted _____
5 the drauft _____
6 autority _____

7 distingish _____
8 missil _____
9 conscribtion _____

2 Use each word/phrase in the box once to make eight compound words or phrases.

unarmed	vast	armed	lethal	military	air	forces	combat	majority
weapon	force	make	nuclear	operation	capability	a distinction		

_____
_____
_____

_____
_____
_____

_____
_____
_____

3 Replace the underlined word(s) with a single word that has a similar meaning.

1 To run an army requires a <u>huge</u> amount of money. v_____
2 The decision will be taken by the <u>armed forces</u>. m_____
3 A brigade is <u>made up</u> of approximately 5,500 men and women. c_____
4 The right to self-defence is one of their <u>central</u> beliefs. f_____
5 There was very little armed <u>fighting</u>. c_____
6 The men are from very <u>different</u> backgrounds. d_____
7 Six soldiers were on duty to <u>protect</u> the camp. g_____
8 Single men <u>make up</u> the majority of the regiment. c_____
9 This knife is a <u>lethal</u> weapon. d_____
10 They don't <u>recognize a difference</u> between men and women. d_____
11 The work <u>includes</u> many different tasks and responsibilities. e_____
12 How many men <u>work</u> in the British army? s_____

4 Complete the text with suitable words.

The British armed (1)_____ (2)_____ of the army, the (3)_____ , and the air (4)_____ . As head of state, the Queen is theoretically in (5)_____ of the armed forces, but in practice they come under the (6)_____ of the British prime minister. There are just under 200,000 men and women (7)_____ in the professional armed forces (often referred to as 'the regulars'), but with even more than that in the (8)_____ . The armed forces are also supported by a number of diverse agencies owned by the Ministry of Defence. The navy is the (9)_____ of the armed forces which is responsible for Britain's nuclear (10)_____ , which (11)_____ four Trident missile submarines.

5 ABOUT YOU AND YOUR COUNTRY Write your answers or ask another student.

1 Has your country got a professional and a reserve army? _____
2 Does your country have military service? _____
3 Does your country have a nuclear capability? _____
4 Have you ever: stood next to a tank? _____ flown in a helicopter? _____
   been in a professional army? _____ dropped from a parachute? _____
   done military service? _____

Remember to test yourself

B For or against the armed forces? 🎧

The armed forces provide protection from an invading enemy and from **internal** conflict; they are called upon to **assist in** international **peacekeeping** operations; and they are used in **civil** emergencies after a national disaster. However, a professional army requires **considerably** more **funding** than a reserve army. **The latter** is only **mobilized** when needed and is therefore much cheaper. The armed forces may also harm a society if they are involved in **counter-productive** (or **merely** unsuccessful) **warfare**.

spotlight	*interior* and *internal*

Interior ADJ, N relates to the inside part of sth (e.g. ADJ the **interior** *walls of the house*; N the **interior** *of a car/building*). OPP **exterior** ADJ, N. **The interior** is the central part of a country, a long way from the coast.
Internal ADJ relates to the inside of sth, including the body (e.g. **internal** *doors/injuries; an* **internal** *enquiry/problem*). OPP **external**. **Internal** is commonly used in reference to things within a country (e.g. **internal** *flights/affairs/markets*). SYN **domestic**.

Glossary

assist (sb) in/with sth	FML help sb to do sth.	**the latter**	the second of two things that have just been mentioned (**the former** refers to the first of two things mentioned).
peacekeeping	intended to stop people fighting (a **peacekeeping force**).		
		mobilize (sth)	prepare (an army) to fight in a war.
civil	connected with the people who live in a country (**civil unrest/war/rights/liberties**).	**counter-productive**	having the opposite effect to the one intended.
		merely	only; simply (used to emphasize what you are saying).
considerably	much; a great deal. **considerable** ADJ.	**warfare**	the activity of fighting a war, often of a particular type (**guerrilla warfare** = fighting in small, unofficial military groups).
funding	money provided for a special purpose (**government funding**).		

6 Circle the correct word(s). Sometimes both words are correct.

1 We could have civil / civic war.
2 He simply / merely wanted to help.
3 They're mobilating / mobilizing the army.
4 I like the interior / internal of the car.
5 It cost considerably / considerately more.
6 We took a domestic / an internal flight.
7 She's got interior / internal injuries.
8 I'm assisting / helping him in his enquiries.

7 Write a single word to complete each sentence.

1 It had the opposite effect to the one we intended, so it was clearly counter-_____ .
2 Most of the time their forces are engaged in guerrilla _____ .
3 The army have been sent there merely as a peacekeeping _____ .
4 There were problems on the coast, but the main area of unrest was in the _____ .
5 People should be allowed to say what they want. It's one of our basic civil _____ .
6 If we want a large modern army, we will need more government _____ .
7 There were two plans mentioned. Was she referring to the former or the _____ ?
8 How quickly can they mobilize the _____ ?
9 Some flights were cancelled – both international and _____ .
10 The bomb exploded in a built-up area, so the damage was _____ .

Remember to test yourself

Review: Institutions

Unit 33

1 Complete each dialogue with a suitable word.

1   Can I see his medical records? ~ No, they're strictly _____.
2   I don't trust that consultant. ~ Why don't you get a second _____?
3   Is there a large scar? ~ No, it was done with keyhole _____.
4   Was the hospital ward clean? ~ Yes, it was absolutely _____.
5   Is there any worthwhile data on this? ~ Yes, they've done clinical _____.
6   Will they contact you about Pat? ~ Yes, they said they'd keep me _____.
7   Can you go straight to a specialist? ~ No, you see your GP and get a _____.
8   Is she still in hospital? ~ No, she's been _____.
9   Has he left hospital? ~ Yes, but he needs time to _____.
10 Were you busy? ~ Yes, we were rushed off our _____.

2 Answer the questions.

1   What's the opposite of *senior*? _____
2   What's the opposite of *be discharged from hospital*? _____
3   What's the medical treatment intended to improve someone's appearance? _____
4   What's a synonym for *recuperate*? _____
5   Acupuncture and homeopathy are examples of what kind of medicine? _____
6   What's a synonym for *meticulous*? _____
7   What's a synonym for *a muddle*? _____
8   *Pay no attention to something* is the same as '_____ no _____ of something'.

A Z **more words**: *antenatal, postnatal, overstretched, inpatient/outpatient,* **intensive** *care, biopsy, in a* **critical** *condition*

Unit 34

1 One word is missing in each sentence. What is it, and where does it go?

1   I believe they will be receiving a government to cover the costs of repairs. _____
2   There are many American living in other countries around the world. _____
3   At what age are you to vote in most countries? _____
4   We will need a very determined person to tomorrow's meeting. _____
5   The councillor will do his best to that the community is well represented. _____
6   The party's says that it will allocate more funds to green issues. _____
7   My cousin works in the voluntary, where people often work for no pay. _____
8   People in high- jobs who appear on TV may need help with presentation skills. _____

2 Complete the dialogues in a suitable way. You only need a single word.

1 Do they let you give your opinion? ~ Yes, we can all have a _____ .
2 Who is the spokesperson? ~ Nobody is speaking on our _____ .
3 Are they listening to your ideas? ~ Yes, they're taking them _____ .
4 Is it paid work? ~ No, it's all done by _____ .
5 Is the research all over the country? ~ Yes, it's _____ .
6 Will they support you? ~ Yes, lots of people will _____ up for us.
7 How much will the department receive? ~ They haven't set the _____ yet.
8 Is the meeting for people who live there? ~ Yes, it's for all local _____ .

A Z more words: ***pressure*** group, support an ***initiative***, ***press*** the government for sth, raise **awareness**, improve the **infrastructure**, chamber

Unit 35

1 Match 1–8 with a–h.

1 smuggle …   a a warrant
2 issue …   b in custody
3 grant …   c workers
4 remand someone …   d diamonds
5 caution …   e someone's passport
6 exploit …   f at a police station
7 forge …   g bail
8 detain someone …   h a suspect

2 Complete the explanations.

1 If the police want to search someone's house, they need to apply for a search _____ .
2 If someone is kept in prison awaiting trial, they are in _____ .
3 Taking or sending goods out of a country illegally is called _____ .
4 If you obtain money from people by deceiving them, that is called _____ .
5 A group of professional criminals is often referred to as a _____ of criminals.
6 Money left with the court to ensure a prisoner will return for trial is called _____ .

A Z more words: *counterfeit, embezzlement, espionage, on the **run**, extradition, **undercover** operation*

Unit 36

1 Complete the table.

Noun	Verb
	abolish
	imprison
deviation	
justification	

Noun	Verb
	segregate
	confine
	rehabilitate
	consent

2 Correct the mistake in each sentence.

1 He's been in a lot of trouble but there are signs that he's turning out a new leaf. ....

2 She committed a terrible crime and she really should be locked out for it. ....

3 I don't believe the death penalty (or capital punish) is justifiable. ....

4 My neighbour and I agreed to share the cost by common consent. ....

5 Robertson was always regarded at a common thief until he turned his life round. ....

6 The business has been on crisis but it seems to be recovering now. ....

7 We are aware that being attacked is an occupying hazard for prison officers. ....

8 We believe that imprisoning these offenders will act as a deterrence. ....

A Z **more words**: *incarcerate, probation,* **solitary** *confinement,* **custodial** *sentence,* **suspended** *sentence, warder*

Unit 37

1 Tick the word(s) that are possible. One, two, or three may be possible.

1 We are concerned about their nuclear *capability* ☐ *weapons* ☐ *military service* ☐.

2 There may be internal *conflict* ☐ *enquiries* ☐ *flights* ☐.

3 He is a member of *the guard* ☐ *the air* ☐ *a peacekeeping* ☐ force.

4 They need to *enlist* ☐ *distinguish* ☐ *make a distinction* ☐ between civilians and the armed forces.

5 The force is *made up* ☐ *consisted* ☐ *composed* ☐ of diverse elements.

6 The government is worried about civil *unrest* ☐ *rights* ☐ *war* ☐.

7 The soldiers discovered a supply of *chemical* ☐ *lethal* ☐ *dead* ☐ weapons.

8 Do you agree with *conscription* ☐ *the draft* ☐ *military service* ☐?

2 One word is missing in each line. What is it, and where does it go?

1 The vast of people are against armed combat if a peaceful solution can be found. ....

2 They had very little respect for the officers command of the troops. ....

3 The paper believes that guerrilla cannot be justified, whatever its aims. ....

4 Attacking that particular state would merely be counter-, I would think. ....

5 We can try to negotiate or face the prospect of armed combat: the would obviously be preferable.
....

6 Our organization has very little money at the moment, so we are hoping to receive government.
....

7 We need to keep some basic supplies reserve. ....

8 The army have been brought in to with the clearing-up operation after the floods. ....

A Z **more words**: *war-torn, veteran, mission, reconnaissance, call sb up, deploy*

Headlines	Meaning
Arms deal probe	**arms** FML weapons, especially those used by the armed forces. **deal** an agreement, especially in business. **probe** an investigation into sth. **probe** v.
Mother's **plea** to **kidnappers**	**plea** FML an urgent and emotional request. **kidnapper** a person who takes sb away illegally and keeps them as a prisoner, usually in order to get money (called a **ransom**). **kidnapping** N. **kidnap** V, N.
Ten-hour **ordeal** for tourists	**ordeal** a difficult or unpleasant experience.
Senate urges caution	**senate** (in the USA and some other countries) one of the two groups of elected politicians; the politicians are called **senators**. **urge sth** forcefully recommend sth (also **urge sb to do sth**).
Bid to **oust** rail **chief**	**bid** an attempt. **bid** v. **oust** (**sb out of sth**) force sb out of a job or position. **chief** (often used in job titles) the most important or one of the most important people in a company or an organization (**police chief**).
Minister vows to quit	**minister** a senior member of a government. **vow** make a formal and serious promise to do sth. **vow** N.
Bomb **blast wrecks** factory	**blast** an explosion (**bomb blast**). **wreck sth** destroy or badly damage sth.
Boost for voters	**boost** a thing that helps or encourages sth. **boost** v.
Go-ahead for road **scheme**	**go-ahead** (usually **the go-ahead**) formal permission to do sth. **scheme** an official plan.
IMG **cease** trading	**cease** FML stop happening or existing. **cease sth** stop doing sth.
Measures to **curb** inflation	**curb sth** limit or control sth.
Politician in death **riddle**	**riddle** a mystery (often a problem that is difficult to solve).
Doctor **cleared** of negligence	**clear sb** (**of sth**) prove that sb is innocent of doing sth wrong.
Injury **blow** for United	**blow** bad news (when something unfortunate has happened).
New flood **alert**	**alert** a warning.
Talks **on brink of** collapse	If sth is **on the brink of** happening, it has reached a point where it is about to happen (often sth very bad).
PM **rules out** referendum	**rule sth out** reject the possibility of sth.
Valuable **gems** stolen	**gems** jewellery.

Certain words often appear in newspaper headlines because they are very short, e.g. *bid, plea, oust, quit.* Other words give stories a more dramatic effect, e.g. *blast* and *boost.* And certain people are often at the centre of news stories, e.g. *ministers* and *senators.*

Remember to test yourself

1 Good news or bad news for the people in the headlines? Write G or B.

1 Minister quits under pressure _____
2 Company ousts chairman _____
3 Go-ahead for doctors _____
4 Ordeal for parents _____

5 Owner sees home wrecked _____
6 New deal for manager _____
7 Boost for farmers _____
8 Further blow for house buyers _____

2 Match the headline words on the left with the correct meaning on the right.

1 vow
2 plea
3 bid
4 cease
5 gems
6 riddle
7 blow
8 probe
9 alert
10 rule out

a jewellery _____
b stop _____
c request _____
d warning _____
e investigation _____
f promise _____
g attempt _____
h bad news _____
i reject _____
j mystery _____

3 Replace the underlined words to create typical headlines.

▶ Senators reject the possibility of more aid   *Senators rule out more aid*
1 New weapons agreement _____
2 Explosion destroys fire station _____
3 Permission for official rail plan _____
4 Company managing director forced from his job _____
5 Encouragement for big banks _____
6 Senior members of government to restrict spending _____
7 Men who took child demand money for her return _____
8 Government strongly advises delay _____
9 Motorcyclist found innocent of child's death _____
10 Firm in serious danger of closure _____

4 Write your own headlines for these news stories (maximum seven words per headline).

▶ There are new warnings about the dangers of certain food.
  NEW FOOD ALERT
1 An explosion has destroyed a new shopping centre.

2 The police have rejected the possibility of a new investigation into the murder.

3 The Prime Minister has promised that he will restrict the amount of money that the government will spend.

4 Senior members of the government are planning a new attempt to force the Prime Minister to resign.

5 There is a mystery surrounding the theft of valuable jewellery.

Remember to test yourself

39 I can understand news journalism

A Common words in news reports 🎧

Amid further **allegations** of a **cover-up**, **sources** at the Home Office refused to comment on claims of a serious **lapse** in security at a nuclear power station.

Discussions about **controversial** new **measures** to control anti-social behaviour are continuing **behind the scenes**.

According to figures from a recent **opinion poll**, the government's popularity is falling.

It **emerged** yesterday that the contents of a **scathing** report on Barkfield Hospital have already been **leaked** to the press. The report **quotes** a senior doctor **as saying that** ...

Glossary

amid (or amidst) sth	while sth else is happening.	**behind the scenes**	without people's awareness or knowledge (**behind closed doors** = in private, not in public).
allegation	a statement, without proof, that sb has done sth wrong. **allege** V.	**according to**	used for saying where ideas or information have come from.
cover-up	an attempt to stop people discovering the truth about sth. **cover sth up** V.	**(opinion) poll**	a process of asking people for their opinion about sth.
source	OFTEN PL a person who provides information, especially for journalists.	**emerge**	(of facts, information, etc.) become known. **emergence** N.
lapse	a small mistake caused by forgetting sth or carelessness.	**scathing**	strongly critical (**scathing attack/remark**).
controversial	causing angry discussion and disagreement. **controversy** N.	**leak sth to sb**	give secret information to journalists or the public. **leak** N.
measure	an official action taken in order to achieve sth.	**quote sb**	repeat the exact words that sb said (**quote sb as saying that ...**).

❶ Complete the dialogues.

1   How do you know about this? ~ It was in a recent _____ poll.
2   How did the man get into the palace? ~ It was a _____ in security apparently.
3   When did they discover this news? ~ It _____ last night.
4   Are these talks in public? ~ No, it's all behind closed _____ .
5   Do many people disagree with it? ~ Yes, it's a very _____ idea.
6   Was she strongly criticized? ~ Yes, it was a _____ attack.
7   Is there proof the man stole it? ~ No, it's just an _____ someone made.
8   Is this information accurate? ~ _____ to *The Times*, it is.

❷ Complete the text with suitable words.

(1)_____ continuing pressure on the government, information has been (2)_____ to the press of a plan to (3)_____ up the fact that Britain cannot meet the European Union's renewable energy targets. (4)_____ to reliable (5)_____ inside Whitehall, officials have informed the government of this fact, and one expert was (6)_____ as saying that Britain might only reach 9 per cent by 2020. Meanwhile, discussions are continuing behind the (7)_____ to see what (8)_____ can be taken to reach the target.

Remember to test yourself

B Figurative language in news reports 🎧

Words connected with *water*, *fire*, *war*, and *sport* are often used figuratively in news reports. For example, if two people are **locked in battle**, it doesn't mean they are literally fighting, but that they are involved in a competition or struggle, e.g. a **legal battle**. These expressions are also called **metaphors**.

	Example	Meaning
WATER	There is certain to be ***a storm of protest*** over the new legislation.	a situation in which a large number of people express strong feelings against sth.
	Refugees are ***flooding*** into the country.	appearing in large numbers at the same time.
	Some people believe the ***tide is now turning*** in the government's favour.	the situation and public opinion are changing.
	The opposition has dismissed the money as ***a drop in the ocean***.	a very small amount compared with what is needed.
FIRE	Police fear the arrest of the two youths could ***spark*** further trouble.	cause sth to start or develop.
	The ministers have had ***a blazing row***.	a very angry argument.
WAR	The headteacher has ***come under attack***.	been strongly criticized. SYN **come under fire**.
	The Board of Directors could be next ***in the firing line***.	in a position in which people can criticize and blame you.
SPORT	The minister has got himself into ***a tight corner***.	a difficult situation.
	MPs are now accusing the government of ***moving the goalposts***.	INF unfairly changing the agreed rules or conditions during a course of action.
	There have been accusations of ***foul play***.	behaviour that is unfair or dishonest.
	Trade Union leaders claim they just want ***a level playing field***.	a situation in which everyone has the same opportunities.

❸ Cross out the incorrect word in each sentence and write the correct word at the end.

1 The Prime Minister could be in the shooting line. _____
2 We sent some money but it's still only a drip in the ocean. _____
3 There was a thunderstorm of protest. _____
4 It was an uphill struggle but I think the wave has turned. _____
5 Tourists are now raining into the town to see the festival. _____
6 They are demanding a flat playing field. _____
7 They're upset that the officials keep moving the goalkeeper. _____
8 The problem is that she has got herself in a very tight bend. _____
9 The producer resigned after a burning row with the director. _____

❹ Complete the sentences.

1 The Prime Minister has come _____ _____ for his handling of the affair.
2 A vicious attack on two young boys nearly _____ a riot earlier this month.
3 The takeover was rather suspicious; I think most people suspect _____ .
4 They expected a _____ protest when they banned smoking in public places.
5 He's made too many mistakes, so now he's got himself in a very _____ .
6 They desperately need aid, but this gift of cash is still only a _____ in the _____ .

40 I can **read human interest stories**

A Amazing but true! 🎧

An operation 55 years later? **Pencil it in**

A German woman who has spent 55 years with the **tip** of a pencil **lodged** in her brain has finally had it removed. Margret Wegner fell over carrying the pencil when she was four. It **punctured** her cheek and went into her brain causing **excruciating** pain, and she has lived with the **ensuing chronic** headaches ever since. At the time, no one **dared** operate, but the **remaining** 2 cms of pencil were removed on Friday in a delicate operation. She is said to be **making a speedy recovery**.

Glossary

pencil sth in	write down details of an arrangement which you may have to change later. This is a **pun** (= the clever or humorous use of a word with more than one meaning).
tip (of sth)	the thin pointed end of sth.
lodged (in sth)	fixed or stuck in sth.
puncture sth	make a small hole in sth (**puncture skin / a tyre**). **puncture** N.
excruciating	extremely painful (**excruciating pain/headaches**).
ensuing	happening after or as a result of another event.
chronic	(especially of a disease) lasting a long time and hard to cure.
remaining	still existing or needing to be dealt with.
make a speedy/ rapid recovery	get well again quickly after an illness or accident.

spotlight *dare*

To **dare** means to be brave enough to do something. It is normally used in questions and negative forms, and can behave like an ordinary verb (e.g. *He **doesn't dare** (**to**) leave.*) or like a modal (e.g. *He **daren't leave**.*).
How dare you *say that!* (= I am very angry that you said that.)
Don't you dare *come near me!* (used to give someone a strong warning)

1 Circle the correct word(s). Both words may be correct.

1 I made a speedy / rapid recovery.
2 The pain was excruciating / crucial.
3 The bone's stuck / lodged in her throat.
4 I've pencilled/penned in the invitation.
5 How dare you do/to do that!
6 I had six; that's the left / remaining one.

2 Replace the underlined words with a single word that has the same meaning.

1 I had an <u>unpleasant and very painful</u> headache. ....
2 Her medical condition is <u>continuous and long-lasting</u>. ....
3 After the fire, we lost sight of him in the <u>resulting</u> panic. ....
4 A piece of glass <u>made a small hole in</u> the tyre. ....
5 I love <u>jokes based on words with two meanings</u>. ....
6 She<u>'s too frightened to</u> drive at night on her own. ....
7 He seems to be making a <u>speedy</u> recovery. ....
8 The <u>end</u> of the cat's tail is white. ....

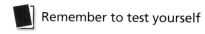 Remember to test yourself

B A survival drama 🎧

Man survives **crocs**[1] **against all odds**

An Australian farmer has described how he spent seven days **sheltering** up a tree above a **crocodile**[1]-**infested swamp**. David George, 53, said he was forced to **take** such **drastic action** after he accidentally **strayed** into the area. His problems began after he fell off his horse; **dazed** and **disorientated**, he hoped the horse would lead him home. 'By the time I **regained my senses**, I was in the middle of a swamp,' he said. He knew he could either **stay put** and wait for a rescue team, or try and get out and **take a chance on** being eaten by a croc. After a long, **gruelling** week, he was spotted by helicopters and rescued.

1

Glossary

against all (the) odds	if sth happens **against all odds**, it happens or succeeds although it seemed impossible or very unlikely.
shelter	stay somewhere that protects you from danger or bad weather.
infested	full of very many insects, animals, etc. (**rat-infested**, **shark-infested**).
swamp	an area in which the ground is very wet or covered in water.
take action	do sth to deal with a situation.
drastic	extreme in a way that has a sudden, violent, or serious effect.
stray	move away from where you should be, without intending to.
dazed	unable to think clearly because of shock or a blow to the head.
disorientated	confused about where you are or which way to go.
regain your senses	think clearly again after a period of confusion.
stay put	INF stay where you are rather than moving away.
take a chance on sth	decide to do sth, even though it involves risk.
gruelling	very difficult and tiring; needing great effort. SYN **punishing**.

❸ Is the meaning the same or different? Write S or D.

1 We had to stay put for an hour.	We couldn't move for an hour.	
2 We found the ring against all odds.	We found the ring against the wall.	
3 Please don't take any risks.	Please don't take any chances.	
4 They found somewhere to shelter.	They found somewhere to relax.	
5 He wandered off the path, into the trees.	He strayed off the path, into the trees.	
6 We took drastic action to prevent losses.	We took some steps to prevent losses.	
7 It was a gruelling experience.	It was a punishing experience.	
8 There are a few sharks in the area.	It's a shark-infested area.	

❹ Complete the dialogues.

1 Did you know where you were? ~ No, I was completely d_____ .

2 Was the land very wet? ~ Yes, they found me by the s_____ .

3 When did you r_____ your senses? ~ Oh, it wasn't long, only a few minutes.

4 How did you respond to the shock? ~ I wandered about; I just felt d_____ .

5 Was it safe to move ahead? ~ No, it was too risky; I decided to s_____ put.

6 You had a very lucky escape. ~ Mmm. I survived against all o_____ .

7 It was an extreme thing to do. ~ Yeah, it was a bit d_____ .

8 It was a frightening situation to be in. ~ Yes; I didn't want to take any c_____ .

Remember to test yourself

41 I can **talk about celebrity**

A Celebrity and the media 🎧

Celebrities 'deserve privacy'

A **survey** on **privacy** and the media has revealed that most people think that there should be little or no **coverage** of the private lives of **celebrities**. This contrasts strongly with the huge success of celebrity magazines, which detail the lives of people **in the public eye**. The **findings** also revealed that people did not want politicians to suffer from press **intrusion**. Certain **tabloids** were **singled out** as being particularly guilty of **prying** into the lives of famous **personalities**.

Glossary

celebrity	1 c a famous person. SYNS **personality**, **celeb** INF. 2 U the state of being famous. SYN **fame**.	**in the public eye**	well known to many people through TV or the press.
deserve sth	If you **deserve sth**, it is right that you should have it, e.g. because of the way you have behaved.	**findings**	PL information learned as the result of research.
survey	an investigation into the opinions or behaviour of a large group of people, usually in the form of questions (**conduct / carry out a survey**).	**intrusion (into sth)**	a thing that comes into sb's life in a negative way. **intrude into sth** v.
		tabloid	a newspaper that gives emphasis to stories about famous people (more serious papers are **broadsheets**).
privacy	the state of being alone and not watched or disturbed by others.	**single sth/sb out**	choose sb/sth from a group for special attention.
coverage	the reporting of news in the press.	**pry into sth**	try to find information about people's private lives.

❶ Tick the correct word(s). More than one word may be correct.

1 She's an international *celebrity* ☐ *personality* ☐ *celeb* ☐.
2 I don't like the way the papers *intrude* ☐ *pry* ☐ *conduct* ☐ into people's private lives.
3 Have you read the *coverage* ☐ *tabloids* ☐ *findings* ☐ today?
4 All he wants in life is *fame* ☐ *privacy* ☐ *intrusion* ☐.
5 She was *singled out* ☐ *intruded* ☐ *deserved* ☐ for special praise.

❷ Complete the text with suitable words.

A recent (1) _____ which was (2) _____ out among 650 young people around New York produced some disturbing (3) _____ on how some teenagers think about celebrity and (4) _____. Many believe that celebrities work hard and (5) _____ to be famous, and that becoming a famous (6) _____ themselves would improve their lives. Lonely teenagers are more likely to follow the lives of people in the public (7) _____.

❸ ABOUT YOU AND YOUR COUNTRY Complete the questions, then write your answers or ask another student.

1 Do you agree that celebrities deserve p_____ ? _____
2 In your country, are there both tabloid and b_____ papers? _____
3 Do they p_____ into the private lives of people in the p_____ eye? _____
4 What do you think are the benefits and disadvantages of f_____ ? _____

📓 Remember to test yourself

B Celebrity headlines 🎧

Rocky **allegedly** back in **rehab**

Football team **rocked** by **scandal**

Newlyweds' marriage **on the rocks**

Rumours of **custody** battle over baby Sahara

Andie **dumps** Gino

Exclusive! Sandie **gives birth to** a girl!

Fellow celebs **rally to** Tom's defence

---

spotlight | *exclusives* and *scoops*

An **exclusive story/interview/photo** etc. is one published or reported only by one newspaper or TV station (**exclusive** N). If a news organization publishes or **broadcasts** (= gives out on TV or the radio) an exciting story before anyone else does, it is called a **scoop** INF. Reporters like to **get a scoop.**

Glossary

allegedly	If sb **allegedly** does sth, another person says they have done it, even though this has not been proved. **allege** v. **allegation** N.	**rumour**	a story or piece of information that may or may not be true.
rehab	the process of helping to cure sb with drug or alcohol addiction.	**custody**	the legal right to look after a child (**have custody of a child**).
rock sb/sth	INF, OFTEN PASSIVE shock or cause upset to sb/sth.	**dump sb**	INF end a romantic relationship with sb.
scandal	a situation in which important people behave in a dishonest or immoral way that shocks people.	**give birth (to sb/sth)**	produce a baby or young animal.
newlyweds	USU. PL a man and woman who have not been married long.	**fellow**	ADJ used to describe sb who is in the same situation as you (**fellow students/workers/passengers**).
on the rocks	INF in difficulties and likely to fail.	**rally (round/ to sb/sth)**	come together to help or support sb/sth.

4 Complete the dialogues with words from the box in the correct form.

rocks	exclusive	rally	fellow	scandal	broadcast	rehab
allegation	rock	rumour				

1 A I heard a _____ that the minister is about to resign. Do you think it's true?
   B Well, there have been _____ that he's involved in a financial _____ .
   A That's terrible. It would really _____ the government, wouldn't it?
   B Yes, and Sky News are going to _____ an _____ interview with him tonight.

2 A You know that guy who was in *Terminator 5*? Can't remember his name.
   B Yeah, I heard his marriage was on the _____ .
   A That's right. Well, evidently he's had drug problems and he's in _____ too.
   B Poor guy. No doubt his _____ celebs will _____ round him.

5 Rewrite the sentence using the word in capitals. The meaning must stay the same.

▶ He is said to have lost all his money. ALLEGEDLY *Allegedly, he's lost all his money.*
1 Lulu has ended her relationship with Rocco. DUMP _____
2 Amelia had a baby boy last week. BIRTH _____
3 Jason has the legal right to look after his daughter. CUSTODY _____
4 Arun is a student in my class. FELLOW _____
5 The journalist wanted to get the story first. SCOOP _____
6 They've just got married. NEWLYWEDS _____

Remember to test yourself

42 I can **discuss political beliefs**

A Political systems 🎧

☞ With **capitalism**, the economy is controlled by companies and individuals (who are **capitalists**), not the state. In Britain, capitalism is **associated with** the **Conservative** Party, which tends to **favour** the **status quo** and is **opposed to radical** change.

☞ With **socialism**, the economy of a country is partly controlled by the state and the wealth is **distributed equally**. In Britain, **socialists** are usually **left-wing**, but not **extremists**.

☞ **Liberalism** is based on a belief in personal and economic freedom, supporting gradual social and political change. **Liberals** who hold such beliefs often vote for **centre parties**.

☞ **Communism** is based on common ownership of **the means of production**, and **communists** believe in a classless society.

spotlight *means*

A **means** is a way of doing or achieving something, e.g. **means of transport/ communication/escape/expression**. The **means of production** is the materials and equipment needed to produce things. A **means of identification** is a way of showing who you are.

Glossary

associated with sth/sb	connected with sth/sb. **association** N.
favour sth/sb	support and agree with sth/sb (also **be in favour of sth/sb**).
status quo	the existing situation (**maintain the status quo**).
opposed to sth/sb	disagreeing strongly with sth/sb. **opposition** N.
radical	1 complete and fundamental. SYN **far-reaching**. 2 (of a person) in favour of political and social change. OPP **reactionary**.
distribute sth	share sth among a number of people. **distribution** N.
equally	in a way that is fair and the same for everyone. **equality** N.
left-wing	OPP **right-wing** (also **on the left/right**).
extremist	a person whose political views are generally not considered to be normal or reasonable. **extreme** ADJ. OPP **moderate**.
centre party	a political party that is not left-wing or right-wing (be **in the centre**).

1 True or false? Write T or F, then correct the false sentences.

▶ A ~~capitalist~~ economy is owned by the people and run by the state. ___F___
   communist

1 People associate liberals with personal freedom _____

2 Socialists believe that wealth should be shared equally. _____

3 A liberal believes in economic freedom and rapid political change. _____

4 The Conservative Party in Britain believes in socialism. _____

5 Socialists believe that everyone should own the means of production. _____

2 Complete the sentences with the opposite meaning to the first half of the sentence.

1 He's left-wing, but she's _____ .
2 She's radical, but he's _____ .
3 He's in favour of it, but she's _____ .
4 He wants change, but she prefers _____ .
5 She has extreme views, but his are _____ .
6 They're on the left and right, but I'm _____ .

3 Complete the words in the sentences.

1 I believe in e_____ of opportunity and the equal d_____ of wealth.
2 Is common ownership of the m_____ of production practical?
3 Would you say you were o_____ the left, the right, or in the centre?
4 I don't think the director is closely a_____ with any political party.
5 In my country we have to carry some means of i_____ with us at all times.

▮ Remember to test yourself

B Political metaphors 🎧

Word + literal meaning	Example of metaphorical use	Metaphorical meaning
crack a line on the surface of sth where it has broken.	*The first **cracks** are appearing in the government.*	a weakness in an idea, a system, or an organization.
driving seat the place where the driver sits.	*People are wondering who **is in the driving seat**.*	be in control of a situation. SYN **pull the strings**.
rock move from side to side.	*The Prime Minister doesn't want MPs to **rock the boat**.*	cause problems by making changes to a situation that is satisfactory as it is.
foundations the structures that form the underground base of a building.	*She **laid the foundations** of the party's success.*	create the basic ideas or principles from which sth can then develop.
depth (especially of water) the deepness of sth.	*Many believe the minister **is out of her depth**.*	be in a situation that is too difficult for you to control.
deep end the end of a swimming pool where the water is deep.	*The MPs **were thrown in at the deep end**. Let's see if they **sink or swim**.*	be faced with a new and difficult task that you're not prepared for. **sink or swim** fail or succeed.
heat sth make sth hot.	*It has started **a heated debate** in parliament.*	an angry discussion (also **heated discussion**).
safe OPP dangerous.	*He got the job because he's **a safe pair of hands**.*	a person you can rely on.
head move in a particular direction.	*The government is **heading in the right direction**.*	making good progress. OPP **heading in the wrong direction**.
microscope an instrument for looking at things which are too small to see.	*The trade secretary could find herself **under the microscope**.*	being watched and examined very carefully.
spin a quick turning movement, round and round. **spin** v.	*No doubt the politicians will give this a positive **spin**.*	a way of giving information to make it appear better, or less bad (the people are **spin doctors**).

4 Circle the correct answer.

1 He's the boss, but it's his wife who pulls the strings / rope .
2 During the first few months, she'll be under the microscope / telescope .
3 As a politician, he's considered to be a safe pair of gloves / hands .
4 Throw them in at the shallow / deep end, then see if they sink / drown or swim.
5 They had a very hot / heated discussion.
6 I wonder what the spin doctors / dentists will do with this information.
7 They've got to remain steady, and not allow anyone to rock the ship / boat .
8 The results indicate that the opposition is leading / heading in the wrong direction.

5 Complete the dialogues in a suitable way.

1 Did they have an easy start? ~ No, they were thrown in ....
2 Is she able to do the job? ~ No, she's out ....
3 Do you think we're making progress? ~ Yes, we're heading ....
4 He created the policies, didn't he? ~ Yes, he laid the ....
5 Is the party still united? ~ No, the first .... are starting to appear.
6 Do you think she's in control? ~ Yes, she's in the driving .... now.
7 Was it dull in parliament? ~ No, there was a very heated ....
8 They managed to twist the facts. ~ Yes, the usual political ....

Remember to test yourself

43 I can **talk about areas of conflict** 🎧

Reporting from a
war zone

The streets were filled with **rubble** and broken glass was everywhere. Food, water, medicine – the necessities of life – were **scarce**, and hospitals **were overwhelmed with** casualties. Apart from the obvious danger of bombing, there was also the threat of unexploded **shells**, **snipers**, and other forms of **random** violence. Soldiers and civilians alike suffered from the tension, and were never far from **breaking point**, but most people refused to **desert** their city. How did I get through that period? **Adrenalin**. That alone kept me going in the face of the **grim** reality that confronted a city **under siege**.

❶ Match 1–8 with a–h.

1 The soldiers were firing .... a sniper
2 He was shot by a .... b rubble
3 The situation was .... c at random
4 I just keep going on .... d under siege
5 Food was .... e grim
6 The city was .... f scarce
7 Life is tough in a war .... g adrenalin
8 The streets were full of .... h zone

❷ Cross out parts of the text and replace them with these words. Write the numbers in the text.

1 grim	2 abandoned	3 sniper
4 lay siege to	5 breaking point✓	6 debris
7 shelling	8 scarce	
9 overwhelmed by		

We were close to ▶ 5 ~~the point where people couldn't deal with the situation~~. Food was in short supply, the situation was unpleasant and depressing, and many people had already left the city for good. Then at 7 a.m. yesterday the attack happened. A man who was just clearing stones, bricks, and glass from a damaged building was shot by a hidden gunman. Amid the ensuing chaos, a small group of rebel soldiers entered the nearby radio station and took control of it. The army immediately began to surround the building. They brought in large guns and started firing at it, then, as night approached, they attacked. The rebels were soon defeated by the superior numbers and firepower of the army.

Glossary

zone	an area or region with a particular feature (a **war/danger zone**).
rubble	broken stones or bricks from a building that has been destroyed (**debris** is similar but is more general and includes wood, glass, etc.).
scarce	not readily available; in short supply. **scarcity** N.
overwhelm sb/ sth	1 present sb or fill sth with too much of sth (**be overwhelmed with/ by**). 2 defeat sb/sth completely).
shell	a metal case full of explosives, to be fired from a large gun (**shell sth** = fire shells at sth).
sniper	a person who shoots at sb from a hidden position.
random	happening without any intended or regular pattern (things that happen **at random** are not ordered or regular).
breaking point	the time when problems have become so great that sb can no longer deal with them (**be at / reach breaking point**).
desert sth	go away from a place and leave it empty. SYN **abandon sth**.
adrenalin	a substance created in the body when you are excited or afraid, giving you more energy.
grim	unpleasant and depressing.
siege	a military operation in which an armed force surrounds a place and stops the supply of food, etc. (**lay siege to sth**, **be under siege**).

 Remember to test yourself

Review: News and current affairs

Unit 38

1 Complete the sentences which explain the headlines.

1 MINISTER OUSTED = A _____ minister has _____ .
2 BOOST FOR TRANSPORT SCHEME = A transport _____ has been given _____ .
3 GO-AHEAD FOR ARMS DEAL = A business _____ on _____ has been given _____ .
4 RANSOM ORDEAL FOR FAMILY = A family is going through a _____ over a ransom.
5 BID TO END KIDNAP = Someone is _____ to end a kidnapping.
6 BLAST WRECKS HOTEL = A hotel has been _____ by _____ .

A Z more words: *Diet puts children in* **peril**   *Inflation cut* **bolsters** *spending*
        Police **foil** *bomb* **plot**   *Women* **heed** *tobacco warnings*   *Record drugs* **haul** *at Heathrow*

Unit 39

1 One word is missing in each line. What is it, and where does it go?

The blazing /\ over the leadership of the Liberal Party is in the headlines   ▶ *row* _____
once again. According sources in Westminster, Harry Jacobs, who has had a   1 _____
strong lead until recently, came under after it was alleged that he had made   2 _____
scathing about the family background of his rival, Ellen Pinter. The comments   3 _____
were to the press by one of Mrs Pinter's supporters, and it is possible that   4 _____
the will now begin to turn in Mrs Pinter's favour, as the tabloid press are   5 _____
beginning to take an interest. She has been as saying that she believes that   6 _____
Mr Jacobs's comments showed a temporary of judgement, and that she felt   7 _____
some sympathy for him as he has clearly put himself in a corner.   8 _____

A Z more words: **grab/hit** *the headlines, stand* **shoulder** *to shoulder, a* **torrent** *of criticism,*
        score an **own goal**, *drop a* **bombshell**, *get caught in the* **crossfire**

Unit 40

1 Complete the words in the story.

The storm was getting closer and we weren't sure whether to (1) s_____ under a tree or run for
the barn. Jan wanted to (2) s_____ put, but I decided to (3) t_____ a c_____
on the barn. Just then, the tree was hit by lightning and a branch fell on Jan. She wasn't unconscious,
but she was obviously very (4) d_____ . After a minute she seemed to (5) r_____ her
senses. The pain was now (6) e_____ , but I didn't (7) d_____ move her in case she had
internal injuries. Thankfully the ambulance arrived within minutes, and as we drove away I could see the
few (8) r_____ branches of the tree on fire. Fortunately Jan made a (9) r_____ recovery.

A Z more words: *on the off* **chance**, *(not) stand a* **chance** *(of doing sth), fancy your* **chance**s, *the*
        chances *are (that), be in with a* **chance**, *give sb/sth half a* **chance**

Unit 41

1 Complete the TV news report using words from the box in the correct form.

| intrusion | scandal | allegation | deserve | exclusive | privacy | allege | coverage | tabloid |

There is continued (1)_____ in the newspapers today of the latest (2)_____ to hit the Democratic Party. However, the minister who is (3)_____ to have awarded a government contract to a company owned by his brother, has hit back at his critics. 'I have done nothing illegal, and do not (4)_____ this', he said. He went on to attack the press for an unjustified (5) _____ into his private affairs, and asked them to respect the (6)_____ of his family. This seems unlikely, as the newspaper who printed the (7)_____ story last week refuses to back down, and the rest of the (8)_____ are now making similar (9)_____ .

A Z **more words:** *a **household** name, prominent, **high-ranking** officers/politicians, stalker/ stalking, **hounded** by the press, the **gutter** press*

Unit 42

1 Rewrite the sentences using the words in capitals. The meaning must remain the same.

1 We had a discussion about socialist policies. WING _____
2 They don't want the situation to change. STATUS _____
3 I don't know who's controlling the situation. DRIVING _____
4 We'll study the document carefully. MICROSCOPE _____
5 I wouldn't be in favour of the proposal. OPPOSED _____
6 He created the basic principles for the policy. FOUNDATIONS _____
7 In our company, everyone has the same rights. EQUALITY _____
8 The prime minister is making good progress. DIRECTION _____

A Z **more words:** ***floating** voter, **cast** your ballot, a **close-run** election, **sweep** to victory, a **landslide** win/victory, exit poll*

Unit 43

1 Complete the definitions.

1 sniper = a person who _____ at someone from a hidden position
2 scarce = not readily _____
3 grim = very _____
4 rubble = broken _____ from a building
5 shell = a metal case full of _____

6 desert somewhere = _____ somewhere
7 random = happening _____ any definite or regular _____ .
8 seige = a _____ operation in which an _____ surrounds a town and tries to _____ it

A Z **more words:** *crossfire, curfew, irreconcilable, call a **truce**, ambush*

44 I can explain job benefits 🎧

Word/phrase	Meaning
benefits	advantages a company offers in addition to the salary. SYN **perks** INF.
benefits **package**	a number of benefits that are offered together.
relocation allowance	**relocation** the process or act of moving to a new place to work. **allowance** money paid to sb to help them, either on a regular basis or for a particular purpose (**food/fuel allowance**).
performance-related bonus scheme	**performance-related** linked to how well sb does in their job. **bonus** extra money paid to sb, often annually or as a reward for sth. **scheme** an official plan.
company **pension** scheme	money paid regularly by a company to help sb when they retire (also **government pension** or **personal/private pension**).
maternity/paternity leave	**maternity leave** a period when a woman temporarily leaves her job to have a baby; **paternity leave** a short period off work allowed to a new father.
expenses	the money sb spends while working that the employer pays back to them later (**travel/travelling expenses**).
30 days' holiday **entitlement**	a thing sb has a right to (often expressed as an amount sb has a right to receive). **be entitled to sth** v.
comprehensive healthcare provision	**comprehensive** including everything or almost everything (**comprehensive car/travel/health insurance**). **healthcare** the service of providing medical care (also **childcare** = the care and supervision of small children). **provision** the act of providing sth (here, private health insurance).
subsidized canteen	If sth is **subsidized**, it is partly paid for by an organization in order to make it cheaper for the people who use it. **canteen** a place where food is served in a company or school.

❶ Find six phrases from the words in the box.

travel	subsidized	maternity	pension	healthcare	relocation
leave	allowance	canteen	expenses	scheme	provision

_____   _____   _____

❷ Write down:

1 three types of insurance you can have: _____ , _____ , _____ .
2 three types of allowance you can have: _____ , _____ , _____ .
3 three types of pension you can have: _____ , _____ , _____ .
4 two types of care that may be provided: _____ , _____ .

❸ Complete the information from this job advertisement with suitable words.

As you would expect from a high-performing council, we offer excellent (1) _____ including:

- government (2) _____ scheme
- performance- (3) _____ bonus scheme
- generous holiday (4) _____
- relocation (5) _____
- healthcare (6) _____
- subsidized (7) _____ with excellent food

Remember to test yourself

45 I can describe ways of working

A Freelance work: the pros and cons 🎧

☺ you are not **accountable to** anyone but yourself

☺ working for a number of employers gives you an **insight into** different companies

☺ it can be more **lucrative**, and it's good not to have to rely **solely** on one company

☺ working from home makes it easier to **juggle** work and family responsibilities

☹ no **guaranteed** income and no **additional** financial benefits (e.g. a company pension)

☹ you will **encounter** quiet periods, a **degree of** isolation, and perhaps loneliness

☹ work can **encroach upon** your home life and your free time

Glossary

the pros and cons	the advantages and disadvantages/**drawbacks**.
accountable to sb	expected to explain all your actions to sb if asked (if you are **not accountable to anyone** you are **your own boss**).
insight into sth	a clear understanding of what sth is like.
lucrative	producing a large amount of money.
solely	only; not involving sb/sth else (**be solely responsible for sth**).
juggle sth	try to manage and balance different jobs and activities in order to fit them successfully into your life.
guarantee sth	promise that sth will happen. **guarantee** N.
additional	more than has been experienced or mentioned before. SYNS **extra**, **further**.
encounter sth	experience sth, especially problems or opposition.
encroach upon sth	FML affect or use up too much of sb's time, rights, personal life, etc.

spotlight *degree*

A **degree of sth** is a certain level or amount of sth, and it is commonly used in certain expressions or patterns:

*It **requires a degree of** skill.*

*I have **a greater degree of** freedom.*

*I can do what I like, **to a degree**. SYN **to an extent**.*

❶ Replace the underlined words with a word or phrase that has a similar meaning.

1 I <u>experienced</u> a few problems. _____

2 There is a certain <u>amount</u> of stress. _____

3 I <u>was my own boss</u>. _____

4 It gave me an <u>understanding of</u> how the company works. _____

5 Initially she had to <u>balance</u> a full-time career with looking after a family. _____

6 There are various <u>advantages and disadvantages</u>. _____

❷ Complete the text with suitable words.

I was a freelance designer for 10 years. I liked being my own (1)_____ and enjoyed the fact that I was (2)_____ responsible for everything I did. Like all freelancers, I (3)_____ a certain (4)_____ of isolation, but I didn't mind that, and the work was quite (5)_____ so I was able to buy a nice house. However, once I had children the work did (6)_____ upon my family life, so in the end I went back to a regular job with a (7)_____ income, plus the (8)_____ benefits of a company car and pension.

❸ ABOUT YOU Have you ever worked freelance? If so, did you enjoy the same advantages and encounter similar problems? Write your answers or talk to another student.

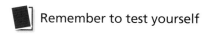 Remember to test yourself

B Working in a team: the pros and cons 🎧

- 😊 a **common goal** is good for **morale** and **fosters team spirit**
- 😊 **collaboration** and **mutual** feedback are **fulfilling** and make people feel **valued**
- 😊 **pooling** diverse skills is generally more productive

- 🙁 if someone doesn't **fit in**, it can be **disruptive** and can **undermine** the work of the team
- 🙁 teams can **stifle** individual **enterprise** and **initiative**

Glossary

common goal	a goal shared by two or more people.
morale	the feeling of confidence and enthusiasm that a person or group has at a particular time (**boost morale** = improve morale).
foster sth	help sth to develop. SYNS **encourage sth**, **promote sth**.
team spirit	the desire among a group to work together and help each other.
collaboration (with sb)	the act of working with others to produce sth.
mutual	used to describe a feeling that two people have for each other equally (**mutual respect/trust**).
fulfilling	giving personal satisfaction. SYN **rewarding**.
value sb/sth	think that sb/sth is important.
pool sth	collect money, ideas, etc. from different people so it or they can be used by all of them (**pool resources**).
fit in (with sb/sth)	be accepted in a situation by the others in a group.
disruptive	causing problems, and making it hard to continue with sth. **disrupt sth** v.
undermine sb/sth	make sb/sth gradually weaker or less effective (**undermine sb's confidence/authority**).
stifle sth	stop sth from happening or developing (**stifle creativity**).
enterprise	the ability to think of new ideas and make them successful.
initiative	the ability to take decisions and act alone (**use your initiative**).

4 Positive or negative? Write P or N.

1 He showed enterprise. _____
2 She was disruptive. _____
3 I don't feel valued. _____
4 It undermined my confidence. _____
5 It boosted my confidence. _____
6 My boss stifles my creativity. _____

5 Find six phrases from the words in the box.

| team | boost | mutual | pool | undermine | stifle | spirit |
| respect | resources | creativity | your authority | morale |

_____   _____   _____

_____   _____   _____

6 Rewrite the sentences without using the underlined words. Keep the meaning the same.

1 He <u>wasn't accepted by the others</u>.   He didn't _____ .
2 She can <u>act on</u> her <u>own</u>.   She can use _____ .
3 I find the work very <u>rewarding</u>.   I find the work very _____ .
4 They <u>did most of it together</u>.   There was a lot of _____ .
5 They <u>shared the same aim</u>.   They had a _____ .
6 We think it will <u>promote</u> team spirit.   We think it will _____ .
7 We can <u>collect ideas from different people</u>.   We can _____ .
8 They have a lot of respect <u>for each other</u>.   They have a lot of _____ .

📓 Remember to test yourself

46 I can **talk about the business world**

A Business takeovers 🎧

Warburg takeover imminent

The battle for Warburg Glass may soon be over. **Former** chairman Matthew Cavendish is now **mounting** a fresh challenge, and has made a **joint bid** for the company with the **backing** of the powerful EPS group. The company has already **rejected** one offer, but an improved **takeover** bid would be attractive to **shareholders** in view of the company's poor recent **dividends**. City analysts believe Cavendish could **clinch the deal** within weeks, and possibly **set off** a new round of **mergers and acquisitions**.

Glossary	
imminent	likely to happen soon.
former	having a particular position in the past (**former president/boss**).
mount sth	organize and begin sth (**mount a challenge/campaign**).
joint	involving two or more people (**joint account/venture**). **jointly** ADV.
bid	an offer to pay a particular price for sth (**make a bid for sth**). **bid** V.
backing	help. SYN **support**. **back sb/sth** V.
reject sth	refuse to accept sth. SYN **turn sth down**. **rejection** N.
shareholder	a person who owns shares in a business or company.
dividend	a portion of a company's profits that is given to shareholders.
clinch sth	succeed in achieving or winning sth (**clinch a deal/victory**).
set sth off	start a process or series of events.

spotlight *merger, takeover, and acquisition*

In a **merger**, two companies agree to join and form a single company. In a **takeover**, one company buys the shares of another public company. The companies may or may not agree to the deal. If they agree, it is a **friendly takeover**; if not, it is a **hostile takeover**. In an **acquisition,** one company buys another company which cannot offer its shares for sale to the public.

❶ Complete the words in the sentences.

1 If we're lucky, we'll c_____ the deal next week.
2 He wants to buy the company and has already made one b_____.
3 If there is more uncertainty, it will s_____ off another wave of selling.
4 Sir Michael is preparing to m_____ a challenge for the leadership.
5 The takeover hasn't happened yet, but it's i_____.
6 If the d_____ is only 50 cents a share, the s_____ won't be happy.

❷ Complete the dialogues with a suitable word.

1 Are you doing this on your own? ~ No, it's a _____ venture with ECL.
2 They didn't reject it, did they? ~ Yes, they _____ it _____ .
3 Has he bought another company? ~ Yes, that's three _____ this year.
4 Is she your current boss? ~ No, she's my _____ boss.
5 Is another _____ bid imminent? ~ Yes, before the end of the week.
6 Are they forming a single company? ~ Yes, there is going to be a _____ .
7 Was it a friendly takeover? ~ No, it was a _____ takeover.
8 Do they need your support? ~ They already have my _____ .

Remember to test yourself

B Describing business activity 🎧

The table includes many phrases that are commonly used in a figurative sense.

Word or phrase	Example	Meaning
go under	*The company may **go under**.*	INF go out of business. SYN **go bankrupt**.
wind sth up	*The board may have to **wind up** the company.*	stop running a business and close it completely.
step down/aside	*The chairman had to **step down**.*	leave an important job.
tighten your belt	*If there is a recession, we will all have to **tighten our belts**.*	spend less money because there will be less available.
go down that road	*The company doesn't want to **go down that** particular **road**.*	take a particular course of action.
wriggle out of sth / doing sth	*They are trying to **wriggle out of** their obligation to customers.*	INF, DISAPPROVING avoid doing sth that you should do.
lure sb	*The company is trying to **lure** passengers away from its rivals.*	DISAPPROVING persuade or tempt sb to do sth by offering them a reward. SYN **entice sb**.
not take sth lying down	*You can be sure that BA **won't take** this situation **lying down**.*	not accept a bad situation without a fight or protest.
tip the balance	*The city's transport links could **tip the balance** in their favour.*	affect the result of sth in one way rather than another.
fuel sth	*The situation is **fuelling fears** that prices could rise again.*	increase sth and make it stronger (**fuel fears/inflation**).
the dust settles	*Wait until **the dust settles**.*	the situation becomes clearer and less disturbed.
on the cards	*A takeover bid is **on the cards**.*	likely to happen.

3 Is the meaning in the sentences the same or different? Write S or D.

1 Don't try and wriggle out of this.	Don't try and interfere in this.	
2 We won't go down that road.	We won't take that lying down.	
3 He decided to step down.	He decided to give up the job.	
4 We may need to tip the balance.	We may need to tighten our belts.	
5 Are they trying to lure customers away?	Are they trying to entice customers away?	
6 Wait until the situation is clearer.	Wait until the dust settles.	
7 We could go under.	We could go bankrupt.	
8 He could wind up the company.	He could expand the company.	

4 Complete the text with suitable words.

The decision by Globus Airlines to open up new routes across the Atlantic is clearly an attempt to (1) _____ customers away from competitors. Closest rival MEDINA has already stated it will not take this move (2) _____ down, but it may have to reduce its prices to tip the (3) _____ once again in its favour. For consumers, of course, this may sound like good news. But is it? If a price war is on the (4) _____ , it will soon start to (5) _____ fears that eventually smaller companies will either go (6) _____ or be taken over. In the long term this may not be good news. We will have to wait and see who is still standing when the dust finally (7) _____ .

Remember to test yourself

47 I can talk about money markets Do Unit 46 first

A Expressing movement in markets 🎧

Word	Example	Meaning
soar	*Share prices have **soared**.*	rise suddenly and quickly. SYN **rocket**.
surge (in sth)	*The market is now expecting a **surge in** the value of the euro.*	a large and sudden increase in the amount or value of sth. **surge** V.
gain	*The dollar made significant **gains**.*	an improvement or increase. OPP **loss**.
hike	*Another **hike in** the rate is possible.*	INF a sudden or significant increase in the level or amount of sth. OPP **cut**.
strengthen	*The yen will **strengthen**.*	become stronger. OPP **weaken**.
rally	*The pound **rallied** later in the day.*	increase in value after a period when it has fallen. SYN **recover / bounce back**.
buoyant	*The market is still **buoyant**.*	confident, successful, and staying at a high level. SYN **healthy**.
snap sth up	*The advice is to **snap up** the shares while you can.*	buy sth quickly, usually while it is cheap or available.
plummet	*The value may **plummet** even more.*	fall suddenly and quickly. SYN **plunge**.
slump	*The price has **slumped** to its lowest level.*	fall by a large amount. **slump** N (**economic slump** OPP **economic boom**).
slash sth	*The Federal Reserve has **slashed** the discount rate.*	reduce sth by a large amount.
wipe sth off sth	*The recession has **wiped** billions **off** the stock markets round the world.*	remove sth from sth, quickly and completely.
turmoil	*The market is still **in turmoil**.*	a state of great confusion.
volatile	*The market **remains volatile**.*	likely to change suddenly. **volatility** N.
turbulence	*There is likely to be short-term **turbulence** in the market.*	a lot of sudden change (also **a bumpy ride** INF). **turbulent** ADJ.

❶ Good or bad news for a company with shares listed on the stock market? Write G or B.

1 We saw a surge in the share value. _____
2 Millions were wiped off the value. _____
3 The company has slashed dividends. _____
4 Investors are snapping up shares. _____
5 Shares rallied yesterday. _____
6 Shares are in for a bumpy ride. _____

❷ Replace the underlined word with an opposite.

1 The pound is <u>strengthening</u>. _____
2 Analysts expect a <u>cut</u> in the interest rate. _____
3 It could lead to an economic <u>boom</u>. _____
4 The share price has <u>soared</u>. _____
5 The market is <u>very stable</u>. _____
6 The market made significant <u>losses</u>. _____

❸ Replace the underlined word(s) with a synonym.

1 The market remains quite <u>healthy</u>. _____
2 The dollar <u>recovered</u> slightly. _____
3 The share price <u>rocketed</u>. _____
4 Shares <u>plunged</u> to their lowest value. _____
5 The markets are in <u>total confusion</u>. _____
6 The market is very <u>unstable</u>. _____

Remember to test yourself

B Reasons to buy and sell shares 🎧

Investors may be given **contradictory** advice about the right time to invest in **equities**. Here, for example, are the thoughts of two experts in the autumn of 2007.

> I would be looking to buy. There is good global growth which will **underpin corporate** profit, and many companies are currently looking strong with few significant **debt burdens**. Current **yields** may be low, but the **underlying outlook** is healthy.

> I would be more cautious. There is a huge credit **bubble** at the moment. As the debt expands, bank lending will **dry up**. There has also been a surge in the yen, which could **trigger** more selling and put markets **under pressure**.

Glossary

investor	a person who buys land, shares, etc. in order to make a profit. **invest** v.
contradictory	saying two different and opposing things. SYN **conflicting**. **contradiction** N. **contradict sb/sth** v.
equities	PL company shares which do not pay a fixed rate of interest.
underpin sth	support or form the basis of sth.
corporate	connected with a large business company. **corporation** N.
debt burden	the responsibility of having to pay back a lot of money.
yield	the total profit or income you get from a business or investment.
underlying	(in finance) An **underlying** number or situation shows what the true amount or level of sth is.
outlook	the probable future for sth.
bubble	(in finance) a temporary and fragile situation caused by a rapid increase in sth (**the bubble will burst** = the situation will end, and people will lose money).
dry up	If sth **dries up**, there is gradually less and less of it.
trigger sth	cause sth to happen.
under pressure	suffering from strain.

4 One letter in one word is missing, unnecessary, or wrong. Find the error and correct it.

1 Analysts are worried that the debit burden is increasing. _____
2 Many believe the credit bubble has already burnt. _____
3 He has just contadicted what he told me earlier. _____
4 The surge in the stock market is good news for inventors. _____
5 Solid growth should underpine the economy. _____
6 The company is planning to move its corporale headquarters. _____
7 Would you advise me to invest in equiries at the moment? _____
8 Some people have received record fields on their investment. _____

5 Complete the sentences using words from the box.

bubble	conflicting	under	invest
debt	underlying	advice	equities
pressure	outlook	burden	burst

1 On the surface the _____ seems uncertain, but the _____ situation is good.
2 They borrowed a lot of money so there is still a significant _____ .
3 They said different things, so I was given _____ .
4 There is always a risk if somebody chooses to _____ in _____ .
5 If the banks go on lending more money, the credit _____ could _____ .
6 If shares continue to lose value, the market is put _____ .

Remember to test yourself

48 I can **talk about personal finance**

A Spending and saving 🎧

Are you good at looking after your money? For instance, do you:

- 🖊 keep a record of your **outgoings**, e.g. **debit card** payments, or **lose track** of what you spend?
- 🖊 keep your account **in credit** all the time, or are you sometimes **overdrawn**?
- 🖊 pay your credit card bills promptly, or do you allow debts to **mount up**?
- 🖊 check all the **transactions** in your **bank statements**, or do you just ignore them?
- 🖊 think you're **thrifty**, or do you **squander** large **sums** of money?

Glossary

outgoings	PL the money a person or business has to spend regularly. OPP **income**.	**transaction**	a piece of business between people. (Here, it is **putting** money **into** your account or **taking** it **out**. SYN **withdrawing** it.)
debit card	a plastic card used for taking money directly from your bank account.		
lose track of sth/sb	not have information about what is happening or where sth/sb is. OPP **keep track of sth/sb**.	**bank statement**	a record of the money paid into and out of a bank account.
		thrifty	careful about spending money. OPP **extravagant**.
credit	If you are **in credit**, there is money in your account. OPP **overdrawn** / **in the red** INF. (If you are **overdrawn**, you have an **overdraft**.)	**squander sth**	waste sth, especially money or time, in a careless way.
		sum (of sth)	an amount of money.
mount up	increase gradually in size. SYN **build up** / **accumulate**.		

spotlight Bank accounts

A **current account** gives immediate access to your money, but pays little interest. A **deposit** or **savings account** pays more interest but without such quick access.

❶ Complete the sentences with suitable words.

1 I'm afraid I _____ track of _____ card payments because I forget to write them down. When I get my monthly bank _____ , I can see all the _____ .
2 I keep a reasonable amount of money in my _____ account – just enough to keep it in _____ – but I put most in a _____ account where I get more interest.
3 I didn't _____ track of my outgoings this month, and now I'm in the _____ .
4 I'm the sensible one with money – very _____ . My brother isn't; he's very _____ .

❷ Complete each dialogue with a single word.

1 Did you take some money out? ~ Yes, I _____ £100.
2 Is there money in your account? ~ No, I'm afraid I'm _____ .
3 Do you know what you spend? ~ Yes, I keep a record of all my _____ .
4 Have you spent too much this month? ~ Yes, and now I've got an _____ .
5 Do you always pay credit card bills? ~ Yes, otherwise debts can _____ up.
6 Does he spend his money carefully? ~ No, he _____ most of it.

 Remember to test yourself

B Looking after your money 🎧

Creating a personal budget

FEW PEOPLE bother to **budget**, which is why so many are in debt. You must **calculate** the total amount of money coming in **per** month, and the total going out, both regular outgoings and all other expenses. Then, **subtract** the expenses **from** the income. If there's a **surplus**, don't spend it: that is your emergency **fund** to keep for **contingencies**.

If there is a **shortfall**, then you must take action. Consider where you can **economize** and **make cutbacks**. Be ruthless, and don't expect anyone else to **subsidize** you and **bail you out**.

spotlight *surplus*

A **surplus** is more of something than is necessary. If it is money, the opposite is a **deficit**; if it is food, petrol, etc., the opposite is a **shortage**.

Glossary

budget	plan how much to spend and what to spend it on (a **budget** is the amount of money available to spend, with a plan for spending it).	**fund**	an amount of money available for a particular purpose.
calculate sth	use numbers to find a total number, amount, or distance. SYN **work sth out. calculation** N.	**contingency**	sth that may or may not happen (**contingency plans / a contingency fund**).
per	for each (used to express the cost or amount of sth for each person, period of time, etc.).	**shortfall**	the difference between what you have and what you need.
		economize	reduce the amount of money, time, goods, etc. that you use. SYN **make cutbacks**.
subtract sth from sth	take one number from another to calculate the difference. SYN **take sth away from sth**.	**subsidize sb**	give money to sb to help them pay for sth. **subsidy** N.
		bail sb out	rescue sb from a difficult situation, often with money.

❸ Circle the odd one out, then say what the other two words have in common.

1	a) shortfall	b) surplus	c) deficit	
2	a) shortage	b) contingency	c) shortfall	
3	a) economize	b) take away	c) subtract	
4	a) economize	b) make cutbacks	c) make contingency plans	
5	a) deficit	b) fund	c) budget	
6	a) work out	b) calculate	c) economize	

❹ Complete the texts with suitable words.

The floods in the spring are now causing severe food (1)_____ throughout the country, and this will leave many farmers with a significant (2)_____ in their income. A few lucky ones may have a (3)_____ fund to help them, but the majority will no doubt be hoping for a government (4)_____ to (5)_____ them out.

I'm not very careful with money and don't often (6)_____ , but I decided to keep a record of my regular outgoings each month. At first I found it quite difficult to (7)_____ all my other expenses, but I managed it after a while. I realized I had a bit of a (8)_____ whenever I had to pay large bills, and would need to make (9)_____ . The most obvious place to start was the car, as it was costing me £100 (10)_____ month.

📓 Remember to test yourself

49 I can **discuss time management**

A Tips for time management 🎧

Time management questionnaire

- Do you **jot down** a list of jobs to do on a daily **basis**, and then **prioritize** them?

- Do you prioritize **ruthlessly**, deciding which tasks you have to **accomplish** that day?

- Do you **stick to** your priorities, **no matter what** happens?
- Do you try to **anticipate** so that you can **schedule** your tasks better?
- Do you **delegate** responsibilities as far as possible?
- Do you set yourself **rigorous** time limits for tasks, and stick to them?

Glossary

jot sth down	write sth quickly.
basis	a particular way in which sth is organized or done (**on a day-to-day basis, on a daily/weekly/ regular basis**).
prioritize	put tasks, problems, etc. in order of importance and do the most important first. **priority** N (**high/low/top priority**).
ruthlessly	in a determined and firm way.
accomplish sth	succeed in doing or completing sth. SYN **achieve sth**.
stick to sth	continue doing sth despite difficulties.
anticipate sth	expect sth will happen and prepare for it. **anticipation** N.
schedule sth	arrange for sth to happen at a particular time. **schedule** N.
delegate sth (to sb)	give part of your work to sb, especially sb in a lower position.
rigorous	strict and severe.

❶ Circle the correct word(s). More than one word may be correct.

1 Once you have prioritized / accomplished your daily list, make sure you do it all.
2 You need to be rigorous / ruthless when deciding what the priorities are.
3 You need to set a time limit, no matter what / whatever happens.
4 I tend to check emails on a daily basis / base, wherever / whatever I am in the world.
5 The organizers hadn't scheduled / anticipated how many people would want to attend.

spotlight · *no matter what, whatever*

No matter what (**when**, etc.) means 'it doesn't matter what (when, etc.)' or 'it isn't important what (when, etc.)'. You can sometimes paraphrase it with **whatever** (**whenever**, etc.).
No matter what happens, don't panic.
= *Whatever* happens, don't panic.
You'll find work **no matter where** *you are.*
= *wherever* you are

❷ Complete the dialogues.

1 How often do you review the figures? ~ Usually on a monthly _____ .
2 He won't give up, even if it's hard. ~ I know, he always _____ to the task.
3 Were you surprised Jack was angry? ~ Yes. I didn't _____ that at all.
4 Has the meeting time been fixed? ~ Yes, it's _____ for 4.00 today.
5 You should get your assistant to do it. ~ I know, I should _____ work more often.
6 Have you got my email address? ~ No, let me just _____ it down.
7 Will you finish the project this week? ~ Yes, I'll do it no _____ what happens.
8 It's been a huge achievement. ~ Yes, we've _____ a great deal.

❸ ABOUT YOU Write answers to the questionnaire, or ask another student.

 Remember to test yourself

B Email stress

Email stress: the new office workers' plague

Over a third of workers say they are **inundated** with a **never-ending stream** of emails and are **stressed out** by the pressure to respond to them **promptly**. Research has found that some employees check their emails every few minutes, leaving them frustrated and **unproductive**. Females feel particularly **hard-hit** by the **deluge**. 'Email is an amazing tool, but it**'s got out of hand**,' says researcher Karen Renaud. She adds that when you **break off from** what you are doing to read your emails, you lose your **train of thought**. The advice is to **set aside** two or three specific email-reading times each day.

Glossary

inundated (with sth)	given so many things that you cannot deal with them. SYNS **overwhelmed**, **swamped**.
never-ending	seeming to last for ever. SYN **interminable**.
stressed out	INF too anxious and tired to be able to relax.
promptly	quickly; without delay. **prompt** ADJ.
unproductive	not producing good results. OPP **productive**.
hard-hit	badly affected by sth (also **severely/badly hit**).
be/get out of hand	be/become impossible to control. OPP **be under control**.
break off (from sth)	stop speaking or doing sth for a time.
train of thought	a linked series of thoughts in your head at one time.
set sth aside	keep sth, especially money or time, for a purpose.

spotlight | Metaphorical use of words

A plague is a fast-spreading disease which often results in death; in the title it is something that causes irritation. A **stream** is a small river, but here it means a continuous flow of things. A **deluge** is a flood or heavy rain, but in the text it means a great quantity of something arriving at the same time.

4 Correct the spelling mistakes.

1 diluge _____ 3 inondated _____ 5 under controll _____
2 interminible _____ 4 severly hit _____ 6 plage _____

5 One word is missing in each sentence. What is it, and where does it go?

▶ I'm feeling very ⟨ out. *stressed*
1 I need to aside money for rent. _____
2 I've lost my of thought. _____
3 We were hard by the price war. _____
4 The work has been never-. _____
5 Our spending has got out hand. _____
6 I had to break from what I was doing. _____
7 The situation is control. _____

6 Complete the questions.   ABOUT YOU

1 If you have a constant s_____ of interruptions,
do you feel o_____/s_____ ? _____
2 Did you get a lot of work done today, or was it a rather
u_____ day? _____
3 Do you agree that people suffer from a d_____ of emails? _____
4 Do you think it's important to reply to emails p_____ ? _____
5 Do you often feel s_____ out because of work or studies? _____
6 What do you think would make you more p_____ at work? _____

7 ABOUT YOU Write your answers to Exercise 6, or ask another student.

 Remember to test yourself

50 I can **discuss workplace disputes**

A An industrial dispute 🎧

Talks between Royal Mail bosses and the CWU union have again ended in **deadlock**, so the union has decided, following the support of its members in the national **ballot**, to **set a date** for strikes as early as next week. They claim it is not just a pay **dispute**, but an attempt to **halt** the **closure** of 2,500 post offices and the further **privatization** of services. For the government, though, there is a great deal **at stake**. If the management gives in to the demands, it could **set a precedent** for other groups, who may feel more **inclined to step up** their own claims for higher wage settlements.

Glossary

deadlock	a failure to reach an agreement or settle an argument (be unable to **break the deadlock**).
ballot	a system of voting in which votes are made in secret (**ballot** (v) a group of people = ask members of a group to vote on sth).
dispute	a disagreement, often official, between people or groups (a **pay/industrial dispute**, **settle a dispute**).
halt sth	prevent sth from continuing.
closure	a situation in which a school, factory, etc. is permanently shut.
privatization	the process of selling an industry so it is no longer owned by the government. OPP **nationalization**. **privatize sth** v.
at stake	If sth is **at stake**, you will lose it if a plan or action is not successful (*there's a lot* **at stake** / *the stakes are high*).
precedent	a thing that happened in the past which is seen as a rule or example to be followed by others in a similar situation.
inclined to do sth	likely to do sth or tending to do sth. **inclination** N.
step sth up	increase the amount of an activity in order to achieve sth.

spotlight *set + noun*

Set is used with many nouns, often meaning to fix something for others to copy, e.g. **set an example**, **set a standard**, **set a record**, **set a precedent**. It can also mean to decide on something, as in **set a date/limit**.

❶ Complete the sentences with a suitable verb.

1 He _____ the standard for others to follow.
2 We must act now in order to _____ the dispute.
3 The union must _____ their members before they can go ahead with strike action.
4 They haven't _____ a date for the next meeting yet.
5 We must find a way to _____ the deadlock.
6 The government has failed to _____ the economic decline, so things look bad.
7 If their demands aren't met, some workers will _____ _____ their call for strike action.

❷ Complete the dialogues with a single word in each space.

1 Is it the only factory to close? ~ No, there have been lots of _____ .
2 Why are they going on strike? ~ It's a _____ over pay I believe.
3 Has this happened before? ~ No, it would set a _____ .
4 Have they reached an agreement? ~ No, the talks ended in _____ .
5 Will the government sell the railways? ~ Yes, there are plans to _____ them.
6 What will happen if you leave? ~ I think others may be _____ to follow.

Remember to test yourself

B Staff disputes 🎧

What would you do in a dispute between members of your own staff? Would you . . .

a) **intervene** at once to **resolve** the problem?

   This would be **proactive**, and a positive way to **tackle the problem**, but is there a risk of **blowing it up out of all proportion**?

b) see if the staff can **sort it out** themselves?

   This could be interpreted as **passing the buck**. But the staff may not want you to **interfere**, so it could be a **wise** thing to do.

c) wait to see if the problem **sorts itself out**?

   Is this sensible or would you just be **procrastinating**?

d) **bury your head in the sand**, as if you're saying, 'What problem?'

Glossary

intervene in sth	get involved in a situation in order to help. **intervention** N.
resolve sth	FML find an acceptable solution to a problem. **resolution** N.
proactive	(of a person or policy) creating or controlling a situation by making things happen, rather than waiting for things to happen.
tackle a problem	do sth to solve a problem.
blow sth (up) out of (all) proportion	make sth more serious than it is.
sort sth out	deal with a problem successfully (if **sth sorts itself out**, the problem is resolved without the need for action from anyone).
pass the buck	make sb else deal with sth that you should deal with.
interfere (in sth)	get involved in a situation in a way that annoys others. **interference** N.
wise (of actions)	sensible; showing good judgement. **wisdom** N. SYN **prudent**. **prudence** N.
procrastinate	FML delay doing sth until later, often because you don't want to do it. **procrastination** N.
bury your head in the sand	pretend a difficult situation doesn't exist.

3 Write the nouns related to these verbs.

1 procrastinate _____   3 resolve _____   5 wise _____

2 interfere _____   4 intervene _____   6 prudent _____

4 Is the speaker pleased or angry with his boss? Write P or A.

1 She tackled the problem. _____   5 She was very prudent. _____

2 She intervened at once. _____   6 She passed the buck. _____

3 She interfered as usual. _____   7 She's usually very proactive. _____

4 She buried her head in the sand. _____   8 She always procrastinates. _____

5 Complete the text.

We recently had a dispute between two employees who wouldn't work together. I could see the problem wasn't going to (1)_____ itself out; I realized that if I didn't (2)_____ and sort it (3)_____, I'd be accused of passing the (4)_____. However, I didn't want to (5)_____ it up out of all (6)_____, so I just had a quiet word with them. It turned out to be a (7)_____ decision, because the problem was (8)_____ quite quickly.

6 ABOUT YOU What would you do in the situation at the top of the page?

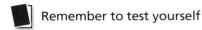 Remember to test yourself

51 I can **talk about office problems** 🎧

MY TOP FIVE **PET HATES**

I can't stand it when colleagues …

- create a paper **jam** in the **photocopier**[1] and leave others to **put it right**
- are always **absent** when the work **piles up** and things are really **hectic**
- **neglect** their own work, but **poke their noses into** other people's business
- **fail to** provide **handover** instructions when they go away on holiday
- constantly **hum**, whistle, **giggle** uncontrollably, **sniff**, etc. right next to me!

Glossary

pet hate	a thing you particularly dislike or find annoying.	**neglect sth**	not do sth, or not give enough attention to sth. **neglect** N.
jam	a situation in which a machine doesn't work because sth is stuck in one position (a **paper jam**). **jam** V (*the photocopier keeps jamming*).	**poke/stick your nose in(to) sth**	INF become involved in sth that does not concern you.
		fail to do sth	not do sth that people expect you to do. SYN **neglect to do sth**.
put sth right	make a situation better after a mistake has made.	**handover**	the act of making sb else responsible for sth. **hand sth over (to sb)** V.
absent (from sth)	not in a place, e.g. because of illness. **absence** N.	**hum**	sing a tune with your lips closed.
pile up	become larger in quantity or amount. SYN **accumulate**.	**giggle**	laugh in a silly way when you're embarrassed, amused, or nervous.
hectic	very busy.	**sniff**	take a quick, noisy breath in through your nose, e.g. when you have a cold.

1 Is the meaning the same or different? Write S or D.

1 The photocopier isn't working.	There's a paper jam in the photocopier.	
2 I mended the fault in the machine.	I put the fault right.	
3 It's one of my pet hates.	It's something I can't stand.	
4 My colleague keeps humming.	My colleague keeps singing.	
5 She was absent this morning.	She wasn't here this morning.	
6 He's always poking his nose in.	He's always neglecting his work.	
7 Work is getting hectic.	Work is really piling up.	
8 I wish she'd stop sniffing.	I wish she'd stop giggling.	

2 Complete the text.

My colleague Barbara had a month off recently; she left very specific (1)_____ instructions for her colleague Doug, so that after such a long (2)_____ , she wouldn't come back to find a mountain of work had (3)_____ . However, Doug's pretty lazy and he (4)_____ to do the things she asked him to. He also (5)_____ his own work and spent most of the time standing round the (6)_____ gossiping, or (7)_____ his nose into other people's business or just (8)_____ at Mark's silly jokes. Barbara's back now, furious with Doug, and, with all the work we have to do, life is as (9)_____ as ever. I don't think Doug will have his job much longer.

3 ABOUT YOU Do you work in an office? If so, do you have any pet hates? Write a list, or tell another student.

Remember to test yourself

Review: Work and finance

Unit 44

1 Complete the dialogues.

1 A Your office is moving to Milan, isn't it?
   B Yes, and I've got a generous _____ allowance, which is great.
2 A Does your company have a bonus _____ ?
   B Yeah, and it's _____-related, which is why I put in such long hours.
3 A When does your maternity _____ start?
   B Next month. And when I come back there is childcare _____ .
4 A Do you use the company _____ at lunchtime?
   B Yes, and it's _____ , so you can get a good meal for €2.
5 A How much holiday are you _____ to?
   B I get 30 days off, but I believe the _____ is increasing to 32 days next year.

A Z more words: ***statutory*** *rights/holidays*, *temporary* ***lay-off***, ***breach*** *of contract, free health* ***screening***, ***share/stock*** *options*

Unit 45

1 Tick the words which are correct. One, two, or three may be correct.

1 There has always been a lot of mutual *trust* ☐ *confidence* ☐ *respect* ☐ .
2 There are several *additional* ☐ *extra* ☐ *further* ☐ factors to consider.
3 It's hard to *juggle* ☐ *encroach upon* ☐ *encounter* ☐ work and family responsibilities.
4 Teamwork requires *a degree* ☐ *an extent* ☐ *an insight* ☐ of respect between colleagues.
5 Colleagues who don't fit in can *undermine* ☐ *pool* ☐ *disrupt* ☐ the work of the team.
6 The project has helped to *foster* ☐ *promote* ☐ *encroach upon* ☐ team spirit.

A Z more words: *make* ***ends*** *meet, networking, the career* ***ladder***, *camaraderie, counterpart,* ***dead-end*** *job, roller coaster*

Unit 46

1 One word is missing from each sentence. Where does it go? Write it at the end.

1 They're in a bad state but, knowing them, they won't take it lying. _____
2 The company is likely to an advertising campaign to improve its profile. _____
3 We have no choice but to our belts in the current climate. _____
4 We could borrow more, but we don't want to go that road. _____
5 The US job figures are fuelling of a global recession. _____
6 It's been chaotic on the markets, but let's just wait till the settles. _____
7 The bid was turned because of insufficient backing by shareholders. _____
8 There is concern that the move will off a fresh round of bids and mergers. _____

A Z more words: *the (financial)* ***muscle***, *go back to the* ***drawing board***, ***grind*** *to a halt, an* ***injection*** *of cash, back on* ***track***

Unit 47

1 Organize the words in the box into the two groups below.

plunge	soar	turbulence	plummet	surge	volatile	slash
boom	buoyant	turmoil	rally	slump	gains	

STABLE OR RISING	UNSTABLE OR FALLING

2 Complete the sentences with suitable words.

1 It's a very good time for _____ to buy shares.
2 The company is struggling under a significant _____ burden.
3 It's a difficult time for the company as they are under a lot of _____.
4 If there is a surge in one currency it could _____ more selling in another currency.
5 Investing in _____ carries more risk than putting your money into a bank account.
6 The market is unstable at present but the _____ is good.
7 Analysts are worried that the credit bubble could _____.
8 Investors are getting _____ signs from the market: one day it suggests things are getting worse, the next day the market rallies.

AZ more words: *ethical* investments, *bonds*, ***portfolio*** of investments, ***negative equity***, ***rights issue***, ***bull market***, ***bear market***

Unit 48

1 Complete the email from a student to her parents.

Dear Mum and Dad

Sorry I haven't been in touch for a while, but things have been really busy at university. Anyway, I'm afraid I've got a confession to make. I've just been looking at my bank (1)_____ , and I feel really stupid. I don't know how it's happened, but I'm in the (2)_____ by a very large amount. In fact, I'm (3)_____ by nearly $500, and even worse, I've already spent the $200 contingency (4)_____ you gave me last term. I know you think I've been (5)_____ money instead of spending it wisely as you've always insisted, but my (6)_____ have been enormous this term: books, a laptop, DVDs (for my studies, of course)... I know I've never been good at keeping to a (7)_____ , but if you will just (8)_____ me out this one last time, I promise I will (9)_____ cutbacks and keep (10)_____ of my spending from now on. Honestly, I will. Really. Honestly and truly.
I'll ring you tonight to talk it over,
Lots of love,
Angelica

AZ more words: *live within your* ***means***, *fritter (money) away*, *take out a* ***mortgage***, *pay sth off*, *extortionate*, *tax* ***rebate***

Unit 49

1 Complete the sentences with suitable verbs.

Improve your time management

If you want to (1)_____ a lot in one day, here's how to do it.

- First of all, (2)_____ your daily tasks, so that important ones are dealt with first.
- As soon as you have your targets for the day, (3)_____ to them.
- Try to (4)_____ any problems; then you are better equipped to deal with them.
- (5)_____ meetings so that they don't interrupt your day too much.
- Always (6)_____ aside time every day for routine tasks such as responding to emails.
- (7)_____ responsibilities so that you don't waste time on trivial things.

A Z **more words**: *workload, absenteeism, backlog, be up to your* **eyes** *in sth, have a lot on your* **plate,** *fall behind* **schedule**

Unit 50

1 Cross out the word which is wrong. Write the correct word at the end.

1   It's a delicate situation and the steaks are high. _____
2   This legal action could make a precedent. _____
3   The union will need to ballet its members before calling a strike. _____
4   They are having further talks to try to set the dispute. _____
5   The government is planning further privatizement of the postal service. _____
6   He may get better, but he's inclinated to be very lazy. _____
7   I was very grateful for the manager's interference in the dispute. _____
8   Don't worry; the problem will sort itself off. _____

A Z **more words**: *grievance, go to arbitration, mediate, take the* **easy** *way out, even-handed, meddle in/with sth*

Unit 51

1 Which words are being defined?

1	_____	sing with your lips closed
2	_____	take a quick, noisy breath in
3	_____	laugh in a silly way
4	_____	not in your place of work, perhaps because of illness
5	_____	very busy
6	_____ *sth*	not give enough attention to something
7	_____	a machine that makes copies of documents
8	_____ *hate*	a thing you particularly dislike
9	_____ *sth right*	make a situation better after a mistake has been made
10	_____ *your* _____ *into sth*	become involved in something that doesn't concern you

A Z **more words**: *aggravating, pester sb,* **know**-*all, whine about things, seethe (with anger),* **drum** *your fingers*

52 I can describe cause and effect

A Actions and reactions 🎧

The **road rage** thing was all **sparked** by a trivial **incident**. The guy behind me kept blowing his horn and it was **driving me mad**. When we stopped at the lights, my passenger Phil **egged me on** to have a word with him. I got out, we started arguing, **one thing led to another** and . . . , well, I kicked his car and **dented**[1] it. He **retaliated** and kicked mine, and Phil, who is easily **provoked**, joined in. I realize I **overreacted**, and I'm shocked at my own behaviour; I think it all **boils down to** the fact that I haven't been well lately. All I can say is that it was an unfortunate **chain of events**, that's for sure . . .

dent v, N

Glossary

road rage	angry or violent behaviour by one driver towards another driver.
spark sth (off)	cause sth to start or develop suddenly.
incident	sth that happens, especially sth unusual or unpleasant.
drive sb mad/crazy/insane	make sb very angry, crazy, etc.
egg sb on	INF encourage sb to do sth, especially sth they should not do.
one thing leads to another	used to suggest that the way one event leads to another is so obvious that it does not need to be stated.
retaliate	do sth harmful to sb because they harmed you first. **retaliation** N.
provoke sb (into sth)	say or do sth that you know will annoy sb so that they react angrily. SYN **goad sb**. **provocation** N.
overreact (to sth)	react too strongly to sth, especially sth unpleasant.
boil down to sth	INF (of a situation) have sth as a main or basic part.
chain of events	a number of connected events that happen one after the other. SYN **sequence of events**.

1 Circle the correct word(s). In some cases, both may be correct.

1 My neighbour's loud music drives / sparks me crazy.
2 She attacked me and, stupidly, I retaliated / egged her on.
3 He was provoked / goaded into a huge argument.
4 It's very common to overreact / boil down to provocation.
5 It was a very unfortunate sequence / chain of events, which ended in court.
6 How exactly did the incident / dent end?
7 One thing led / went to another, and I found myself the owner of a new car.
8 Don't mention her ex-boyfriend; it will only drive / provoke her again.

2 Complete the questions, then write your answers, or ask another student.   ABOUT YOU

1 Have you ever witnessed a r_____ rage i_____?   _____
2 Have you ever kicked something and d_____ it?   _____
3 Do you tend to remain calm, or do you o_____ in difficult situations?   _____
4 What kinds of things d_____ you mad?   _____

📖 Remember to test yourself

B Causes, reasons, and results 🎧

A What **aroused** the police's suspicions?
B Well, Sims had a clear **motive**: revenge.

A What was the **outcome** of the discussion?
B We were eventually **coerced into** agreeing.

A The flood had **a knock-on effect** on tourism.
B Yes, it was bound to have **repercussions**.

A What **prompted** you to ring Nina?
B **No reason** – just fancied a chat.

A We're considering various **spin-offs**.
B That should **generate** more income.

A Has the smoking ban **come into effect**?
B Yes, it's already **made a** big **difference**.

---

spotlight *effect*

If a law or regulation **comes into effect**, it begins to apply or be used. **Knock-on effects** cause events to happen one after another in a series. An **adverse** or **detrimental effect** is a negative or unpleasant one (OPP a **beneficial** effect).

---

❸ Match 1–8 with a–h.

1 We don't want to feel _____
2 The incident aroused _____
3 I believe it will make a big _____
4 The decision had an adverse _____
5 The move will have serious _____
6 The suspect had a clear _____
7 The company is planning commercial _____
8 The move generated considerable _____

a income.
b effect.
c spin-offs.
d repercussions.
e suspicion.
f coerced.
g difference.
h motive.

❹ One word is missing in each sentence. What is it, and where does it go?

1 The house took a long time to build, but the end is fantastic. _____
2 What made you ring Robert? ~ Oh, reason. _____
3 The new law came effect at the beginning of June. _____
4 Too much sunlight can have a effect on your skin. _____
5 Current levels of deforestation will have long-term. _____
6 I'm not really sure what him to resign so suddenly. _____
7 What was the final of the talks in Bali? _____
8 One indirect result or knock-on will be price rises throughout the economy. _____

Remember to test yourself

53 I can **talk about truth and lies**

A A story about lying 🎧

I **was** once **economical with the truth** on a job application form. I lied about my employment record, **talked up** my skills, and **embellished** my previous salary by a few thousand. Oh, and I **glossed over** one rather **unpalatable** truth, **namely** that I'd been sacked from my last job. But trying to **sustain** the lies at the interview was a nightmare. My interviewer soon **detected** something was wrong, and a friendly chat **deteriorated** into an awful **interrogation**. And after a series of awkward questions, he **caught me out**; I felt utterly **humiliated**. **Needless to say**, I've never done it since.

Glossary

be economical with the truth	say things that are only partially true (used as a euphemism for 'lie': see page 203).
talk sth up	describe sth in a way that makes it sound better than it is.
embellish sth	make a statement or story more interesting by adding details that are not always true.
gloss over sth	deliberately avoid talking about sth unpleasant, or say as little as possible about it.
unpalatable	unpleasant and hard to accept.
namely	used to introduce more exact information about a subject.
sustain sth	make sth continue for some time.
detect sth	discover or notice sth, especially sth that is hard to see or hear.
deteriorate	become worse. **deterioration** N.
interrogation	the process of asking sb a lot of questions, especially in an aggressive way. **interrogate sb** V.
catch sb out	make sb make a mistake which shows they have been lying.
humiliated	feeling ashamed because you have lost the respect of other people. **humiliate sb** V. **humiliation** N.
needless to say	obviously.

1 Complete the words and circle the stressed syllable.

▶ e c o (n o) m i c a l
1 embel_____
2 s____st____n

3 h____m____l____ted
4 int_____og_____ion
5 int_____og_____

6 unp_____t____ble
7 d____t____ct
8 n____m____ly

2 Complete the dialogue.

A Did you know that Johnny Savill's got the sack? Evidently he was, well, let's just say he was '(1)_____ with the truth' about a few things.

B Well, I can't say I'm surprised. When I worked with him he often (2)_____ things up, especially when our sales were down. And I think he was a bit dishonest – he would (3)_____ the facts, or (4)_____ over the things he didn't want you to know about. And his relationship with Mrs Kilgarriff has really (5)_____ lately because she was obviously suspicious of him.

A Yeah, evidently he was called in to see her yesterday and she virtually (6)_____ him, asking him loads of difficult questions, and eventually she (7)_____ him out. He must have felt really (8)_____ – he's a very proud guy. In the end, he just couldn't (9)_____ all those lies. Well who could, faced with Mrs Kilgarriff? But (10)_____ say, I'm not sorry for him. He deserved it.

Remember to test yourself

B Quotes about truth and lies 🎧

- When war is **declared**, truth is the first **casualty**. *Arthur Ponsonby*

- The most dangerous of all **falsehoods** is a slightly **distorted** truth. *C. G. Lichtenberg*

- **Level with** your child by being honest. Nobody spots a **phoney** quicker than a child. *Mary MacCracken*

- There are only two ways of telling the complete truth: **anonymously** and **posthumously**. *Thomas Sowell*

- Tell the truth so as to **puzzle** and **confound** your **adversaries**. *Henry Wotten*

- We are never **deceived**; we deceive ourselves. *Johann Wolfgang von Goethe*

Glossary

declare war / a ceasefire	announce the start of war or a ceasefire.
casualty	sth that is destroyed or sb who suffers when sth else happens.
distort sth	twist or change facts, etc. so that they are no longer true.
level with sb	INF tell the truth and not hide any important facts.
phoney	INF a person who is not honest or sincere. **phoney** ADJ, INF.
anonymously	in such a way that the speaker's name is kept secret. **anonymity** N.
posthumously	after sb has died.
puzzle sb	make sb feel confused because they don't understand sth. SYNS **baffle sb**, **confound sb** FML. **puzzled** ADJ.
adversary	FML an enemy or opponent.
deceive sb	trick sb by behaving dishonestly (also **deceive yourself** refuse to admit that sth unpleasant is true SYN **delude yourself**). **deceit** N. SYN **deception** N.

spotlight   Types of lie

A **falsehood** FML is a lie. A **white lie** is a small lie, especially one you tell to avoid hurting someone. A **half-truth** is a statement which only gives some of the facts. A **fib** INF is an unimportant lie.

3 Write the words in the correct column in the table.

| phoney | a white lie | falsehood | confound sb | fib | deceit |
| adversary | level with sb | declare sth | distort sth | | |

Formal	Informal	Neutral

4 Complete the dialogues.

1 Did she sign her name on the letter? ~ No, she sent it _____ .
2 Why did Erich lose his job? ~ He was a _____ of the financial cutbacks.
3 He was awarded the medal _____ . ~ Yes, his widow accepted it on his behalf.
4 I eat loads of vegetables. ~ That's a _____ -truth. They're all on your pizzas!
5 What's the latest news? ~ The rebels have _____ a ceasefire.
6 Did you understand what she said? ~ No, I was a bit _____ , actually.
7 I'm good enough to win. ~ You're just _____ yourself; you won't.
8 Was it true what he said? ~ No, he _____ the facts. I was very angry.

5 ABOUT YOU Look at the quotes again. Do you agree with them? Write your answers, or discuss with another student.

Remember to test yourself

54 I can **discuss problems and solutions**

A Problems in general 🎧

Word	Example	Meaning
minor	*The design is a **minor** problem.*	not important. OPP **major**.
growing	*Obesity is a **growing** problem.*	increasing in size, amount, or degree.
urgent	*Lack of funds is an **urgent** issue.*	requiring immediate action.
perennial	*Noise is a **perennial** problem.*	always existing and not seeming to change.
insoluble	*The problem seems **insoluble**.*	unable to be solved. SYN **insurmountable** FML.
arise	*Various problems have **arisen**.*	start to exist. SYN **occur / come up**.
raise sth	*I **raised** the problem of staffing.*	mention sth for people to discuss.
confront sb	*There are a number of problems **confronting** the head teacher.*	If problems **confront sb**, they appear and have to be dealt with by sb. SYN **face sb**.
confront sth	*She's had to **confront** the fact that she can no longer walk.*	deal with a problem or difficult situation. SYN **face up to sth**.
address sth	*We've got to **address** the lack of experience in the team.*	think about a difficult situation and decide how to deal with it.
get to grips with sth	*I'm just beginning to **get to grips with** my new job.*	begin to understand and deal with sth difficult.
tackle sth	*They must **tackle** inflation.*	make a big effort to deal with a problem.
overcome sth	*The company had to **overcome** a number of financial difficulties.*	succeed in dealing with a problem that has been preventing you from achieving sth.
exacerbate sth FML	*We must be careful not to **exacerbate** the problem.*	make an existing problem worse. SYN **aggravate sth**.

1 Replace the underlined word with a synonym.

1   The problem is <u>increasing</u>. ....
2   She's had to <u>confront</u> her fear. ....
3   When did the problem <u>occur</u>? ....
4   Drugs can <u>aggravate</u> the problem. ....
5   It is an <u>insurmountable</u> problem. ....
6   The problem <u>facing</u> us is huge. ....

2 Complete the gaps in the dialogues with one word.

1   Have they aggravated the problem? ~ Yes, they've made it ....
2   Is it an .... problem? ~ No, we can deal with it later.
3   Have they discussed finance? ~ Yes, I .... it at the last meeting.
4   Has she .... her shyness? ~ Yes, and the difference is amazing.
5   Have they solved the problem? ~ No, but they've begun to get to .... with it.
6   It's a .... problem, isn't it? ~ Yes, it never seems to go away.
7   Are they .... the problem? ~ Yes, I think they're making a real effort.
8   Is it a major problem? ~ No, it's just a .... matter really.

3 ABOUT YOUR COUNTRY Are these things problems in your country? If so, which adjectives above might describe the problem, and what is being done about them?

litter on the streets   graffiti on walls   increasing household waste
pollution in town centres   parking in town centres   vandalism   bullying in schools

Remember to test yourself

B Teenage problems and solutions 🎧

How parents can deal with teenage problems

1 Teenagers are never satisfied with their appearance and this can **dent** their **self-esteem**. Don't **make light of** these worries even if they seem **trivial** to you. Explain that others don't notice the details that we notice in ourselves.

2 Some teenagers **take** failure **in their stride**, while others let it **get them down**. Help your teen to **keep things in perspective**. Explain that everyone has **setbacks** in life, and **reassure** them that you**'re behind** them 100 per cent, **regardless of** what happens.

3 Some teenagers – boys especially – find it difficult to identify and **articulate** how they feel. Keep **channels of communication** open at all times and respect their ideas.

Glossary

dent (sb's confidence, reputation, etc.)	damage sb's confidence, etc.	**keep sth in perspective**	not allow a problem to have too much importance.
self-esteem	the way you feel about yourself (**high/low self-esteem**).	**setback**	a problem that delays or prevents progress.
		reassure sb	say or do sth that makes sb less worried. SYN **set sb's mind at rest**.
make light of sth	treat sth as unimportant. OPP **take sth seriously**.	**be behind sb/sth**	give your support to sb/sth.
trivial	not important or serious.	**regardless of sth**	without being affected or influenced by sth.
take sth in your stride	accept and deal with a difficult situation without letting it worry you.	**articulate sth**	FML express your thoughts clearly in words. **articulate** ADJ.
get sb down	If sth **gets you down** it makes you feel sad or depressed.	**channel of communication**	a system or method for sending or obtaining information.

4 Complete the gaps in the sentences with a single word.

1 His poor exam results have not been good for his self-_____ .
2 It's upsetting, but she mustn't let it _____ her _____ .
3 She expresses herself very well; she's always been extremely _____ .
4 His mother will support him _____ of what he does, because she loves him.
5 Bullying is not a _____ issue; it's a very serious problem.
6 Parents must ensure there is an open _____ of communication with their kids.

5 Complete the conversation with a suitable word or words.

A Carrie's teacher told her that she isn't good enough to become a doctor, and it has (1)_____ her confidence.

B I'll bet it has. And Carrie's not good at taking these things in (2)_____ , is she?

A No. And when you're her age, it's difficult to keep things in (3)_____ .

B Yeah. But I'm sure her mother has tried to set her mind (4)_____ .

A Oh yes, she's been right (5)_____ her, and has (6)_____ her that everything is OK. She's also tried to make (7)_____ of the teacher's remarks by suggesting that he didn't mean it.

B Yes, but even so, it must be a real (8)_____ for her. I hope she gets over it quickly.

6 ABOUT YOU Have you experienced any of the teenage problems above, either as a teenager yourself or as a parent? What other problems do teenagers often have, and how should parents respond? Write your answers or talk to another student.

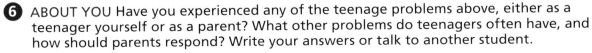 Remember to test yourself

55 I can describe **old and new**

A An old house 🎧

… we saw this amazing, **dilapidated** house, **formerly** owned by a wealthy family but then **abandoned** at the end of the century. Some features like the oak staircase are very well **preserved**, but most of it is pretty **run-down** and has **fallen into decay**. It could be a lot of fun **renovating** it, though. It has old **stables**, which I'd like to convert into an **ultra-modern** kitchen. There are also the **ruins** of a **medieval tower**[1]! I'd love to **trace** the history of the place …

Glossary

dilapidated	(of a building) old and in very bad condition. SYNS **run-down**, **ramshackle**.
formerly	in earlier times. SYN **previously**.
abandon sth	leave a place, vehicle, etc. empty without planning to return.
preserve sth	keep sth in its original state or in good condition. **preservation** N.
fall into decay/ disrepair	gradually be destroyed through lack of care.
renovate sth	repair and decorate an old building, car, etc. SYN **do sth up** INF.
stables	buildings in which horses are kept.
ultra-(modern)	extremely (modern) (also **ultra-cautious**).
ruins	parts of a building that remain after it has been destroyed. (**Remains** are parts of objects and buildings that have been discovered recently. **Human/animal remains** are bones or dead bodies.)
medieval	connected with **the Middle Ages** (= about 1000 to 1450).
trace sth (back) (to sth)	find the origin or cause of sth.

❶ Cross out the word that is wrong in each sentence. Write the correct word at the end.

1 The company deals in extra-modern, contemporary furniture. ....

2 The weather has meant that the building is in a poor state of destruction. ....

3 They discovered the ruins of a dead sheep at the end of the field. ....

4 She keeps the horses in the estables at night. ....

5 The war left the whole area on ruins, with countless run-down buildings. ....

6 Mumbai, formally known as Bombay, has a population of 15 million. ....

❷ Complete the dialogues. More than one word may be correct.

1 The building used to be a prison, didn't it? ~ No, it was .... a hospital.

2 Are you going to do the place ....? ~ Yes, we plan .... it.

3 It's in a bad state, isn't it? ~ Yes, it's very ....

4 It fell into .... years ago. ~ Yes, it was .... by the owner.

5 We can restore it to its original condition. ~ Yes, we should .... old buildings.

6 It dates from the .... Ages, I believe. ~ That's right, it's ....

7 Why is he using the internet so much? ~ He wants to .... his family history.

8 That style's very fashionable just now. ~ Yes, it's .... modern.

Remember to test yourself

B Old and new objects 🎧

Brand new Sasko G5000 mobile phone – **cutting-edge** technology at its very best.

Innovative anti-snore **device** – clips on to sleeper's nose for a good night's sleep.

Up-to-date guidebook to Korea – **second-hand** but **good as new**.

Genuine antique grandfather clock. The 8-day mechanism is **in mint condition**.

Reproduction ancient Egyptian statue of the goddess Bastet.

Fully reconditioned exercise bike with original **packaging** and instructions.

Glossary

brand new	completely new.	**genuine**	exactly what it appears to be; real. SYN **authentic**.
cutting-edge (technology)	the most advanced (technology) in the field.	**antique**	old, and often very valuable. **antique** N.
innovative	featuring or introducing new ideas, methods, etc.	**in mint condition**	new or as good as new. SYN **in perfect condition**.
device	an object or piece of equipment designed to do a particular job.	**reproduction**	a thing made as a copy of an earlier object or style. **reproduce sth** v.
up to date	modern (**out of date** = old-fashioned, or without the most recent information and therefore no longer useful).	**ancient**	belonging to a period of history from thousands of years ago.
second-hand	not new; owned by sb else before.	**reconditioned**	(of a machine) repaired so that it is in good condition.
(as) good as new	in very good condition (also **like new** ADV).	**packaging**	materials used to wrap and protect goods sold in shops.

❸ Complete the phrases.

1 _____ of date   3 _____ as new   5 brand _____
2 in _____ condition   4 cutting _____   6 second-_____

❹ Complete the sentences.

1 A battery charger is an extremely useful energy-saving _____ .
2 It's a beautifully made, 18th-century _____ clock. At least, I hope it's genuine!
3 There were earrings like it thousands of years ago in _____ Greece, and now they make _____ of them and sell them in tourist shops.
4 We bought a second-hand lawnmower – it was fully _____ , and it was fantastic value.
5 I don't want a copy of the clock: I want a _____ antique.
6 Shops often sell more goods if they're displayed in attractive _____ .
7 Our small factory _____ antique clocks and we sell them on the internet.
8 They want something really _____ to date, and they're awarding a prize for the most _____ design.

Remember to test yourself

56 I can talk about **success and failure**

A Success 🎧

JANE	Maximo, your pizza chain's been a **resounding** success. How did things **turn out** so well for you? What's **the secret of your success**?
MAXIMO	Well, I had **a stroke of luck** early on. I hired a talented young chef who was really keen to **fulfil his potential**, and basically he **never put a foot wrong**. We had to work together to **overcome** all the **obstacles in our way** – we nearly **came unstuck** when the first restaurant was flooded – but eventually we **made it**.
JANE	You **made a** big **breakthrough** after you were on that TV show, didn't you?
MAXIMO	Yes, we **went from strength to strength** after that. Still, you can never relax …

Glossary

resounding	very great (**a resounding success/defeat/win/victory**).
turn out (well/badly)	happen in a particular way, often unexpectedly.
the secret of (your) success	a way of doing things that has brought success.
a stroke of sth	an unexpected but important event (**a stroke of luck**).
potential	qualities that exist and can be developed (**fulfil/realize your potential** = use your natural abilities to achieve what you hoped to achieve).
not put a foot wrong	not make a single mistake.

overcome sth	succeed in controlling or dealing with a problem.
obstacle	a situation or event that makes it hard for you to achieve sth.
in sb's/the way	stopping sb from doing sth.
come unstuck	INF fail completely.
make it	succeed in achieving a goal; become successful.
breakthrough	an important development that may lead to an achievement or agreement (**make/achieve a breakthrough**).
go from strength to strength	become more and more successful.

1 Make six phrases using words from the box.

a resounding	come	the secret	turn out	a stroke	fulfil
of luck	unstuck	of your success	your potential	victory	badly

....

....

2 Good or bad? Write G or B.

1 We went from strength to strength. ....

2 There were obstacles in our way. ....

3 They came unstuck. ....

4 She never put a foot wrong. ....

5 They had a breakthrough. ....

6 They overcame the obstacles. ....

3 Complete the sentences.

1 He's very successful, but he's had to .... various personal problems during his life.

2 I passed my exam. However, I think it was a .... of luck.

3 The company struggled at first; now they're going from strength ....

4 You must ask him for the .... of his success.

5 There's a long way to go, but things have .... out well so far.

6 The film industry is a tough business, but I believe she has the .... to go on and make it.

📓 Remember to test yourself

B Failure 🎧

A Did Don **make a go of** the business?
B No, he was **way out of his depth**.

A It's a **tricky** situation to deal with.
B Yes, Sue's really **up against it**.

A I'm afraid the marriage is **going downhill**.
B And it started so well. That's sad.

A So Carla **came bottom** in the exams.
B Yeah, and I only just **scraped through**.
Mum thinks we've **let her down**.

A That boxer **is past it**, surely.
B Yeah, but he still wants to **make a comeback**.

A I hear the film was a **flop**.
B Afraid so – an **unmitigated** disaster.

spotlight   *way*

Way can be used informally to mean 'by a large amount' or 'very far'.
*It cost **way** over $1,000.* = a lot more than $1,000
*The others were **way** ahead of me.* = a long way ahead of me

Glossary

make a go of sth	INF make sth succeed, especially a business or marriage.
out of your depth	unable to do or understand sth because it is too hard.
tricky	difficult to do or deal with (**a tricky situation/question/ problem**).
up against it	INF facing difficult problems or opposition.
go downhill	get worse in quality, health, etc. SYN **deteriorate**.
come bottom	receive the lowest score in an exam. OPP **come top**.
scrape through (an exam)	only just succeed in passing an exam.
let sb down	make sb disappointed because you haven't behaved well or done what you said you would do.
be past it	INF be too old to do what you used to be able to do.
comeback	If a person in public life **makes a comeback**, they start doing sth again which they had stopped doing.
flop	INF a film, play, book, party, etc. that is not successful. **flop** V, INF.
unmitigated	complete (used to describe sth bad). SYN **absolute**.

4 Tick the words or phrases which are informal.

1 Did she make a go of it? _____
2 The play was a flop. _____
3 She's past it. _____
4 He let me down. _____
5 I'm really up against it. _____
6 That's way too expensive. _____

5 Circle the correct word(s). Sometimes both words are correct.

1 Embarrassingly, I got / came bottom in the end-of-year progress tests.
2 He's determined to stay and make / have a go of his marriage.
3 The team started well but they've deteriorated / gone downhill recently.
4 He's away / way too old to be driving.
5 She wants to do / make a political comeback at the next election.
6 The show was an unmitigated / absolute disaster; I didn't know what to do with myself.

6 One word is missing in each speaker's utterance. Where does it go? Write it at the end.

1 I don't like to tell him he's past. _____ ~ Hmm, it's a situation. I don't envy you. _____
2 Any chance he'll make comeback? _____ ~ No, his last film badly. _____
3 Did she top in the public vote? _____ ~ Yes, but she was against it. _____
4 He himself down in the exam. _____ ~ Yes, he only just through. _____
5 Her interview was an unmitigated. _____ ~ Yes, she was way of her depth. _____

📓 Remember to test yourself

57 I can describe the past, present, and future

A Thinking about time 🎧

- **Time flies** *when you get older.*
- *I get depressed* **from time to time**.
- *I will go to university* **in due course**.
- **It's about time** *I start**ed** a pension.*
- **At one time** *I wanted to be a journalist.*
- *I* **do** *everything* **at the last minute**.

- **In retrospect**, *I wish I'd gone to university.*
- **For the time being** *I'm happy where I am.*
- *My parents are a bit* **behind the times.**
- *I've become more tolerant* **over time.**
- *Elvis Presley was a bit* **before my time.**
- **With hindsight** *I should've worked harder.*

Glossary

time flies	time seems to pass very quickly.	**in retrospect**	thinking now about the past, often with a different view from the one you had then. SYN **looking back**.
from time to time	sometimes but not regularly. SYN **now and again**.		
in due course	at the right time and not before.	**for the time being**	for a short period of time but not permanently.
it's about time	used to say that sth should happen soon or should have happened already (notice the past tense). SYN **it's high time**.	**behind the times**	old-fashioned in ideas, ways, etc.
		over time	gradually.
at one time	in the past but not now.	**before your time**	before you were born or before you can remember.
do sth at the last minute	do sth at the latest possible time before sth else happens. SYN **leave sth to/till the last minute**.	**with hindsight**	with the ability to understand a situation only after it has happened (**with the benefit of hindsight**).

1 Find nine time phrases in the box.

at the last	over	in	with	behind	at	retrospect	from time		for the time
in due	the times	minute	one time	course	hindsight	time	being	to time

2 Complete the sentences.

1   In _____ , I don't think I made the most of my time at university.
2   With the benefit of _____ it was probably a mistake for me to leave my last job.
3   The trouble with Angel is that he _____ everything to the last _____ .
4   Listen, it's _____ time you started taking these exams seriously.
5   My mum used to love punk music, but it's a bit _____ my _____ .
6   The time has _____ since I've been in Greece. I've loved every minute of it.
7   The university says they'll give us the date of the exams in due _____ .
8   _____ one time I wanted to be a professional footballer. I think I'm a bit old for that now.
9   Your English won't improve immediately; it happens _____ time.
10 This dictionary will be fine _____ the time _____ .

3 ABOUT YOU Read the statements at the top again. Are they true for you? If not, write answers that are true for you using the phrases in bold, or talk to another student.

Remember to test yourself

B Time words which are similar in meaning 🎧

Word	Example	Meaning
during **throughout**	*It rained **during** the day.* *It rained **throughout** the day.*	at a point within a period of time. continuously within a period of time.
age **era**	*We're living in the nuclear **age**.* *When Mandela was released, it was the beginning of a **new era**.*	a particular period of history. a period of time with a particular quality or character.
extend sth **prolong sth**	*They're going to **extend** my visa.* *The drugs will **prolong** her life.*	increase the length of time of sth. make sth last longer. OPP **curtail** FML.
interval **gap** **break**	*Buses run at regular **intervals**.* *There's a fifteen-minute **interval**.* *We met again after a ten-year **gap**.* *I get a **coffee break** and **lunch break** at work.*	a period of time between two events or two parts of sth, e.g. a play. a period of time when sth stops. a short period of time when you stop what you are doing and rest.
spell **stage** **phase**	*I did a **spell of** work there.* *I stopped for water at one **stage**.* *It's just a **phase** that most teenagers go through.* *It's an early **stage**/**phase** of the project.*	a short period of time or of a particular activity. a period that forms part of an activity. a difficult period of time that sb/sth passes through (**stage** is also possible). a period of time that forms part of a process or the development of sth.
pass **elapse** **go by**	*Two years **passed** / **elapsed** / **went by** before I saw her again.* *Time **passed** / **went by** slowly.*	all the verbs describe the process of time; **elapse** is FML; **pass** and **go by** are often used with an adverb to describe how time happens.
soon or **shortly**	*He **soon** realized it was a mistake.* *I'll be with you **soon**/**shortly**.* *I left **soon**/**shortly** after Dina.* *He left **shortly** before midnight.*	quickly (after sth happens). in a short period of time from now. a short period after sb/sth. a short period before sb/sth.

❹ Circle the correct word(s). Both words may be correct.

1 There's bound to be a gap / an interval during the concert.
2 We're off soon / shortly but I'll give you a ring tomorrow.
3 Several days went by / elapsed before the solicitor rang me again.
4 She had a short spell / stage working for an oil company.
5 I woke up twice during / throughout the night.
6 She's reached a critical stage / phase in her career.
7 The late 70s was the height of the 'punk music' age / era.
8 I'm afraid we will have to curtail / prolong the meeting until 9.00.

❺ Complete the text with suitable time words.

I went to university in 1995, and I worked incredibly hard (1)_____ the time I was there.
I decided I needed a (2)_____ after that, so I travelled round Europe, spending nine months
in France. (3)_____ the time I was there, I had a short
(4)_____ of work teaching English. It was the most interesting (5)_____ of my life.
When I came back, I decided that as we were living in the computer (6)_____ , I'd get a job
in IT. It was a terrible mistake. I (7)_____ realized I didn't want to sit at a computer all day,
and although the company offered to (8)_____ my contract, I decided to quit. So, after a
three-year (9)_____ , I retrained as a teacher, and came to work in Finland. Almost five years
have (10)_____ since I made that decision.

📓 | Remember to test yourself

Review: Concepts

Unit 52

1 Circle the correct word.

1 An **outcome** is a cause / result of something.

2 You can **dent** a car / book .

3 **Coerce** means force / encourage someone.

4 **Repercussions** are usually good / bad .

5 You **provoke** a person / an object .

6 You can **generate** an income / a loss .

7 A **motive** is a design / reason .

8 A **detrimental** effect is positive / negative .

A Z **more words:** *pressurize sb, lie behind sth, **after**-effect, **domino** effect, the **upshot**, incite, induce*

Unit 53

1 Make words from the jumbled letters. Use the definitions to help you.

▶ HAFOLODES   a formal word for a lie. _falsehood_

1 MAHITEDULI   feeling ashamed because you have lost the respect of others. ....

2 HENOPY   a person who is not honest or sincere. ....

3 OGITERINTRAON   the process of asking somebody a lot of difficult questions. ....

4 MONYAOYNUSLA   in such a way that the speaker or writer's name is kept secret. ....

5 BESHELMIL   make a story more interesting by adding false details. ....

6 VADRYRESA   a formal word for an enemy or opponent. ....

7 PAUNALATELB   unpleasant and hard to accept. ....

8 MEYANL   used to introduce more exact information about a subject. ....

A Z **more words:** *a **pack** of lies, a **tall story**, **lie** through your teeth, **true** to your word, too good to be **true**, nothing could be further from the **truth***

Unit 54

2 Complete the crossword. The letters in the grey squares spell out another word. What is it?

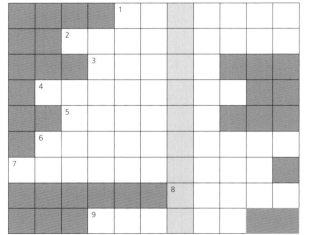

1 not serious or important
2 always existing and never seeming to change
3 occur, come up
4 deal with a problem or difficult situation
5 make a big effort to deal with a problem
6 able to express your thoughts clearly in words
7 make things worse
8 make .... of something = treat something as unimportant
9 requiring immediate attention

A Z **more words:** *predicament, dilemma, in a **quandary**, be at your **wit**s' end, **teething** troubles, **grapple***

Unit 55

1 Is the meaning of the words in italics the same or different? Write S or D.

1 The painting is *genuine / authentic*. …
2 It's *a brand new / an innovative* car. …
3 They want to *preserve it / do it up.* …
4 The building is quite *dilapidated / ramshackle*. …
5 I collect *ancient / antique* clocks. …
6 These shoes are *completely / brand* new. …
7 Beijing was *previously / formerly* called Peking. …
8 They want to *abandon / preserve* the place. …

A Z **more words:** *an **old** hand, a **new**comer, **new**fangled, new **blood**, be on its/your **last** legs, archaic*

Unit 56

1 Complete the words in the text.

At 17, Rob Greig was a very successful amateur golfer. Everyone said he had the (1) p_____
to go on and (2) m_____ it in the professional game, so after a (3) r_____ success in
the British Open last year, and just three days after his 18th birthday, Rob turned professional. He soon
realized how different the professional game was. 'There were experienced players out there ten years
older than me, so I knew I was up (4) a_____ it,' said Rob. 'At first it was obvious I was
(5) w_____ out of my (6) d_____ and I felt that I was (7) l_____ myself
down.' But Rob was determined not to let any (8) o_____ get in his (9) w_____ . He
kept working at his game to (10) o_____ the weaknesses, and his big (11) b_____
came last year in the Italian Open. He didn't put a foot (12) w_____ in the four rounds and
won by three clear shots. Since then he has gone from strength to (13) s_____ , and is now
really starting to (14) f_____ his enormous potential.

A Z **more words:** *an **overnight** success, an **out-and-out** failure/success, **pull** sth off, attain sth, backfire, pinnacle*

Unit 57

1 Complete the sentences in a suitable way.

1 I got to the station just as the train was leaving! In retrospect, I _____ .
2 Jack knows it's a major operation, but it could prolong _____ .
3 We left the cinema shortly _____ .
4 The children are 5, 12, and 17, so they're at different stages _____ .
5 He promised he would come and fix the tap, and in due course _____ .
6 I work weekdays mostly, but from time to time _____ .
7 The ceremony was very long and we _____ throughout it.
8 He was released from prison after two years, and with hindsight _____ .

A Z **more words:** *have **time** to kill, **third** time lucky, be (living) on **borrowed** time, **once** upon a time, nine **times** out of ten*

58 I can use everyday language

A An informal conversation 🎧

> DAN   I thought the **do** at Coleen's would be **a good laugh**, but actually it was **a bit of a drag**.
>
> TIM   Yeah, **lousy** I thought. And asking people to pay twenty **quid** was a bit of a **rip-off**. There wasn't much to eat either, but then Coleen is a bit **tight-fisted**, isn't she?
>
> DAN   She can be. And who was that **vile bloke** in the black leather jacket? He was awful.
>
> TIM   Yeah, he was **a pain**, wasn't he? He spent ages **moaning** about his flatmate, and then when I got up and went to the **loo**, he **pinched** my drink.
>
> DAN   **What a nerve!**

Glossary (*all these items are informal*)

do	a friendly informal meeting or party. SYN **get-together**.	**vile**	very bad or unpleasant (a **vile smell**). SYN **disgusting**.
a (good) laugh	an enjoyable experience.	**bloke**	a man. SYN **guy**.
a (bit of a) drag	a boring or annoying occasion or situation.	**a (real) pain**	an annoying person or situation. SYN **a pain in the neck**.
lousy	bad, unpleasant, or of poor quality (**a lousy film, lousy weather**).	**moan (about sth)**	complain (about sth) in a way that annoys people.
quid	a pound (£) in money (PL **quid** NOT ~~quids~~).	**loo**	a toilet.
rip-off	a thing that is not worth what you pay for it. **rip sb off** V.	**pinch sth**	steal sth. SYN **nick sth**.
tight-fisted	not generous with money. SYNS **tight, stingy**.	**What a nerve!**	used to say you think sb's behaviour is rude or inappropriate. SYN **What a cheek!**

❶ Replace the underlined word(s) with an informal equivalent.

1   It was a <u>man</u> in the street. ....
2   Who <u>stole</u> your pen? ....
3   He's always <u>complaining</u>. ....
4   What a <u>horrible</u> smell. ....

5   He is so <u>mean</u>. ....
6   It was ten <u>pounds</u>. ....
7   The film was <u>terrible</u>. ....
8   He's gone to the <u>toilet</u>. ....

❷ Complete the dialogues with a single word.

1   Is he very annoying?
2   Was the party enjoyable?
3   Did the company overcharge you?
4   Was the trip boring?
5   What a .... !
6   Are they having a do at the office?

~ Yes, he's a real ....
~ Yes, it was a good ....
~ Yeah, it was a ....
~ Yes, it was a bit of a ....
~ Yeah, it was incredibly rude, wasn't it?
~ Yeah, just an informal ....

Remember to test yourself

B Common informal words in spoken English 🎧

Word	Example	Meaning
darling/love	***Darling***, *have we got any eggs?* *What would you like,* ***love***?	used to address sb you love, and by some people in shops as a friendly way of addressing customers, particularly women.
broke	*I'm completely* ***broke***.	not having any money.
starving	*What's for lunch? I'm* ***starving***.	very hungry. SYN **dying for sth to eat**.
kip	*I might have a* ***kip*** *after lunch.*	a short sleep.
posh	*They stayed in a very* ***posh*** *hotel.*	elegant and expensive.
nosy (also **nosey**)	*I'm careful what I say to Cath; she's very* ***nosy***.	DISAPPROVING interested in things that don't concern you.
bug	*She picked up a* ***bug*** *on holiday.*	an infectious illness.
be into sth	*They're both* ***into*** *extreme sports.*	be very interested in sth as a hobby.
hammer sb	*Our team got absolutely* ***hammered*** *yesterday. We lost 5–1.*	defeat sb very heavily (often used when talking about sport). SYN **thrash sb**.
con sb	*I think that builder* ***conned*** *us.*	deceive and trick sb, especially in order to get money from them.
flak	*He's taken a lot of* ***flak*** *over this issue.*	criticism. SYN **stick**.
daft	*It was rather a* ***daft*** *thing to say.*	silly (sometimes in an amusing way).
ta	*Here's your change. ~* ***Ta***.	thanks. SYN **cheers**.
dodgy	*His idea sounds a bit* ***dodgy***.	causing suspicion; possibly dishonest.
laid-back	*He's very* ***laid-back***.	calm and relaxed. SYN **easy-going**.
racket	*What a terrible* ***racket***!	a large amount of noise. SYN **din**.

3 Write one word to describe the topic of conversation in each sentence.

1 He's got a bug. _____
2 What a racket next door! _____
3 I need a kip. _____
4 She's broke at the moment. _____
5 I'm starving. _____
6 Will he get much stick for this? _____

4 Replace one informal word with an equivalent informal word or phrase.

1 Here's your coffee. ~ Cheers. _____
2 What's that din? _____
3 I got a lot of stick for what I did. _____
4 When's dinner? I'm starving. _____
5 Do you need the car, love? _____
6 We were thrashed yesterday. _____

5 Complete the dialogues with a suitable informal word.

1 Do you want to go out this evening? ~ I can't afford to – I'm _____ .
2 What a stupid comment. ~ Yes, it was a bit _____ .
3 Is he fairly easy-going? ~ Oh yes, very _____ .
4 This is none of her business. ~ Well, tell her not to be so _____ .
5 Are you still feeling tired? ~ Yes, I think I'll go and have a _____ .
6 Did he really need money for the bus? ~ No, I think he _____ us.
7 He's a rather suspicious-looking bloke. ~ Yes, he looks a bit _____ .
8 I didn't know she was ill. ~ Yes, she picked up a _____ in Crete.
9 Do they go to the beach a lot? ~ Yes, they're both _____ surfing.
10 Their house looks very expensive. ~ Yes, it's a very _____ place.

Remember to test yourself

59 I can use idioms and set phrases (1)

A Discussing problems 🎧

A I'm having a hard time with this German course. New words seem to **go in one ear and out the other**. And when I want to say something, **my mind goes a complete blank**.
B Well, it takes time to learn a language, but you'll **get there** in the end.
A Yeah, **it's no good** moaning about it. Maybe I **could do with** some extra lessons.
B That's a possibility. Do you **have anyone in mind**?
A Not **off the top of my head**, no.
B Well, **your best bet is to** talk to your teacher. She may know someone who could do it.

Glossary

go in one ear and out (of) the other	If sth **goes in one ear and out of the other**, you forget it very quickly.
my mind goes (a complete) blank	= suddenly I cannot remember sth.
get there	be successful (**get somewhere** = make progress; **get nowhere** = make no progress).
it's no good + -ing	used to say that it is not useful doing sth. SYNS **there's no point in** + -ing, **it's no use** + -ing.
I (you/he, etc.) could do with sth	I (/you/he, etc.) need sth.
have sb/sth in mind	be thinking of sb/sth for a particular purpose.
off the top of my head	without thinking about sth carefully.
your best bet (is to …)	used when advising sb what to do. SYN **the best thing (to do is …)** .

spotlight   *idioms* and *set phrases*

An **idiom** is a group of words whose overall meaning is different from the meanings of the individual words, e.g. **under the weather** (= slightly ill). Idioms are commonly used in informal English.
A **set phrase** is a group of words which function as a complete unit, e.g. **sorry to keep you waiting**. The meaning may be easy to understand, but the same idea might be expressed differently in your own language.

❶ One word is missing. Where does it go? Write it at the end.

1 It's no worrying about it. _____
2 That's just off the of my head. _____
3 It goes in one and out the other. _____
4 Marty could with some help. _____
5 My went a complete blank. _____
6 I think he's feeling under weather. _____

❷ Complete the idiom or set phrase in each dialogue.

1 We need someone for the extra work. ~ True. Do you have anyone in _____ ?
2 What shall I do? ~ Off the top of my _____ , I'm not sure.
3 Did she ask you a question? ~ Yes, my mind went a complete _____ .
4 What shall we do? ~ Your best _____ is to ring the station.
5 They're making very slow progress. ~ Yes, but they'll get _____ eventually.
6 Has Marc gone to bed? ~ Yes, he was feeling a bit under the _____ .
7 Didn't we say we'd meet at 4 o'clock? ~ Yes. I'm sorry to _____ .
8 Can you remember the instructions? ~ No. They went in one ear _____ .

❸ ABOUT YOUR LANGUAGE How would you translate these idioms and set phrases into your own language? Write a translation, or talk to someone who speaks your language.

Remember to test yourself

B Idiomatic responses 🎧

Idiom or set phrase	Meaning
A Bob's coming, isn't he? B **Don't hold your breath**.	used to say you don't expect sth to happen even though sb said it would.
A Are they sure to win the election? B Yeah. It's **a foregone conclusion**.	used to say that sth is a result that is certain to happen.
A Are you going to the party? B **You bet**.	used to emphasize that you are keen to do sth.
A It's very cold today. B **You can say that again**.	used to agree completely with what sb has just said.
A Have you got Saturday off? B **No such luck**, I'm afraid.	used to express your disappointment that sth is not going to happen.
A Sal said she's too busy to help us. B **A likely story**.	used ironically to say you don't believe what sb has told you.
A Where's Patsy? B **I haven't the faintest idea**.	used to say you don't know sth. SYNS **Don't ask me. Your guess is as good as mine**.
A You look very stressed. B Yes, **it's been one of those days**.	used to say you have had a hard day.
A Shall I apply for that job? B **You've got nothing to lose**.	used to say there is no reason for sb not to do sth.
A Rani's going out with a film star. B **You're kidding**.	used to say that you think sth cannot be true and must be a joke. SYNS **You're joking. You can't be serious**.
A I hurt my toe, then I burnt my hand. B Oh dear. **It's not your day**, is it?	used when several unpleasant or unfortunate things happen on the same day.
A Can we go in if we're not members? B **No way**.	used to say that sth is not at all possible or not allowed. SYN **no chance**.

4 Circle the correct word/phrase.

1 **A likely story** is one that you think is probably true / false .
2 If you reply **Don't ask me**, it means you don't know the answer / don't want to answer .
3 If you say **You're kidding**, you think the other person is being / not being serious.
4 **No way** means it's not practical / possible .
5 **I haven't the faintest idea** means I don't care / I don't know .
6 **Don't hold your breath** means you expect / don't expect something to happen.

5 Complete a suitable idiom in response to these statements or questions.

1 I've just won the lottery! ~ You ....
2 Could I borrow your Dad's car? ~ No ....
3 Why did they leave so early? ~ No idea. Your guess ....
4 Has it been busy in the office today? ~ Yes, it's been ....
5 Are you going to the wedding? ~ Yes, you ....
6 Do you think they'll win? ~ Definitely. It's a ....
7 I won some money. Did you? ~ No such ....
8 Shall we enter for the competition? ~ Why not? We've got nothing ....
9 It's hot in here, isn't it? ~ Yes, you can ....
10 My car broke down this morning, and a tooth fell out this afternoon. ~ It's not ....

Remember to test yourself

60 I can **use idioms and set phrases (2)** Do Unit 59 first

A Commenting on a situation 🎧

Some idioms and set phrases are commonly used to express an opinion about a situation.

> We can borrow money if need be, but it's **a last resort**.

> She wouldn't admit her mistake because she didn't want to **lose face**.

> She's trying her best, but I think she's **fighting a losing battle**.

> I've got a new computer, and frankly **it's more trouble than it's worth**.

> I think my nephew will do well as long as he **keeps his feet on the ground**.

> You can eat what you like and drinks are free. Sounds **too good to be true**, doesn't it?

> He's got his own flat, but his mum still cooks for him – he's got **the best of both worlds**.

> She's always terribly serious. I think she needs to **let her hair down** a bit.

> The trouble with Rolf is that – most of the time – he **lives in a world of his own**.

Glossary

a last/final resort	an action you will take if there is no other option (**as a last resort** SYN **if all else fails**).
it's more trouble than it's worth	used to say the disadvantages of sth are greater than the advantages.
the best of both worlds	a situation in which you have the advantages of two things without any disadvantages.
lose face	look stupid or be less respected because of sth you have done.
keep your feet on the ground	remain sensible and realistic about life.
let your hair down	relax and enjoy yourself.
fight a losing battle	try to do sth that will almost certainly fail.
too good to be true	used to express doubts about a surprisingly good situation.
live/be in a world of your own	spend your time imagining things, and not be aware of things around you.

1 Cover the text and glossary, then complete these set phrases and idioms.

1 let your hair ....
2 if all else ....
3 fight a losing ....
4 it's more trouble than it's ....
5 too good to be ....
6 live in a world ....
7 the best of both ....
8 keep your feet on the ....

2 Complete each dialogue with a suitable set phrase or idiom.

1 Is Karen a bit of a dreamer? ~ Yes, she lives in ....
2 You don't want to use your savings? ~ No, that's a last ....
3 He thinks he can achieve anything. ~ Yes, he needs to ....
4 So you may have to sell your car. ~ Yes, if all ....
5 Did he try to cover up his mistake? ~ Yes, he didn't want to ....
6 You mean everything is free? ~ Yes, it sounds too ....
7 She looks as if she's enjoying herself ~ Yes, she's really ....
8 It's near the sea but close to the city. ~ Great, so you've got ....

3 ABOUT YOUR LANGUAGE How would you translate these idioms into your own language? Write your answers, or talk to someone who speaks your language.

Remember to test yourself

B Adding tone and emphasis 🎧

Some idioms and set phrases add extra politeness or emphasis, or prepare the listener for what you are going to say, or give a more personal interpretation of the message.

Idiom or set phrase	Meaning
*Do you know if they're married, **by any chance?***	used to add politeness to a question (also: *Do you **happen to** know if they're married?*).
***If you don't mind my/me asking**, how much did it cost?*	used before a question which you think may be sensitive.
*We'd like to see you, but **the thing is**, we don't know what time we'll get there.*	used to introduce an explanation, and often one that suggests there is a problem.
*I think the film is **every bit as** good **as** his last one.*	used to emphasize the comparative; equally good, bad, interesting, etc.
*I may get the job – **you never know**.*	used to say that you can never be certain about future events, so anything is possible.
***Guess what**! Ed and Sue are getting married.*	used before giving sb surprising or exciting news.
*He doesn't look rich, but **believe it or not**, he owns a castle in Bavaria.*	used to introduce information which is true but surprising.
*He's been working since 7 o'clock this morning, so **no wonder** he's tired.*	used to emphasize the fact that sth is not surprising.
*Where **on earth** did you get those boots?*	used after *wh*- questions to indicate surprise, and sometimes annoyance, about sth.
*I would say, **all things being equal**, that women are better communicators than men.*	used to say that sth is true if there are no other factors affecting it.
*The room is empty but, **for some reason**, we're not allowed to use it.*	used to say, often with slight annoyance, that you don't know the reason or don't understand it.
***I have to admit**, he's very good at his job.*	used to agree reluctantly that sth is true.

4 Complete the idiom or set phrase in each sentence.

1 _____ what! I've got a new job.
2 I don't think he has the ability to do it, but you never _____ .
3 What on _____ are you doing here?
4 I made a special trip to the post office, but for _____ reason, they closed early.
5 I have to _____ , France are a good team – even though I'm English!
6 He won all his matches, so no _____ he's delighted.
7 All things being _____ , I think we'll lose.
8 We went trekking in the desert and, _____ it or not, it started raining!

5 Add a suitable idiom or set phrase to these sentences. Put an arrow to show where it goes.

1 Do you know if it's open? _____
2 How old are you? _____
3 She looks about 20, but she's only 13. _____
4 He's been very ill, so he looks thin. _____
5 I'm hoping to go, but I've got a meeting on the same day. _____
6 There are many exceptions, but I think men are better cooks than women. _____
7 The book is as violent as all his others. _____
8 It was a beautiful day, but the beach was deserted; I can't think why. _____

Remember to test yourself

61 I can **use set phrases with two key words** 🎧

These set phrases consist of two words belonging to the same grammatical category, joined by *and*, *or*, and *to*. The word order is fixed, i.e. *back and forth*, not *forth and back*. Many are made up of synonyms or opposites.

Example	Meaning
We've been going **back and forth** all day.	from one place to another and then back again, many times.
First and foremost we need a plan.	more than anything else.
I thought **long and hard** before taking the job.	for a long time.
They'll be here **sooner or later**.	at some time in the future.
You're wearing your jumper **back to front**.	with the back where the front should be.
I enjoy the **hustle and bustle** of city life.	busy and noisy activity.
I learnt how to use a computer by **trial and error**.	a process of trying to solve a problem in different ways until you are successful.
What are our **aims and objectives**?	things you want to achieve.
That's against the **rules and regulations**.	rules.
Who is responsible for **law and order**?	safe and peaceful conditions in society when people obey the law.
Max was very **bright and cheerful** today.	happy and lively.
The children got home **safe and sound**.	safely; not harmed, damaged, lost, etc.
I'm **sick and tired of** this weather.	bored with or annoyed about sth, and wanting it to stop. SYN **fed up with sth**.
He badly needs a job, so he can't really afford to **pick and choose**.	choose only those things that you like or want.
They were **pushing and shoving** behind us.	**shove** push in a rough way.

1 Write eight set phrases using words from the box.

push	pick	back	first	long	sooner
rules	front	sick	regulations	foremost	
choose	tired	later	hard	shove	

....
....
....
....

spotlight   *bribery* and *corruption*

Bribery is the offering of money or another incentive to sb to persuade them to take part in an activity, usually something dishonest. **bribe sb** v. **Corruption** is illegal or dishonest behaviour, especially on the part of sb in power. **corrupt** ADJ. The two words are often used together.
*There are still allegations of **bribery and corruption** in the police force.*

2 Complete the set phrase in each sentence.

1   I saw Joelle earlier. She's very bright and .... today.
2   There's no law and .... in the place: just bribery and .... everywhere.
3   They said 4 o'clock, so they should be here sooner or ....
4   First and ...., we have got to establish our aims and ....
5   I used to love the hustle and .... of city life, but I'm sick and .... of it now.
6   I didn't have the instructions, so I just worked it out by trial and ....
7   It was a terrible flight, but we finally got here safe and ....
8   I'm moving stuff from Pete's flat to my flat, and I've been back and .... all day.

Remember to test yourself

62 I can **use similes** 🎧

We form most similes with *as* + adjective + *as* + noun, and some with verb or noun + *like* + noun. Similes with *as* emphasize the meaning of the adjective. (Note that the first *as* is often omitted.)

Key word	Simile
gold	*The kids were **as good as gold** today.* = well behaved
feather	*I picked up the little girl – she was **as light as a feather**.*
bat	*I'm afraid I'm **blind as a bat**.* (used humorously)
post	*My father is **deaf as a post**.* (used humorously)
ox	*John will carry it – he's **as strong as an ox**.*
rake	*My sister's **as thin as a rake**.*
mouse	*The baby's been **as quiet as a mouse**.*

Key word	Simile
sheet	*Ken went **as white as a sheet**.* = white with fear or illness
beetroot	*Sally went **as red as a beetroot**.* = very embarrassed
bone	*The ground is **as dry as a bone** at the moment.*
cake	*The new model is **selling like hot cakes**.* = selling very quickly or in large numbers
log	*I **slept like a log** last night.* = slept very well
dream	*The plan **worked like a dream**.* = was very successful
sieve	*Sometimes I've got **a mind like a sieve**.* = a bad memory

❶ Complete the similes.

1 He's been as quiet as a ....
2 I'm sure this new computer game will sell like hot ....
3 We badly need rain because the garden is as dry as a ....
4 When I picked her up she was as light as a ....
5 My father always sleeps like a ....
6 She can't remember what she did with it; she's got a mind like a ....
7 My builder is as strong as an ....
8 I fitted a new ink cartridge and the printer's working like a .... now.

❷ Choose a suitable simile to describe these people and things.

1 My grandfather can't hear a thing. ....
2 My grandmother can't see a thing. ....
3 My girlfriend needs to put on weight. ....
4 The plan was very successful. ....
5 She looked horrified. ....
6 The children behaved very well. ....
7 She was very embarrassed. ....
8 He often forgets things. ....

Remember to test yourself

63 I can use a range of phrasal verbs

A Phrasal verbs with more formal equivalents 🎧

Phrasal verb	More formal equivalent
If you **talk** someone **into** doing something,	you **persuade** them to do it.
If you **talk** someone **out of** doing something,	you **dissuade** them **from** doing it.
If you **bring** a topic **up** in a conversation,	you **raise** the topic.
If you **get** your ideas **across** to someone,	you **communicate with** them clearly.
If you **butt in** on a conversation,	you **interrupt** a conversation.
If someone **drags out** a discussion,	they **prolong** it (= make it longer than necessary).
If you **own up** to something,	you **confess** to it (= admit you did sth wrong).
If someone **goes on at** you,	they **criticize** you for sth you have done.
If you **hit back at** someone who has criticized you,	you **retaliate** (against them).
If the government **does away with** a tax,	it **abolishes** it.
If you **call off** a meeting,	you **cancel** it.
If you **make up for** something,	you **compensate for** it (= do sth good to balance the bad effects of it).
If someone **makes out** that they're rich,	they **claim** that they are rich (= say that they are rich even though it may not be true).
If you are **taken in** by someone's charm,	you are **deceived** by it.
If you have a row with someone and then **make it up with** them,	you **are reconciled** with them (= become friends with them after a disagreement).
If you **take** a machine **apart**,	you **dismantle** it (also **take it to pieces**).

1 Find a verb in the text below with the same meaning as these verbs.

▶ called it off *cancelled it*   2 make out ....   4 bring up ....   6 drag out ....
1 get across ....   3 went on at ....   5 butted in ....   7 hit back at him ....

Memo to Alex Parker	From Joey Cassani

I'm afraid I've had a problem with Adam Lewis at SBP. I organized a meeting with him, but he cancelled it ✓ at the last minute. He did the same this week, so I decided to raise the issue with him. I tried to explain politely that we couldn't carry on like this, but he interrupted continually and I wasn't able to communicate my message clearly. He even tried to claim that I'd been late for meetings myself (which was completely untrue), and he criticized me for other things too. Anyway, I didn't want to prolong the discussion, as I knew I might retaliate; so in the end I left it.

2 Rewrite the sentences using the word in capitals at the end as part of a phrasal verb.

1 I never expected him to confess to the crime. UP ....
2 Nothing can compensate for the loss of earnings. MAKE ....
3 She tried to dissuade me from giving up my job. OUT ....
4 Do you think they'll ever abolish the monarchy? DO ....
5 He isn't easily deceived. IN ....
6 Try and persuade him to come. INTO ....
7 Did they dismantle the shed? TAKE ....
8 Have they made friends again? UP ....

Remember to test yourself

B Phrasal verbs in context 🎧

> I **bumped into** Sue in town last week and she was **asking after** you. We arranged to meet for dinner last night, but she didn't **show up**. I guess something must've **cropped up** . . .

> I was aching all over and I realized I must be **going down with** the flu. I was hoping to **shake it off** with painkillers, but once the effects **wore off**, I felt dreadful. I was in bed for days and even **missed out on** my best friend's wedding.

> My brother's brilliant at **picking up** languages; he can **get by** in German, Italian, and Swedish, whereas with me, it takes ages for things to **sink in**. But I started learning Spanish last year – I've really **stuck at** it and I feel I'm getting somewhere now.

spotlight | Phrasal verbs: meanings and forms

Many phrasal verbs have more than one meaning and construction, e.g. **pick up** and **pick sb/sth up**.
Sales have **picked up** (= improved).
The wind **picked up** (= got stronger).
She **picked** *me* **up** (= collected me in her car).
This radio can't **pick up** *the World Service* (= receive an electronic signal).
You can also **pick up** (= acquire) an illness or a bad habit.

Glossary

bump into sb	meet sb by chance.
ask after sb	ask sb how sb else is, or what they are doing.
show up	arrive where you have arranged to meet sb. SYN **turn up**.
crop up	happen unexpectedly. SYN **come up**.
go down with sth	become sick or ill with sth. SYN **catch** sth.
shake sth off	get rid of sth, such as an illness or a problem.
wear off	(of a pain, a feeling, or an effect) gradually disappear or stop.
miss out on sth	miss an opportunity to do or have sth.
pick sth up	learn a new skill easily and without effort.
get by	If you **get by** in a language, you can speak at a basic level.
sink in	become completely understood or able to be remembered.
stick at sth	continue to work in a determined way to achieve sth.

❸ Correct any mistakes in the sentences. Be careful: some sentences are correct.

1 She's fluent in Russian, and she can go by in Hungarian too. _____
2 I meant to ring him, but something cropped out and it slipped my mind. _____
3 You'll only make progress if you really stick at your studies. _____
4 My life is so dull. I always have the feeling I'm missing out of something. _____
5 Did you bump in her or had you arranged to meet? _____
6 I think she's very fond of you; she always asks after you when I see her. _____

❹ Replace the underlined verbs with a phrasal verb with the same meaning.

1 After three hours, he <u>arrived</u> without a word of apology. _____
2 You can't use your mobile in the mountains – it's impossible to <u>receive</u> a signal. _____
3 I just can't <u>get rid of</u> the feeling that someone is watching me. _____
4 He had to say it several times before the news <u>was completely understood</u>. _____
5 It's not that easy to <u>acquire</u> a language just by living in the country. _____
6 All the people I work with seem to have <u>caught</u> the flu. _____
7 Once I'd had the injection, the pain started to <u>gradually disappear</u>. _____
8 As the breeze started to <u>get stronger</u>, we set off for the cottage. _____

Remember to test yourself

> I'm not very keen on the flat, or the area. **Mind you**, it's better than my last place. **Incidentally**, do you know how Marek's getting on in his new flat?

ASMA   Do you think you'll go back to the same hotel?

BRAD   Well, **as a matter of fact** we were a bit disappointed the last time we were there. **By and large** the staff were still very nice, but the food has really gone downhill.

SIMON   The company is likely to move its headquarters to Brussels. **As for** Deborah, she'll probably have to get a job with another insurance firm.

TANYA   Yes, or **alternatively**, she could stay with the company in the UK, but in a different branch.

> I don't think Alistair should apply for the job in Munich. He doesn't have that much experience; and **in any case**, he doesn't speak German.

> **It's true** that Peter was only trying to help. **Even so**, he shouldn't have got involved.

> I may get the bus, or take a taxi if necessary. **At any rate**, I'll be there on time, so don't worry. And **as I was saying**, if you would like me to bring anything, just let me know.

Glossary

mind you	INF used to add a further comment which is usually a contrast or a surprise, but can also be an explanation. SYN **still**.
incidentally	used to change the conversation to a different topic. SYN **by the way**.
as for	used to start talking about sb or sth new that is connected with what you were talking about before.
alternatively	used to introduce an idea that is a second choice or possibility.
it's true	used to agree with an idea made by the previous speaker (but often before disagreeing). SYN **I agree**.
even so	used to introduce a counter-argument or return to one the speaker has already made. SYNS **all the same**, **nevertheless**.
as a matter of fact	used to say what you really think, or to introduce information which is not what the listener expects to hear. SYNS **actually**, **to be honest**, **to tell you the truth**.
by and large	used to introduce a generalization. SYNS **to a large extent**, **on the whole**, **broadly speaking**.
in any case	used to introduce an additional point and one that is often conclusive or the most important. SYNS **besides**, **anyway**.
at any rate	used to say that sth is true or sth will happen in spite of other things mentioned. SYNS **anyway**, **anyhow**.
as I was saying	used to return the conversation to sth you said earlier.

spotlight   *anyway*

In spoken English, **anyway** can mean **in any case** (*see above*) or **at any rate** (*see above*), but it is commonly used to change the topic of conversation:

Yes, next year could be a difficult time. ***Anyway****, let's not worry about that now. What would you like to eat?*

Remember to test yourself

1 Complete the phrases with words from the box to form ten discourse markers.

| case | extent | honest | you | rate | speaking | fact | so | same | whole |

1 mind _____
2 at any _____
3 even _____
4 as a matter of _____

5 on the _____
6 in any _____
7 broadly _____

8 to be _____
9 to a large _____
10 all the _____

2 Correct the error in the discourse marker in each sentence.

1 Broad speaking, it was very interesting. _____
2 We had a fantastic time. All same, I was glad to get home. _____
3 We can take the bags, or alternative leave them here. _____
4 I don't like the sea because the water is dirty. In every case, I can't swim very well. _____
5 To say you the truth, I didn't like it very much. _____
6 The restaurant's great, but as I was telling, it's not good for kids. _____

3 Replace the underlined word/phrase with a different word/phrase that has the same meaning.

1 I think he was from the Czech Republic. By the way, what was his name again? _____
2 The film has had great reviews, but to tell you the truth, I didn't like it. _____
3 To a large extent, you can get by without speaking the language. _____
4 I was disappointed with broadband. Still, it's faster than it was before. _____
5 We can't give Mike a lift – he lives miles away. And in any case, the car's full. _____
6 I agree some of the definitions could be shorter. Nevertheless, it's a good dictionary. _____
7 I may find out the results this Wednesday, or I may have to wait until the weekend.
   At any rate, I'll phone you as soon as I know. OK? _____
8 It's a lovely gallery, but as a matter of fact, we were only there for an hour. _____

4 Complete the sentences and dialogues with suitable discourse markers from the box.

| by the way | alternatively | to be honest | as for | by and large |
| all the same | besides | mind you | it's true | |

1 I read that public transport was very cheap, but _____ I thought it was quite expensive.
2 We might go to a camping site. _____ we could just stay in a B & B each night.
3 _____ that a lot of people drop litter, which is very anti-social. _____ , you can't start sending people to prison for that kind of offence.
4 It wasn't a great place to stay. _____ , it didn't cost a lot.
5 A I've packed lots of jumpers so I'm prepared for the cold weather.
   B Good, you'll need them. _____ , what time does the plane take off?
6 I've been told there's a very good Chinese restaurant in the main square. _____ somewhere to stay, I'm afraid I can't help you.
7 You won't want to climb that hill – it's very steep. And _____ , it's too far away.
8 It can be cold in winter, but _____ it doesn't snow much.

5 ABOUT YOUR LANGUAGE Look at the texts on page 162 and try to translate the discourse markers into your own language. Remember it is spoken language.

Remember to test yourself

65 I can use vague language 🎧

You can use the vague language below when you don't want or need to be precise.

A How long will the trip take?
B Three weeks **or thereabouts**.

A He earns **stacks of** money, doesn't he?
B Mmm, **somewhere in the region of** €100,000.

A He's **something to do with** advertising.
B Yes, **or something along those lines**.

A She looks a lot older. Is she ill **or something**?
B I don't know; I'm **kind of** worried about her.

A We'll buy that car **somehow or other**.
B I've got £1,000, **give or take** a few quid.

A How much did you pay for that **stuff**?
B Oh, fifty **odd**, I think.

Glossary

or thereabouts	used after a number, quantity, etc. to show that it is approximate. SYN **or so**.
stacks of sth	INF a large quantity of sth. SYNS **tons/loads/bags of sth** INF.
(somewhere) in the region of	(used before a number) approximately. SYN **round about**.
something to do with (sth)	in some way connected with (sth).
kind of	INF to some extent, but in a way that is hard to explain. SYN **sort of**.
somehow (or other)	in some way or by some means, although you don't know exactly how.
give or take sth	used for talking about numbers which are not exact.
stuff	INF used to refer to things when it is obvious what you are talking about, or you don't know the name, or the name isn't important.
(-)odd	INF (after a number) a little more or less than the number (*thirty-odd people*).

1 One word is missing in each sentence. Where does it go? Write it at the end.

1 The whole trip cost somewhere the region of €380. _____
2 She was just sort pretending to be ill; in fact she wasn't. _____
3 We seem to have of rice; I'd better make paella. _____
4 There were about 100 people or of that sort. _____
5 We'll leave at seven, give take a few minutes. _____
6 I've got a meeting tonight but I'll finish my essay by tomorrow or other. _____
7 I'll send a card or letter, or something along those. _____
8 Could you give me a ring about 6.30 tonight? _____

> **spotlight** *or something*
>
> You can use these phrases when you are being vague.
> *She's a nurse **or something like that / or something along those lines**.*
> *He works in publishing **or something / or something of that sort**.*

2 Rewrite the sentence, making it more vague. Use the word at the end of the line, and make any necessary changes.

▶ We invited a hundred to the wedding. SO We invited a hundred or so to the wedding.
1 I've completed 50 per cent of the project. ROUND _____
2 He looks depressed. KIND _____
3 His job is in marketing. DO _____
4 Do you know who all those CDs and DVDs belong to? STUFF _____
5 I imagine we'll get forty-nine people at the meeting. ODD _____
6 We've got vegetables so I'd better make some soup. TONS _____
7 She must be getting on for 80, I would say. THEREABOUTS _____
8 We could get him a book for his birthday. SOMETHING _____

Remember to test yourself

66 I can **use sayings and proverbs**

A Famous last words 🎧

Some sayings are concise ways of explaining something, or commenting on a situation.

Example	Meaning
A He thinks the exam will be easy. B Oh, **famous last words**.	used when you think sb is being too confident about something that is going to happen.
A Are tickets available? B Yes, but it's **first come, first served.**	people will be served or dealt with in the order in which they arrive or ask for sth.
A She ought to pass easily. B Yes, but **you can never tell**.	you can never be sure about sth because things are not always what they appear to be.
A She's not going to apply again. B No, **once bitten, twice shy**, I guess.	after an unpleasant experience, you are careful to avoid sth similar.
A You should tell him he's wrong. B Hmm, **easier said than done**.	it is easy to talk about something, but it is much more difficult to do it.
A Can anyone come this evening? B Yes, **the more the merrier**.	if there are more people or things, the situation will be better and more enjoyable.
A How's the new job? B **So far, so good**.	used to say that everything is fine at the moment but you know things may become more difficult.
A Barry never writes or phones. B Well, **out of sight, out of mind** – I suppose.	used to say that sb stops thinking about people when they are not with them.
A I met two of your colleagues today. B Oh, it's **a small world**, isn't it?	used to express your surprise when you meet sb you know unexpectedly, or when you are talking to sb and realize they know people who you know.
A He said you were a hypocrite. B Well, that's **the pot calling the kettle black**.	used about sb who criticizes people for faults that they have themselves.

❶ Cross out the wrong word and write the correct one to form the saying.

1 It's a little world. _____
2 Once eaten twice shy. _____
3 The more the happier. _____
4 Famous last phrase. _____

5 So far, no good. _____
6 First come, are served. _____
7 Out of eyes, out of mind. _____
8 Easier spoken than done. _____

❷ Complete the saying in each sentence.

1 He'll never get married again: once bitten, _____ .
2 We'll have tougher times ahead but so far, _____ .
3 Since I've been here I've met four people I know. It's a small _____ .
4 When she's with you she makes you feel important, but out of sight, _____ .
5 I think he'll do well, but you know, you can _____ .
6 They want to limit the numbers, but in my opinion the more _____ .
7 She suggested I tried asking for a rise, but that's easier _____ .
8 Air passengers are given seats on the basis of first come, _____ .
9 He said that I look stupid when I dance. Talk about the pot _____ .

❸ ABOUT YOUR LANGUAGE How would you translate these sayings into your own language? Write a translation, or talk to another student who speaks your language.

Remember to test yourself

B Practice makes perfect 🎧

Many sayings give advice, or say something that is generally true.

Example	Meaning
He tends to get what he wants because **money talks**[1].	If you have a lot of money, you will have more power and influence than other people.
He treats her very badly but she doesn't realize; **love is blind**[2] in her case.	When you love somebody, you cannot see their faults.
Don't worry – **lightning never strikes twice (in the same place)**[3].	An unusual or unpleasant event won't happen in the same place or to the same person twice.
Don't say anything at the moment: **let sleeping dogs lie**[4].	Avoid mentioning a particularly difficult subject which may cause trouble.
She spends hours at the piano, but **practice makes perfect**.	If you do sth repeatedly, you will become very good at it.
I haven't heard from my son for weeks, but usually **no news is good news**.	If you haven't had any news, then it's probable that nothing has gone wrong and things are fine.
It seems cruel to do it, but in this case **the end justifies the means**.	Bad or unfair methods of doing sth are acceptable if the results of the action are good or positive.
You mustn't do that: **two wrongs don't make a right**.	If sb does sth bad to you, that is not a reason to do sth bad to them.
Let's do this together: **two heads are better than one**.	Two people can achieve more than one person working alone.
He thinks **blood is thicker than water**.	Family relationships are stronger than any other.
He can say what he likes, but **actions speak louder than words**.	What a person actually does is more important than what they say they will do.
He believes in an **eye for an eye (and a tooth for a tooth)**.	Used to say that you should punish somebody by doing to them what they have done to you.
Don't forget that **charity begins at home**.	You should help and care for your own family first before you start helping others.
She may be very attractive, but **beauty is only skin-deep**.	How someone looks is less important than their character.
They finally turned up at 8.30, but **better late than never**.	It is better to arrive late or achieve sth late, than not arrive or achieve anything at all.
The mountain road is dangerous so go slowly – **better safe than sorry**.	It is better to be careful than to take a risk or act too quickly and later regret it.
Live and let live – that's my **motto**.	Accept other people's opinions and ways of life, even if they are different from your own. A **motto** is a phrase which expresses the beliefs of a person or organization.
Enjoy yourself: **you're only young once**.	Young people should enjoy themselves because in later life they will have more to worry about.
In my view **prevention is better than cure**.	It is better to stop something bad from happening than try to deal with it after it has happened.

Remember to test yourself

4 Look at the sayings on page 166. Write down two which are connected with each of these topics.

1   family: ....
2   relationships: ....
3   morality: ....
4   tolerance: ....
5   progress: ....

5 Write down six sayings using words from the box.

cure	actions	love	better than	louder than	blood	words	water
lightning	charity	at home	never	is	prevention	blind	strikes
is	begins	twice	speak	thicker than	is		

....

....

....

6 Complete these sayings.

1   Better late than ....
2   Better safe than ....
3   You're only young ....
4   Let sleeping dogs ....
5   Practice makes ....
6   Two heads are ....

7   No news is ....
8   The end ....
9   Two wrongs ....
10 Lightning never ....
11 Prevention is better ....
12 An eye ....

7 Use a suitable saying to respond to each of these situations.

▶   I came down slowly – I didn't want to fall over. Better safe than sorry!
1   He works on his English for three hours every day. ....
2   Shall we work on this problem together? ....
3   When she finishes university she wants to travel round Europe. ....
4   I would always go to my family for help before asking friends. ....
5   He went to hospital over three hours ago, but we haven't heard anything. ....
6   Why does he get a seat first just because he owns lots of companies? ....
7   If he takes my exercise book, I'll take his dictionary. ....
8   They finally got here, but they missed the first part. ....
9   We don't share the same opinions on things, but I just accept it. ....
10 It's a very sensitive subject with Amélie. Should I say something? ....
11 She doesn't seem to see her husband's faults. ....
12 After what he did to me, I'll get my revenge. ....

8 ABOUT YOU Which sayings on page 166 do you think are generally true or represent good advice? Write your answers or ask another student.

9 ABOUT YOUR LANGUAGE How would you translate these sayings into your own language? Do you have equivalent sayings? Write a translation, or talk to another student who speaks your language.

Remember to test yourself

Review: Spoken English

Unit 58

1 One letter in one word is wrong in each line. Cross out the mistake and correct it.

1   Would you believe it! Someone's ticked my bike again! ....

2   Madonna got a lot of flan from the press last year. ....

3   I'm not feeling too good – I think I must have a rug. ....

4   He tried to borrow €200 from me – what a creek! ....

5   They were making a terrible jacket so I asked them to turn it down. ....

6   It's no good trying to get him to pay; he's really light. ....

7   Have you got anything in the fridge? I'm lying for something to eat. ....

8   I like most parties, but that one was a bit of a drug; in fact I left early. ....

2 Complete the email using words from the box in the correct form.

cheek	lousy	broke	neck	stick	guy	laugh	moan	back	bloke

Hi Sven
Hope you had a nice weekend – it's a pity you weren't here because we had a really good
(1)........................ on Saturday night at Erno's. We were completely (2)........................ after
going to that night club on Friday, so we decided to stay in and we invited Kim, Des, and a
couple of other (3)........................ round for a drink. One of these other (4)........................ ,
whose name was Phil, was a real pain in the (5)........................ – he just kept
(6)........................ all evening about everything: football, the state of the country, the
weather, on and on . . . and then he started giving Erno some (7)........................ because he
didn't think Erno's cooking was very good (in fact, he's right, it is pretty (8)........................),
but we thought it was a bit of a (9)........................ , especially as he'd done nothing to help.
Anyway, you know Erno, he's pretty (10) laid-........................ – he just smiled and then he
started to laugh, and then he couldn't stop, and soon we were all laughing . . .

A Z more words: **off colour**, to **nip** out/round, it's bust, **clear** off!, a doddle/cinch, a **tip-off / tip**
sb off

Unit 59

1 Cross out the incorrect word in each response.

1   Do you think he'll be on time? ~ Your guess is as good as mine is.

2   Mark's split up with Jessica. ~ You're not kidding! I don't believe it.

3   You look completely worn out. ~ Yes, it's been one of those bad days.

4   What time will Gerry be back? ~ Don't you ask me. He never tells me a word.

5   Did you get tickets for the match? ~ No any such luck, I'm afraid.

6   Have you had the test results back? ~ No, but there's no use of worrying.

7   Did you speak to Jack about his room? ~ Yes, but it goes in one ear and out the other ear.

8   Should I try ringing the bank again? ~ Well, you've got nothing for to lose.

A Z more words. Look at idioms under 'far' in your dictionary, e.g. go **far**, not **far** off. Make a list of
all the other useful idioms in your notebook.

Unit 60

1 Complete the dialogue.

A How are things going at home?

B Well, we've got new neighbours upstairs and – guess (1)_____ – they're every
   (2)_____ as annoying as the last lot who lived there.

A Oh, how awful. Why?

B Well, believe it or (3)_____ , this family have even worse taste in music and play it till three
   in the morning.

A No (4)_____ you're fed up. What on (5)_____ can you do about it?

B I'm moving – the whole business is more trouble than it's (6)_____ .

A Yes, you'd just end up fighting a losing (7)_____ and feel frustrated. And you never
   (8)_____ , living somewhere else might be just the change you need.

2 Put the words in order to make sentences.

1 equal / things / centre / in / rather / being / the / I'd / live / all _____
2 of / in / to / world / own / she / live / seems / a / her _____
3 as / is / exercise / what / as / bit / eat / important / every / you _____
4 he / for / him / reason / I / answer / but / rang / some / didn't _____
5 you / asking / me / if / charge / did / you / much / how / don't / they / mind / ? _____
6 let / down / great / week / to / hard / hair / after / a / it's / your _____

A Z more words: *pay **lip service** to sth, **pull** the wool over someone's eyes, get the **wrong** end of
the stick, turn a **blind** eye to sth, a new **lease** of life, can't make **head** nor tail of sth*

Unit 61

1 One word is wrong in each sentence. Cross it out and write the correct word at the end.

1 I love having the option to pick and select the songs on my iPod.   _____
2 You've got your jumper on backwards to front; turn it round.   _____
3 It is crucial that our aims and objects are absolutely clear.   _____
4 There's something exciting about the hustle and hassle of a big city.   _____
5 We ended up going back and fourth several times till we found the shop. _____
6 She's a delightful colleague – always so light and cheerful.   _____
7 I had to give in and obey the rules and regulators in the institution.   _____
8 I couldn't do it at first, but you eventually get there by trial and mistake. _____

A Z more words: ***take** it or leave it, **prim** and proper, **down and out**, **short** and sweet, **scrimp**
and save, **odds and ends***

Unit 62

1 Complete the similes.

1 The children were as .... as gold.

2 She's as .... as a mouse.

3 The ground is as .... as a bone.

4 My son's as .... as an ox.

5 I went as .... as a beetroot.

6 The software package worked like a ....

7 I've got a memory like a ....

8 She sleeps like a ....

A Z **more words:** *dead* as a doornail/dodo, *safe* as houses, *sick* as a parrot, *tough* as old boots, *easy* as pie, *hard* as nails, be like *gold dust*

Unit 63

1 Match the phrasal verbs with a more formal synonym on the right.

do away with	own up	crop up
take sth apart	take sb in	drag sth out
hit back	butt in	turn up

prolong sth	arrive	interrupt
deceive sb	abolish	dismantle sth
retaliate	confess	happen unexpectedly

....

....

....

A Z **more words:** Look up the phrasal verbs related to *live, drop, stand, catch,* and *talk.* Write down any meanings and examples which are new to you.

Unit 64

1 Circle the correct phrase. Sometimes, both phrases are correct.

1 A Have you started your art course yet?

  B As a matter of fact / By the way , I'm doing the course on digital photography.

2 A What did you think of the meeting?

  B Well, on the whole / by and large, I thought it was pretty successful. Mind you / Besides , I thought Caroline was a bit irritating – she didn't keep to the point at all.

  A Yes, to be honest / all the same , I've always found her very difficult.

3 A I'm not sure how long I'll be away, but I'll be back by the weekend at any rate / anyhow .

  B That's good – oh, incidentally / even so , what time are you leaving?

4 A Hi, Sue, I'm just having a few problems with my computer; it keeps crashing.

  B Try turning it off and on again; alternatively / to tell you the truth , ring technical support.

5 I agree / It's true he was only using me as an example, but even so / even if it was very insensitive.

6 I don't really want to go in this weather. At any rate / Besides it's too far away.

A Z **more words:** having *said* that, on *top* of sth/sb, as a *rule*, to *say* nothing of sth, *above* all, *talking* of sb/sth

Unit 65

1 Complete the sentences using vague language.

1   I must've seen twenty horses or _____ .
2   His parents aren't old; I'd say they were fifty _____ .
3   Their farm is somewhere in the _____ of 500 acres.
4   I can't really afford a new car, but I'll find the money _____ or other.
5   The whole project will take nine months, give or _____ a week or two.
6   His job is _____ to do with the railways.
7   What's all that _____ doing on the floor?
8   He's a pharmacist or something along those _____ .

A Z **more words**: *whats-his/her-name, whatsit, thingummy/thingamujig, whatnot, whatchamacallit, doodah*

Unit 66

1 Write a proverb or saying using the word in capitals. The meaning must be the same as in the sentence.

1   Accept other people's opinions and ways of life, even if they differ from yours.
    LIVE _____
2   It's easy to talk about something but a lot harder to do something about it.
    SAID _____
3   Two people working together can achieve more than one.
    HEADS _____
4   If you have a bad experience, you don't want something like it to happen again.
    SHY _____
5   Family relationships are stronger than other relationships.
    THICKER _____
6   If someone does something bad to you, you won't improve things by doing something bad to them.
    RIGHT _____

2 Complete the sentences.

1   He's pretty well off, and as they say, _____ talks – he gets what he wants.
2   I'm still waiting to hear from the hospital, but I guess that _____ news is _____ news.
3   Don't get into another row with the neighbours – just let _____ dogs lie.
4   If you want to come camping with us next week, please do – the more the _____ !
5   Don't forget to lock the doors when you leave – better _____ than _____ .
6   It's hard to find a seat in the library – it's first _____ , first _____ , so get there early!
7   My driving is gradually improving and I'm a bit safer – I guess _____ makes perfect.
8   She only rings me at New Year – it's a case of out of _____ , out of _____ .

A Z **more words**: ***waste*** *not, want not; nothing* ***ventured****, nothing gained;* ***touch*** *wood;* ***absence*** *makes the heart grow fonder;* ***familiarity*** *breeds contempt;* ***ignorance*** *is bliss*

67 I can **write a formal letter**

A Useful phrases for formal letters 🎧

> 2 Grampian Close
> HELENSBURGH
> G84 7PP
> 30th June 2001

Scottish Property Services Ltd
3 Union Terrace
GLASGOW

Phrase	Use/Meaning
Opening a letter	
I am writing to inform you that I will be leaving at the end of June.	used for giving information.
I am writing to inform you of my intention to terminate my **lease**.	**intention** (**to do sth**) a plan to do sth **terminate sth** end or stop sth. **lease** a legal agreement for renting a property.
I am writing to enquire whether . . .	used for asking a question or making a request.
I regret to inform you that . . .	used for giving bad news.
I am delighted to inform you that . . .	used for giving good news.
I am writing in response to your **appeal for** aid in . . .	used for replying to an advertisement, etc. **appeal for sth** an urgent or sincere request for people to give money, help, etc.
Please accept my sincere condolences.	used for expressing apologies, sympathy, etc. **sincere** expressing what you really think or feel. SYN **genuine**. **condolences** the things you say to show sympathy when sb has just died.

Opening a reply to a letter	
Further to our meeting last week, . . . *Following* our conversation on 5 May, . . . *In reply to* your letter of 7 July, . . . *With reference to* your letter of 3 June, . . .	used to refer to a previous conversation with the receiver, or a letter/email from them.
Thank you for your letter *concerning* . . .	**concerning** about. SYN **regarding**.

Referring to something in a letter	
Please find enclosed a copy of . . . *As you will see from* my CV, I . . .	used to refer to sth in the body of the letter or included with it.
I would like to draw your attention to . . .	used to refer to sth in the body of the letter, or sth that is relevant to the subject of the letter.

Closing a letter	
Should you require any further information, please do not hesitate to contact me.	commonly used at the end of a formal letter or offer (*should* here is a more formal equivalent of *if*).
I would be grateful if you could contact me as soon as possible.	used to make a request, or ask for action to be taken.
I look forward to meeting you. I look forward to **hearing from you.**	used to end a formal letter (**hearing from you** is used when you expect a reply).

Remember to test yourself

1 Circle the correct word(s).

1 Please accept my sincere condolence/condolences on the death of your father.
2 As you will see/read from my CV, I have extensive experience in marketing.
3 I am delighted/delighted to inform you that your application has been successful.
4 I look toward/forward to hearing from you.
5 Following/Following to our earlier conversation, I have now looked at the plan.
6 Thank you for your letter concerning/concerned the sale of your property.
7 Would/Should you require any further information, do not hesitate to contact me.
8 I am writing in response for/to your appeal for assistance at Longhurst Farm in July.

2 Write a more formal word or phrase with a similar meaning to the words in italics.

1 I am writing to *ask* / .... whether there has been any progress with my application.
2 I *am sorry* / .... to *tell* / .... you that the International Sustainability conference has been cancelled.
3 I am writing to inform you of my *plan* / .... to *end* /.................... my lease.
4 *If* / .... you *need* / .... any *more* / .... information, please *feel free* / .... to *get in touch with* / .... me.
5 *After* / .... our *chat* / .... yesterday, *it would be good* / .... if you could send me the details *about* / .... the proposed changes.

3 One word is missing from each sentence. What is it, and where does it go?

1 I am writing in to your article about supermarket packaging. ....
2 We look forward hearing from you. ....
3 I am writing reply to your letter of 17 October.
4 Thank you for your letter the pre-service training course at CDQ. ....
5 Please enclosed a copy of my birth certificate. ....
6 I am writing in reply to your for donations following the tsunami disaster. ....
7 Please accept my sincere on the death of your grandfather. ....
8 I would like to your attention to the final clause of the lease. ....
9 As you see from my CV, I have extensive experience in sales and marketing. ....
10 With to your letter of 17 May, I am enclosing the documents you requested. ....

4 Write sentences suitable for formal letters.

▶ Ask a customer to get in touch with you before the weekend.
   I would be grateful if you could contact me before the weekend.
1 Start a letter explaining that you saw an advertisement for a receptionist in yesterday's paper.

2 Point out that you have included a photocopy of your driving licence in the envelope.

3 Mention a conversation you had with your client yesterday, and tell them that you now have the necessary documents.

4 Say that you are happy to give any more information needed about your qualifications if they are needed.

5 Say that you would like the company to send you a brochure and price list.

6 Explain to an interview candidate that they have been given the job.

Remember to test yourself

B Advice on writing formal letters 🎧

When writing a formal letter, firstly **state** your purpose in the opening paragraph in a **straightforward** manner. The **body** of the letter should contain one or more paragraphs, each dealing with a separate aspect of the **subject matter**. The final paragraph should **spell out** what you want to happen next.

It is crucial to adopt a suitable **tone**. Be clear, **concise**, and **to the point**, avoiding **superfluous** matter, but not too **blunt** or **abrupt**. Keep the language **plain** and simple where possible. Refer to **sample** letters on the internet for further guidance.

Glossary

state sth	write or say sth clearly or firmly.	**to the point**	relevant and without any extra information. SYN **pertinent**.
straightforward	uncomplicated and easy to understand. OPP **convoluted**.	**superfluous**	unnecessary.
body	the main part of a book, article, text, etc.	**blunt**	saying what you think even if it offends or upsets people.
subject matter	the ideas or information in a book, letter, painting, etc.	**abrupt**	speaking or acting with few words and in a way that seems unfriendly or rude. SYNS **brusque**, **curt**.
spell sth out	explain the details of sth in a simple, clear way.		
tone	the general attitude or feeling expressed in a piece of writing.	**plain**	without unnecessary detail; clear.
concise	expressed clearly and without using any unnecessary words.	**sample**	an example, or small amount, of sth to show what all of it is like.

5 According to the text above, are the following positive (P) or negative (N)?

1   The information was superfluous. _____
2   She writes in plain English. _____
3   The letter sounds curt. _____
4   It was to the point. _____
5   His style is very straightforward. _____
6   I thought his email was quite abrupt. _____
7   The information was pertinent. _____
8   The tone was brusque. _____
9   It was written in a convoluted way. _____
10   Her response was very blunt. _____

6 Complete the dialogues with a suitable word.

1   Did he say what he needed? ~ Yes, he _____ it very clearly.
2   Her tone is rather brusque, isn't it? ~ Yes, I find it rather _____ .
3   Did you find some model letters? ~ Yes, I found some _____ letters on a website.
4   He should tell her the problem clearly. ~ That's right; he's got to _____ it out.
5   Did you enjoy the programme? ~ No, I wasn't interested in the _____ matter.
6   Was the complaint in the introduction? ~ No, I put it in the _____ of the letter.
7   Is that detail really necessary? ~ No, it's _____ .
8   Is the letter easy to follow? ~ Yes, it's very _____ .

7 ABOUT YOU AND YOUR COUNTRY Is the advice in the text similar to the advice you would give for formal letters in your own language? Where is it the same, and where does it differ?

Remember to test yourself

68 I can use formal link words 🎧

In addition to the many link words you already know, e.g. *however, although, furthermore, since,* etc., there are a limited number of link words and phrases which are mostly used in formal written English.

It is our understanding that the residents of Alton Court received a full apology from the council in writing **prior to** the meeting that was held on 7 June. **In view of** the limited inconvenience they suffered, this was felt to be adequate; **thus** no further action was taken. **With regard to** Mr Wilson, however, the council acknowledges some damage was caused to his property, **albeit** very minor, and therefore agrees to pay the full costs incurred by Mr Wilson, **notwithstanding** the burden it will inevitably place on the council's resources. **In conclusion**, we sincerely hope this brings an end to the matter.

Glossary

prior to sth	before sth.
in view of sth	used to introduce the reason for a decision. SYN **considering sth**.
thus	therefore. SYN **hence**.
with/in regard to sb/sth	relating to a particular person or subject. SYNS **concerning sth, regarding sth**.
albeit	although.
notwithstanding	in spite of.
in conclusion	used in writing or a formal speech to show that you are about to finish what you are saying.

spotlight   *hitherto* and *henceforth*

Hitherto means 'up to this time'.
Hitherto *we had had no problems of this kind.*
Henceforth means 'from this time on'.
*Jason Dean Williams (**henceforth** referred to as 'the accused') . . .*

❶ Replace the underlined word(s) with a more formal equivalent.

1   He was only seven, <u>so</u> he couldn't be held responsible for his actions. ....
2   I agreed, <u>although</u> with some reluctance, that I would accompany them. ....
3   The meeting will go ahead <u>in spite of</u> the planned protests. ....
4   We were told <u>before</u> the meeting. ....
5   His performance was extraordinary <u>considering</u> his advancing years. ....
6   <u>Up to this time</u>, the species was unknown. ....

❷ Complete the sentences with a suitable link word or phrase.

1   Deoxyribonucleic acid (............ referred to as DNA) carries genetic information.
2   They did not have valid tickets, ... they were not allowed to board the train.
3   .... our conversation yesterday, I had not met either man.
4   Work on the new extension will commence next month. .... the roof, the contractors have assured us that the necessary repairs will be carried out immediately.
5   .... the complaints received, we still have complete faith in both the company and the Managing Director.
6   .... , the board would like to thank everyone for attending the meeting and making such a positive contribution.

Remember to test yourself

69 I can use academic English 🎧

A Public examinations

Exam requirements

Some public examinations in English consist of a written paper in which candidates are required to produce a piece of **discursive** writing. They may be asked to present and develop an **argument**, **evaluate** ideas, **summarize** information, etc. Candidates are **assessed** on a number of **criteria**, including their ability to write in an organized and **coherent** way, their **command of** a range of **stylistic** features, and their ability to write in an appropriate **register**. Some tasks may also involve the use of **narrative**.

---

spotlight   *present v*

The verb **present** (stress on second syllable) can be used to show or describe something in speech, e.g. at a **conference**, where there are talks on different subjects, or in writing. **presentation** N.
*I'm **presenting** the new product at the sales **conference**.*
*He didn't **present** his ideas very coherently in his essay.*

Glossary

discursive	discussing different ideas.
argument	a set of reasons that sb uses to show that sth is true or correct.
evaluate sth	form an opinion of sth after careful thought. **evaluation** N. SYN **assess sth** V, **assessment** N.
summarize sth	give a short statement that brings together the main points of sth. SYN **sum sth up**. **summary** N.
criterion (PL **criteria**)	a standard or principle by which sth is judged.
coherent	(of writing) clear and comprehensible, with each part following on logically from the one before. OPP **incoherent**. **coherence** N.
command of sth	a knowledge of sth and an ability to use it well.
stylistic	connected to the way a writer or artist does sth. **style** N.
register	the words, grammar, and style that sb uses in a particular situation, e.g. *formal*.
narrative	a description of events, especially in a novel. SYN **story** (the person is a **narrator**).

1 Circle the correct word(s). Sometimes both words may be correct.

1   He asked me to sum up / summarize the main points.
2   Having read her essay, what was your command / assessment of it?
3   The events in the novel are described by a narrative / narrator.
4   We had to assess / evaluate the plans.
5   The single most important criterion / criteria was experience.
6   The chairman came to my conference / presentation and thanked me afterwards.
7   It was an interesting argument / register, but I'm not sure I agree with it.
8   You have to be able to propose / present your ideas on paper.

2 Complete the sentences.

1   I decided to write a _____ because I'm quite good at telling stories.
2   You should provide a brief _____ of your ideas at the end of the talk.
3   I couldn't follow what the writer was trying to say because it was so _____ .
4   The use of metaphors is an important _____ feature of the writing.
5   What are your _____ for choosing the best candidate for the job?
6   To write an academic essay, you need a very good _____ of the language.
7   Most academic essays are written in a formal style and _____ .
8   I'm not very good at discussing ideas on paper, so I avoid _____ essays.

 Remember to test yourself

B Basics of academic writing 🎧

In a piece of academic writing, the writer will do at least some of the following:

- **outline** their main ideas
- **explore** certain ideas in greater depth
- **highlight** important facts
- **adopt** a particular **stance** or point of view
- **exemplify** certain points
- **draw conclusions**

They may also compare and contrast, **condemn** or **condone**, explain, describe, analyse, **hypothesize**, **assert**, **justify**, and – to the irritation of some people – **sit on the fence**.

Glossary

outline sth	give a description of the main points involved in sth. **outline** N.
explore sth	examine, discuss, or think about sth carefully. SYN **analyse sth**.
highlight sth	emphasize sth to give it more attention.
adopt sth	decide to take and support a particular point of view, plan, etc.
stance (on sth)	an opinion that sb has about sth and expresses publicly. SYN **position**.
exemplify sth	give an example to make sth clearer. SYN **illustrate sth**.
conclusion	a decision reached after discussion and examination of any evidence (**reach / draw / come to a conclusion**). **conclude** V.
condemn sth/sb	say publicly that you think sth or sb is bad or wrong. **condemnation** N.
condone sth	accept or forgive behaviour that most people think is wrong.
hypothesize	suggest a possible explanation for sth, but without knowing whether it is really true. **hypothesis** N.
assert sth	state clearly that sth is true. SYN **claim sth**. **assertion** N.
justify sth	show that sth is right or reasonable. **justification** N.
sit on the fence	IDIOM avoid deciding or saying which side of an argument you support.

3 Complete the sentences with a form of the word in capitals.

1 There was universal .... of the attack. CONDEMN
2 What .... did you draw? CONCLUDE
3 It may be unwise to .... at this stage. HYPOTHESIS
4 I felt he .... the point very well. EXAMPLE
5 He was correct in his .... that the man was guilty. ASSERT
6 What was his .... for that argument? JUSTIFY

4 Rewrite the sentences on the left using a single verb or noun for the underlined words in 1–7, and a phrase in 8. Keep the meaning the same.

1 She gave a general picture of her ideas. She ....
2 She had one possible explanation. She had one ....
3 She gave special emphasis to certain points. She ....
4 She wouldn't accept or forgive his behaviour. She wouldn't ....
5 She didn't take and support a clear stance. She didn't ....
6 She went on to analyse the idea in more depth. She went on to ....
7 She couldn't show her ideas were reasonable. She couldn't ....
8 In the end, she wouldn't agree or disagree. In the end, she ....

Remember to test yourself

Far from the Madding Crowd by Thomas Hardy

SYNOPSIS: After inheriting her **prosperous** uncle's farm, Hardy's **protagonist**, Bathsheba Everdene, becomes an independent woman. But her beauty attracts many admirers: farm worker Gabriel Oak, landowner William Boldwood, and handsome soldier Frank Troy, whom she later marries. However, Troy is a selfish man who allows his earlier love, Fanny Robin, to die in poverty while giving birth to his child. Boldwood is madly jealous of Troy, and later in the novel this is the reason for his **downfall** when, in a jealous rage, he kills Troy. Gabriel asks for **mercy** to be shown him, and, on the grounds of **insanity**, Boldwood escapes death but is sent to prison. The novel ends with Bathsheba marrying Gabriel.

COMMENTARY: Incidents such as Fanny's pregnancy and **pitiful** death, and Boldwood's act of murderous violence, **convey** Hardy's growing taste for tragedy. But **unlike** Tess in the later *Tess of the D'Urbervilles*, **fate** still favours Bathsheba. She finally finds contentment with Gabriel, who **embodies** the best qualities of the rural community in the fight against the growth of industrialism, which Hardy finds so **alien**.

Another theme in the novel is the danger and destruction **inherent in** romantic love and marriage. Hardy **exposes** the irrationality and **betrayals** of romantic relationships, and implies that the true basis of a happy marriage is **companionship** and a common interest. For some it is also an early example of feminist literature. Bathsheba is **portrayed** as an independent woman with the courage to **defy** convention and run a farm herself. Her passionate nature leads her into errors of judgement, but Hardy **endows** her with the **resilience**, intelligence, and good luck to overcome the mistakes of youth.

Glossary

synopsis	a short summary of the plot of a book, film, etc.
prosperous	rich and successful. SYN **affluent**. **prosperity** N.
protagonist	the main character in a book, film, etc.
downfall	A person's **downfall** is the complete loss of their money, power, etc.
mercy	a kind or forgiving attitude towards sb you have the power to harm or punish. **merciful** ADJ. OPP **merciless**.
insanity	the state of being seriously mentally ill. **insane** ADJ. OPP **sane**.
commentary	a written explanation or discussion of sth such as a book.
pitiful	deserving, or causing you to feel, pity.
convey sth	communicate ideas and feelings.
unlike	used to contrast one person or thing with another.
fate	a power that is believed to control everything and that cannot be changed.
alien	strange, difficult to understand, and often unacceptable.
inherent (in sth)	If sth is **inherent in sth**, it is a natural part of it and cannot be removed from it. SYN **intrinsic**.

expose sth	tell the true facts about sth and show it to be bad or wrong.
betrayal	the act of being disloyal to sb who trusts you. **betray** V.
companionship	a friendly and comfortable relationship between people.
portray sb/sth	describe sb/sth in a piece of writing. SYN **depict sb/sth**. **portrayal** N.
defy sth/sb	refuse to obey a law or rule, or a person. **defiance** N. **defiant** ADJ.
resilience	the ability to recover and become strong again after a difficult or unpleasant situation. **resilient** ADJ.

spotlight — *embody/represent sth, endow sb with sth*

If a character in a book **embodies** or **represents** something, they show or express a particular idea or quality (**embodiment** N). If the writer **endows** a character **with** something, they give the character a particular quality or feature.
*He **embodies** the spirit of hopefulness.*
*She is the **embodiment** of beauty.*
*The author **endows** the hero **with** great powers.*

 Remember to test yourself

1 Add the related words.

1 betray _____ N
2 portray _____ N
3 defy _____ N
4 embody _____ N
5 prosperous _____ N
6 insane _____ N
7 resilience _____ ADJ
8 mercy _____ ADJ
9 pity _____ ADJ

2 Circle the correct word(s).

1 A commentary on a novel is a synopsis / an explanation of the main events.
2 If something is alien to you, it is easy / difficult to understand.
3 If you expose someone, you tell the truth / lies about them.
4 A pitiful story is likely to make you feel sad / proud.
5 Resilience is the ability / inability to recover from a big disappointment.
6 If you are defiant, you agree / refuse to do something.

3 Replace the underlined word(s) with another word that has a similar meaning in the context.

1 Could you just give me a summary of the novel? _____
2 She is portrayed as a very virtuous character. _____
3 In the end she died a rather sad death. _____
4 He was one of the more affluent landowners. _____
5 Generosity was one of her intrinsic qualities. _____
6 There were fears he might be mad. _____
7 In the novel she embodies the forces of change. _____
8 She misses the enjoyment of being with other people. _____

4 Complete the synopsis of the novel with words from the box, in the correct form.

| fate | represent | downfall | mercy | protagonist | depict | unlike |
| endow | convey | defy | betray | embodiment | | |

Tess is the (1)_____ in Hardy's novel that bears her name, *Tess of the D'Urbervilles*. She is (2)_____ in the novel as a daughter of nature, and Hardy (3)_____ her with so many noble qualities that she is one of his most sympathetic characters. But time and again she has to endure suffering and the brutality of the industrial age. This brutality is (4)_____ in the character of Alec D'Urberville, who is the (5)_____ of evil in the novel. The other man in her life is Angel Clare, an intelligent young freethinker, who (6)_____ convention and is happy to work on a farm rather than go to university. He and Tess fall in love and marry, but when Tess tells him that she has previously had a child, Angel feels (7)_____ and leaves her. (8)_____ is sometimes kind to Hardy's heroines, but not in this case. Tess goes back to Alec, but when Angel returns from Brazil and forgives her, she brings about her own (9)_____ by stabbing Alec to death. But (10)_____ Boldwood at the end of Hardy's earlier novel *Far from the Madding Crowd*, Tess is shown no (11)_____ . She is executed for her crime, although the final incident is only (12)_____ to us by a black flag being waved over the prison.

5 ABOUT YOU What was the last novel you read? Can you give a synopsis of it? Write it down, or tell another student.

Remember to test yourself

71 I can use scientific English

A Research 🎧

Scientific method

SCIENTIFIC RESEARCH proposes **hypotheses** as explanations of **phenomena**, and then designs experimental studies to gather **empirical** evidence and test them out. These **procedures** must be repeatable in order to predict future results with some certainty. A **facet** shared by other fields of enquiry is the **conviction** that the process must also be **objective** in order to reduce a **biased** interpretation of the results. Another basic expectation is to document, **archive**, and share all data so that it is available for **scrutiny** by other scientists. There is then the opportunity to **verify** the results by **replicating** them.

1 Complete the tables.

ADJECTIVE	NOUN
objective	....
biased	....
empirical	....

VERB	NOUN
verify	....
....	hypothesis
....	scrutiny

2 Replace the underlined word with a word of similar meaning.

1 Objectivity is just one <u>aspect</u> of the problem.
   f...............
2 The results came under close <u>examination</u>.
   s...............
3 At the moment it's just a working <u>theory</u>.
   h...............
4 His views are completely <u>objective</u>.
   u...............
5 Their personal <u>belief</u> is that the drug is safe.
   c...............
6 Can we <u>duplicate</u> this experiment?
   r...............

Glossary

hypothesis (PL **hypotheses**) a possible explanation of sth, based on a few facts but not yet proven to be true. SYN **theory. hypothesize** V. **hypothetical** ADJ.

phenomenon (PL **phenomena**) a thing that happens or exists, especially sth that is not fully understood.

empirical based on experiments or experience, not just ideas (**empirical evidence/knowledge/ research**). **empiricism** N.

procedure a way of doing sth, especially the usual or correct way.

facet (of sth) a particular part of sth. SYN **aspect (of sth)**.

conviction a strong opinion or belief (**political/ moral conviction**).

objective based on fact and not influenced by personal feelings or opinion. SYN **unbiased**. OPP **subjective. objectivity** N.

biased influenced by personal feelings. OPP **unbiased/objective. bias** N.

archive sth put documents in an **archive** (a set of historical documents).

scrutiny careful and thorough examination (**come under close/careful scrutiny**). SYN **inspection. scrutinize sth** V.

verify sth check or show that sth is true and accurate. **verification** N.

replicate sth copy sth exactly. SYN **duplicate sth**.

3 Complete the sentences.

1 Experiments must follow a clear ....
2 Violence in society is not a new ....
3 We need to .... experiments so that we can verify other people's results.
4 Do you have any .... evidence to support your theory?
5 All the published results are kept in an .... in the library.
6 It's a .... report and lacks objectivity.

Remember to test yourself

B Genetics 🎧

GENE THERAPY: *Genes* are the basic physical and functional **units** of **heredity**, and *gene therapy* is a technique for correcting **defective** genes responsible for diseases. It works by **inserting** a normal gene into the *genome* (the complete set of genes in a living cell) to replace an **abnormal** gene. A carrier **molecule** called a *vector* must be used to deliver the therapeutic gene to the patient's target **cells**. But there are many limitations:

- the rapidly dividing nature of many cells means that gene therapy may be **short-lived**;
- the normal gene may be attacked and **repelled** by the patient's **immune system**;
- gene therapy works best on disorders arising from the **mutation** of a single gene.

Glossary

genetics the scientific study of the ways in which different characteristics are passed from one generation to the next. **genetic** ADJ.

heredity the process by which physical and mental characteristics are passed from parents to their children. **hereditary** ADJ.

defective having a fault or faults. SYN **faulty**. **defect** N.

insert sth (into sth) put sth into sth else or between two things. **insertion** N.

abnormal different from what is expected, and often harmful or unwanted.

molecule the smallest unit (of two or more **atoms**) that a substance can be divided into, without changing its chemical nature. **molecular** ADJ.

cell the smallest unit of living matter that can exist; all plants and animals are made up of **cells** (**blood cells**, **brain cells**).

short-lived only lasting for a short time. OPP **long-lived**.

repel sth successfully fight or drive away sth that is attacking you.

immune system the system in your body that produces substances to help it fight against infection and disease (giving **immunity**).

mutation (in biology) a process in which genetic material changes in structure when it is passed on. **mutate** V.

spotlight *unit*

A **unit** can be a thing, person, or group that is complete in itself but can also form part of something larger.
*The **basic unit** of society is the family.*
*A **maternity unit** in a hospital.*

4 Circle the correct word(s).

1 The unit is defective / defaulty.
2 Is this particularly disnormal / abnormal?
3 The ward is in the maternity unit / system.
4 Arthritis can be heredity / hereditary.
5 The effects are short-living / short-lived.
6 It's your immune / immunity system.

5 Complete the sentences.

1 _____ therapy has been used to restore the function of ageing brain _____ in monkeys.
2 The problem was caused by the _____ of the genes as they were passed on.
3 Doctors _____ a tube into the patient's stomach.
4 The body has to be able to _____ the abnormal cells that are attacking it.
5 A _____ disorder is a disease caused by an abnormality in someone's DNA.
6 If an illness is passed from parents to their children, it's a problem of _____ .
7 The technique involves the _____ of genes for nerve growth into the brain.
8 In _____ science, a _____ is a stable unit comprising two or more atoms.

Remember to test yourself

Skyscrapers: design and construction

Every skyscraper is designed within physical **constraints** such as climate and geology, and then has to **comply with** the most **stringent** safety regulations. It also has to **meet the needs of** its **occupants**, and satisfy the aesthetic objectives of both owner and architect.

Design engineers translate the architect's vision into a detailed plan that is structurally sound. As each skyscraper is unique, models of the building must undergo **rigorous** tests in wind tunnels to **determine** whether they can **withstand** the effects of high winds. If tests show the building will **sway** excessively, designers may add mechanical devices to **counteract** or restrict **motion**.

In the construction, engineers dig a massive hole in the rock and then establish the **footings**[1], which form the base that **anchors** the building. Steel or **reinforced concrete** columns are inserted in the footings, and concrete is poured on top.

Vertical supports are put in place by **cranes**[2]; these support the vertical **load**. Horizontal **beams** and steel **girders** are then placed at a 90 degree **angle** to the vertical columns; these hold the building together. Exterior walls merely enclose the structure, and are constructed by attaching **panels**[3] of material such as glass or metal to the building's framework. This is often done by **bolting** them to **brackets** secured to the floors or support columns. ■

Glossary

constraint	a thing which limits your freedom to do sth (**physical/financial/political constraints**). SYN **restriction**. **constrain** V.
comply with sth	obey a rule, order, law, etc. **compliance** N.
stringent	(of a law, rule, etc.) very strict.
meet the needs of sb/sth	satisfy the needs of sb/sth.
occupant	a person who lives or works in a particular room or building (**residents** live or stay in a building, but don't work in a building).
rigorous	done carefully and with great attention to detail. SYN **thorough**.
determine sth	calculate sth exactly. SYN **establish sth**.
withstand sth	be strong enough to be unharmed by great heat, cold, pressure, etc. SYNS **resist sth, stand up to sth**.
sway	move slowly from side to side.
counteract sth	do sth to reduce or prevent the bad effects of sth.
motion	the act or process of moving (sth can be **in motion**).
anchor sth	fix sth firmly in position so that it cannot move.
reinforced	made stronger, especially by the addition of another material.
concrete	a mixture of sand, cement, small stones, and water, which forms a hard building material.
vertical	going straight up or down from a surface.
load	the amount of weight pressing down on sth (a **vertical load**).
beam	a long piece of wood or metal, used to support a weight above.
girder	a strong metal beam in large buildings.
angle	the space between two lines or surfaces that join (**angle sth** V move or position sth so it is not straight; it is **at an angle**).
bolt sth to sth	fasten sth to sth with a **bolt** (= a long piece of metal).
bracket	a piece of metal or wood fixed to a wall to support sth.

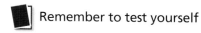 Remember to test yourself

1 Circle the odd one out.

1 a) restriction   b) compliance   c) constraint
2 a) stringent   b) rigorous   c) thorough
3 a) beam   b) girder   c) bracket
4 a) motion   b) anchor   c) sway
5 a) counteract   b) determine   c) establish
6 a) withstand   b) resist   c) comply
7 a) angle   b) concrete   c) steel
8 a) occupant   b) constraint   c) resident
9 a) panels   b) crane   c) footings
10 a) bracket   b) bolt   c) load

2 Replace the underlined word(s) with a single word of similar meaning.

1 We haven't managed to <u>determine</u> the extent of the damage.
2 The building is <u>moving from side to side</u>.
3 You can't do anything once it is <u>in motion</u>.
4 We hope the structure will be able to <u>stand up to</u> the pressure.
5 They hope this will <u>satisfy</u> the needs of the planners.
6 Most architects have to operate with various financial <u>restrictions</u>.
7 Basically, the fence comprises six <u>rectangular pieces of wood</u>.
8 We need to <u>firmly fix</u> it to the ground.
9 High-rise buildings have to comply with <u>very strict</u> fire regulations.
10 They have very <u>thorough</u> tests before they are given the go-ahead.

3 Complete the texts with suitable words.

With a skyscraper, the effects of the wind are a greater problem than the weight of the structure, so designers have to ensure that the building can (1)_____ strong winds, and will not (2)_____ enough to cause the (3)_____ physical or emotional discomfort.

In the design, engineers will have to (4)_____ whether the steel (5)_____ are strong enough to support the vertical (6)_____ . If not, engineers will have to (7)_____ the pressure of the weight, and one common method is to add more (8)_____ concrete around the supports in order to stiffen the central core of the building.

Remember to test yourself

73 I can **use abbreviations** 🎧

A Electronic messaging

NB Abbreviations in text messaging are changing all the time.

Text Language Guidelines

- VOWELS are often removed, e.g. **WKND** = weekend, **sry** = sorry, **pls** = please, **xlnt** = excellent, **thx/tnx** = thanks, **msg** = message, **spk** = speak, **yr** = your OR you're

- WORDS can be omitted, especially articles, prepositions, and pronouns.

- SINGLE LETTERS replace words with the same sound: **b** = be, **c** = see, **d** = the, **n** = in OR and, **r** = are, **u** = you

- SINGLE NUMBERS replace words and parts of words with the same sound: **8** = -ate, e.g. **GR8** = great, **l8r** = later; **4** = for, -fore e.g. **b4** = before; **2** = to, too

- / is used to show missing letters, e.g. **w/** = with, **w/o** = without, **s/t** = something

- COMMON ABBREVIATIONS (also used in chatrooms and email) **2day, 2nite, 2moro** = today, tonight, tomorrow

ttyl = talk to you later
asap = as soon as possible
bfn OR **b4n** = bye for now
hand = have a nice day
cul8r = see you later
fyi = for your information
atb = all the best
btw = by the way
lol = lots of love OR laughing out loud
imho = in my humble opinion (humorous, = in my opinion, though I am not an important person)
x = kiss

myob = **mind your own business**
iirc = if I remember/**recall** correctly

gtg = (I've) got to go (now)
prolly OR **prbly** = probably

- EMOTICONS (you have to read some of these **sideways** by turning your head to the left)
☺ or **:)** = happy or amused (a **smiley**)
;) = **winking** (showing you are joking)
☹ or **: (** = unhappy or displeased
:-/ = doubtful or confused
;-x = my lips are **sealed** (I won't tell anyone)

Glossary

mind your own business	a rude way of telling sb not to ask questions about or get involved in sth you don't want them to know about. SYN **it's none of your business**.
recall sth	remember sth. SYN **recollect sth. recollection** N.
sideways	to, towards, or from the side.
wink (at sb) *see picture*	
seal sth	close sth very firmly so that nothing can get in or out.

 Remember to test yourself

1 Cross out any wrong words. Write the correct word(s) at the end.

1   imho = in my ~~humorous~~ opinion _____ humble
2   btw = by the ~~weekend~~ _____ way
3   fyi = for your ~~interest~~ _____ information
4   hand = have a nice ~~drink~~ _____ day
5   : (= unhappy or tired _____
6   ttyl = ~~turn~~ to you later _____ talk
7   2day = ~~two days~~ _____ today
8   lol = lots of ~~laughs~~ _____ love
9   ;-x = my ~~letters~~ are sealed _____ lips
10 :-/ = doubtful or concerned _____
11 myob = ~~make~~ your own business _____ mind
12 iirc = if I ~~read~~ correctly _____ recall

2 Translate the messages into standard English.

Hi, thx 4 yr msg. R u goin 2 c Sally ths
wknd? Pls giv her lol :) Alice

_____

Hi cn u fone me asap? S/t important 2 tel
u! ;-x atb Suzie

_____

Dinr lst nite wz xlnt. tnx ☺ Wil u b n 2nite?
Hope 2 cul8r Joe

_____

Cd u spk 2 yr dad b4 d wknd? Iirc he wil b
n 2moro. Lol Steffi

_____

Sry bt im prolly goin 2 b l8 4 d mtng. Wil rng
u w/ mor info l8r. Strt w/o me. Bfn Zoe

_____

3 Write these words or phrases in text messaging language.

►   today _2day_
1   great _____
2   thanks _____
3   see you later _____
4   in my humble opinion _____
5   excellent _____
6   before _____
7   lots of love _____
8   without _____
9   I won't tell anyone _____
10 tomorrow _____

B Common abbreviations 🎧

The abbreviations used here in spoken English are all pronounced as individual letters.

Abbreviations used in written English		Spoken or written abbreviations	
sae	stamped (self-)addressed envelope	**B & B**	bed and breakfast = a small hotel and the service provided.
PS	postscript (written at the end of a letter to add extra information)		closed-circuit television, often used in a building to prevent crime.
encl.	document(s) enclosed	**CEO**	chief executive officer
inc. **incl.**	(in advertisements) included / including, e.g. *batteries not* **inc.** inclusive, e.g. *12–24 June* **incl.**	**PC**	**politically correct** (of language or behaviour) aiming to avoid offending anyone, e.g. *It's more* **PC** *to refer to old people as elderly.*
attn or **fao**	for the attention of, e.g. *Sales Dept* **attn** *Doug Smith*	**HQ**	**headquarters** = the main offices of an organization.
PTO	please turn over	**ETA**	estimated time of arrival
RSVP	(on invitations) please reply (from French 'Répondez s'il vous plaît')	**IQ**	intelligence quotient = a measure of sb's intelligence using special tests (**a high/low IQ**).
c/o	care of (used on a letter to sb staying at another person's house)	**TLC**	INF tender loving care = the sympathy and support you show sb to make them feel better.
NB	used to make sb notice some important information (from Latin 'nota bene')	**DIY**	do-it-yourself = home repairs and decoration you do yourself rather than paying sb to do it.

4 True or false? Write T or F.

1 You use NB to highlight something. ....
2 You write your address on an sae. ....
3 Big companies usually have an HQ. ....
4 'incl.' and 'encl.' mean the same. ....

5 You see ETA on travel information. ....
6 PTO means 'please take over'. ....
7 RSVP means 'tell me if you can come'. ....
8 You have to pay someone for DIY. ....

5 Complete the texts with suitable abbreviations.

Mary Collins, (1) ....
Mr and Mrs E Brooks,
34 Sydney Hill,
Devon
TX7 5GN

(3) .... Jeff Sergeant,
DELTA,
87 Riverside,
Milton Keynes
MY6 2AJ

... a room reservation for
12–14 July
(5) .... , i.e.
leaving 15 July ...

See you soon, love Mina
(2) .... I nearly forgot –
Jackie's pregnant again!

As requested, I have enclosed an (4) ....
for further details of the campaign.

6 Complete the sentences with suitable abbreviations.

1 He has risen through the company to become the .... – with all the stress that entails.
2 She's quite hard of hearing – which is a more .... way of saying 'deaf'.
3 He's had a terrible time – he really needs a bit of .... Let's invite him for a drink.
4 We found a gorgeous little .... in a remote village. The owners were really kind.
5 I'm sure they'll get the pickpocket – there is .... all over the town.
6 Just having a high .... doesn't mean you'll be any more successful than anyone else.

Remember to test yourself

Review: Written English

Unit 67

1 Find five pairs of synonyms in the box.

straightforward	complicated	abrupt	unnecessary	brusque
convoluted	easy to understand	relevant	superfluous	pertinent

.... / .... / ....

.... / .... / ....

.... / ....

A Z more words: *indent, pompous, waffle, to whom it may* **concern**

Unit 68

1 Complete the table with a formal link word and its less formal equivalent.

although	prior to	in spite of	albeit	in view of	thus
considering	notwithstanding	before	therefore		

Formal link word(s)	Less formal equivalent

A Z more words: *nonetheless, likewise, herewith, herein*

Unit 69

1 Complete the tables.

Verb	Noun
evaluate	
condemn	
assert	
summarize	
	hypothesis
	justification
	example
	outline

2 Yes or no? Write Y or N.

1 If someone committed a serious crime, would most people condone it? ....

2 If you adopt a stance, do you sit on the fence? ....

3 If you explore an issue, do you analyse it? ....

4 If you write a narrative, does it need to be coherent? ....

5 If you highlight an issue, do you condemn it? ....

6 If someone has a good command of English, do they use appropriate register? ....

7 If you have to outline an argument, should you give a lot of detail? ....

8 If you write a discursive essay, are you producing an outline of a story? ....

A Z **more words**: *account for sth, cross-reference, **cite** your sources, plagiarism, elucidate, acknowledgements*

Unit 70

1 Complete the crossword. The letters in the grey squares spell out another word. What is it, and what does it mean?

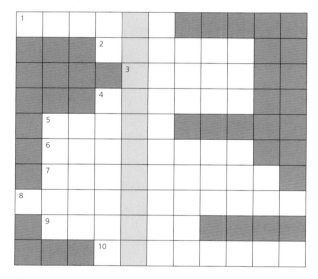

1 portray someone or something in a piece of writing
2 communicate ideas and feelings to someone
3 a kind willingness to forgive someone you have power over
4 express or show an idea or quality
5 strange and difficult to understand
6 a complete loss of power, money, etc.
7 a description of someone or something in a piece of writing
8 the main character in a book, film, etc.
9 be disloyal to someone who trusts you in a way that hurts them
10 a summary of something longer, like a book or film

A Z **more words**: *parody, allusion, analogy, understatement, anticlimax, flashback*

Unit 71

1 One word is either wrong or missing in these definitions. Make any necessary corrections.

1 A phenomenon happens or exists, and is usually fully understood. ....

2 A procedure is a way of describing something. ....

3 A cell is the largest unit of living matter that can exist. ....

4 Someone who is biased is not influenced by their feelings and opinions. ....

5 In biology, mutation is a process in which genetic material declines when it is passed on. ....

6 If you replicate something, you replace it. ....

7 If you repel something, you unsuccessfully fight something that is attacking you. ....

8 A conviction is a weak opinion or belief. ....

2 Complete the sentences using the correct form of the word in capitals.

1   We can only _____ at this point.   HYPOTHESIS
2   This disease is often _____ .   HEREDITY
3   We will _____ the information carefully.   SCRUTINY
4   They think it's a _____ gene.   DEFECT
5   Her views are objective and completely _____ .   BIAS
6   We need _____ of these details.   VERIFY
7   It doesn't guarantee _____ .   IMMUNE
8   It's a branch of _____ science.   MOLECULE

A Z **more words**: *adjacent, binary, correlation, fusion, induce, linear, synthesis, spectrum, segment, residue*

Unit 72

1 One word is missing in each sentence. What is it, and where does it go?

1   The central core of a building is often made of reinforced. _____
2   Large steel are placed between the vertical columns to hold the building together. _____
3   The exterior walls are made by attaching made of glass or metal to the building. _____
4   Skyscrapers undergo rigorous tests to whether they can withstand high winds. _____
5   All support beams are lifted by and then put in place. _____
6   The design has to with strict safety regulations before construction begins. _____
7   All buildings have to conform to physical imposed by climate and geology. _____
8   Mechanical devices may be added to or resist motion. _____
9   All construction has to go through the most safety checks. _____
10 The building's support columns are usually in the footings. _____

A Z **more words**: *aggregate, bond/bonding, cladding, welding, rivet, axis, contraction, density*

Unit 73

1 What do these abbreviations stand for?

1   B & B = _____
2   PTO = _____
3   HQ = _____
4   CCTV = _____
5   DIY = _____
6   CEO = _____
7   PC = _____
8   c/o = _____
9   fao = _____
10 IQ = _____
11 ETA = _____
12 TLC _____

A Z **more abbreviations**: *A & E, AGM, AOB, DOB, IMF, WHO, YHA, VSO, VIP*

74 I can use prefixes

A Mis-, inter-, ill- 🎧

Professor Morton's lecture was terrible:
- ✏ he **miscalculated** the time
- ✏ it was full of **misconceptions**
- ✏ his handout was full of **misprints**
- ✏ he **misjudged** the audience
- ✏ there was no **interaction** with the audience
- ✏ his jokes completely **misfired**
- ✏ it was **ill-informed** and **ill-prepared**

Prefix	Word and meaning	Other words
mis- = bad(ly) or wrong(ly)	**miscalculate sth** estimate a time, amount, etc. wrongly. **misconception** a **concept** (= idea) which is not based on correct information or is not clearly understood. **misconceived** ADJ. **misprint** a small mistake, e.g. a spelling mistake in a book, paper, etc. **misjudge sth/sb** make a wrong judgement about sth or sb. **misfire** (of a plan or joke) go wrong.	**misdiagnose sth** be wrong about what illness sb has. **misinform sb** (**about sth**) give sb the wrong information about sth. **mismanage sth** manage or deal with sth badly. SYN **mishandle sth**. **mislay sth** lose sth for a time. SYN **misplace sth**. **mistreat sth/sb** treat sth/sb in a bad or cruel way.
inter- = between; from one to another	**interaction** the activity of being with and talking to people; the way that people react to each other. **interact** (**with sb**) V.	**interdependent** consisting of parts that depend on each other. **interrelated** (of two things) closely related and affecting each other.
ill- + PP = badly (ill- is an adverb but can act like a prefix)	**ill-informed** having little or no knowledge of sth. **ill-prepared** badly planned or organized.	**ill-treated** treated in a cruel or unkind way. **ill-advised** not sensible; likely to have a bad effect.

❶ 📓 Cover the table. Write the prefixes.

1	_____ action	5	_____ dependent	9	_____ lay
2	_____ conception	6	_____ treat	10	_____ advised
3	_____ diagnose	7	_____ fire	11	_____ related
4	_____ prepared	8	_____ informed	12	_____ judge

❷ Complete the sentences on the right using a word beginning with *mis-*, *ill-*, or *inter-*.

1 I was given inaccurate information. I was _____ .
2 They dealt with the situation badly. The situation was _____ .
3 The animals were handled in a cruel manner. The animals were _____ .
4 She hardly knew anything about the topic. She was _____ .
5 Someone lost the documents. The documents were _____ .
6 The newspaper's full of typing mistakes. The article was full of _____ .
7 Most people's ideas about it are wrong. Most people's ideas are _____ .
8 They didn't identify the illness accurately. The illness was _____ .
9 I thought I had enough, but I got it wrong. I thought I had enough, but I _____ .
10 The two things affect one another. The two things are _____ .

📓 Remember to test yourself

B Re-, de-, anti-, over-, under- 🎧

Prefix	Example	Other words
re- again	*We need to* **reappraise** *the idea.* = examine the idea again to see if it needs changing. SYN **reassess**.	**refuel** put more fuel in a plane. **rewrite, reconstruct, reinvent, retell**
de- 1 indicating reversal or removal	*That is now* **declassified** *information.* = officially no longer secret. OPP **classified.** *I* **defrosted** *the fridge.* = removed ice from the fridge.	**depopulated** (of an area) from which all or most of the people have moved away. OPP **populated.** **decentralize, destabilize** **decaffeinated** with the caffeine removed.
de- 2 indicating reduction	*The currency was* **devalued.** = the value of the currency was officially reduced.	**depreciate** become less valuable over time.
anti- 1 opposed to	*We went on an* **anti-war** *demonstration.* = opposed to war.	**anti-racism, anti-drugs policy, anti-** **virus software**
anti- 2 preventing; curing	*He took* **anti-inflammatory** *drugs.* = used to reduce swelling and pain.	**anti-depressants** drugs used to treat depression.
over- indicating 'too much/many'	*Why do airlines* **overbook** *flights?* = sell more tickets than are in fact available.	**overrated** If sth is **overrated**, it is believed by some people to be better than it is. OPP **underrated.** **overdose** N, **overemphasize, overload**
under- indicating 'not enough'	*The child was* **undernourished.** = unhealthy because of a lack of food. SYNS **malnourished, underfed.**	**underprivileged** having less money and fewer advantages than most people. SYN **disadvantaged.**

spotlight *un-* and *under-*

There is a difference between **un-** and **under-**.
An **unemployed** person doesn't have a job; an **underemployed** person doesn't have enough work
to do, or their skills are not made use of. More examples: **uncooked/undercooked, undeveloped/**
underdeveloped, unpaid/underpaid, unsold and **undersold** = sold at a price lower than the real value.

3 Find the end of each word. Circle the ones which can be preceded by *de-*.

racismfrostprivilegeddepressantpopulatedassessclassifiedfuelfedvaluebook

4 Circle the correct form(s). Sometimes both words are correct.

1 unsold / undersold

2 underadvantaged / disadvantaged

3 anti-war / overwar

4 underrated / overrated

5 unprivileged / underprivileged

6 unpaid / underpaid

5 Complete the dialogues.

1 Will this cream reduce the swelling? ~ Yes, it's ....

2 Is there enough work for Joe in the factory? ~ No, he's rather ....

3 Has the painting gone up in value? ~ No, sadly it has actually ....

4 I keep getting computer viruses. ~ You need some ....

5 We should consider that plan again. ~ I agree; it's time to .... it.

6 My chicken's still red in the middle. ~ Don't eat it – they've .... it.

7 Why was she rushed to hospital? ~ She was on drugs and took an ....

8 That child is terribly thin, isn't he? ~ Yes, if you ask me, he's ....

Remember to test yourself

75 I can use suffixes

A -ize and -ify 🎧

The suffixes -ize (also -ise) and -ify are added to adjectives and nouns to form verbs, indicating 'become or make something like (the adjective or noun)'. Adding -ify may change the spelling of the verb.

Noun/Adj	Example with -ize	Meaning
legal ADJ	Some people want to **legalize** drugs.	make sth legal.
nation N	The government is planning to **nationalize** the railways.	put an industry or company under the control of the government. OPP **privatize**.
vandal N (person)	Youths have **vandalized** the bus shelter.	damage or destroy sth for no reason. **vandalism** N.
character N	The coastline is **characterized** by very steep cliffs.	give sth its typical quality or feature. **characteristic** ADJ.
visual ADJ	I can't **visualize** what the room will look like.	form a picture of sth in your mind. SYN **imagine**.

Also: **economize, popularize, modernize, personalize, commercialize, finalize, specialize, industrialize, socialize, generalize, familiarize, itemize, equalize, standardize, symbolize**

Noun/Adj	Example with -ify	Meaning
intense ADJ	The news has **intensified** speculation that the chairman may resign.	**intense** (of feelings) very strong. If you **intensify sth**, you make it greater in strength or degree. SYN **heighten sth**.
solid N, ADJ	When the liquid cools, it **solidifies**.	become solid or make sth solid.
pure ADJ	These tablets **purify** the water.	If sth is **pure** it isn't mixed with anything. If you **purify** sth, you remove any dirty substances to make it pure.
quantity N	It's hard to **quantify** how much I need.	express sth as an amount or number.
peace N	One of the men tried to **pacify** the angry crowd.	make sb who is angry become quiet and calm. SYN **placate sb**.

Also: **electrify, simplify, identify, exemplify** (= give examples), **clarify** (= make sth clear)

❶ What are the verbs related to these nouns or adjectives?

1 character .... 4 symbol .... 7 electric ....
2 solid .... 5 legal .... 8 peace ....
3 clear .... 6 industrial .... 9 example ....

❷ Replace the underlined words with a verb ending in -ize or -ify in the correct form.

1 We will all have to spend less money. ....
2 The presence of the police heightened the tension in the crowd. ....
3 After all these years, I can't imagine what his sister will look like. ....
4 All the bus shelters have been damaged by gangs of youths. ....
5 The promise of action did not placate the angry demonstrators. ....
6 We need to remove any dirty or harmful substances from the water. ....
7 First they nationalized the railway, now they plan to sell it off. ....
8 Can we express in an amount how much damage has been done? ....

Remember to test yourself

3 ABOUT YOUR COUNTRY Write your answers or ask another student.

Has your government recently nationalized or privatized any industries? ....

Do you have much vandalism? What things are vandalized? ....

Is there currently anything against the law that you would like to legalize? ....

Does your country specialize in making any particular type of product? If so, what? ....

B -proof, -free 🎧

Buy our **foolproof** guide to dressing for your body shape.

Interested in **tax-free** earnings or **inflation-proof savings**? Contact us today.

Take the heat out of cooking with our **ovenproof** dishes.

Buy a plasma TV and get 12 months' **interest-free** credit.

Magnetic childproof safety locks.

No other lock compares!

Glossary

foolproof	If sth is **foolproof** it is so well designed that it cannot go wrong or be used wrongly (a **foolproof** machine/method).
tax-free	**Tax-free** earnings are earnings on which you don't have to pay tax.
inflation-proof savings	savings that are safe because they are guaranteed to go up as much as inflation.
ovenproof	able to be used safely inside an oven.
interest-free	**Interest-free** credit is a loan that you don't have to pay interest on.
magnetic	ADJ, **magnet** N (*see picture*).
childproof	If sth is **childproof** it is designed so that children cannot open or use it.

spotlight   *-proof, -free*

-proof means safe against the thing mentioned, e.g. a **waterproof** coat doesn't let water through; a **soundproof** room doesn't let sound through; a **bullet-proof** vest (*see picture*) protects the wearer from bullets (also **bullet-proof armour/windows**).

-free means without the thing mentioned, e.g. if you buy **duty-free** cigarettes you don't have to pay **duty** (= tax); a **trouble-free** life is a life without worry or anxiety.

4 Choose the best noun from the right for each of the adjectives on the left.

trouble-free	tax-free	room	perfume
soundproof	foolproof	locks	life
childproof	duty-free	income	method

5 Complete the sentences with a suitable word.

1 If you're doing some cooking, use the other dishes; these aren't ....

2 You can buy most fridges and freezers with .... credit.

3 Anyone can use this machine: it's ....

4 Famous people sometimes travel in cars with .... windows for security.

5 You need to make sure that any savings you have are ....

6 My feet are wet. These boots aren't ....

Remember to test yourself

76 I can use words with prepositions

A Noun + preposition 🎧

Noun	Example with a preposition	Meaning
excerpt	*She's reading an **excerpt from** her latest novel.*	a short piece taken from a book, piece of music, etc. SYN **extract** (from a film it is a **clip**).
remedy	*What's the **remedy for** this crisis? It is used as a **remedy for** colds.*	1 a way of dealing with a problem. SYN **solution**. 2 a treatment to cure an illness, reduce pain, etc.
aptitude	*I have no **aptitude for** languages.*	natural skill or ability in doing sth.
restriction	*Are there **restrictions on** parking here?*	a law or rule that limits what you can do, or what can happen.
compilation	*The CD is a **compilation of** her best singles.*	different items, especially music or writing, that are brought together in a performance, CD, or book.
disregard	*He shows a complete **disregard for** his own safety.*	a lack of care or concern about sth (you can also **have no regard for sth**).
complex	*He has a **complex about** his nose.*	an abnormal worry or concern about sth.
substitute	*You can use honey as a **substitute for** sugar.*	a thing that you use or have instead of the one you usually use or have.
grudge	*He has a **grudge against** his boss.*	a feeling of dislike for sb because of sth they have done to you.
involvement	*They have some **involvement with** a number of companies.*	the act of participating in sth.
ban	*There's a total **ban on** smoking.*	a rule that says sth is not allowed.

---

spotlight   *control of/over sth/sb*

You can **gain/keep/lose control of sth/sb**. *The army has **gained control of** the city.*

You can also **have control over sb/sth**. *The parents **have no control over** their children.*

---

❶ Circle the correct word.

1 a grudge for / against someone
2 a ban on / of alcohol
3 a substitute for / of something
4 a complex on / about something
5 have control over / about something

6 an aptitude for / about something
7 a disregard of / for something
8 involvement with / for something
9 an extract from / for something
10 a remedy for / of something

❷ Complete the sentences with a suitable noun.

1 He's a thoughtless man, and has absolutely no _____ for other people's feelings.
2 The album is largely a _____ of her old songs.
3 I had to read an _____ from her autobiography.
4 Barry has had a _____ against me ever since I was promoted over him.
5 I've never had an _____ for figures or mental arithmetic.
6 They showed a couple of _____ from Almodóvar's latest film.
7 Is there any _____ on the number of books we can borrow from the library?
8 She's lost _____ of the movement in her left arm.

📓 Remember to test yourself

B Adjective or verb + preposition 🎧

Having **embarked on** industrial action, the air traffic controllers are now **intent upon** causing maximum disruption, and most flights will be **subject to** long delays.

Some of the workers remain stubbornly **resistant to** change, but they are no longer **representative of** the majority, who now seem **reconciled to** the new proposals.

Problems may **stem from** the fact that a new computer isn't always fully **compatible with** existing equipment, and people may have to learn to **live with** this.

The way these women are **dependent on** their husbands, and still **subservient to** them, is **reminiscent of** life in the 19th century.

Glossary

embark on sth	start to do sth new or difficult.
intent upon/on sth	determined to do sth.
subject to sth	likely to be affected by sth, especially sth bad.
stem from sth	be the result of sth.
compatible with sth/sb	able to be used with sth or exist with sb without causing problems.
live with sth	accept an unpleasant situation.
resistant to sth	opposed to sth and trying to stop it happening.
representative of sth/sb	typical of a particular group or thing.
reconciled to sth	able to accept a bad situation that you cannot change. SYN **resigned to sth**.
dependent on sb/sth	needing sb/sth in order to survive or be successful.
subservient to sb	always obeying sb and doing what they want.
reminiscent of sth/sb	tending to remind people of sth/sb.

❸ Match 1–6 with a–f.

1 He's a representative …
2 The times are subject …
3 They plan to embark …
4 The two are not compatible …
5 He is still intent …
6 The difficulties stem …

a on a new venture.
b with each other.
c upon winning the competition.
d of the group.
e from the earlier injury.
f to change.

❹ Complete the dialogues with a suitable word.

1 Would you say he's typical? ~ Yes, he's fairly _____ of the group.
2 Does he need Marion? ~ Yes, he's completely _____ on her.
3 Does she do whatever he tells her? ~ Yes, she's totally _____ to him.
4 Do they accept the changes? ~ I think they're _____ to them now.
5 He's determined to succeed, isn't he? ~ Yes, he seems _____ on pursuing his goals.
6 Are the trains running on time yet? ~ No, they're still _____ to delays.
7 He can't change his situation, can he? ~ No, he'll just have to _____ with it.
8 They hate any kind of change. ~ Yes, they're extremely _____ to it.
9 Why don't they get on with each other? ~ It _____ from a row they had ages ago.
10 It's quite a strange piece of music. ~ Yes, it's _____ of 1980s rock music.

Remember to test yourself

77 I can use prepositional phrases

A A range of prepositional phrases 🎧

A Did she get the job **on merit**?
B Yes, **on balance** she was the right choice.

A The journey must have been boring.
B **On the contrary**, it was fantastic!

A **On reflection** I wish we'd stayed in London.
B Yes, I wouldn't have moved **by choice**.

A She rings me every day **without fail**.
B She must be very keen on you!

A Do you have to travel **at short notice**?
B Yes, I get a call and have to leave **at once**.

A Is that a new camera?
B Yes. I got it **in exchange for** my TV.

A There's a job going at the studios.
B Yeah, Basil mentioned it **in passing**.

A I can't be bothered to cook.
B Well, **at the very least**, have a burger.

Glossary

on merit	according to how good sb is, and for no other reason.	**at short notice**	with very little warning (also **at a moment's notice**).
on balance	after considering all the facts. SYN **all things considered**.	**at once**	immediately. SYN **right away**, **straightaway**.
on the contrary	used for emphasizing that sth is true even though it is the opposite of what has been suggested.	**in exchange for sth**	If you give sb sth **in exchange for** sth, you give them sth and they give you sth of a similar value or type.
on reflection	after thinking carefully about sth.		
by choice	as a thing you have chosen.	**in passing**	If you say sth **in passing**, you say it while you are talking about sth else.
without fail	1 always. 2 When you tell sb to do sth **without fail**, you are telling them they must do it (*Be home by 10.00 without fail!*).	**at the very least**	as an absolute minimum.

1 Circle the correct word.

1 He came in / at a moment's notice.
2 On / In balance, that's the best one.
3 She mentioned it on / in passing.
4 He comes every day without fail / failing.

5 She got the job in / on merit alone.
6 We have to leave right way / away.
7 No, on / in the contrary, we loved the show!
8 She got it in exchange / change for a favour.

2 Complete the sentences using words from left and right.

at	on	at	by
without	on	at	in

once	fail	exchange for	balance
the very least	choice	short notice	reflection

1 I drive to work, but I'd never do it _____ if I could avoid it.
2 You should take the dessert out of the freezer and serve it _____ .
3 I thought I understood it, but _____ I realized it was more complicated.
4 They should give me my money back or _____ offer to exchange the shoes.
5 We're offering her a free room in our house _____ looking after our child.
6 I need you to finish this project by tomorrow morning, _____ .
7 It may be difficult to find someone to do the job _____ , but we'll try.
8 I would say that, _____ , the best thing is to do nothing for the moment.

Remember to test yourself

B More phrases 🎧

GOVERNMENT **OUT OF TOUCH WITH** PUBLIC MOOD

Road named **in honour of** Nelson Mandela

Giant insurance firm **under investigation** for fraud

GENE THERAPY TRIAL **ON HOLD**

Statue unveiled **in memory of** Mother Theresa

Couple found **in possession of** cocaine

New shopping centre **under construction**

Traffic flow improved **by means of** better public transport

UNIONS WORK HARD TO KEEP GOVERNMENT **IN OFFICE**

Film release delayed **out of respect for bereaved** family

Glossary	
out of touch (with sth)	no longer having recent knowledge or information about sth. OPP **in touch** (also **out of luck**, **out of sight**).
in honour of sb/sth	in order to show respect and admiration for sb or sth.
giant	(of a company) very large and successful.
on hold	delayed until a later time or date.
in memory of sb/sth	in honour of, and to remind people of, sb who has died.
in possession of sth	FML having or holding sth.
by means of sth	FML with the help of sth.
in office	in a position of authority, especially in government (also **in power**, **in danger**, **in trouble**).
out of respect (for sb)	because of consideration and respect felt for sb.
bereaved	If sb is **bereaved**, a close friend or relative has recently died.

spotlight *under*

Under can mean 'in the process of something', e.g.:
under investigation (= in the process of being investigated),
under discussion,
under construction,
under attack.

❸ Tick the words which are possible. One, two, or three my be possible.

1 The government has been *in power* ☐ *out of touch* ☐ *in office* ☐ for years.
2 Following the attack, several men are now *under investigation* ☐ *under suspicion* ☐ *on hold*.
3 The suspect was found *in possession of* ☐ *by means of* ☐ *in honour of* ☐ stolen goods.
4 I attended the ceremony *in honour of* ☐ *out of respect for* ☐ *in memory of* ☐ those who died.
5 She is *in touch* ☐ *out of luck* ☐ *out of sight* ☐ with the feelings of the general public.

❹ One word is missing from each line. What is it, and where does it go? Write it at the end.

1 We have had to put our holiday plans on for the moment because of work. ....
2 Out respect for the bereaved family, hundreds turned up at the funeral. ....
3 I'm afraid I can't help as I'm really out of with this area of research. ....
4 The demonstrators will be in serious if the army starts to attack them. ....
5 The multi-storey car park has been construction for six months. ....
6 He works for a engineering company; it's a multinational and doing very well. ....
7 She opened the can by of a special device designed for the disabled. ....
8 We caught a glimpse of the rabbit before it ran of sight into the bushes. ....

Remember to test yourself

78 I can use a range of adjectives

A Synonyms and opposites 🎧

Marcus Campion was nearing the end of a **distinguished** career. He was a man of **exceptional** talent, and had been one of the most **eminent** lawyers of his generation, but he felt **perplexed** and uneasy as he considered his latest case. 'This Mabbutt is a **bizarre** character I'll admit, and his story is somewhat **implausible**,' remarked Campion to his army of admiring young colleagues. 'But is it really **conceivable** that he could kill his young wife and daughter?' Campion had defended **wicked** men in the past, but now the prospect of it made him feel quite **dejected**. He sat down with a heavy heart. ♩

Glossary

distinguished	successful, and admired and respected by others. SYN **illustrious**.
exceptional	unusually good. SYN **outstanding**.
perplexed	confused because you are unable to understand sth. SYNS **puzzled**, **baffled**.
bizarre	very strange and unusual. SYN **weird**.
implausible	not reasonable or likely to be true. OPP **plausible**. (A **convincing** story makes you believe it is true. OPP **unconvincing**.)
conceivable	able to be imagined or believed; possible. OPP **inconceivable**.
wicked	bad and morally wrong. SYN **evil**.
dejected	unhappy and depressed. SYN **despondent**.

spotlight Fame

Someone who is **eminent** is famous and respected, often for being good at a profession. If someone or something is **notorious**, they are well known for being bad (e.g. a **notorious** criminal). SYN **infamous** FML.

❶ Circle the correct word(s). Sometimes both words are correct.

1 No one knows why he made that decision. We were all rather dejected / perplexed .
2 After the mistakes we've made, it's conceivable / inconceivable we'll lose the election.
3 It was an unusual story, but it sounded quite plausible / convincing .
4 Al Capone was a notorious / an infamous American gangster.
5 I couldn't tell you what the film was about; it was exceptional / bizarre .
6 Two of my uncles had illustrious / distinguished careers in the navy.

❷ Write the answers.

1 a synonym for *infamous* _____
2 a synonym for *evil* _____
3 the opposite of *convincing* _____
4 a synonym for *perplexed* _____
5 the opposite of *conceivable* _____
6 a synonym for *weird* _____
7 the opposite of *plausible* _____
8 a synonym for *dejected* _____
9 a synonym for *illustrious* _____
10 a synonym for *outstanding* _____

❸ Complete the words in the sentences.

1 He was a w_____ man and responsible for the death of many innocent people.
2 She looked very d_____ when I saw her this morning, after the defeat yesterday.
3 She's an e_____ scientist as well as being a well-known writer.
4 I was completely b_____ by his directions; I couldn't understand them at all.
5 He played an o_____ game – he was easily the best player on the pitch.
6 There's a b_____ story in the paper about a man who lives underwater.

Remember to test yourself

B Adjectives easily confused 🎧

Adjective	Example	Meaning
concluding **conclusive**	*It's in the **concluding** chapter.* *Do we have **conclusive** proof?*	(of the final chapter/section of sth) ending. showing sth to be definitely true.
tasteful **tasty**	*The room was very **tasteful**.* *The soup was very **tasty**.*	(especially of clothes, furniture, etc.) attractive and of good quality. having a pleasant taste (**tasteless** is the opposite of **tasty** and **tasteful**).
naked **nude** **bare**	*The child was almost **naked**.* *She posed as a **nude** model for Picasso.* *They walked in **bare** feet.*	not wearing clothes. used to talk about the naked human form in art (**in the nude** = naked). (of a part of the body) not covered by clothes (**bare head/arms/legs**).
exhausted **exhaustive**	*He was **exhausted** after the run.* *It's an **exhaustive** investigation.*	extremely tired. SYN **worn out**. extremely thorough and complete.
comprehensive **comprehensible** SYN **intelligible**	*They gave me a **comprehensive** list of hotels in the area.* *It's a clear and **comprehensible** document.*	including all or almost all the facts or details that may be necessary. able to be understood. OPPS **incomprehensible**, **unintelligible**.
invaluable **worthless**	*Her advice was **invaluable**.* *That vase is **worthless**.*	very useful or valuable. having no worth or value. SYN **valueless**.
childlike **childish**	*He has a **childlike** enthusiasm.* *Her behaviour is very **childish**.*	APPROVING having qualities typical of a child. DISAPPROVING behaving in a silly way.
negligent **negligible**	*They have proved that the doctors were **negligent**.* *The damage was **negligible**.*	FML not taking enough care over sth you are responsible for. so small as to be of no importance.

❹ Correct the mistakes. Three sentences have no mistakes.

1 In some countries women can't walk around with naked arms. _____
2 She was crying just because she lost her pen. That's a bit childlike, isn't it? _____
3 Police have carried out an exhaustive search for the missing girl. _____
4 He wouldn't give me any money for it – he said it was invaluable. _____
5 The police found a nude body in the lake. _____
6 The fish dish was very tasty. _____
7 Someone has scratched the side of my car, but the damage is negligent. _____
8 He used naked models in many of his paintings. _____
9 We were completely worn out after all that gardening. _____

❺ Complete the adjective in each sentence.

1 They've done some research but we'll have to wait for a more *comp*_____ study.
2 She still has a *child*_____ quality about her, which is lovely.
3 There is no *concl*_____ evidence that Parker was at the scene of the crime.
4 They carried out an *exhaust*_____ study into the causes of the disaster.
5 All the decor was very *tast*_____ and it created a charming atmosphere.
6 The heroine gets killed in the *concl*_____ chapter of the book.
7 Anyone could follow her instructions: they were clear and *comp*_____ .
8 They found that one of the police officers was *negli*_____ in his duties.

79 I can **use different types of adverb**

A Commenting 🎧

A I can't believe that Martin still commutes to London every day: it's an awful journey.

B I know. But **apparently** he really likes his job. And **presumably** he earns a lot more working in London.

A Yeah, I guess so. But **ultimately** I think he does it for his career, not the money.

B Well, **to be perfectly honest**, I think he's mad.

A Yes, it's **obviously** not what we would choose. You want to be able to spend time with your family, **naturally**, and I wouldn't commute to London because … well, **basically** I'm too lazy. But Martin's different. His career means **practically** everything to him.

B True. But **strangely enough**, he wasn't all that ambitious when we were at school.

Glossary

apparently	according to what you have heard or read. SYN **evidently**.
presumably	used to say that you think sth is probably true.
ultimately	finally, when everything has been considered.
to be (perfectly) honest	used when saying what you really think about sth. SYNS **frankly**, **personally**.
obviously	used when giving information that you expect other people to know already or agree with. SYN **clearly**.
naturally	used to say that sth is normal and not surprising. SYN **of course**.
basically	used when giving the most important fact. SYN **essentially**.
practically	almost. SYN **virtually**.
strangely (enough)	used to show that sth is surprising. SYNS **oddly/curiously** (enough).

❶ Replace the underlined word(s) with another word or phrase that keeps the same meaning.

1 Sharon rang a couple of minutes ago. <u>Apparently</u>, the others missed the train. _____

2 They said the restaurant was always busy, but <u>surprisingly</u> it was almost empty. _____

3 <u>Virtually</u> all the shops were closed when I got into town. _____

4 He promised to come, but <u>I would think that</u> he'll turn up later. _____

5 We got there early <u>essentially</u> because we weren't sure when it started. _____

6 I got her a ticket but, <u>to be perfectly honest</u>, I don't think she's interested. _____

❷ Complete the sentences with a suitable word or phrase.

1 I know he won't be happy, but f_____ I don't care what he thinks.

2 A_____ we can't get tickets until tomorrow. That's what he told me.

3 We can all say what we think, but u_____ it's your decision.

4 There are eight of us, so o_____ we'll need two cars.

5 We're both chefs, so n_____ we talk about food quite a lot.

6 I usually feel nervous before I give a talk, but c_____ e_____ I felt fine today.

Remember to test yourself

B Stating a perspective or viewpoint 🎧

Word	Example	Meaning
commercially	***Commercially**, the film was a flop, but I really enjoyed it.*	= from the point of view of sales or profit. SYN **financially**. **commercial** ADJ.
traditionally	***Traditionally** it was men who went out to work, but that's changing.*	= according to past custom. **traditional** ADJ.
logically	***Logically**, we should consult a lawyer if there is a legal problem.*	= if we are to act sensibly and with sound reasons. **logical** ADJ. **logic** N.
socially	***Socially**, it's good for children to mix with other kids in a playgroup.*	= from the point of view of making friends. **social** ADJ.
realistically	***Realistically**, people won't give up their cars unless public transport is greatly improved.*	= if we are sensible about what can be achieved, we have to conclude that ... **realistic** ADJ.
officially	***Officially**, we can't go in until 10 a.m., but they might open earlier.*	= according to the rules, or what we have been told. OPP **unofficially**.
indirectly	*The changes aren't aimed at us, but we will be affected **indirectly**.*	= as an additional effect or consequence. OPP **directly**.
technically	***Technically** her performance was very good, but I didn't personally enjoy it.*	= from the point of view of her technical skill. **technical** ADJ. **technique** N.
physically **mentally**	***Physically** the work isn't difficult ... ... but **mentally** it's very tough.*	= considering the effect on the body. = considering the effect on the mind.
theoretically	***Theoretically** we could still lose the championship.*	used to say that sth could possibly happen or be true, but is unlikely.
as far as sth **is concerned**	***As far as** money is **concerned**, we can manage.*	used to give facts or an opinion about an aspect of sth.

---

spotlight ... *speaking*

This word can be added to some adverbs when an area of activity is being defined.
*Technically **speaking**, he was good.   Financially **speaking**, it was a disaster.*

---

❸ Replace the underlined words with a single adverb.

1   <u>According to the rules</u>, nobody is allowed in without a ticket. ....
2   <u>In terms of the profit we made</u>, the festival was a great success. ....
3   <u>In terms of what we can actually achieve</u>, 80 per cent is probably the maximum. ....
4   <u>For the good of society</u> this legislation will bring considerable improvements. ....
5   <u>In terms of technique</u>, she is very competent. ....
6   <u>It's reasonable and sensible that</u> the money should be divided between her sons. ....
7   <u>It is possible that</u> we could work on Sunday, but we'd be exhausted. ....
8   <u>It's the custom that</u> the festival is held on the last weekend in May. ....

❹ Complete the sentences with a suitable word or phrase.

1   As far as the environment is ...., it could be very damaging.
2   Physically the job is quite easy but .... it demands a lot of concentration.
3   The job cuts are in a different department but they will affect us ....
4   He's a natural athlete, but technically .... he still has a lot to learn.
5   .... children sing songs outside people's homes. It happens every year.
6   .... money is concerned, it's been quite successful.

Remember to test yourself

C Adverbs with different or overlapping meanings 🎧

I worked in the tax office **briefly**, but it seemed like **forever**.

I don't know **precisely** how it happened, but I could see she was **truly** sorry about it.

She said she did it **purely** to get experience, but it wasn't **strictly** true.

The restaurant is **invariably** full, but it's **primarily** for tourists.

It wasn't **simply** my fault; we're both **equally** responsible.

Things have changed **somewhat** since I was there, but it's still **relatively** unspoilt.

Glossary

briefly	1 for a short time. 2 in a few words (*he explained* **briefly**).
forever	for a long time; for all time (*nothing lasts* **forever**).
purely	completely and only (**purely by chance**). SYN **simply**.
strictly	exactly and completely (also used to emphasize that sth must happen in all circumstances: *Smoking in the lift is* **strictly** *prohibited.*).
simply	just; only (also, absolutely: *He was* **simply** *brilliant.*).
equally	to the same degree (also used to introduce a second point which is as important as the first).
precisely	exactly and correctly (also used to emphasize that sth is very true or obvious: *He's very young; that's* **precisely** *why he needs my help.*).
truly	sincerely (also used to emphasize a particular quality: *a* **truly** *remarkable man*).
invariably	used to emphasize that sth is always true or always happens.
primarily	mainly. SYNS **chiefly, predominantly**.
somewhat	fairly; quite (can be used after a verb or before an adjective).
relatively	to a fairly large degree in comparison with sth else.

5 Tick the correct word(s). More than one may be correct.

1 It was *relatively* ☐ *strictly* ☐ *somewhat* ☐ unusual, but not that strange.
2 She studies physics *simply* ☐ *equally* ☐ *purely* ☐ because she enjoys it.
3 I'm not sure she is being *strictly* ☐ *precisely* ☐ *equally* ☐ honest.
4 It's not a huge place but it's *invariably* ☐ *relatively* ☐ *precisely* ☐ big.
5 He spoke *relatively* ☐ *briefly* ☐ *chiefly* ☐ about his childhood.
6 I'm always punctual, but she's *precisely* ☐ *invariably* ☐ *primarily* ☐ late.
7 His voice is *simply* ☐ *predominantly* ☐ *truly* ☐ remarkable.
8 Camping here is *truly* ☐ *somewhat* ☐ *strictly* ☐ forbidden.

6 Complete the sentences with a suitable adverb.

1 She's worked all over the world, but _____ in North and South America.
2 I'm unlucky with the weather. It _____ rains when I go on holiday.
3 She came to stay with us _____ last year; just for a few days.
4 I don't like getting there too early, but _____ I don't want to be late.
5 She's doing well now, but her success won't last _____ .
6 I was _____ sorry to hear about her mother's accident.
7 Pavel knows _____ what we need, so he's getting everything.

Remember to test yourself

80 I can **use euphemisms** 🎧

> My neighbour's **getting on a bit**; she's **visually impaired** and rather **hard of hearing**. I feel very sorry for her as well because her husband **passed away** recently and she had to have her cat **put to sleep**.

> It says here that two soldiers were injured during a **friendly fire** incident. There's nothing 'friendly' about it – just another of those terrible euphemisms, like '**collateral damage**'.

> There's more talk of **downsizing** at work. If I were the boss, I'd **let** Godfrey **go**; he's **not exactly bright** – and I've seen him **helping himself to** the office stationery.

A **euphemism** is a mild or less direct word or phrase that people use to refer to something embarrassing or unpleasant, sometimes to make it seem more acceptable than it is, e.g. *I don't know what I'd do **if anything happened to him*** (= if he died). Euphemisms often refer to death, war, age, and sex.

Glossary

getting on (a bit)	INF (of a person) quite old.	**not exactly bright**	a way of saying that sb is unintelligent (also **not exactly clever/practical**, etc.).
visually impaired	having poor eyesight.		
hard of hearing	unable to hear very well.		
pass away	die. SYN **pass on**.	**help yourself to sth**	DISAPPROVING steal sth.
put sth to sleep	kill a sick or injured animal with drugs so that it dies without pain. SYN **put sth down**.	**friendly fire**	If sb is killed or injured by **friendly fire**, they are hit by a bomb or weapon fired by their own side.
downsizing	the dismissing of employees to reduce costs. **downsize** V.	**collateral damage**	death or injury to ordinary citizens, and possibly damage to buildings as well, during the course of a war.
let sb go	dismiss sb or make them redundant.		

❶ Complete the dialogues.

1 Was it a _____ incident? ~ Yes, hit by weapons from our own side.
2 She's hopeless at housework. ~ Yes, she's not exactly _____ , is she?
3 Did he catch what you said? ~ No, I think he's a bit _____ of _____ .
4 Will he lose his job? ~ Yes, they'll have to _____ him _____ .
5 Is your grandmother still alive? ~ No, she _____ two years ago.
6 There's not much money left. ~ No, I think Eric's been _____ himself to it.
7 Was the dog badly injured? ~ Yes, I'm afraid they had to _____ it to _____ .
8 He can't see very well, can he? ~ No, he's visually _____ .

❷ Rewrite the sentences using the words in capitals. Make any necessary changes.

1 Did she just take a couple of pens? HELP _____
2 The company is cutting the number of workers. DOWNSIZE _____
3 The animal was killed by the vet. DOWN _____
4 My dog Barty is very stupid. CLEVER _____
5 The president's pretty old. ON _____
6 There were many killed and injured in the bombing. COLLATERAL _____

Remember to test yourself

Review: Aspects of language

Unit 74

1 Cross out the wrong answer or answers.

1 I think he was mis................................... .
   a) informed   b) advised   c) understood   d) diagnosed

2 The children were under................................... .
   a) advantaged   b) nourished   c) privileged   d) fed

3 It's an anti-................................... march.
   a) drugs   b) racism   c) war   d) virus

4 The two things are inter................................... .
   a) dependent   b) similar   c) related   d) place

5 I think she was ill-................................... .
   a) handled   b) advised   c) treated   d) prepared

A Z **more words**: *ill-conceived, interlinked, misquote, demobilize, overexpose, oversubscribed, relaunch, reinstate, reinvest*

Unit 75

1 Rewrite the sentences using the word in capitals with an appropriate suffix. The meaning must stay the same.

1 The hurricane is getting stronger as it heads towards land. INTENSE

2 You don't have to pay tax on this income. TAX

3 This kind of vegetation is typical of the region. CHARACTER

4 The building contains a system which removes pollution from the air. PURE

5 You can't hear a thing outside the studio. SOUND

6 He needs to give a better explanation of his intentions. CLEAR

7 If you leave that in the sun, it'll just go hard. SOLID

8 The plan I've devised can't possibly go wrong. FOOL

A Z **more words**: *institutionalize, harmonize, rationalize, liquidize, vilify, magnify, falsify*

Unit 76

1 Complete the sentences with a suitable preposition.

1 In your country, are children largely subservient _____ their parents? _____
2 Do most drivers show a total disregard _____ the speed limit? _____
3 What would you like to see a ban _____ in your country? _____
4 Do parents usually have a firm control _____ their teenagers? _____
5 Are most people resistant _____ advice on healthy eating? _____
6 Do people in your country generally have an aptitude _____ languages? _____
7 Do many people embark _____ a new career in middle age? _____
8 Do you agree that there is no substitute _____ hard work? _____

2 ABOUT YOUR COUNTRY Write your answers, or ask another student.

[A Z] **more words**: *allegiance to sb/sth, craving for sth, safeguard against sth, proportionate to sth, susceptible to sth, settle for sth*

Unit 77

1 Cross out the noun which does not follow the preposition at the beginning.

1 *on:* balance / passing / merit / reflection
2 *at:* once / choice / short notice / the very least
3 *in:* the contrary / office / power / possession of
4 *out of:* respect / sight / luck / discussion
5 *under:* suspicion / danger / investigation / attack

[A Z] **more words**: *on **account** of, out of **action**, in **accordance** with, on **hand**, out of **bounds**, under **duress**, off the **subject***

Unit 78

1 Complete the crossword.

					1	E								
		2				E								
			3			E								
4						E								
	5					E								
		6				E								
7						E								
	8					E								
		9				E								

1 bizarre
2 famous and respected in a professional capacity
3 unhappy and depressed
4 impossible to imagine or believe
5 including all or most of the facts or details necessary
6 lacking flavour
7 failing to take enough care over something you are responsible for
8 baffled
9 not wearing clothes

[A Z] **more words**: Use the synonyms feature boxes in the *Oxford Advanced Learner's Dictionary*, and look at: *artificial, dirty, exciting, nervous, serious, wrong.*

Unit 79

1 Use adverbs from the box to complete the sentences.

| invariably | indirectly | officially | purely | apparently | briefly | virtually | ultimately |

1 I met her _____ by chance outside the hairdresser's.
2 People who play chess are _____ good at logic puzzles.
3 She spoke _____ about her father, but I was disappointed. I wanted to hear more.
4 The outcome of the election is _____ certain; the polls give Lawson a 20 per cent lead.
5 The rise in interest rates is bound to affect us, at least _____ .
6 He had a difficult choice to make but, _____ , it was his decision and his alone.
7 I thought she had spread the rumour but _____ it was nothing to do with her.
8 He got us into the concert free, but _____ we should have paid.

2 Tick the best sentence ending. In some cases, both may be correct.

1 I'd invited too many people, and realistically
     a I should have realized that ☐.
     b I rang and told some not to come ☐.

2 The evening was freezing, but oddly enough
     a I took my coat ☐.
     b I hardly noticed ☐.

3 There wasn't enough food, but frankly
     a it was too late to do anything ☐.
     b I didn't care ☐.

4 Sue has a son, so naturally
     a I invited him too ☐.
     b she brought him ☐.

5 The guests were predominantly
     a from my neighbourhood ☐.
     b late arriving ☐.

6 By midnight I was practically
     a doing the washing up ☐.
     b asleep ☐.

A Z **more words:** *undoubtedly, ostensibly, supposedly, outwardly, numerically, overtly*

Unit 80

1 Complete the dialogues, explaining the literal meaning of the euphemisms. Look at the example first.

▶ He's getting on a bit. ~ You mean he *'s quite old* .
1 She's not exactly bright. ~ You mean she _____ .
2 He's visually impaired. ~ You mean he _____ .
3 The company are downsizing. ~ You mean they _____ .
4 They were hit by friendly fire. ~ You mean by _____ .
5 The cat has been put to sleep. ~ You mean it _____ .
6 He's a bit hard of hearing. ~ You mean he _____ .
7 I think she helped herself to the money. ~ You mean she _____ .
8 There's been some collateral damage. ~ You mean some _____ .

A Z **more words:** *put sb/sth out of their* **misery**, **do** *sb in, men's/ladies' (room), in the* **family** *way,* **throw** *up, give up the* **ghost**

Vocabulary building

The related forms of many words are included within the glossaries in the individual units (to find them, use the word list on pages 236–56). Other related forms are included in the tables below. The items in bold are all taught in the book, and the related forms all have a closely related meaning.

1 Adjectives and nouns

ADJECTIVE	NOUN
addicted	addiction, **addict**
additional	addition
alien, alienated	alienation
anonymous	**anonymity**
aromatic	**aroma**
attentive, inattentive	**attention**
bereavement	**bereaved**
blunt	bluntness
chaotic	**chaos**
compatible, incompatible	compatibility, incompatibility
concise	conciseness
cruel	cruelty
discreet, **indiscreet**	discretion, indiscretion
distracted	distraction
ecstatic	ecstasy
elated	elation
faithful	**faith**
familiar, unfamiliar	familiarity
flammable/inflammable	**flame**
hysterical	hysteria
jubilant	jubilation
neutral	neutrality
normal, **abnormal**	normality, abnormality
notorious	notoriety
nude	nudity, **nude**
precise	**precision**
proportionate	**proportion**
ruthless	ruthlessness
scandalous	**scandal**
secretive	secrecy, **secret**
snobbish	snobbery, **snob**
spiritual	**spirit**
subservient	subservience
subtle	subtlety
transparent	transparency
trivial	triviality
visible, **invisible**	visibility, invisibility
wicked	wickedness

2 Verbs and nouns

VERB	NOUN
accomplish	accomplishment
acquire	acquisition
allocate	allocation
compile	**compilation**
confront	confrontation
contribute	**contribution**, contributor
desert	desertion
detain	detention
detect	detection
distort	distortion
divert	diversion
embark	embarkation
impose	imposition
indulge	indulgence
photocopy	**photocopier**
proceed	**procedure**
propose	proposal, proposition
pursue	pursuit
reassure	reassurance
substitute	**substitute**, substitution
subtract	subtraction
suppress	suppression

 Test yourself

3 Nouns, verbs, and adjectives

NOUN(S)	VERB	ADJECTIVE
accumulation	**accumulate**	cumulative
adjustment	**adjust**	adjustable
appreciation	**appreciate**	appreciative
association	associate	**associated**
authenticity	authenticate	**authentic**
bend	**bend**	bent
comparison	**compare**	**comparable**, comparative
control	control	controlled, uncontrolled
description	**describe**	descriptive, **indescribable**
disruption	**disrupt**	**disruptive**
exhaustion	exhaust	**exhausted**
exploration	**explore**	exploratory
exposure	**expose**	exposed
favour	**favour**	favourable, unfavourable
flirt (person)	**flirt**	flirtatious
forgiveness	**forgive**	forgivable, **unforgivable**
inclusion	**include**	**inclusive**
indication	**indicate**	indicative
intrusion	**intrude**	intrusive
justification	**justify**	**justifiable**, justified
mixture	**mix**	mixed
opposition	oppose	**opposed**, opposing
possession	possess	possessive
provocation	**provoke**	provocative
purification	**purify**	**pure**
puzzle	**puzzle**	**puzzled**
quantity	**quantify**	quantifiable
reinforcement	reinforce	**reinforced**
reminiscence	reminisce	**reminiscent**
retaliation	**retaliate**	retaliatory
stimulation	**stimulate**	stimulating
symbolism, symbol	**symbolize**	symbolic

Answer key

Unit 1

1 1 D 2 S 3 S 4 D 5 D 6 D 7 S 8 S

2
1 ambiguity/ambiguities
2 precision
3 synonymous
4 interchangeable
5 interpretation
6 self-explanatory

3
1 literal
2 figurative
3 making
4 *Both answers are correct.*
5 sarcasm
6 mocked
7 ironic
8 *Both answers are correct.*

4
1 disapproving
2 literary
3 made
4 slang, current, dated/old-fashioned
5 pejorative/derogatory
6 figuratively

Unit 2

1
1 second thoughts
2 on my mind
3 get out of
4 believe this
5 flying
6 two minds
7 ulterior
8 tied up

2
1 crawling
2 thick
3 sweet
4 tied up
5 dawned

3
1 How did you **get** him …
2 keep you **going** until …
3 that will **make** it …
4 fishing that **brought** people …
5 it won't **keep** after tomorrow
6 to **put** them into words
7 that will **do** for …

4
1 brings
3 get
3 come
4 leave
5 do
6 keep
7 make
8 leave
9 get
10 push

Unit 3

1
1 cut
2 barbed
3 expectancy
4 pin
5 clips
6 polish
7 spare
8 passer

2
1 licence
2 kin
3 fancy
4 rhymes
5 weekend
6 certificate
7 fruit/slot

4 built-up, worn out, thick-skinned, panic-stricken, narrow-minded, bad-tempered

5
1 narrow-minded
2 last-minute
3 tongue-tied
4 single-minded
5 off-putting
6 broad-minded/open-minded

6 *Possible answers:*
1 Were there many dropouts?
2 There was a five-mile tailback.
3 It was a setback (for him) when he failed the exam.
4 We had a two-hour hold-up.
5 There was a breakdown on the motorway.
6 It was awful after the break-up.
7 What was the turnout?
8 The outbreak of war was inevitable.

7
1 turnout
2 write-off
3 let-down
4 break-up
5 tailbacks
6 outlay

Unit 4

1
1 go out, spread, die down
2 light, put out
3 catch, fire, burst, go up

2
1 caught
2 broke
3 spread
4 burst
5 on
6 put it out
7 setting

3
1 gone out
2 die down
3 went out
4 put, out
5 broke out
6 burst into
7 forest
8 spreading

5
1 considerable
2 principal
3 widespread
4 fierce/widespread
5 utter
6 classic

6
1 honour
2 faces
3 summary
4 effort
5 criticism
6 chaos
7 accent
8 escape

7
1 Torrential
2 gale-force
3 utter/total
4 considerable/great
5 concerted
6 main/principal
7 extensive/widespread
8 fierce/strong/widespread

8 *These words are not correct:*
1 c 2 a 3 c 4 b 5 a

9
1 eyesore, entirely
2 holds, take
3 made
4 settle, back
5 such thing
6 reached, entirely
7 prospect
8 offence, reach

Unit 5

1 1 reflect (4)   4 absorb (3)
  2 absorbed (1)   5 count (1)
  3 counted (2)   6 reflected (1)

2 1 shrugged   4 favour   6 circumstances
  2 owes   5 nodded   7 stamped
  3 raised

3 1 We could see our faces reflected **in** the water.
  2 She proposed **that we** leave the children behind. OR She proposed **leaving** the children behind.
  3 You can take dogs into shops in certain circumstance**s**.
  4 There were ten people there, **not** counting the two of us.
  5 He proposed **taking** the car. OR He proposed **that we** take the car.
  6 I'll need to reflect **on** what he said.

4 1 count myself lucky
  2 in favour of
  3 under the circumstances
  4 reflected badly on everyone

5 *The correct prepositions are:*
  1 conducive **to** sth
  2 fraught **with** (danger)
  3 devoid **of** sth
  4 immune **to** sth

Unit 6

1 1 reputable   5 inexcusable
  2 inclusive   6 uneventful
  3 inexplicable   7 apologetic
  4 comparable   8 indescribable

2 1 They excel at/in sport.
  2 I think he was a worthy winner.
  3 The party was uneventful.
  4 The flat is unfurnished.
  5 The trip was pointless.
  6 It's an interesting vase but it's worthless.
  7 The movement has a large following.
  8 There is increasing recognition of its value. OR People increasingly recognize its value.

3 1 housing   6 pointless
  2 noticeable   7 following
  3 apologetic   8 furnished
  4 inclusive
  5 unforgivable/inexcusable

4 1 finalize   4 handling   7 comparable
  2 excel   5 pointless   8 heartless
  3 emotive   6 mistook

6 1 to **keep** himself
  2 defend **myself**
  3 origin **of**
  4 **make** the confession

5 assured **me/him/us, etc.** it would
6 commit **himself**

7 *Possible answers:*
  1 Where did this originate?
  2 I want to simplify the procedure.
  3 There is a lot of alcohol abuse. OR Alcohol abuse is very common.
  4 Does the research give us an/any/some indication of a link?
  5 He's got to make a commitment.
  6 Did she make a confession?
  7 The boy suffered racial abuse.
  8 I was surprised at the severity of the conditions.

Unit 7

1 *Possible answers:*
  Frail people are often **doddery** (when they walk).
  A **paunch** is a fat **stomach**.
  Freckles are on your **skin**.
  Hair can be **ginger**.
  Chubby means a bit **fat**.
  You wear a **brace** on your **teeth**.

2 1 show off   4 straighten
  2 getting on for, gorgeous   5 stick out
  3 cheeks   6 cute

3 1 true   4 notice   7 better
  2 help you   5 more   8 can't
  3 positive   6 don't notice

4 1 pay   5 stripes
  2 unflattering 6 key
  3 features   7 draw
  4 hips   8 exaggeration

Unit 8

1 1 B   2 B   3 G   4 G   5 B   6 B   7 B   8 G

2 1 leaping/jumping   5 misinterpret
  2 look out   6 not necessarily
  3 observant   7 gestures, excessive
  4 display/show   8 combination

3 *These words are correct:*
  1 make   3 stroke   5 with
  2 fist   4 arms   6 someone

4 1 implication
  2 flirting
  3 leant/leaned, fancied/fancies
  4 stubborn/obstinate
  5 implies, mind, generalize
  6 fiddle

Unit 9

1 1 limping   5 chase
  2 stagger   6 marched
  3 dash   7 charged/dashed
  4 galloped   8 tiptoed/crept

2
1 had a pronounced limp
2 made a dash for cover
3 went for a stroll along the beach
4 broke into a gallop
5 led the charge
6 the car chase

3
1 sluggish
2 Bend
3 supple/agile
4 alternate
5 thought up/devised
6 constant
7 strenuous/arduous
8 recurrent

4
1 constant
2 alternate
3 loosen up / warm up
4 press-ups
5 sprint
6 fear

Unit 10

1
1 beeping
2 rattling
3 squelching
4 slam
5 creak
6 pitched
7 rustling
8 rumbling

2
1 creaks
2 rustling
3 beeping
4 high
5 screeching
6 slamming
7 rumble
8 rattle

3
1 mice squeak
2 owls hoot
3 dogs bark
4 wolves howl
5 dogs growl
6 cocks crow
7 bees buzz

4 1 P 2 N 3 N 4 N 5 P 6 N 7 P 8 N

5
1 roar
2 howling/roaring
3 bark, bite
4 squeaky
5 hooted
6 buzzing

Unit 11

1
1 sight/eyesight
2 discomfort
3 blinking
4 eliminate
5 glare
6 blurred

2
1 Sore, tired or burning eyes are classic symptoms of eye **strain**.
2 If your eyes are dry and **irritated**, try using eye drops.
3 He must be very **short-sighted** because he can't read the dictionary definitions.
4 You should get up and walk about to **ease/alleviate** the problem of back pain.
5 Make a conscious effort to **blink** more often to prevent dry eyes.
6 Whenever I make too much noise in the office, my colleague glares **at** me.

3
1 haze
2 spectacular, breathtaking
3 caught sight of, spotted
4 stand, keep
5 only just, barely
6 came into, disappeared from

4
1 I was only just able to make out the boat on the horizon.
2 As I turned the corner, the house came into view/sight.
3 Those stars are invisible without a telescope.
4 We could only just see the trees through the fog.
5 She eyed me very suspiciously.
6 The thief left the building and vanished into thin air.
7 I caught a glimpse of the thief as he ran out of the building. OR I glimpsed the thief as…
8 We watched the boat until eventually it disappeared from sight.

Unit 12

1 1 P 2 U 3 P 4 U 5 U 6 P 7 P 8 P

2
1 squeeze
2 stimulate
3 stroking
4 slid
5 steadily
6 pinch
7 applied
8 fingertips

3
1 flavour
2 unappetizing
3 pungent
4 musty
5 aroma
6 water
7 nauseating
8 insipid

4
1 appetizing
2 mouth-watering
3 delicate
4 pungent
5 gone off
6 disgusting
7 appetite
8 stench/smell
9 subtle

Unit 13

1 sprain your ankle
high blood pressure
hay fever
upset stomach
nasty rash
dislocated shoulder
splitting headache
itchy scalp
mouth ulcer

2
1 blisters
2 rash
3 diarrhoea
4 itch
5 constipated
6 pulled

4 1 T 2 F 3 T 4 T 5 F 6 T 7 T 8 T

5
1 dose
2 term
3 date
4 aspirin
5 limit
6 effects

6
1 lethargic
2 disorder/upset/ache
3 enclosed
4 expectations
5 persistent
6 discarded

Unit 14

1
1 happy-go-lucky
2 within reason
3 have a go at
4 considerate
5 passion
6 a real chatterbox/ really chatty
7 down-to-earth

2
1 attribute/quality
2 affection
3 go
4 pretentious
5 spontaneous
6 integrity

3
1 N   3 P   5 N   7 P   9 P
2 P   4 P   6 N   8 N   10 P

4
1 make   3 conceited   5 nose
2 struck   4 take   6 assertive

5
1 conscientious   4 ruthless
2 assertive   5 trustworthy
3 shrewd

6
1 misled
2 distant/stand-offish
3 diffident
4 impulsive/rash
5 cunning
6 deceptive

7
1 virtue, vice   5 surface, cover
2 sceptical   6 traits
3 cynical   7 naivety
4 cruel

Unit 15

1
1 P 2 N 3 N 4 P 5 P 6 N 7 P 8 N

2
lose your temper   desperately unhappy
over the moon   hit the roof
close to tears   go mad

3
1 stunned
2 his temper
3 desperation
4 heartbroken/devastated
5 the roof
6 ecstatic/euphoric/elated
7 tears
8 hysterical

4
1 uneasy   3 suppress   5 guarded
2 reveal   4 vulnerable 6 innermost

5
1 heart
2 wasn't in it
3 gave it away
4 on her sleeve, pent-up
5 heart

Unit 16

1
1 N 2 P 3 N 4 P 5 N 6 P

2
1 complimentary   5 inevitably
2 resented   6 strain
3 hostility   7 tough
4 sticking

3
1 instant   4 face(s)
2 up   5 goes
3 compliment

5
1 He's fully accepted ~~to~~ our decision. –
2 She feels she can confide ~~with~~ me. in
3 I think they all respect ~~for~~ him. –
4 The ~~initially~~ problem was money. initial
5 I regret his ~~reluctant~~ to go. reluctance
6 It took time to ~~hold~~ their respect. gain/
win/earn

6
1 How are things? 6 respect
2 reluctant   7 ups and downs
3 appreciates   8 looking up
4 Initially   9 way things are
5 accepts   10 bond, make sacrifices

Unit 17

1
1 courageous   4 inspirational
2 humble   5 dignity
3 bravery   6 idolize

2
1 I looked up to my father.
2 I want to follow in his footsteps.
3 Why did she have a go at him?
4 He dedicated himself to helping the poor.
5 She was my inspiration.
6 He was Paula's idol/hero.

4
1 hypocritical   4 malicious
2 rebellious   5 spiteful
3 idealistic   6 despicable

5
1 snob   5 idealist
2 gossip   6 hypocrite
3 rebel   7 vulgar/coarse/crude
4 bully

Unit 18

1
peer pressure, nature or nurture?, play a
part, broken home, deprived childhood, a
beneficial effect

2
1 P 2 P 3 N 4 N 5 P 6 N

3
1 home   4 nature   7 part
2 deprived 5 impact   8 incentive
3 pressure 6 model

5
1 set   3 make   5 do
2 kick up   4 pull   6 lay down

6
1 threatening
2 on and on (about them)
3 nagging
4 a mess
5 gave in / capitulated
6 unappealing

Unit 19

1
1 inoffensive   4 perceive
2 courteous   5 downwards
3 etiquette   6 chopsticks

2
1 customary
2 frowned
3 manners
4 viewed
5 considered
6 Customs
7 regarded, respectful
8 offensive
9 discourteous/disrespectful
10 etiquette

4
1 ~~put his foot in it~~
2 *All three are possible.*
3 ~~cheek~~
4 ~~her foot in it~~
5 *All three are possible.*
6 ~~comments, disgrace~~
7 *All three are possible.*
8 ~~an insolence~~

5
1 class
2 manners
3 behaviour
4 foot
5 put
6 downright
7 remark/comment
8 exception
9 taste

Unit 20

1
1 artichoke
2 pomegranate
3 beetroot
4 cinnamon
5 papaya
6 fennel
7 ginger
8 squash
9 almonds
10 radishes
11 lentils
12 bean sprouts

2
1 Raisins and sultanas are types of dried fruit.
2 Sage and coriander are herbs.
3 Almonds and cashews are types of nut.
4 Papaya and passion fruit are tropical fruits.
5 Ginger and cinnamon are spices.

4 cheese grater, lemon squeezer, kitchen scales, food processor, garlic crusher, deep fat fryer

5
1 colander
2 wok
3 corkscrew
4 ladle
5 sieve
6 whisk

6
1 lemon/lime/orange
2 cheese
3 flour
4 rice/fish/vegetables
5 fruit, vegetables, meat, bread, etc.
6 meat and some vegetables

7
1 grapes
2 chickens
3 fish
4 bread
5 cheese
6 pear
7 cake
8 nut

8
1 made a meal of it
2 to have his cake and eat it
3 chalk and cheese
4 eat my words
5 a fish out of water
6 fishy/a bit fishy (to me)

Unit 21

1
1 streets
2 wander
3 easy
4 it all
5 track
6 atmosphere
7 around
8 batteries

2
1 undergone
2 flourishing
3 remarkably
4 unique
5 unspoilt
6 remote

3
1 thriving
2 stunning
3 diverse
4 off the beaten track/isolated
5 trek
6 retain
7 unwind/take it easy/chill out
8 restored

4
1 easy
2 remote
3 restoration
4 laze
5 wander
6 cobbled
7 away from it

Unit 22

1
1 edge
2 effects
3 -biting
4 out of
5 twist
6 unanimously
7 adaptation
8 -tingling
9 ghost
10 applaud

2
1 audience
2 brilliant/sensational
3 acclaim
4 cast
5 set
6 phenomenally
7 nail-biting/gripping
8 clapping

3 1 D 2 S 3 S 4 S 5 D 6 S 7 S 8 D

4
1 deadly, stiff
2 clichéd
3 wooden
4 feeble
5 unconvincing
6 rubbish
7 death, mediocre
8 dire

Unit 23

1 1 F 2 F 3 T 4 F 5 T 6 T 7 F 8 T

2
1 round
2 drawn
3 victories
4 draw
5 runners-up
6 got through
7 the rest
8 knocked out

3
1 we **dominated** the first half
2 put us **under** a lot
3 we gave **away** a
4 went **to** pieces
5 let us **down**
6 no **chance** of
7 could be **relegated**

4 1 run
2 chance
3 promoted
4 verge of victory
5 unbeaten this season
6 form
7 on top/dominant

Unit 24

1 1 field   5 obtain/acquire
2 site   6 camping site
3 attract   7 wildlife
4 copy/imitate   8 scenery

2 1 process   4 countryside
2 nest, shed   5 seeds
3 plant, stem, roots   6 cottage, slopes

3 1 B   2 G   3 B   4 B   5 B   6 G

4 1 spade
2 my feet up
3 mow the lawn
4 cut back this bush
5 compost to the soil
6 plant some roses
7 hedge round the field
8 the weeding
9 fertile

Unit 25

1 1 around   3 focused   5 from
2 his   4 an   6 browse

2 1 search of   6 on impulse
2 after   7 drop
3 tag   8 off
4 shop around   9 browsing
5 minute/moment

3 bargain hunting, drug addict, compulsive
gambler, crippling debts, shopping spree,
leisure pursuit

4 1 heading   4 outweigh
2 indulge   5 outnumber
3 gadget   6 addicted to

Unit 26

1 1 hosts   5 socializes
2 disposable   6 drown out
3 away   7 contribution
4 time-consuming

2 1 laid on   5 warmed up
2 beforehand   6 livened up
3 contributed   7 deafening
4 gatecrashers   8 clearing up

3 1 in company   5 awkward
2 got/was drunk   6 warm welcome
3 loner   7 cliquey
4 do/party tonight   8 accompany you

4 1 join in   5 get-together/do
2 doubt   6 do/get-together, fancy
3 pop   7 company
4 own company   8 clique

Unit 27

1 1 transform
2 amend, adapt, reform
3 restore, revert, reverse
4 evolve, assimilate, transition

2 1 transition   5 go/revert
2 restore   6 adapt/adjust
3 evolution   7 irreversible
4 reversal   8 assimilate

3 1 N   2 N   3 P   4 N   5 P   6 P

4 1 subtle
2 sweeping/wholesale/major
3 refreshing
4 enforce
5 implement
6 bring about / cause

5 1 pursue   6 ongoing
2 sweeping   7 consultation
3 resistance   8 implemented
4 consulted   9 obvious
5 welcome

Unit 28

1 1 B   3 G   5 B   7 B   9 G
2 B   4 B   6 G   8 B   10 B

2 1 dryer
2 charge (up)
3 consume
4 appliances
5 conserve
6 batteries, still, charger
7 saving
8 consumer

4 1 environmentally-friendly, eco-friendly
2 in season
3 food miles, our carbon footprint
4 maximize
5 enterprise, venture
6 *All three are possible.*

5 1 groundbreaking   5 disposed
2 recycling   6 minimizes
3 venture   7 miles
4 recycle   8 season

Unit 29

1 1 S   2 D   3 S   4 D   5 S   6 S   7 S

2 1 out, extinct   4 in, wild
2 decline, gradual   5 reserve, habitat
3 danger, breed   6 species, becoming

3 1 ~~divested~~ diverted
2 ~~putting~~ taking
3 ~~puts~~ poses
4 ~~genes pool~~ gene pool
5 ~~in~~ on/upon
6 ~~over~~ after
7 ~~fund~~ funds
8 ~~threaten~~ threat

4 1 likelihood   4 rhino
2 territory   5 territorial
3 poaching   6 poverty

Unit 30

1 invasion, invasive
cure, curable/incurable
resumption
conventional
vaccination, vaccinate
diagnose, diagnostic
transplant

2 1 No   3 Yes   5 No   7 No   9 Yes
2 No   4 No   6 Yes   8 No   10 No

3 1 b   3 h   5 g   7 c   9 f
2 i   4 e   6 j   8 a   10 d

4 1 wiped out, eradicated
2 restricted, transplant
3 vaccinate, vaccine
4 conventional, advances
5 rate, survival
6 carry out/perform, confined

Unit 31

1 1 scroll up a document
2 enter your password
3 use computer jargon
4 hack into someone's computer
5 anti-virus protection
6 e-learning
7 do a web search
8 block spam from your inbox

2 1 password   4 google   7 viruses
2 username   5 links   8 filters
3 log on/in   6 search

3 1 T   2 F   3 T   4 T   5 F   6 T

4 1 downloaded   5 virtual
2 registered   6 dreamt/thought
3 videoblog, rated   7 downloaded
4 uploaded   8 format

Unit 32

1 1 emigrated   5 fled
2 seek   6 prejudice, migrants
3 refuge   7 seek/take
4 ethnic

2 1 There's no limit on the number of people granted political **asylum** in this country.
2 Racial and sexual **discrimination** is against the law in matters of employment.
3 Economic **migration** to richer countries has existed for centuries.
4 There's been a rise in the **deportation** of illegal workers back to their home countries.
5 Nearly half a million people were forced to **flee** their homes during the civil war, and many of them **took** refuge in the mountains, away from the fighting.
6 Many families **were** uprooted against their will to make way for the new road.

3 1 ~~for~~ towards
2 ~~acclimated~~ acclimatized
3 ~~nostalgic~~ nostalgia
4 ~~stereoscope~~ stereotype
5 ~~integrity~~ integration
6 ~~natural~~ native

4 1 used/accustomed   6 desire
2 native   7 integrate
3 faith   8 hostility/animosity
4 shock   9 peace
5 stereotypical   10 hang

Unit 33

1 1 protect someone's confidentiality, get hold of something, clinical trial, enrol on a course, strictly confidential, cosmetic surgery

2 1 register   6 access
2 hours   7 charge
3 referred   8 surgery
4 referral   9 medicine
5 opinion   10 negligence

4 1 S   2 S   3 D   4 S   5 D   6 S   7 D   8 D   9 S

5 1 kept   4 junior
2 surgery   5 spotlessly
3 rushed   6 convalescence

Unit 34

1 1 resident   5 charity
2 ensure   6 allocate
3 voluntary   7 manifesto
4 council   8 councillor

2 1 manifestos   4 ~~volunteer~~ voluntary
2 ~~to~~ in   5 ~~for~~ of
3 ~~make~~ take   6 ~~out~~ up

3 1 councillors, behalf   4 stick/stand, take
2 councils, charity   5 grant
3 have   6 citizens

4 1 *All three are possible.*
  2 transport, road
  3 profile
  4 chairman, chairperson
  5 spokesperson, spokesman
  6 eligible, ineligible

5 1 police   4 agency   7 eligible
  2 promotes   5 budget   8 mayor
  3 chair   6 network

Unit 35

1 *The following activities are illegal:*
smuggling, fraud, forgery, drug-trafficking.

2 1 defrauding   5 organized
  2 trafficking   6 forgery
  3 exploit   7 enticed, proceeds
  4 smuggle

4 1 a constable
  2 an inspector/the chief constable
  3 the chief constable
  4 a magistrate/judge
  5 the police/a police constable/officer/
   a policeman
  6 a solicitor
  7 a judge/magistrate
  8 someone awaiting trial / prisoner
  9 a prisoner/someone awaiting trial

5 1 about   6 custody
  2 police   7 solicitor
  3 detained   8 magistrate
  4 grounds   9 released
  5 cautioned

Unit 36

1 1 up
  2 me as a friend
  3 over a new leaf.
  4 justifiable
  5 imprisonment
  6 abolition of the law
  7 occupational hazard
  8 reoffenders

2 1 rehabilitate   4 abolish
  2 deterrent   5 revenge
  3 capital   6 crisis

3 *These are correct:*
  1 confined   4 self-assessment
  2 deviate   5 agreement/consent
  3 prisoners/inmates   6 exclusively

4 1 therapy   5 proportion
  2 segregation   6 mutual
  3 cells   7 therapeutic
  4 consent   8 contained

Unit 37

1 1 civilian   6 authority
  2 weapon   7 distinguish
  3 nuclear   8 missile
  4 enlisted   9 conscription
  5 the draft

2 unarmed combat   military operation
  vast majority   air force
  armed forces   make a distinction
  lethal weapon   nuclear capability

3 1 vast
  2 military
  3 composed
  4 fundamental
  5 combat
  6 diverse
  7 guard
  8 comprise
  9 deadly
  10 distinguish/differentiate
  11 encompasses
  12 serve

4 1 forces   7 enlisted/serving
  2 consist   8 reserves
  3 navy   9 branch
  4 force   10 capability/weapons
  5 command   11 comprises/comprise
  6 authority/command

6 1 civil   5 considerably
  2 simply/merely   6 a domestic/an internal
  3 mobilizing   7 internal
  4 interior   8 assisting/helping

7 1 productive   6 funding
  2 warfare   7 latter
  3 force   8 army / armed forces
  4 interior   9 domestic/internal
  5 rights/liberties   10 considerable

Unit 38

1 1 B   2 B   3 G   4 B   5 B   6 G   7 G   8 B

2 1 f   3 g   5 a   7 h   9 d
  2 c   4 b   6 j   8 e   10 i

3 1 New arms deal
  2 Blast wrecks fire station
  3 Go-ahead for rail scheme
  4 Company chief ousted
  5 Boost for big banks
  6 Ministers to curb spending
  7 Kidnappers demand ransom
  8 Government urges delay
  9 Motorcyclist cleared of child's death
  10 Firm on brink of closure

4 *Possible answers:*
1 Blast wrecks new shopping centre
2 Police rule out new murder probe
3 Prime Minister vows to curb government spending
4 Ministers bid to oust PM
5 Riddle surrounding stolen gems

Unit 39

1 1 opinion   5 controversial
   2 lapse   6 scathing
   3 emerged   7 allegation
   4 doors   8 According

2 1 Amid/Amidst   5 sources
   2 leaked   6 quoted
   3 cover   7 scenes
   4 According   8 measures

3 1 ~~shooting~~ firing
   2 ~~drip~~ drop
   3 ~~thunderstorm~~ storm
   4 ~~wave~~ tide
   5 ~~raining~~ flooding
   6 ~~flat~~ level
   7 ~~goalkeeper~~ goalposts
   8 ~~bend~~ corner
   9 ~~burning~~ blazing

4 1 under attack/fire   4 storm of
   2 sparked   5 tight corner
   3 foul play   6 drop, ocean

Unit 40

1 1 *Both are correct.*   4 pencilled
   2 excruciating   5 do
   3 *Both are correct.*   6 remaining

2 1 excruciating   5 puns
   2 chronic   6 daren't
   3 ensuing   7 rapid
   4 punctured   8 tip

3 1 S   2 D   3 S   4 D   5 S   6 D   7 S   8 D

4 1 disorientated   5 stay
   2 swamp   6 odds
   3 regain   7 drastic
   4 dazed/disorientated   8 chances

Unit 41

1 1 *All three are correct.*
   2 intrude/pry
   3 coverage/tabloids
   4 fame/privacy
   5 singled out

2 1 survey   5 deserve
   2 carried   6 personality/celebrity
   3 findings   7 eye
   4 fame

3 1 privacy   3 pry, public
   2 broadsheet   4 fame

4 1 rumour, allegations, scandal, rock, broadcast, exclusive
   2 rocks, rehab, fellow, rally

5 1 Lulu has dumped Rocco.
   2 Amelia gave birth to a baby boy last week.
   3 Jason has custody of his daughter.
   4 Arun is a fellow student.
   5 The journalist wanted to get a scoop.
   6 They're newlyweds.

Unit 42

1 1 T
   2 T
   3 F; A liberal believes in economic freedom and **gradual** political change.
   4 F; The Conservative Party in Britain believes in **capitalism**.
   5 F; **Communists** believe that everyone should own the means of production.

2 1 right-wing
   2 reactionary
   3 opposed to it/against it
   4 (to maintain) the status quo
   5 moderate
   6 in the centre

3 1 equality, distribution
   2 means
   3 on
   4 associated
   5 identification

4 1 strings   5 heated
   2 microscope   6 doctors
   3 hands   7 boat
   4 deep, sink   8 heading

5 1 at the deep end
   2 of her depth
   3 in the right direction
   4 foundations
   5 cracks
   6 seat
   7 debate/discussion
   8 spin

Unit 43

1 1 c   2 a   3 e   4 g   5 f   6 d   7 h   8 b

2 We were close to > 5 ~~the point where people couldn't deal with the situation~~. Food was 8 ~~in short supply~~, the situation was 1 ~~unpleasant and depressing~~, and many people had already 2 ~~left~~ the city for good. Then at 7 a.m. yesterday the attack happened. A man who was just clearing 6 ~~stones, bricks, and glass~~ from a damaged building was shot by a 3 ~~hidden gunman~~. Amid the ensuing chaos, a small group of rebel soldiers entered the nearby radio station and took control of it. The army immediately 4 <del>began to surround</del> the building. They brought in large guns and started 7 <del>firing at</del> it, then, as night approached, they attacked. The rebels were soon 9 <del>defeated by</del> the superior numbers and firepower of the army.

Unit 44

1 travel expenses   pension scheme
subsidized canteen   healthcare provision
maternity leave   relocation allowance

2 1 car, travel, health
2 relocation, food, fuel
3 company, government, private/personal
4 healthcare, childcare

3 1 benefits ('perks' is too informal for a job advertisement)
2 pension
3 related
4 entitlement
5 allowance
6 provision
7 canteen

Unit 45

1 1 encountered
2 degree
3 was accountable to no one OR wasn't accountable to anyone
4 insight into
5 juggle
6 pros and cons

2 1 boss
2 solely
3 encountered
4 degree
5 lucrative
6 encroach
7 guaranteed
8 additional/extra/further

4 1 P   2 N   3 N   4 N   5 P   6 N

5 team spirit   pool resources
boost morale   undermine your authority
mutual respect   stifle creativity

6 1 He didn't fit in.
2 She can use her initiative.
3 I find the work very fulfilling.
4 There was a lot of collaboration.
5 They had a common goal.
6 We think it will foster team spirit.
7 We can pool our resources.
8 They have a lot of mutual respect.

Unit 46

1 1 clinch   4 mount
2 bid   5 imminent
3 set   6 dividend, shareholders

2 1 joint   5 takeover
2 turned it down   6 merger
3 acquisitions   7 hostile
4 former   8 backing

3 1 D   2 D   3 S   4 D   5 S   6 S   7 S   8 D

4 1 lure/entice   5 fuel
2 lying   6 bankrupt/under
3 balance   7 settles
4 cards

Unit 47

1 1 G   2 B   3 B   4 G   5 G   6 B

2 1 weakening
2 hike
3 slump
4 plummeted/plunged
5 volatile/in turmoil/turbulent
6 gains

3 1 buoyant
2 rallied/bounced back
3 soared
4 plummeted
5 turmoil
6 turbulent/volatile

4 1 <del>debit</del> debt
2 <del>burnt</del> burst
3 <del>contadicted</del> contradicted
4 <del>inventors</del> investors
5 <del>underpine</del> underpin
6 <del>corporale</del> corporate
7 <del>equiries</del> equities
8 <del>fields</del> yields

5 1 outlook, underlying
2 debt burden
3 conflicting advice
4 invest, equities
5 bubble, burst
6 under pressure

Unit 48

1 1 lose, debit, statement, transactions
2 current, credit, savings/deposit
3 keep, red
4 thrifty, extravagant

2 1 withdrew   4 overdraft
2 overdrawn   5 mount/build
3 outgoings   6 squanders

3 1 *Surplus* is different; *shortfall/deficit* mean an amount that is less than you need.
2 *Contingency* is different; *shortfall/ shortage* both mean not having enough of something.
3 *Economize* is different; *take away/subtract* mean to take one number from another.
4 *Make contingency plans* is different; *economize/make cutbacks* mean to reduce the amount you spend.
5 *Deficit* is different; *budget/fund* mean an amount of money you have available to spend.
6 *Economize* is different: *work out/calculate* mean to find the total number/amount of something.

4 1 shortages   6 budget
2 shortfall   7 work out
3 contingency   8 shortfall/deficit
4 subsidy   9 cutbacks
5 bail   10 per

Unit 49

1 1 prioritized   4 basis, wherever
2 *Both are correct.*   5 anticipated
3 *Both are correct.*

2 1 basis   5 delegate
2 sticks   6 jot
3 anticipate   7 matter
4 scheduled   8 accomplished/achieved

4 1 deluge   4 severely hit
2 interminable   5 under control
3 inundated   6 plague

5 1 I need to **set** aside money for rent.
2 I've lost my **train** of thought.
3 We were hard **hit** by the price war.
4 The work has been never-**ending**.
5 Our spending has got out **of** hand.
6 I had to break **off** from what I was doing.
7 The situation is **under** control.

6 1 stream, overwhelmed/stressed/swamped
2 unproductive
3 deluge
4 promptly
5 stressed
6 productive

Unit 50

1 1 set   4 set   6 halt
2 settle   5 break   7 step up
3 ballot

2 1 closures   4 deadlock
2 dispute   5 privatize
3 precedent   6 inclined (OR likely)

3 1 procrastination   4 intervention
2 interference   5 wisdom
3 resolution   6 prudence

4 1 P   2 P   3 A   4 A   5 P   6 A   7 P   8 A

5 1 sort   5 blow
2 intervene   6 proportion
3 out   7 wise/prudent/sensible
4 buck   8 resolved

Unit 51

1 1 S   2 S   3 S   4 D   5 S   6 D   7 S   8 D

2 1 handover
2 absence
3 piled up/accumulated
4 failed/neglected
5 neglected
6 photocopier
7 poking
8 giggling
9 hectic

Unit 52

1 1 drives
2 retaliated
3 *Both words are correct.*
4 overreact
5 *Both words are correct.*
6 incident
7 led
8 provoke

2 1 road, incident   3 overreact
2 dented   4 drive

3 1 f   2 e   3 g   4 b   5 d   6 h   7 c   8 a

4 1 The house took a long time to build, but the end **result** is fantastic.
2 A What made you ring the doctor?
B Oh, **no** reason.
3 The new law came **into** effect at the beginning of June.
4 Too much sunlight can have a **detrimental** effect on your skin.
5 Current deforestation will have long-term **repercussions/consequences**.
6 I'm not really sure what **prompted** him to resign so suddenly.
7 What was the final **outcome/result** of the talks in Bali?
8 One indirect result or knock-on **effect** will be price rises throughout the economy.

Unit 53

1 1 embellish   5 interrogated
2 sustain   6 unpalatable
3 humiliated   7 detect
4 interrogation   8 namely

2
1. economical
2. talked
3. embellish
4. gloss
5. deteriorated
6. interrogated
7. caught
8. humiliated
9. sustain
10. needless to

3 Formal: falsehood, confound sb, adversary, declare sth
Informal: phoney, fib, level with sb
Neutral: a white lie, deceit, distort

4
1. anonymously
2. casualty
3. posthumously
4. half
5. declared
6. baffled/puzzled
7. deceiving/deluding
8. distorted

Unit 54

1
1. growing
2. face up to
3. arise/come up
4. exacerbate
5. insoluble
6. confronting

2
1. worse
2. urgent
3. raised
4. overcome
5. grips
6. perennial
7. tackling/confronting
8. minor

4
1. esteem
2. get her down
3. articulate
4. regardless
5. trivial
6. channel

5
1. dented
2. her stride
3. perspective
4. at rest
5. behind
6. reassured
7. light
8. setback

Unit 55

1
1. ~~extra~~ ultra-
2. ~~destruction~~ preservation
3. ~~ruins~~ remains
4. ~~estables~~ stables
5. ~~on ruins~~ in ruins
6. ~~formally~~ formerly

2
1. formerly/previously
2. up, renovate
3. run-down/dilapidated/ramshackle
4. decay/disrepair, abandoned ('neglected' is also possible here)
5. preserve
6. Middle, medieval
7. trace
8. ultra-

3
1. out
2. mint/perfect
3. good
4. cutting edge
5. new
6. hand

4
1. device
2. antique
3. ancient, reproductions
4. reconditioned
5. genuine
6. packaging
7. reproduces
8. up, innovative

Unit 56

1 a resounding victory, come unstuck, the secret of your success, turn out badly, a stroke of luck, fulfil your potential

2 1 G 2 B 3 B 4 G 5 G 6 G

3
1. overcome
2. stroke
3. to strength
4. secret
5. turned
6. potential

4 *The informal words and phrases are:*
1. make a go of it
2. flop
3. past it
4. –
5. up against it
6. way

5
1. came
2. make
3. *Both words are correct.*
4. way
5. make
6. *Both words are correct.*

6
1. I don't like to tell him he's past **it**. ~ Hmm, It's a **tricky** situation. I don't envy you.
2. Any chance he'll make **a** comeback? ~ No, his last film **flopped** badly.
3. Did she **come** top in the public vote? ~ Yes, but she was **up** against it.
4. He **let** himself down in the exam. ~ Yes, he only just **scraped/got** through.
5. Her interview was an unmitigated **disaster**. ~ Yes, she was way **out** of her depth.

Unit 57

1 at the last minute, over time, in retrospect, with hindsight, behind the times, at one time, from time to time, for the time being, in due course

2
1. retrospect
2. hindsight
3. leaves, minute
4. about/high
5. before my time
6. flown
7. course
8. At
9. over
10. for the time being

4
1. an interval
2. *Both words are correct.*
3. *Both words are correct.*
4. spell
5. during
6. *Both words are correct.*
7. era
8. prolong

5
1. throughout/during
2. break
3. During
4. spell
5. phase/stage/time
6. age
7. soon
8. extend
9. gap
10. elapsed/passed/gone by

Unit 58

1
1 bloke/guy
2 nicked/pinched
3 moaning
4 vile/disgusting
5 tight-fisted/tight/stingy
6 quid
7 lousy
8 loo

2
1 pain (in the neck)　4 drag
2 laugh　　　　　　 5 cheek/nerve
3 rip-off　　　　　　6 get-together

3
1 illness　　3 sleep　　5 food
2 noise　　　4 money　　6 criticism

4
1 Cheers = Ta
2 din = racket
3 stick = flak
4 starving = dying for something to eat
5 love = darling
6 thrashed = hammered

5
1 broke　　5 kip　　　8 bug
2 daft　　　6 conned　9 into
3 laid-back　7 dodgy　10 posh
4 nosy

Unit 59

1
1 It's no **good/use** worrying about it.
2 off the **top** of my head
3 in one **ear** and out the other
4 could **do** with
5 My **mind** went a complete blank
6 under **the** weather

2
1 mind　　　　5 there/somewhere
2 head　　　　6 weather
3 blank　　　　7 keep you waiting
4 bet　　　　　8 and out the other

4
1 false
2 don't know the answer
3 not being
4 possible
5 I don't know
6 don't expect

5
1 're joking/'re kidding'/can't be serious
2 way/chance
3 is as good as mine
4 one of those days
5 bet
6 foregone conclusion
7 luck
8 to lose
9 say that again
10 your day.

Unit 60

1
1 down　　4 worth　　　7 worlds
2 fails　　5 true　　　　8 ground
3 battle　6 of your own

2
1 a world of her own
2 resort
3 keep his feet on the ground
4 else fails
5 lose face
6 good to be true
7 letting her hair down
8 the best of both worlds

4
1 Guess　4 some　　7 equal
2 know　 5 admit　　8 believe
3 earth　6 wonder

5
1 Do you know if it's open, **by any chance**? OR Do you **happen to** know if it's open?
2 How old are you, **if you don't mind me/ my asking**?
3 She looks about 20, but **believe it or not**, she's only 13. OR … but she's only 13, **believe it or not**.
4 He's been very ill, so **no wonder** he looks thin.
5 I'm hoping to go, but **the thing is**, I've got a meeting on the same day.
6 There are many exceptions, but **all things being equal**, I think men are better cooks than women.
7 The book is **every bit as** violent as all his others.
8 It was a beautiful day, but **for some reason**, the beach was deserted; I can't think why.

Unit 61

1 push and shove　　long and hard
pick and choose　　sooner or later
back to front　　　rules and regulations
first and foremost　sick and tired

2
1 cheerful　　　　　5 bustle, tired
2 order, corruption　6 error
3 later　　　　　　　7 sound
4 foremost, objectives　8 forth

Unit 62

1
1 mouse　　4 feather　7 ox
2 cakes　　5 log　　　8 dream
3 bone　　6 sieve

2
1 He's deaf as a post.
2 She's blind as a bat.
3 She's as thin as a rake.
4 It worked like a dream.
5 She went/was as white as a sheet.
6 They were as good as gold.
7 She went/was as red as a beetroot.
8 He's got a mind like a sieve.

Unit 63

1 1 communicate
    2 claim
    3 criticized
    4 raise
    5 interrupted
    6 prolong
    7 retaliate

2 1 I never expected him to **own up** to the crime.
    2 Nothing can **make up for** the loss of earnings.
    3 She tried to **talk me out of** giving up my job.
    4 Do you think they'll ever **do away with** the monarchy?
    5 He isn't easily **taken in**.
    6 Try and **talk** him **into** com**ing**.
    7 Did they **take** the shed **to pieces / apart**?
    8 Have they **made up**?

3 1 ~~go by~~ get by
    2 ~~cropped out~~ cropped up
    3 *Correct*
    4 ~~missing out of~~ missing out on
    5 ~~bump in~~ bump into
    6 *Correct*

4 1 turned up/showed up
    2 pick up
    3 shake off
    4 sank in
    5 pick up
    6 gone down with
    7 wear off
    8 pick up

Unit 64

1 1 mind you   6 in any case
    2 at any rate   7 broadly speaking
    3 even so   8 to be honest
    4 as a matter of fact 9 to a large extent
    5 on the whole   10 all the same

2 1 **Broadly** speaking   4 In **any** case
    2 All **the** same   5 To **tell** you the truth
    3 alternative**ly**   6 as I was **saying**

3 1 Incidentally
    2 to be honest/as a matter of fact/actually
    3 On the whole/By and large/Broadly speaking
    4 Mind you
    5 besides/anyway
    6 It's true; even so/all the same
    7 Anyway/Anyhow
    8 actually/to be honest/to tell you the truth

4 1 to be honest   5 By the way
    2 Alternatively   6 As for
    3 It's true, All the same 7 besides
    4 Mind you   8 by and large

Unit 65

1 1 somewhere **in** the region
    2 sort **of** pretending to be ill
    3 have **stacks/tons/loads/bags** of rice
    4 or **something** of that sort
    5 give **or** take a few minutes
    6 tomorrow **somehow** or other
    7 along those **lines**.
    8 **round** about 6.30

2 1 I've completed **round about** 50 per cent of the project.
    2 He looks **kind of** depressed.
    3 His job is **something to do with** marketing.
    4 Do you know who all **that stuff** belong**s** to?
    5 I imagine we'll get fifty-**odd** people at the meeting.
    6 We've got **tons of** vegetables so I'd better make some soup.
    7 She must be getting on for 80 **or thereabouts**, I would say.
    8 We could get him a book **or something** (**like that / along those lines**) for his birthday.

Unit 66

1 1 It's a **small** world.
    2 Once **bitten**, twice shy.
    3 The more the **merrier**.
    4 Famous last **words**.
    5 So far, so **good**.
    6 First come, **first** served.
    7 Out of **sight**, out of mind.
    8 Easier **said** than done.

2 1 twice shy
    2 so good
    3 world
    4 out of mind
    5 never tell
    6 the merrier
    7 said than done
    8 first served
    9 calling the kettle black

4 1 blood is thicker than water; charity begins at home.
    2 love is blind; beauty is only skin-deep.
    3 two wrongs don't make a right; the end justifies the means.
    4 live and let live; let sleeping dogs lie.
    5 two heads are better than one; practice makes perfect.

5 Prevention is better than cure.
    Actions speak louder than words.
    Love is blind.
    Blood is thicker than water.
    Lightning never strikes twice.
    Charity begins at home.

6
1. never
2. sorry
3. once
4. lie
5. perfect
6. better than one
7. good news
8. justifies the means
9. don't make a right
10. strikes twice
11. than cure
12. for an eye

7
1. Practice makes perfect.
2. Two heads are better than one.
3. You're only young once.
4. Blood is thicker than water.
5. No news is good news.
6. Money talks.
7. Two wrongs don't make a right.
8. Better late than never.
9. Live and let live.
10. Let sleeping dogs lie.
11. Love is blind.
12. An eye for an eye.

Unit 67

1
1. condolences
2. see
3. delighted to
4. forward
5. Following
6. concerning
7. Should
8. to

2
1. enquire
2. regret, inform
3. intention, terminate
4. Should, require, further, do not hesitate, contact
5. Following/Further to, conversation, I would be grateful, concerning

3
1. I am writing in **response** to your article about supermarket packaging.
2. We look forward **to** hearing from you.
3. I am writing **in** reply to your letter of 17 October.
4. Thank you for your letter **concerning/ regarding** the pre-service training course at CDQ.
5. Please **find** enclosed a copy of my birth certificate.
6. I am writing in reply to your **appeal** for donations following the tsunami disaster.
7. Please accept my sincere **condolences** on the death of your grandfather.
8. I would like to **draw** your attention to the final clause of the lease.
9. As you **will** see from my CV, I have extensive experience in sales and marketing.
10. With **reference** to your letter of 17 May, I am enclosing the documents you requested.

4 *Possible answers:*

1. I am writing in response to your advertisement for a receptionist in yesterday's paper.
2. Please find enclosed a photocopy of my driving licence.

3. Following/Further to our conversation yesterday, I now have the necessary documents.
4. Should you require any further information about my qualifications, please do not hesitate to contact me.
5. I would be grateful if you could send me a brochure and price list.
6. I am delighted to inform you that your application has been successful/ that you have been given the job/post.

5
| 1 N | 3 N | 5 P | 7 P | 9 N |
| 2 P | 4 P | 6 N | 8 N | 10 N |

6
1. stated
2. abrupt/curt/rude
3. sample
4. spell
5. subject
6. body
7. superfluous/irrelevant
8. straightforward

Unit 68

1
1. thus/hence
2. albeit
3. notwithstanding
4. prior to
5. in view of
6. Hitherto

2
1. henceforth
2. thus/hence
3. Prior to
4. With regard to/Regarding/Concerning
5. Notwithstanding
6. In conclusion

Unit 69

1
1. sum up / summarize
2. assessment
3. narrator
4. assess/evaluate
5. criterion
6. presentation
7. argument
8. present

2
1. narrative
2. summary
3. incoherent
4. stylistic
5. criteria
6. command
7. register
8. discursive

3
1. condemnation
2. conclusion
3. hypothesize
4. exemplified
5. assertion
6. justification

4
1. She **outlined** her ideas.
2. She had one **hypothesis**.
3. She **highlighted** certain points.
4. She wouldn't **condone** his behaviour.
5. She didn't **adopt** a clear **position**.
6. She went on to **explore** the idea in more depth.
7. She couldn't **justify** her ideas.
8. In the end, she **sat on the fence**.

Unit 70

1
1. betrayal
2. portrayal
3. defiance
4. embodiment
5. insanity
6. resilient
7. merciful/merciless
8. pitiful

5 prosperity

2 1 an explanation 4 sad
2 difficult 5 ability
3 the truth 6 refuse

3 1 synopsis 5 inherent
2 depicted 6 insane
3 pitiful 7 represents
4 prosperous 8 companionship

4 1 protagonist 7 betrayed
2 depicted 8 Fate
3 endows 9 downfall
4 represented 10 unlike
5 embodiment 11 mercy
6 defies 12 conveyed

Unit 71

1 objective, objectivity
biased, bias
empirical, empiricism
verify, verification
hypothesize, hypothesis
scrutinize, scrutiny

2 1 facet 4 unbiased
2 scrutiny 5 conviction
3 hypothesis 6 replicate

3 1 procedure 4 empirical
2 phenomenon 5 archive
3 duplicate/replicate 6 biased/subjective

4 1 defective 4 hereditary
2 abnormal 5 short-lived
3 unit 6 immune

5 1 Gene, cells 5 genetic
2 mutation 6 heredity
3 insert/inserted 7 insertion
4 repel/fight 8 molecular, molecule

Unit 72

1 1 b 3 c 5 a 7 a 9 b
2 a 4 b 6 c 8 b 10 c

2 1 establish 6 constraints
2 swaying 7 panels
3 moving 8 anchor
4 withstand/resist 9 stringent
5 meet 10 rigorous

3 1 withstand/stand up to/resist
2 sway
3 occupants/residents
4 determine/establish
5 girders/supports
6 load
7 counteract
8 reinforced

Unit 73

1 1 ~~humorous~~ humble
2 ~~weekend~~ way
3 ~~interest~~ information
4 ~~drink~~ day
5 ~~tired~~ displeased
6 ~~turn~~ talk
7 ~~two days~~ today
8 ~~laughs~~ love (OR laughing out loud)
9 ~~letters~~ lips
10 ~~concerned~~ confused
11 ~~make~~ mind
12 ~~read~~ remember/recall

2 Hi, thanks for your message. Are you going to see Sally this weekend? Please give her lots of love. ;) Alice
Dinner last night was excellent. Thanks ☺ Will you be in tonight? Hope to see you later. Joe
Sorry, but I'm probably going to be late for the meeting. I will ring you with more information later. Please start without me. Bye for now, Zoe
Hi, can you phone me as soon as possible? I have something important to tell you! My lips are sealed. All the best, Suzie
Could you speak to your dad before the weekend? If I recall/remember correctly, he will be in tomorrow. Lots of love, Steffi.

3 1 gr8 5 xlnt 8 w/o
2 thx 6 b4 9 ;-x
3 cul8r 7 lol 10 2moro
4 imho

4 1 T 2 T 3 T 4 F 5 T 6 F 7 T 8 F

5 1 c/o 3 attn/fao 5 incl.
2 PS 4 sae

6 1 CEO 3 TLC 5 CCTV
2 PC 4 B & B 6 IQ

Unit 74

1 1 interaction 7 misfire
2 misconception 8 ill-informed
3 misdiagnose 9 mislay
4 ill-prepared 10 ill-advised
5 interdependent 11 interrelated
6 mistreat 12 misjudge

2 1 misinformed
2 mishandled/mismanaged
3 mistreated/ill-treated
4 ill-informed
5 mislaid/misplaced
6 misprints
7 misconceived
8 misdiagnosed
9 miscalculated
10 interrelated

3 racism/frost/privileged/depressant/populated/
assess/classified/fuel/fed/value/book
defrost, depopulated, declassified, devalue

4 1 *Both forms are correct.*
2 disadvantaged
3 anti-war
4 *Both forms are correct.*
5 underprivileged
6 *Both forms are correct.*

5 1 anti-inflammatory
2 underemployed
3 depreciated
4 anti-virus software
5 reassess/reappraise/reconsider
6 undercooked
7 overdose
8 undernourished/underfed

Unit 75

1 1 characterize   6 industrialize
2 solidify   7 electrify
3 clarify   8 pacify
4 symbolize   9 exemplify
5 legalize

2 1 economize   5 pacify
2 intensified   6 purify
3 visualize   7 privatize
4 vandalized   8 quantify

4 a trouble-free life, a soundproof room,
childproof locks, tax-free income, a
foolproof method, duty-free perfume

5 1 ovenproof   4 bulletproof
2 interest-free   5 inflation-proof
3 foolproof   6 waterproof

Unit 76

1 1 against   5 over   8 with
2 on   6 for   9 from
3 for   7 for   10 for
4 about

2 1 regard   5 aptitude
2 compilation   6 clips
3 extract/excerpt 7 restriction
4 grudge   8 control

3 1 d 2 f 3 a 4 b 5 c 6 e

4 1 representative   6 subject
2 dependent   7 live
3 subservient   8 resistant
4 reconciled/resigned 9 stems
5 intent   10 reminiscent

Unit 77

1 1 at   4 fail   7 on
2 On   5 on   8 exchange
3 in   6 away

2 1 by choice   5 in exchange for
2 at once   6 without fail
3 on reflection   7 at short notice
4 at the very least 8 on balance

3 1 *All three are possible.*
2 under investigation/under suspicion
3 in possession of
4 *All three are possible.*
5 in touch

4 1 We have had to put our holiday plans on
hold for the moment because of work.
2 Out **of** respect for the bereaved family,
hundreds turned up at the funeral.
3 I'm afraid I can't help as I'm really out of
touch with this area of research.
4 The demonstrators will be in serious
trouble if the army starts to attack them.
5 The multi-storey car park has been **under**
construction for six months.
6 He works for a **giant** engineering
company; it's a multinational and doing
very well.
7 She opened the can by **means** of a special
device designed for the disabled.
8 We caught a glimpse of the rabbit before
it ran **out** of sight into the bushes.

Unit 78

1 1 perplexed
2 conceivable
3 *Both are correct.*
4 a notorious/an infamous
5 bizarre
6 *Both are correct.*

2 1 notorious   6 bizarre
2 wicked   7 implausible
3 unconvincing   8 despondent
4 puzzled/baffled   9 distinguished
5 inconceivable   10 exceptional

3 1 wicked   4 baffled
2 despondent/dejected 5 outstanding
3 eminent   6 bizarre

4 1 ~~naked~~ bare
2 ~~childlike~~ childish
3 *Correct*
4 ~~invaluable~~ worthless/valueless
5 ~~nude~~ naked
6 *Correct*
7 ~~negligent~~ negligible
8 ~~naked~~ nude
9 *Correct*

5 1 comprehensive   5 tasteful
2 childlike   6 concluding
3 conclusive   7 comprehensible
4 exhaustive   8 negligent

Unit 79

1 1 Evidently
2 curiously (enough)/strangely (enough)/
oddly (enough)
3 Practically
4 presumably
5 basically
6 frankly/personally

2 1 frankly 4 obviously
2 Apparently 5 naturally
3 ultimately 6 curiously enough

3 1 Officially
2 Financially/Commercially (speaking)
3 Realistically
4 Socially
5 Technically
6 Logically
7 Theoretically (speaking)
8 Traditionally

4 1 concerned 4 speaking
2 mentally 5 Traditionally
3 indirectly 6 As far as

5 1 relatively/somewhat
2 simply/purely
3 strictly
4 relatively
5 briefly/chiefly
6 invariably
7 simply/truly
8 strictly

6 1 primarily/chiefly/predominantly
2 invariably
3 briefly
4 equally
5 forever
6 truly
7 precisely

Unit 80

1 1 friendly fire 5 passed away
2 practical 6 helping
3 hard of hearing 7 put it to sleep
4 let him go 8 impaired

2 1 Did she help herself to a couple of pens?
2 The company is downsizing.
3 The animal was put down.
4 My dog Barty is not exactly clever.
5 The president's getting on.
6 There was a lot of collateral damage.

Answer key to review units

Expanding your vocabulary

Unit 1

1 1 ambiguous
2 transparent/self-explanatory
3 old-fashioned
4 poke fun
5 disapproving
6 precise
7 interchangeable/synonyms/synonymous
8 virtually

Unit 2

1 1 It suddenly dawned on me who had stolen my mobile.
2 I'm in two minds about the job.
3 In his haste, he sent the vase flying.
4 She ate some chocolate, which kept her going until she was rescued.
5 The laptop's a bargain and comes with free software.
6 Do many people try to get out of paying tax?
7 That/It was sweet of you to do that for me.
8 Changing his job is the last thing on his mind.

Unit 3

1 1 look
2 shoes, equipment
3 off-putting
4 hold-up
5 passer-by, next of kin
6 car
7 setback, break-up
8 drawing pin

2 1 open-minded
2 last-minute
3 nursery rhymes
4 shortcut OR short cut
5 turnout
6 absent-minded
7 spare part
8 shake-up
9 breakdown
10 barbed wire

Unit 4

1 1 **caught** fire
2 broken **out**
3 **spread** rapidly
4 gale-**force** winds
5 advance **warning**
6 a **narrow** escape
7 put it **out**
8 growing **concern**
9 face the **prospect**
10 held **responsible**

2 1 considerable/great
2 real
3 reach
4 point
5 fierce/widespread/strong
6 make
7 concern
8 compromise
9 honour
10 familiar
11 brief

Unit 5

1 1 lick
2 count
3 reflect
4 absorb
5 shrug
6 stamp
7 favour
8 circumstances
9 raise
10 propose
11 hung
The word in the grey squares is 'information'.

Unit 6

1 apologetic
occupied
forgivable/unforgivable
defenceless, defensive
finalize
excel
pointless
emotive/emotional
heartless
severity

The body

Unit 7

1 1 h 2 f 3 a 4 b 5 g 6 c 7 e 8 d

2 1 ~~attracted~~ drew
2 ~~make~~ create
3 ~~loosen~~ straighten
4 ~~enhance~~ exaggerate
5 ~~going~~ getting
6 ~~unflattering~~ flattering
7 ~~for~~ to
8 ~~cover~~ conceal/hide

Unit 8

1 1 flirting
2 fancied
3 fiddling
4 contact
5 conclusion(s)
6 leaning
7 folded
8 going
9 misinterpreted

Unit 9

1 *Possible answers:*
1 Perhaps because they had injured their leg or foot.
2 If someone was riding it in a race.
3 For pleasure. / To enjoy yourself.
4 So that no one could hear or see you.
5 Not usually.
6 Not usually.
7 To give yourself some variety.
8 Do some exercise. / Work out at the gym.

Unit 10

1
1	rattled	5	beeped	8	squelched
2	rumbled	6	screech	9	creaking
3	rustled	7	slammed	10	pitched
4	splashing				

2
1	roar	4	rattle	7	buzz
2	creak	5	screech	8	slam
3	howl	6	bark		

Unit 11

1
1 barely   5 tears
2 breathtaking   6 blinking
3 blurred   7 spectacular
4 warily   8 alleviate

Unit 12

1 TOUCH: tap, vigorous, squeeze, stroke, slide, pinch
SMELL: stench, fragrance, aroma, musty, pungent
TASTE: bland, insipid, peppery

Unit 13

1
1 effects   5 persist   8 lethargic
2 excess   6 itchy   9 blisters
3 upset   7 dose   10 ulcer
4 sprained
The phrase in the grey squares is 'expiry date'.

2 *These words are correct:*
1 long-term, short-term
2 persistent, splitting
3 dose, dosage
4 the speed limit, all my expectations
5 an itchy scalp, a nasty rash
6 Drowsiness, Lethargy

You and other people

Unit 14

1 cynicism   naivety
scepticism   spontaneity
affectionate   passionate
charisma   virtuous

2
1 What did you make of him?
2 I think you ought to give it a go.
3 I'll do anything within reason.
4 He's sceptical about the figures.
5 I took to him after a while.
6 He strikes me as very bright.
7 He really got up my nose.
8 He's a real character. / He's a character.
9 On the surface it seemed sensible.
10 Don't judge a book by its cover.

Unit 15

1
1 reveal/disclose
2 uneasy/uncomfortable
3 devastated/heartbroken
4 ecstatic / over the moon
5 hit the roof / went mad
6 suppress / bottle up
7 cautious/guarded

Unit 16

1
1 an instant **dislike** to me
2 talking about me **behind** my back
3 everything to **gain/win/earn** his respect
4 a strain **on** me
5 and **confide** in my boss
6 he **resented** the fact
7 really **tough** decision
8 decided to stick **up** for myself
9 but as time has gone **by**,
10 feel that **things** are looking up

Unit 17

1
1	idolize	5	criticize	8	principles
2	rebel	6	idealist	9	heroine
3	crude	7	footsteps	10	down
4	inspire				

The word in the grey squares is 'dedication'.

Unit 18

1 *These are correct:*
1 a mess, a fuss
2 broken, deprived
3 beneficial, detrimental
4 *All three are correct.*
5 an unappealing
6 *All three are correct.*

Unit 19

1 1 P 2 N 3 N 4 P 5 N 6 N 7 N 8 P

2
1 put
2 foot
3 exception
4 customary/usual, regard/view/consider, upper, middle, regard/view/consider
5 frown
6 etiquette/custom

Leisure and lifestyle

Unit 20

1 1 d 2 e 3 a 4 f 5 b 6 h 7 c 8 g

2 *Suggested answers:*
You can use a corkscrew to open a bottle of wine.
You beat eggs with a whisk.
A raisin is a kind of dried fruit.
You drain things with a colander.
Lentils are a kind of pulse.
You can braise things in a casserole.
You use a ladle to serve soup.
A cashew is a kind of nut.
You use a wok to stir-fry food.
Sage is a kind of herb.

Unit 21

1 Lisbon is surrounded by seven hills, and from most of them you have **stunning** views of this **remarkable** city, which has managed to **retain** so much of its **diverse** architecture and cultural heritage. But it is also a modern, **thriving** European capital, and in recent years many of the old buildings have been **restored**. For tourists, one of the most popular parts is the Alfama, where you can **wander** around and **soak up** the charms of the old town. The Chiado district is famous for shops and restaurants, but for really **vibrant** night life, head for the Bairro Alto. Then after all that, you can **unwind** on the nearby beaches of Cascais and Estoril: wonderful places to **recharge your batteries**.

2 1 *unique:* the **only** one of its kind
2 *off the beaten track:* **far** away from other people and houses
3 *unspoilt:* beautiful because it hasn't **changed**
4 *cobbled streets:* streets with a surface of old round **stones**
5 *take it easy:* **relax** and do very little
6 *trek:* a long hard **walk**
7 *undergo something:* experience a process of **change**
8 *charm:* very **attractive/pleasant** qualities or features

Unit 22

1 1 biting 4 miscast 7 tears/death
2 audiences 5 clichés 8 rubbish
3 edge 6 effects

2 **negative:** dire, tedious, mediocre, feeble, unconvincing, atrocious
positive: sensational, fabulous, phenomenal, brilliant, extraordinary

Unit 23

1 *These are correct:*
1 promoted, relegated
2 under pressure, off form
3 a last, a great, an outside
4 home, a neutral venue
5 through, knocked out
6 runners-up

2 1 drawn, eliminated / knocked out
2 victory, last
3 run, unbeaten, form
4 top, gave away

Unit 24

1

M	C	O	M	P	O	S	T	S	
E	L		R			S	P		
A	A	B	B	U	S	H	H	A	W
D	W	U	N			E	D	I	
O	N	L		E		D	E	L	
W	M	B	H	E	D	G	E	S	D
W	O	F	E	R	T	I	L	E	L
E	W						E	I	
E	E	N	R	I	C	H		D	F
D	R	O	O	T	S			S	E

2 1 roots 7 enrich
2 wildlife 8 fertile
3 seeds 9 hedge
4 meadow 10 prune
5 bulb 11 lawnmower, shed
6 weed 12 spade

Unit 25

1 1 impulse 4 around 7 gambler
2 pursuit 5 spree 8 debts
3 addict 6 hunting 9 tag

2 1 ~~before~~ after 5 ~~out~~ off
2 ~~minutes~~ minute 6 ~~addict~~ addicted
3 ~~for~~ on 7 ~~to~~ for
4 ~~induct~~ indulge 8 ~~searching~~ search

Unit 26

1 1 socialize 6 pop 10 make
2 loner 7 lay 11 host
3 company 8 liven 12 get-together
4 join 9 drowns 13 away
5 awkward
8 ~~deterrence~~ deterrent

A changing world

Unit 27

1 1 irreversible 3 ongoing 5 gone back
2 subtle 4 sweeping 6 practice

Unit 28

1 How to be **green**: dos and don'ts
- Eat locally produced fruit and vegetables to reduce food **miles**.
- Try to eat fruit and vegetables that are in **season**.
- **Recycle** most of your waste rather than throwing it away.
- Use energy-**saving** light bulbs, which **emit** less CO_2.
- Use **rechargeable** batteries.
- Don't use a tumble **dryer**: it **consumes/uses** masses of energy.
- Maximize natural light in order to **minimize** the use of electric lights.
- Don't leave electrical appliances such as TVs on **standby**.
- Avoid things which are **disposable** and designed to be thrown away after use.

Unit 29

1 1 deforestation 5 captivity
2 wiped 6 wild
3 extinction 7 reserves
4 habitat 8 toll

Unit 30

1 1 eradicated, wiped out 5 limit, restrict
2 invasive 6 condition
3 bed, a wheelchair 7 resume
4 *All three are possible.* 8 parts, organs

Unit 31

1 1 log in/on OR log on/off
2 cyberspace OR cybercafé
3 scroll up OR scroll down (OR scroll bar)
4 e-business OR e-learning
5 a virtual community OR virtual office OR virtual reality
6 upload something OR download something

2 1 videoblog 3 camcorder 5 install
2 password 4 upload

Unit 32

1 1 flee 6 discrimination
2 native 7 faith
3 refuge 8 peace
4 asylum 9 nostalgia
5 shock

Institutions

Unit 33

1 1 confidential
2 opinion
3 surgery
4 spotless/immaculate
5 trials
6 informed
7 referral
8 discharged
9 recuperate/convalesce/recover
10 feet

2 1 junior
2 be admitted to hospital
3 cosmetic surgery / plastic surgery
4 convalesce ('recover' would also be possible)
5 complementary
6 fastidious
7 a mix-up ('a mess' would also be possible)
8 take no notice of sth

Unit 34

1 1 a government **grant**
2 American **citizens**
3 are you **eligible** to vote
4 to **chair** tomorrow's meeting
5 to **ensure** that (also **see** that)
6 The party's **manifesto**
7 voluntary **sector**
8 high-**profile** jobs

2 1 say 4 volunteers 7 budget
2 behalf 5 nationwide 8 residents
3 seriously 6 stand/stick

Unit 35

1 1 d 2 a 3 g 4 b 5 h 6 c 7 e 8 f

2 1 warrant 3 smuggling 5 gang
2 custody 4 fraud 6 bail

Unit 36

1 abolition, abolish
imprisonment, imprison
deviation, deviate
justification, justify
segregation, segregate
confinement, confine
rehabilitation, rehabilitate
consent, consent

2 1 turning ~~out~~ over
2 locked ~~out~~ up
3 capital ~~punish~~ punishment
4 ~~common~~ mutual consent
5 regarded ~~at~~ as
6 ~~on~~ in crisis
7 ~~occupying~~ occupational hazard
8 ~~deterrence~~ deterrent

Unit 37

1 1 capability/weapons
  2 *All three are possible.*
  3 the air / a peacekeeping
  4 distinguish / make a distinction
  5 made up / composed
  6 *All three are possible.*
  7 chemical/lethal
  8 *All three are possible.*

2 1 the vast **majority**
  2 officers **in** command
  3 guerrilla **warfare**
  4 counter-**productive**
  5 the **former** would
  6 government **funding**
  7 **in** reserve
  8 to **assist** with / to **help** with

News and current affairs

Unit 38

1 *Possible answers:*
  1 A government minister has been forced out of his/her job.
  2 A transport plan has been given encouragement.
  3 A business agreement on weapons has been given approval.
  4 A family is going through a very bad experience over a ransom.
  5 Someone is trying/attempting to end a kidnapping.
  6 A hotel has been destroyed by an explosion.

Unit 39

1 1 According **to**
  2 under **attack/fire**
  3 scathing **remarks**
  4 were **leaked** to the press
  5 the **tide** will now
  6 has been **quoted** as saying
  7 a temporary **lapse** of judgement
  8 a **tight** corner

Unit 40

1 1 shelter
  2 stay
  3 take a chance
  4 dazed/disorientated
  5 regain
  6 excruciating
  7 dare
  8 remaining
  9 rapid

Unit 41

1 1 coverage
  2 scandal
  3 alleged
  4 deserve
  5 intrusion
  6 privacy
  7 exclusive
  8 tabloids
  9 allegations

Unit 42

1 *Possible answers:*
  1 We had a discussion about left-wing policies.
  2 They want to maintain the status quo.
  3 I don't know who's in the driving seat.
  4 We'll put the document under the microscope.
  5 I'd be opposed to the proposal.
  6 He laid the foundations for the policy.
  7 There is equality in our company.
  8 The prime minister is heading in the right direction.

Unit 43

1 1 shoots
  2 available
  3 unpleasant and depressing
  4 bricks and stones
  5 explosives
  6 leave / go away from
  7 without, pattern
  8 military, army / armed force, capture

Work and finance

Unit 44

1 1 relocation
  2 scheme, performance
  3 leave, provision
  4 canteen, subsidized
  5 entitled, entitlement

Unit 45

1 1 trust, respect
  2 *All three are possible.*
  3 juggle
  4 a degree
  5 undermine, disrupt
  6 foster, promote

Unit 46

1 1 take it lying **down**
  2 likely to **mount** (OR **launch**) an advertising campaign
  3 no choice but to **tighten** our belts
  4 to go **down** that road
  5 fuelling **fears** of a global recession
  6 wait till the **dust** settles
  7 The bid was turned **down**
  8 the move will **set** off a fresh round

Unit 47

1 **Rising and stable:** soar, surge, boom, buoyant, rally, gains
  Falling and unstable: plunge, turbulence, plummet, volatile, slash, turmoil, slump

2 1 investors 5 equities/shares
2 debt 6 outlook
3 pressure 7 burst
4 trigger 8 conflicting/contradictory

Unit 48

1 1 statement 6 outgoings
2 red 7 budget
3 overdrawn 8 bail
4 fund 9 make
5 squandering (OR wasting) 10 track

Unit 49

1 1 achieve/accomplish
2 prioritize
3 stick/keep
4 anticipate
5 Schedule/Timetable/Organize/Arrange
6 set
7 Delegate

Unit 50

1 1 ~~steaks~~ stakes
2 ~~make~~ set
3 ~~ballet~~ ballot
4 ~~set~~ settle
5 ~~privatizement~~ privatization
6 ~~inclinated~~ inclined
7 ~~interference~~ intervention
8 ~~off~~ out

Unit 51

1 1 hum 6 neglect
2 sniff 7 photocopier
3 giggle 8 pet
4 absent 9 put
5 hectic 10 poke your nose

Concepts

Unit 52

1 1 result 4 bad 7 reason
2 car 5 a person 8 negative
3 force 6 an income

Unit 53

1 1 humiliated 5 embellish
2 phoney 6 adversary
3 interrogation 7 unpalatable
4 anonymously 8 namely

Unit 54

1 1 trivial 6 articulate
2 perennial 7 exacerbate
3 arise 8 light
4 confront 9 urgent
5 tackle
The word in the grey squares is 'insoluble'.

Unit 55

1 1 S 2 D 3 D 4 S 5 D 6 S 7 S 8 D

Unit 56

1 1 potential
2 make
3 resounding ('remarkable' is also possible)
4 against
5 way ('well' is also possible)
6 depth
7 letting
8 obstacles
9 way
10 overcome
11 breakthrough
12 wrong
13 strength
14 fulfil

Unit 57

1 *Possible answers:*
1 should have set out earlier / should have left earlier / should have taken a taxi.
2 his life considerably/ by several years.
3 after the film ended. / after 10.00.
4 of development.
5 he did. / he turned up.
6 I (have to) work on Saturdays/Sundays.
7 had to stand / were very bored
8 he shouldn't have been let out. / that was too short.

Spoken English

Unit 58

1 1 ~~ticked~~ nicked 5 ~~jacket~~ racket
2 ~~flan~~ flak 6 ~~light~~ tight
3 ~~rug~~ bug 7 ~~lying~~ dying
4 ~~creek~~ cheek 8 ~~drug~~ drag

2 1 laugh 7 stick/flak
2 broke 8 lousy/vile/
3 blokes/guys disgusting
4 guys/blokes 9 cheek
5 neck 10 back
6 moaning

Unit 59

1 1 Your guess is as good as mine ~~is~~.
2 You're ~~not~~ kidding! I don't believe it.
3 Yes, it's been one of those ~~bad~~ days.
4 Don't ~~you~~ ask me. He never tells me a word.
5 No ~~any~~ such luck, I'm afraid.
6 No, but there's no use ~~of~~ worrying.
7 No; it goes in one ear and out the other ~~ear~~.
8 Well, you've got nothing ~~for~~ to lose.

232 REVIEW ANSWER KEY

Unit 60

1 1 what   4 wonder   7 battle
   2 bit   5 earth   8 know
   3 not   6 worth

2 1 All things being equal, I'd rather live in
    the centre. OR I'd rather live in the centre,
    all things being equal.
   2 She seems to live in a world of her own.
   3 Exercise is every bit as important as what
    you eat. OR What you eat is every bit as
    important as exercise.
   4 I rang him but for some reason he didn't
    answer. OR I rang him but he didn't
    answer for some reason.
   5 How much did they charge you, if you
    don't mind me asking?
   6 It's great to let your hair down after a
    hard week. OR After a hard week, it's
    great to let your hair down.

Unit 61

1 1 pick and **choose**
   2 **back** to front
   3 aims and **objectives**
   4 hustle and **bustle**
   5 back and **forth**
   6 **bright** and cheerful
   7 rules and **regulations**
   8 trial and **error**

Unit 62

1 1 good   4 strong   7 sieve
   2 quiet   5 red   8 log
   3 dry   6 dream

Unit 63

1 do away with / abolish
   own up / confess
   crop up / happen unexpectedly
   take sth apart / dismantle
   take sb in / deceive
   drag sth out / prolong
   hit back / retaliate
   butt in / interrupt
   turn up / arrive

Unit 64

1 *These phrases are correct:*
   1 As a matter of fact
   2 on the whole / by and large, Mind you, to
    be honest
   3 at any rate / anyhow, incidentally
   4 alternatively
   5 I agree / It's true, even so
   6 Besides

Unit 65

1 1 so/thereabouts
   2 odd / something / or thereabouts
   3 region
   4 somehow
   5 take
   6 something
   7 stuff
   8 lines

Unit 66

1 1 Live and let live.
   2 Easier said than done.
   3 Two heads are better than one.
   4 Once bitten, twice shy.
   5 Blood is thicker than water.
   6 Two wrongs don't make a right.

2 1 money   4 merrier   7 practice
   2 no, good   5 safe, sorry   8 sight, mind
   3 sleeping   6 come, served

Written English

Unit 67

1 straightforward / easy to understand
   complicated/convoluted
   abrupt/brusque
   unnecessary/superfluous
   relevant/pertinent

Unit 68

1 albeit, although
   prior to, before
   notwithstanding, in spite of
   in view of, considering
   thus, therefore

Unit 69

1 evaluate, evaluation
   condemn, condemnation
   assert, assertion
   summarize, summary
   hypothesize, hypothesis
   justify, justification
   exemplify, example
   outline, outline

2 1 N   2 N   3 Y   4 Y   5 N   6 Y   7 N   8 N

Unit 70

1 1 depict   5 alien   8 protagonist
   2 convey   6 downfall   9 betray
   3 mercy   7 portrayal   10 synopsis
   4 embody
   The word in the grey squares is 'commentary'.

Unit 71

1 1 **not** usually fully understood
2 ~~describing~~ doing
3 ~~largest~~ smallest
4 ~~not~~
5 ~~declines~~ changes
6 ~~replace~~ copy
7 ~~unsuccessfully~~
8 ~~weak~~ strong

2 1 hypothesize   5 unbiased
2 hereditary   6 verification
3 scrutinize   7 immunity
4 defective   8 molecular

Unit 72

1 1 The central core of a building is often made of reinforced **concrete**.
2 Large steel **girders** are placed between the vertical columns to hold the building together.
3 The exterior walls are made by attaching **panels** made of glass or metal to the building.
4 Skyscrapers undergo rigorous tests to **determine/establish/assess** whether they can withstand high winds.
5 All support beams are lifted by **cranes** and then put in place.
6 The design has to **comply** with strict safely regulations before construction begins.
7 All buildings have to conform to physical **constraints** imposed by climate and geology.
8 Mechanical devices may be added to **counteract** or resist motion.
9 All construction has to go through the most **stringent/rigorous/thorough** safety checks.
10 The building's support columns are usually **anchored** in the footings.

Unit 73

1 1 bed and breakfast
2 please turn over
3 headquarters
4 closed-circuit television
5 do-it-yourself
6 chief executive officer
7 politically correct
8 care of
9 for the attention of
10 intelligence quotient
11 estimated time of arrival
12 tender loving care

Aspects of language

Unit 74

1 1 ~~advised~~   4 ~~similar, place~~
2 ~~advantaged~~   5 ~~handled~~
3 ~~virus~~

Unit 75

1 1 The hurricane is **intensifying** as it heads towards land.
2 This income is **tax-free**.
3 This kind of vegetation **characterizes** the region.
4 The building contains a system which **purifies** the air.
5 The studio is **soundproof**.
6 He needs to **clarify** his intentions.
7 If you leave that in the sun, it will just **solidify**.
8 The plan I've devised is **foolproof**.

Unit 76

1 1 to   4 over   7 on
2 for   5 to   8 for
3 on   6 for

Unit 77

1 1 ~~passing~~   4 ~~discussion~~
2 ~~choice~~   5 ~~danger~~
3 ~~the contrary~~

Unit 78

1 1 weird   6 tasteless
2 eminent   7 negligent
3 dejected   8 perplexed
4 inconceivable 9 naked
5 comprehensive

Unit 79

1 1 purely   4 virtually   7 apparently
2 invariably   5 indirectly   8 officially
3 briefly   6 ultimately

2 1 a   3 a and b   5 a
2 b   4 a and b   6 b

Unit 80

1 *Possible answers:*
1 's unintelligent
2 's got very poor eyesight.
3 're dismissing/sacking people
4 our own side
5 's dead OR 's been killed by the vet
6 can't hear (very well) OR 's rather deaf
7 stole it
8 ordinary citizens/people have been killed/injured

List of spotlight boxes

Unit	Title of spotlight box	Page
1B	*make fun of someone*	11
3B	Adjectives with -*minded*	15
3C	*outbreak, outlay,* etc.	16
4A	Collocation	17
4C	*entirely*	19
6A	Different related forms	22
7A	Suffix -*en*	29
7B	Expressions with *attention*	29
9A	Verbs and nouns	32
9B	Expressions with *constant*	33
10A	Ergative verbs	34
11A	-*sighted*	36
11B	Ways of seeing	37
12A	Adverbs of manner	38
12B	Adjectives ending in -*y*	39
13B	*exceed* and related forms	41
14C	*cynical, sceptical*	47
15A	*desperate* and related forms	48
15B	Other expressions with *heart*	49
16A	*tough*	50
16B	*accept*	51
17B	*principles* and *values*	53
18B	*expect*	55
19A	*consider, regard, view, perceive*	56
21	*relax*	64
22B	Boredom	67
23B	*chance*	69
24A	*nature*	70
25B	Prefix *out-*	73
26B	*company*	75
27B	Adjective + *change*	81
28B	-*friendly*	83
29A	*extinct, extinction*	84
30A	*rate*	86
31A	*e-* and *cyber-*	88
32A	*migration*	90
32B	Getting used to things	91
33B	A stay in hospital	95

Unit	Title of spotlight box	Page
34B	Gender	97
35B	The police	99
36B	*self-*	101
37A	*comprise, make up, consist of, compose*	102
37B	*interior* and *internal*	104
38	Headline words	108
40A	*dare*	112
41B	*exclusives* and *scoops*	115
42A	*means*	116
45A	*degree*	122
46A	*merger, takeover,* and *acquisition*	124
48A	Bank accounts	128
48B	*surplus*	129
49A	*no matter what, whatever*	130
49B	Metaphorical use of words	131
50A	*set* + noun	132
52B	*effect*	139
53B	Types of lie	141
56B	*way*	147
59A	*idioms* and *set phrases*	154
61	*bribery* and *corruption*	158
63B	Phrasal verbs: meanings and forms	161
64	*anyway*	162
65	*or something*	164
68	*hitherto* and *henceforth*	175
69A	*present* v	176
70	*embody/represent sth, endow sb with sth*	178
71B	*unit*	181
74B	*un-* and *under-*	191
75B	-*proof, -free*	193
76A	*control of/over sth/sb*	194
77B	*under*	197
78A	Fame	198
79B	*… speaking*	201
80	Euphemisms	203

Word list / Index

Numbers are unit numbers, not page numbers

a likely story /ə ˈlaɪkli ˌstɔːri/ 59
a real character /ə ˌriːəl ˈkærəktə(r)/ 14
a real effort /ə ˌriːəl ˈefət/ 4
a real eyesore /ə ˌriːəl ˈaɪsɔː(r)/ 4
a real pain /ə ˌriːəl ˈpeɪn/ 58
a small world /ə ˌsmɔːl ˈwɜːld/ 66
a tight corner /ə ˌtaɪt ˈkɔːnə(r)/ 39
abandon /əˈbændən/ 43, 55
abnormal /æbˈnɔːml/ 71
abolish /əˈbɒlɪʃ/ 36, 63
abolition /æbəˈlɪʃn/ 36
about *as in* be about to do sth 35
abrupt /əˈbrʌpt/ 67
absence /ˈæbsəns/ 51
absent /ˈæbsənt/ 51
absent-minded /ˌæbsənt ˈmaɪndɪd/ 3
absolute ADJ /ˈæbsəluːt/ 56
absorb /əbˈzɔːb/ 5
abuse N /əˈbjuːs/ 6
abuse V /əˈbjuːz/ 6
accent /ˈæksənt/ 4
accept /əkˈsept/ 16
access N, V /ˈækses/ 33
accident-prone /ˈæksɪdnt ˌprəʊn/ 30
acclaim /əˈkleɪm/ 22
acclaimed /əˈkleɪmd/ 22
acclimatized *as in* get acclimatized 32
accompany /əˈkʌmpəni/ 26
accomplish /əˈkʌmplɪʃ/ 49
according to /əˈkɔːdɪŋ ˌtuː, tə/ 39
account *as in* current/deposit account 48
accountable to /əˈkaʊntəbl ˌtuː, tə/ 45
accumulate /əˈkjuːmjəleɪt/ 48, 51
accustomed *as in* get accustomed 32
achieve /əˈtʃiːv/ 49
acquire /əˈkwaɪə(r)/ 24
acquisition /ˌækwɪˈzɪʃn/ 46
action *as in* take action 40
actions speak louder than words /ˈækʃnz ˌspiːk ˌlaʊdə ðən ˈwɜːdz/ 66
actually /ˈæktʃuəli/ 64
adapt to /əˈdæpt ˌtuː, tə/ 27
adaptation /ˌædæpˈteɪʃn/ 22
addict *as in* drug addict 25
addicted to sth /əˈdɪktɪd tə ˌ.../ 25
additional /əˈdɪʃənl/ 45
address V /əˈdres/ 54
adjust /əˈdʒʌst/ 11
adjust to /əˈdʒʌst ˌtuː, tə/ 27
adjustment /əˈdʒʌstmənt/ 11
admit sb to hospital /ədˌmɪt ˌ... tə ˈhɒspɪtl/ 33
adopt /əˈdɒpt/ 69
adrenalin /əˈdrenəlɪn/ 43
advance /ədˈvɑːns/ 30
adversary /ˈædvəsəri/ 53

adverse effect /ˌædvɜːs ɪˈfekt/ 52
advertising agency /ˈædvətaɪzɪŋ ˌeɪdʒənsi/ 34
affection /əˈfekʃn/ 14
affectionate /əˈfekʃənət/ 14
affluent /ˈæfluənt/ 70
after sth /ˈɑːftə ˌ.../ 25
against all (the) odds /əˌgenst ˌɔːl ði ˈɒdz/ 40
age /eɪdʒ/ 57
agency /ˈeɪdʒənsi/ 34
aggravate /ˈægrəveɪt/ 54
agile /ˈædʒaɪl/ 9
agility /əˈdʒɪləti/ 9
agree entirely /əˌgriː ɪnˈtaɪəli/ 4
aims and objectives /ˌeɪmz ənd əbˈdʒektɪvz/ 61
air force /ˈeə ˌfɔːs/ 37
albeit /ˈɔːlbiːt/ 68
alcoholic /ˌælkəˈhɒlɪk/ 25
alert N /əˈlɜːt/ 38
alien /ˈeɪliən/ 70
all the same /ˌɔːl ðə ˈseɪm/ 64
all things being equal /ˈɔːl ˌθɪŋz ˌbiːɪŋ ˈiːkwəl/ 60
all things considered /ˈɔːl ˌθɪŋz kənˈsɪdəd/ 77
allegation /ˌæləˈgeɪʃn/ 39, 41
allege /əˈledʒ/ 39, 41
allegedly /əˈledʒɪdli/ 41
alleviate /əˈliːvieɪt/ 11
allocate /ˈæləkeɪt/ 34
allowance /əˈlaʊəns/ 44
almonds /ˈɑːməndz/ 20
alongside /əˈlɒŋsaɪd/ 31
aloof /əˈluːf/ 14
alternate V /ˈɔːltəneɪt/ 9
alternatively /ɔːlˈtɜːnətɪvli/ 64
ambiguity /ˌæmbɪˈgjuːəti/ 1
ambiguous /æmˈbɪgjuəs/ 1
amend /əˈmend/ 27
amendment /əˈmendmənt/ 27
amid /əˈmɪd/ 39
amidst /əˈmɪdst/ 39
an eye for an eye /ən ˌaɪ fər ən ˈaɪ/ 66
an eye for an eye and a tooth for a tooth /ən ˌaɪ fər ən ˈaɪ ən ə ˌtuːθ fər ə ˈtuːθ/ 66
analyse /ˈænəlaɪz/ 69
anchor V /ˈæŋkə(r)/ 72
ancient /ˈeɪnʃnt/ 55
angle N, V /ˈæŋgl/ 72
animosity /ˌænɪˈmɒsəti/ 32
ankle /ˈæŋkl/ 13
anonymity /ˌænəˈnɪməti/ 53
anonymously /əˈnɒnɪməsli/ 53
anti- /ˈænti/ 74
anti-depressant /ˌænti dɪˈpresənt/ 74

anti-drugs policy /ˌænti ˈdrʌgz ˌpɒləsi/ 74
anti-inflammatory /ˌænti ɪnˈflæmətri/ 74
anti-racism /ˌænti ˈreɪsɪzəm/ 74
anti-spam filter /ˌænti ˈspæm ˌfɪltə(r)/ 31
anti-virus protection /ˌænti ˈvaɪrəs prəˌtekʃn/ 31
anti-virus software /ˌænti ˈvaɪrəs ˌsɒftweə(r)/ 74
anti-war /ˌænti ˈwɔː(r)/ 74
anticipate /ænˈtɪsɪpeɪt/ 49
anticipation /ænˌtɪsɪˈpeɪʃn/ 49
antique N, ADJ /ænˈtiːk/ 55
anyhow /ˈenihaʊ/ 64
anyway /ˈeniweɪ/ 64
apart *as in* take sth apart 63
apologetic /əˌpɒləˈdʒetɪk/ 6
apologize /əˈpɒlədʒaɪz/ 6
appalled /əˈpɔːld/ 15
apparently /əˈpærəntli/ 79
appeal N /əˈpiːl/ 67
appeal for /əˈpiːl fə(r)/ 67
appealing /əˈpiːlɪŋ/ 18
appetite /ˈæpɪtaɪt/ 12
appetizing /ˈæpɪtaɪzɪŋ/ 12
applaud /əˈplɔːd/ 22
applause /əˈplɔːz/ 22
appliance /əˈplaɪəns/ 28
apply pressure to /əˌplaɪ ˈpreʃə tə/ 12
appreciate /əˈpriːʃieɪt/ 16
appreciation /əpriːʃiˈeɪʃn/ 16
aptitude /ˈæptɪtjuːd/ 76
archive N, V /ˈɑːkaɪv/ 71
arduous /ˈɑːdjuəs/ 9
argument /ˈɑːgjumənt/ 69
arise /əˈraɪz/ 54
armed combat /ˌɑːmd ˈkɒmbæt/ 37
armed forces /ˌɑːmd ˈfɔːsɪz/ 37
arms /ɑːmz/ 38
arms *as in* folded arms 8
army /ˈɑːmi/ 37
aroma /əˈrəʊmə/ 12
arouse /əˈraʊz/ 52
artichoke /ˈɑːtɪtʃəʊk/ 20
articulate ADJ /ɑːˈtɪkjulət/ 54
articulate V /ɑːˈtɪkjuleɪt/ 54
as a favour /ˌæz ə ˈfeɪvə(r)/ 5
as a matter of fact /ˌæz ə ˌmætər əv ˈfækt/ 64
as far as sth is concerned /ˌæz ˌfɑːr əz ˈ... ɪz kənˈsɜːnd/ 79
as blind as a bat /ˌæz ˌblaɪnd əz ə ˈbæt/ 62
as deaf as a post /ˌæz ˌdef əz ə ˈpəʊst/ 62
as dry as a bone /ˌæz ˌdraɪ əz ə ˈbəʊn/ 62
as for /ˈæz fə(r)/ 64

VOWELS: æ cat | ɑː father | e ten | ɜː bird | ə about | ɪ sit | iː see | i many | ɒ got | ɔː saw | ʌ up | ʊ put | uː too | u actual | aɪ my | aʊ now | eɪ say | əʊ go | ɔɪ boy | ɪə near | eə hair | ʊə pure

as good as gold /ˌəz ˌɡɒd əz ˈɡəʊld/ 62
as I was saying /ˈæz aɪ wəz ˌseɪɪŋ/ 64
as light as a feather /ˌəz ˌlaɪt əz ə ˈfeðə(r)/ 62
as quiet as a mouse /ˌəz ˌkwaɪət əz ə ˈmaʊs/ 62
as red as a beetroot /ˌəz ˌred əz ə ˈbiːtruːt/ 62
as strong as an ox /ˌəz ˌstrɒŋ əz ən ˈɒks/ 62
as thin as a rake /ˌəz ˌθɪn əz ə ˈreɪk/ 62
as time went by /əz ˌtaɪm went ˈbaɪ/ 16
as white as a sheet /ˌəz ˌwaɪt əz ə ˈʃiːt/ 62
as you will see from my CV . . . /ˌæz ju wɪl ˌsiː frəm ˌmaɪ ˌsiː ˈviː/ 67
asap (= as soon as possible) /ˌeɪ ˌes ˌeɪ ˈpiː/ 73
ask a favour /ˌɑːsk ə ˈfeɪvə(r)/ 5
ask after /ˈɑːsk ˌɑːftə(r)/ 63
aspect /ˈæspekt/ 71
assert /əˈsɜːt/ 69
assertion /əˈsɜːʃn/ 69
assertive /əˈsɜːtɪv/ 14
assess /əˈses/ 69
assessment /əˈsesmənt/ 69
assimilate /əˈsɪməleɪt/ 27
assimilation /əsɪməˈleɪʃn/ 27
assist /əˈsɪst/ 37
associated with /əˈsəʊʃieɪtɪd wɪð/ 42
association /əsəʊʃiˈeɪʃn/ 42
assurance /əˈʃʊərəns/ 6
assure /əˈʃʊə(r)/ 6
astute /əˈstuːt/ 14
asylum /əˈsaɪləm/ 32
at a moment's notice /ət ə ˌməʊmənts ˈnəʊtɪs/ 77
at an angle /ət ən ˈæŋɡl/ 72
at any rate /ət ˈeni ˌreɪt/ 64
at ease as in put sb at ease 33
at home /ət ˈhəʊm/ 23
at once /ət ˈwʌns/ 77
at one time /ət ˈwʌn ˌtaɪm/ 57
at random /ət ˈrændəm/ 43
at short notice /ət ˌʃɔːt ˈnəʊtɪs/ 77
at stake /ət ˈsteɪk/ 50
at the last minute /ət ðə ˌlɑːst ˈmɪnɪt/ 57
at the very least /ət ðə ˌveri ˈliːst/ 77
atb (= all the best) 73
8 (= -ate) 73
atom /ˈætəm/ 71
atrocious /əˈtrəʊʃəs/ 22
attack as in under attack 77
attention /əˈtenʃn/ 7
attn 73
attract /əˈtrækt/ 24
attract sb's attention /əˌtrækt ˌ... əˈtenʃn/ 7
attribute N /ˈætrɪbjuːt/ 14
audience /ˈɔːdiəns/ 22
authentic /ɔːˈθentɪk/ 55
authority /ɔːˈθɒrəti/ 37
away /əˈweɪ/ 23

away as in get away from it all 21
away as in right away 77
awkward /ˈɔːkwəd/ 26

B & B (= bed and breakfast) /ˌbiː ən ˈbiː/ 73
b (= be) 73
b4 (= before) 73
b4n (= bye for now) 73
back V /bæk/ 46
back as in behind sb's back 16
back and forth /ˌbæk ən ˈfɔːθ/ 61
back down /ˌbæk ˈdaʊn/ 4
back to front /ˌbæk tə ˈfrʌnt/ 61
backing /ˈbækɪŋ/ 46
bad run /ˌbæd ˈrʌn/ 23
bad taste as in be in bad taste 19
bad-tempered /ˌbæd ˈtempəd/ 3
badly hit /ˌbædli ˈhɪt/ 49
baffle /ˈbæfl/ 53
baffled /ˈbæfld/ 78
bags of /ˈbæɡz əv/ 65
bail /beɪl/ 35
bail sb out /ˌbeɪl ˌ...ˈaʊt/ 48
balance as in on balance 77
balance as in tip the balance 46
ballot N, V /ˈbælət/ 50
ban N /bæn/ 76
bank /bæŋk/ 37
bank statement /ˈbæŋk ˌsteɪtmənt/ 48
bankrupt as in go bankrupt 46
barbed wire /ˌbɑːbd ˈwaɪə(r)/ 3
bare /beə(r)/ 78
barely /ˈbeəli/ 11
bargain hunting /ˈbɑːɡɪn ˌhʌntɪŋ/ 25
bark N, V /bɑːk/ 10
basic unit /ˈbeɪsɪk ˌjuːnɪt/ 71
basically /ˈbeɪsɪkli/ 79
basis /ˈbeɪsɪs/ 49
bat /bæt/ 62
batteries as in recharge your batteries 21
battery charger /ˈbætəri ˌtʃɑːdʒə(r)/ 28
battle as in fight a losing battle 60
battle as in locked in battle 39
be about to do sth /ˌbiː əˌbaʊt tə ˈduː ˌ.../ 35
be behind sb/sth /ˌbi bɪˈhaɪnd ˌ.../ 54
be bullied /ˌbi ˈbʊlid/ 17
be carried away /ˌbi ˌkærɪd əˈweɪ/ 26
be composed of /ˌbi kəmˈpəʊzd əv/ 37
be confined to a wheelchair /ˌbi kənˌfaɪnd tu ə ˈwiːltʃeə(r)/ 30
be confined to bed /ˌbi kənˌfaɪnd tə ˈbed/ 30
be cruel to be kind /ˌbi ˌkruːəl tə bi ˈkaɪnd/ 14
be detained in custody /ˌbi dɪˌteɪnd ɪn ˈkʌstədi/ 35
be distracted by sth /ˌbi dɪˈstræktɪd baɪ ˌ.../ 25
be drawn against /ˌbi ˈdrɔːn əˌɡenst/ 23
be drawn to /ˌbi ˈdrɔːn tə/ 14
be economical with the truth /ˌbiː iːkəˌnɒmɪkl wɪð ðə ˈtruːθ/ 53

be entitled to /ˌbiː ɪnˈtaɪtld ˌtuː, tə/ 44
be getting on for /ˌbi ˈɡetɪŋ ˌɒn fə(r)/ 7
be humiliated /ˌbi hjuːˈmɪlieɪtɪd/ 60
be in a mess /ˌbiː ɪn ə ˈmes/ 18
be in a world of your own /ˌbiː ɪn ə ˌwɜːld əv jɔːr ˈəʊn/ 60
be in bad taste /ˌbi ɪn ˌbæd ˈteɪst/ 19
be in favour of /ˌbi ɪn ˈfeɪvər əv/ 42
be in poor taste /ˌbi ɪn ˌpɔː ˈteɪst/ 19
be in the driving seat /ˌbi ɪn ðə ˈdraɪvɪŋ ˌsiːt/ 42
be in the red /ˌbi ɪn ðə ˈred/ 48
be in two minds about /ˌbi ɪn ˌtuː ˈmaɪndz əˌbaʊt/ 2
be into sth /ˌbiː ˌɪntə ˈ.../ 58
be locked in battle /ˌbi ˌlɒkt ɪn ˈbætl/ 39
be off /ˌbiː ˈɒf/ 25
be on top /ˌbi ˌɒn ˈtɒp/ 23
be on your best behaviour /ˌbiː ˌɒn jɔː ˌbest bɪˈheɪvjə(r)/ 19
be out of hand /ˌbiː ˌaʊt əv ˈhænd/ 49
be out of your depth /ˌbiː ˌaʊt əv jɔː ˈdepθ/ 42
be overdrawn /ˌbiː əʊvəˈdrɔːn/ 48
be overwhelmed by /ˌbiː əʊvəˈwelmd baɪ/ 43
be past it /ˌbi ˈpɑːst ɪt/ 56
be promoted /ˌbi prəˈməʊtɪd/ 23
be put out /ˌbi ˌpʊt ˈaʊt/ 19
be reconciled with /ˌbi ˈrekənsaɪld wɪð/ 63
be referred to sb /ˌbi rɪˈfɜːd tə ˌ.../ 33
be relegated /ˌbi ˈrelɪɡeɪtɪd/ 23
be the last thing on sb's mind /ˌbi ðə ˌlɑːst ˌθɪŋ ɒn ˌ... ˈmaɪnd/ 60
be thrown in at the deep end /ˌbi ˌθrəʊn ˌɪn ət ðə ˈdiːp ˌend/ 42
be tied up /ˌbi ˌtaɪd ˈʌp/ 2
be under siege /ˌbiː ˌʌndə ˈsiːdʒ/ 43
be uprooted /ˌbiː ʌpˈruːtɪd/ 32
beam /biːm/ 72
bean sprouts /ˈbiːn ˌspraʊts/ 20
bear sth in mind /ˌbeə ˌ... ɪn ˈmaɪnd/ 8
beat /biːt/ 20
beautiful /ˈbjuːtɪfl/ 21
beauty is only skin-deep /ˈbjuːti ɪz ˌəʊnli ˌskɪn ˈdiːp/ 66
bee /biː/ 10
beep N, V /biːp/ 10
beetroot /ˈbiːtruːt/ 20, 62
before sb's time /bɪˌfɔː ˌ... ˈtaɪm/ 57
beforehand /bɪˈfɔːhænd/ 26
behalf as in on behalf of sb 34
behaviour as in be on your best behaviour 19
behind as in be behind sb/sth 54
behind closed doors /bɪˌhaɪnd ˌkləʊzd ˈdɔːz/ 39
behind sb's back /bɪˌhaɪnd ˌ... ˈbæk/ 16
behind the scenes /bɪˌhaɪnd ðə ˈsiːnz/ 39

behind the times /bɪˌhaɪnd ðə ˈtaɪmz/ 57
believe it or not /bɪˌliːv ɪt ɔː ˈnɒt/ 60
belt *as in* tighten your belt 46
bending /ˈbendɪŋ/ 9
beneficial effect /benɪˌfɪʃl ɪˈfekt/ 18
benefits /ˈbenɪfɪts/ 44
bereaved /bɪˈriːvd/ 77
besides /bɪˈsaɪdz/ 64
best *as in* the best of both worlds 60
best *as in* the best thing 59
bet *as in* your best bet 59
betray /bɪˈtreɪ/ 70
betrayal /bɪˈtreɪəl/ 70
better late than never /ˌbetə ˌleɪt ðən ˈnevə(r)/ 66
better safe than sorry /ˌbetə ˌseɪf ðən ˈsɒri/ 66
better still /ˌbetə ˈstɪl/ 28
bfn (= bye for now) 73
bias /ˈbaɪəs/ 71
biased /ˈbaɪəst/ 71
bid N, V /bɪd/ 38, 46
bid *as in* make a bid for 46
big chance /ˌbɪg ˈtʃɑːns/ 23
bigoted /ˈbɪgətɪd/ 3
birth *as in* give birth 41
birth certificate /ˈbɜːθ səˌtɪfɪkət/ 3
birth rate /ˈbɜːθ ˌreɪt/ 30
bit of a drag /ˌbɪt əv ə ˈdræg/ 58
bite your fingernails /ˌbaɪt jɔː ˈfɪŋgəneɪlz/ 8
bizarre /bɪˈzɑː(r)/ 78
blame *as in* take the blame 4
bland /blænd/ 12
blast /blɑːst/ 38
blazing row /ˌbleɪzɪŋ ˈraʊ/ 39
blink V /blɪŋk/ 11
blister /ˈblɪstə(r)/ 13
block spam /ˌblɒk ˈspæm/ 31
bloke /bləʊk/ 58
blood is thicker than water /ˌblʌd ɪz ˌθɪkə ðən ˈwɔːtə(r)/ 66
blood pressure /ˈblʌd ˌpreʃə(r)/ 13
blow /bləʊ/ 38
blow sth out of proportion /ˌbləʊ ... ˌaʊt əv prəˈpɔːʃn/ 50
blunt /blʌnt/ 67
blurred vision /ˌblɜːd ˈvɪʒn/ 11
boast V /bəʊst/ 10
boat *as in* rock the boat 42
body /ˈbɒdi/ 5, 67
boil down to sth /ˈbɔɪl ˌdaʊn tə ,.../ 52
bolt V, N /bɒlt/ 72
bond /bɒnd/ 16
bone /bəʊn/ 62
bonus /ˈbəʊnəs/ 44
book *as in* don't judge a book by its cover 14
boom *as in* economic boom 47
boost N, V /buːst/ 38
boost morale /ˌbuːst məˈrɑːl/ 45
bored out of your mind /ˌbɔːd ˌaʊt əv jɔː ˈmaɪnd/ 22
bored stiff /ˌbɔːd ˈstɪf/ 22
bored to death /ˌbɔːd tə ˈdeθ/ 22

bored to tears /ˌbɔːd tə ˈtɪəz/ 22
boring /ˈbɔːrɪŋ/ 22
boss *as in* your own boss 45
bottle sth up /ˌbɒtl ,... ˈʌp/ 15
bounce back /ˌbaʊns ˈbæk/ 47
brace /breɪs/ 7
bracket N /ˈbrækɪt/ 72
braise /breɪz/ 20
branch /brɑːntʃ/ 37
brand new /ˌbrænd ˈnjuː/ 55
brave /breɪv/ 17
bravery /ˈbreɪvəri/ 17
breadwinner /ˈbredwɪnə(r)/ 20
break /breɪk/ 57
break down /ˌbreɪk ˈdaʊn/ 3
break into a gallop /ˌbreɪk ˌɪntu ə ˈgæləp/ 9
break off from sth /ˌbreɪk ˈɒf frəm ,.../ 49
break out /ˌbreɪk ˈaʊt/ 3, 4
break the deadlock /ˌbreɪk ðə ˈdedlɒk/ 50
break up /ˌbreɪk ˈʌp/ 3
break-up /ˈbreɪk ˌʌp/ 3
breakdown /ˈbreɪkdaʊn/ 3
breaking point /ˈbreɪkɪŋ ˌpɔɪnt/ 43
breakthrough /ˈbreɪkθruː/ 56
breath *as in* don't hold your breath 59
breathtaking /ˈbreθteɪkɪŋ/ 11
breed /briːd/ 29
bribe V /braɪb/ 61
bribery /ˈbraɪbəri/ 61
brief summary /ˌbriːf ˈsʌməri/ 4
briefly /ˈbriːfli/ 79
bright *as in* not exactly bright 80
bright and cheerful /ˌbraɪt ən ˈtʃɪəfl/ 61
brilliant /ˈbrɪliənt/ 22
bring sb somewhere /ˈbrɪŋ ... ˌsʌmweə(r)/ 2
bring sth about /ˌbrɪŋ ... əˈbaʊt/ 27
bring sth up /ˌbrɪŋ ,... ˈʌp/ 63
broad-minded /ˌbrɔːd ˈmaɪndɪd/ 3
broadcast V /ˈbrɔːdkɑːst/ 41
broadly speaking /ˌbrɔːdli ˈspiːkɪŋ/ 64
broadsheet /ˈbrɔːdʃiːt/ 41
broke /brəʊk/ 58
broken home /ˌbrəʊkən ˈhəʊm/ 18
browse /braʊz/ 25
browser /ˈbraʊzə(r)/ 31
brusque /bruːsk/ 67
btw (= by the way) 73
bubble /ˈbʌbl/ 47
buck *as in* pass the buck 50
budget N /ˈbʌdʒɪt/ 34
budget N, V /ˈbʌdʒɪt/ 48
bug /bʌg/ 58
build up /ˌbɪld ˈʌp/ 48
built-up /ˌbɪlt ˈʌp/ 3
bulb (= light bulb) /bʌlb/ 28
bulb (= plant) /bʌlb/ 24
bullet-proof /ˈbʊlɪt ˌpruːf/ 75
bully N, V /ˈbʊli/ 17
bump into sb /ˌbʌmp ˌɪntə ,.../ 63
bumpy ride /ˌbʌmpi ˈraɪd/ 47
buoyant /ˈbɔɪənt/ 47

burden *as in* debt burden 47
burst into flames /ˌbɜːst ˌɪntə ˈfleɪmz/ 4
burst into tears /ˌbɜːst ˌɪntə ˈtɪəz/ 4
bury your head in the sand /ˌberi jɔː ˌhed ɪn ðə ˈsænd/ 50
bush /bʊʃ/ 24
butt in /ˌbʌt ˈɪn/ 63
butterfly /ˈbʌtəflaɪ/ 24
buy sth on impulse /ˌbaɪ ,... ɒn ˈɪmpʌls/ 25
buzz V /bʌz/ 10
buzz about /ˌbʌz əˈbaʊt/ 10
by and large /ˌbaɪ ən ˈlɑːdʒ/ 64
by any chance /ˌbaɪ ˌeni ˈtʃɑːns/ 60
by chance *as in* purely by chance 70
by choice /ˌbaɪ ˈtʃɔɪs/ 77
by common consent /ˌbaɪ ˌkɒmən kənˈsent/ 36
by means of /ˌbaɪ ˈmiːnz əv/ 77
by mutual consent /ˌbaɪ ˌmjuːtʃuəl kənˈsent/ 36
by the way /ˌbaɪ ðə ˈweɪ/ 64

c (= see) 73
cake *as in* have your cake and eat it 20
cake *as in* sell like hot cakes 62
calculate /ˈkælkjuleɪt/ 48
calculation /kælkjuˈleɪʃn/ 48
call sth off /ˌkɔːl ,... ˈɒf/ 63
camcorder /ˈkæmkɔːdə(r)/ 31
cancel /ˈkænsl/ 63
canteen /kænˈtiːn/ 44
capital punishment /ˌkæpɪtl ˈpʌnɪʃmənt/ 36
capitalism /ˈkæpɪtəlɪzəm/ 42
capitalist /ˈkæpɪtəlɪst/ 42
capitulate /kəˈpɪtʃuleɪt/ 18
captivity *as in* in captivity 29
car chase /ˈkɑː ˌtʃeɪs/ 9
carbon footprint /ˌkɑːbən ˈfʊtprɪnt/ 28
carried away *as in* be/get carried away 26
carry out (= implement) /ˌkæri ˈaʊt/ 27
carry out (a procedure) /ˌkæri ˈaʊt/ 30
carry out (a survey) /ˌkæri ˈaʊt/ 41
case *as in* in any case 64
cashews /ˈkæʃuːz, kæˈʃuːz/ 20
casserole /ˈkæsərəʊl/ 20
cast /kɑːst/ 22
casualty /ˈkæʒuəlti/ 53
catch /kætʃ/ 63
catch a glimpse of /ˌkætʃ ə ˈglɪmps əv/ 11
catch fire /ˌkætʃ ˈfaɪə(r)/ 4
catch sb out /ˌkætʃ ... ˈaʊt/ 53
catch sight of /ˌkætʃ ˈsaɪt əv/ 11
cause /kɔːz/ 27
caution V /ˈkɔːʃn/ 35
cautious /ˈkɔːʃəs/ 15
CCTV (= closed circuit television) /ˌsiː ˌsiː ˌtiː ˈviː/ 73
cease /siːs/ 38

VOWELS: æ cat | ɑː father | e ten | ɜː bird | ə about | ɪ sit | iː see | i many | ɒ got | ɔː saw | ʌ up | ʊ put | uː too | u actual |
aɪ my | aʊ now | eɪ say | əʊ go | ɔɪ boy | ɪə near | eə hair | ʊə pure

238

celeb /sə'leb/ 41
celebrity /sə'lebrəti/ 41
cell (= prison cell) /sel/ 36
cell (e.g. blood cell) /sel/ 71
centre party /'sentə ˌpɑːti/ 42
CEO (= chief executive officer) /ˌsiː ˌiː 'əʊ/ 73
certificate as in birth certificate 3
chain of events /ˌtʃeɪn əv ɪ'vents/ 52
chair N, V /tʃeə(r)/ 34
chairman /'tʃeəmən/ 34
chairperson /'tʃeəpɜːsn/ 34
chairwoman /'tʃeəwʊmən/ 34
chalk as in like chalk and cheese 20
chance /tʃɑːns/ 23
chance as in by any chance 60
chance as in purely by chance 79
chance as in take a chance on sth 40
change /tʃeɪndʒ/ 27
channel of communication /ˌtʃænl əv kəmjuːnɪ'keɪʃn/ 54
chaos as in total/utter chaos 4
character /'kærəktə(r)/ 14
characteristic /ˌkærəktə'rɪstɪk/ 75
characterize /'kærəktəraɪz/ 75
charge N, V /tʃɑːdʒ/ 9
charge sth /'tʃɑːdʒ ˌ.../ 28
charge sth up /ˌtʃɑːdʒ ˌ... ʌp/ 28
charger /'tʃɑːdʒə(r)/ 28
charisma /kə'rɪzmə/ 14
charismatic /ˌkærɪz'mætɪk/ 14
charity /'tʃærəti/ 34
charity begins at home /ˌtʃærəti bɪˌɡɪnz ət 'həʊm/ 66
charity organization /'tʃærəti ɔːɡənaɪˌzeɪʃn/ 34
charm /tʃɑːm/ 21
charming /'tʃɑːmɪŋ/ 21
chase N, V /tʃeɪs/ 9
chatterbox /'tʃætəbɒks/ 14
chatty /'tʃæti/ 14
cheek (= rude behaviour) /tʃiːk/ 19, 58
cheeky /'tʃiːki/ 19
cheerful as in bright and cheerful 61
cheers /tʃɪəz/ 58
cheese as in like chalk and cheese 20
chemical weapon /ˌkemɪkl 'wepən/ 37
chemotherapy /kiːməʊ'θerəpi/ 30
chickens as in don't count your chickens 20
chief /tʃiːf/ 38
chief constable /ˌtʃiːf 'kʌnstəbl/ 35
chiefly /'tʃiːfli/ 79
childcare /'tʃaɪldkeə(r)/ 44
childish /'tʃaɪldɪʃ/ 78
childlike /'tʃaɪldlaɪk/ 78
childproof /'tʃaɪldˌpruːf/ 75
chill out /ˌtʃɪl 'aʊt/ 21
chocoholic /ˌtʃɒkə'hɒlɪk/ 25
choice as in by choice 77
choose as in pick and choose 61
chop V /tʃɒp/ 20
chopsticks /'tʃɒpstɪks/ 19
chore /tʃɔː(r)/ 24
chronic /'krɒnɪk/ 40

chubby /'tʃʌbi/ 7
chubby cheeks /ˌtʃʌbi 'tʃiːks/ 7
cinnamon /'sɪnəmən/ 20
circumstance /'sɜːkəmstəns/ 5
citizen /'sɪtɪzn/ 34
city-wide /ˌsɪti 'waɪd/ 34
civil /'sɪvl/ 37
civilian N, ADJ /sə'vɪliən/ 37
claim V /kleɪm/ 63, 69
clap /klæp/ 22
clarify /'klærəfaɪ/ 75
class as in lower/middle/upper/ working class 19
classic example /'klæsɪk ɪgˌzɑːmpl/ 4
classified /'klæsɪfaɪd/ 74
clean as in spotlessly clean 33
clear /klɪə(r)/ 29
clear sb of /'klɪə ˌ... əv/ 38
clear sth up /ˌklɪə ˌ... ʌp/ 26
clear up /ˌklɪər 'ʌp/ 26
clearly /'klɪəli/ 79
clenched fist /ˌklentʃt 'fɪst/ 8
cliché /'kliːʃeɪ/ 22
clichéd /'kliːʃeɪd/ 22
clinch V /klɪntʃ/ 46
clinical trial /ˌklɪnɪkl 'traɪəl/ 33
clip N /klɪp/ 31, 76
clique /kliːk/ 26
cliquey /'kliːki/ 26
close to tears /ˌkləʊs tə 'tɪəz/ 15
closure /'kləʊʒə(r)/ 50
clue as in I haven't a clue 59
c/o /'keər əv/ 73
coarse /kɔːs/ 17
cobbled streets /ˌkɒbld 'striːts/ 21
cock /kɒk/ 10
coerce /kəʊ'ɜːs/ 52
coercion /kəʊ'ɜːʃn/ 52
coffee break /'kɒfi ˌbreɪk/ 57
coherence /kəʊ'hɪərəns/ 69
coherent /kəʊ'hɪərənt/ 69
coincide with /ˌkəʊɪn'saɪd wɪð/ 31
coincidence /kəʊ'ɪnsɪdəns/ 31
colander /'kʌləndə(r)/ 20
collaboration /kəlæbə'reɪʃn/ 45
collateral damage /kəˌlætərəl 'dæmɪdʒ/ 80
collocation /kɒlə'keɪʃn/ 4
combat /'kɒmbæt/ 37
combination /kɒmbɪ'neɪʃn/ 8
combine /kəm'baɪn/ 8
come across as /'kʌm əˌkrɒs əz/ 14
come bottom /ˌkʌm 'bɒtəm/ 56
come in /ˌkʌm 'ɪn/ 2
come into effect /ˌkʌm ˌɪntu: ɪ'fekt/ 52
come into sight /ˌkʌm ˌɪntə 'saɪt/ 11
come into view /ˌkʌm ˌɪntə 'vjuː/ 11
come top /ˌkʌm 'tɒp/ 56
come under attack /ˌkʌm ˌʌndər ə'tæk/ 39
come under fire /ˌkʌm ˌʌndə 'faɪə(r)/ 39
come unstuck /ˌkʌm ʌn'stʌk/ 56
come up /ˌkʌm 'ʌp/ 54, 63
come with /'kʌm ˌwɪð/ 2
comeback /'kʌmbæk/ 56

command N /kə'mɑːnd/ 69
command V /kə'mɑːnd/ 37
comment /'kɒment/ 19
commentary /'kɒməntri/ 70
commercial /kə'mɜːʃl/ 79
commercialize /kə'mɜːʃəlaɪz/ 75
commercially /kə'mɜːʃəli/ 79
commit /kə'mɪt/ 6
commitment /kə'mɪtmənt/ 6
common goal /ˌkɒmən 'ɡəʊl/ 45
communicate with /kə'mjuːnɪkeɪt ˌwɪð/ 63
communism /'kɒmjunɪzəm/ 42
companionship /kəm'pænjənʃɪp/ 70
company /'kʌmpəni/ 26
comparable /'kɒmpərəbl/ 6
compare /kəm'peə(r)/ 6
compatible with /kəm'pætəbl ˌwɪð/ 76
compensate for /'kɒmpənseɪt ˌfɔː(r), fə(r)/ 63
compilation /kɒmpɪ'leɪʃn/ 76
complementary medicine /kɒmplɪˌmentri 'medsn/ 33
complex /'kɒmpleks/ 76
compliance /kəm'plaɪəns/ 72
compliment N, V /'kɒmplɪmənt/ 16
complimentary /kɒmplɪ'mentri/ 16
comply with /kəm'plaɪ ˌwɪð/ 72
compose /kəm'pəʊz/ 37
composed as in be composed of 37
compost /'kɒmpɒst/ 24
comprehensible /kɒmprɪ'hensəbl/ 78
comprehensive /kɒmprɪ'hensɪv/ 44, 78
comprise /kəm'praɪz/ 37
compulsive /kəm'pʌlsɪv/ 25
con V /kɒn/ 58
conceal /kən'siːl/ 7
conceited /kən'siːtɪd/ 14
conceivable /kən'siːvəbl/ 78
concept /'kɒnsept/ 74
concern as in main/principal/growing concern 4
concerned as in as far as sth is concerned 79
concerning /kən'sɜːnɪŋ/ 67, 68
concerted effort /kənˌsɜːtɪd 'efət/ 4
concise /kən'saɪs/ 67
conclude /kən'kluːd/ 69
concluding /kən'kluːdɪŋ/ 78
conclusion /kən'kluːʒn/ 69
conclusions as in jump/leap to conclusions 8
conclusive /kən'kluːsɪv/ 78
concrete /'kɒnkriːt/ 72
condemn /kən'dem/ 69
condemnation /kɒndem'neɪʃn/ 69
condition /kən'dɪʃn/ 30
condolences /kən'dəʊlənsɪz/ 67
condone /kən'dəʊn/ 69
conduct (a survey) /kən'dʌkt/ 41
conference /'kɒnfərəns/ 69
confess /kən'fes/ 6, 63
confession /kən'feʃn/ 6
confide in /kən'faɪd ˌɪn/ 16
confidential /kɒnfɪ'denʃl/ 33

CONSONANTS: b **b**ad | d **d**id | f **f**all | g **g**et | h **h**at | j **y**es | k **c**at | l **l**eg | m **m**an | n **n**ow | p **p**en | r **r**ed | s **s**ee | t **t**ea | v **v**an | w **w**et | z **z**oo | ʃ **sh**oe | ʒ vi**si**on | tʃ **ch**ain | dʒ **j**am | θ **th**in | ð **th**is | ŋ si**ng**

confidentiality /ˌkɒnfɪdenʃiˈæləti/ 33
confine /kənˈfaɪn/ 36
confined as in be confined to bed / a
   wheelchair 30
confinement /kənˈfaɪnmənt/ 36
conflicting /kənˈflɪktɪŋ/ 47
confound /kənˈfaʊnd/ 53
confront /kənˈfrʌnt/ 54
conscientious /ˌkɒnʃiˈenʃəs/ 14
conscription /kənˈskrɪpʃn/ 37
consent N, V /kənˈsent/ 36
consent as in by common/mutual
   consent 36
consequences /ˈkɒnsɪkwənsɪz/ 52
conservation /ˌkɒnsəˈveɪʃn/ 28
Conservative /kənˈsɜːvətɪv/ 42
conserve /kənˈsɜːv/ 28
consider /kənˈsɪdə(r)/ 19
considerable /kənˈsɪdərəbl/ 37
considerable difficulty /kənˌsɪdərəbl
   ˈdɪfɪkəlti/ 4
considerably /kənˈsɪdərəbli/ 37
considerate /kənˈsɪdərət/ 14
considered as in all things
   considered 77
considering /kənˈsɪdərɪŋ/ 68
consist of /kənˈsɪst əv/ 37
constable /ˈkʌnstəbl/ 35
constant /ˈkɒnstənt/ 9
constipated /ˈkɒnstɪpeɪtɪd/ 13
constipation /ˌkɒnstɪˈpeɪʃn/ 13
constrain /kənˈstreɪn/ 72
constraint /kənˈstreɪnt/ 72
construction as in under
   construction 77
consult /kənˈsʌlt/ 27
consultation /ˌkɒnslˈteɪʃn/ 27
consultative /kənˈsʌltətɪv/ 27
consume /kənˈsjuːm/ 28
consumer /kənˈsjuːmə(r)/ 28
consumption /kənˈsʌmpʃn/ 28
contingency /kənˈtɪndʒənsi/ 48
contradict /ˌkɒntrəˈdɪkt/ 47
contradiction /ˌkɒntrəˈdɪkʃn/ 47
contradictory /ˌkɒntrəˈdɪktəri/ 47
contrary as in on the contrary 77
contribute /kənˈtrɪbjuːt/ 26
contribution /ˌkɒntrɪˈbjuːʃn/ 26
control /kənˈtrəʊl/ 76
control as in under control 49
controversial /ˌkɒntrəˈvɜːʃl/ 39
controversy /ˈkɒntrəvɜːsi,
   kənˈtrɒvəsi/ 39
convalesce /ˌkɒnvəˈles/ 33
convalescence /ˌkɒnvəˈlesns/ 33
convention /kənˈvenʃn/ 30
conventional /kənˈvenʃənl/ 30
convey /kənˈveɪ/ 70
conviction /kənˈvɪkʃn/ 71
convincing /kənˈvɪnsɪŋ/ 22, 78
convoluted /ˈkɒnvəluːtɪd/ 67
copy N, V /ˈkɒpi/ 24
coriander /ˌkɒriˈændə(r)/ 20
corkscrew /ˈkɔːkskruː/ 20
corner as in a tight corner 39
corporate /ˈkɔːpərət/ 47
corporation /ˌkɔːpəˈreɪʃn/ 47

corrupt /kəˈrʌpt/ 61
corruption /kəˈrʌpʃn/ 61
cosmetic surgery /kɒzˌmetɪk
   ˈsɜːdʒəri/ 33
cottage /ˈkɒtɪdʒ/ 24
could as in I could do with 59
council /ˈkaʊnsl/ 34
councillor /ˈkaʊnsələ(r)/ 34
count /kaʊnt/ 5
counter-productive /ˌkaʊntə
   prəˈdʌktɪv/ 37
counteract /ˌkaʊntərˈækt/ 72
countryside /ˈkʌntrisaɪd/ 24
courage /ˈkʌrɪdʒ/ 17
courageous /kəˈreɪdʒəs/ 17
courteous /ˈkɜːtiəs/ 19
courtesy /ˈkɜːtəsi/ 19
cover sth up /ˌkʌvə ˌ... ˈʌp/ 39
cover-up /ˈkʌvər ʌp/ 39
coverage /ˈkʌvərɪdʒ/ 41
crack N /kræk/ 42
crafty /ˈkrɑːfti/ 14
crane /kreɪn/ 72
crawl /krɔːl/ 2
crazy as in drive sb crazy 52
creak N, V /kriːk/ 10
create /kriˈeɪt/ 27
create an illusion /kriˌeɪt ən ɪˈluːʒn/ 7
credit /ˈkredɪt/ 48
creep /kriːp/ 9
crime as in organized crime 35
crippling /ˈkrɪplɪŋ/ 25
crisis as in in crisis 36
criteria /kraɪˈtɪəriə/ 69
criterion /kraɪˈtɪəriən/ 69
criticism /ˈkrɪtɪsɪzəm/ 4
criticize /ˈkrɪtɪsaɪz/ 17, 63
croc /krɒk/ 40
crocodile /ˈkrɒkədaɪl/ 40
crop up /ˌkrɒp ˈʌp/ 63
crow /krəʊ/ 10
crude /kruːd/ 17
cruel /ˈkruːəl/ 6
cruel as in be cruel to be kind 14
crush V /krʌʃ/ 20
cul8r (= see you later) 73
culture shock /ˈkʌltʃə ˌʃɒk/ 32
cunning /ˈkʌnɪŋ/ 14
curable /ˈkjʊərəbl/ 30
curb V /kɜːb/ 38
cure N, V /kjʊə(r)/ 30
curiously enough /ˌkjʊəriəsli ɪˌnʌf/ 79
current as in in current use 1
current account /ˈkʌrənt əˌkaʊnt/ 48
curt /kɜːt/ 67
curtail /kɜːˈteɪl/ 57
custody /ˈkʌstədi/ 35, 41
custom /ˈkʌstəm/ 19
customary /ˈkʌstəməri/ 19
cut N /kʌt/ 47
cut sth back /ˌkʌt ˌ... ˈbæk/ 24
cutbacks as in make cutbacks 48
cute /kjuːt/ 7
cutting edge /ˌkʌtɪŋ ˈedʒ/ 55
cutting-edge technology /ˌkʌtɪŋ ˌedʒ
   tekˈnɒlədʒi/ 55
cyber- /ˈsaɪbə/ 31

cyber-café /ˈsaɪbə ˌkæfeɪ/ 31
cyberspace /ˈsaɪbəspeɪs/ 31
cynical /ˈsɪnɪkl/ 14
cynicism /ˈsɪnɪsɪzəm/ 14

d (= the) 73
daft /dɑːft/ 58
damage as in extensive/widespread
   damage 4
damp /dæmp/ 11
danger as in in danger 29, 77
danger zone /ˈdeɪndʒə ˌzəʊn/ 43
dank /dæŋk/ 12
dare V /deə(r)/ 40
darling /ˈdɑːlɪŋ/ 58
dash N, V /dæʃ/ 9
date as in out of / up to date 55
date as in set a date 50
dated /ˈdeɪtɪd/ 1
dawn on /ˈdɔːn ˌɒn/ 2
day as in it's not sb's day / it's been
   one of those days 59
dazed /deɪzd/ 40
de- /diː/ 74
deadlock /ˈdedlɒk/ 50
deadly dull /ˌdedli ˈdʌl/ 22
deadly weapon /ˌdedli ˈwepən/ 37
deafening /ˈdefnɪŋ/ 26
deal N /diːl/ 38
death rate /ˈdeθ ˌreɪt/ 30
debate as in heated debate 42
debit card /ˈdebɪt ˌkɑːd/ 48
debris /ˈdebriː/ 43
debt burden /ˈdet ˌbɜːdn/ 47
decade /ˈdekeɪd/ 30
decaffeinated /diːˈkæfɪneɪtɪd/ 74
decay as in fall into decay 55
deceit /dɪˈsiːt/ 53
deceive /dɪˈsiːv/ 14, 53, 63
deceive yourself /dɪˈsiːv jɔːˌself/ 53
decentralize /diːˈsentrəlaɪz/ 74
deception /dɪˈsepʃn/ 53
deceptive /dɪˈseptɪv/ 14
declare a ceasefire /dɪˌkleər ə
   ˈsiːsfaɪə(r)/ 53
declare war /dɪˌkleə ˈwɔː(r)/ 53
declassified /diːˈklæsɪfaɪd/ 74
decline as in gradual/steady
   decline 29
dedicate /ˈdedɪkeɪt/ 17
dedicated /ˈdedɪkeɪtɪd/ 17
dedication /ˌdedɪˈkeɪʃn/ 17
deep end /ˌdiːp ˌend/ 42
deep fat fryer /ˌdiːp ˌfæt ˈfraɪə(r)/ 20
deep-fry /ˌdiːp ˈfraɪ/ 20
defect /ˈdiːfekt/ 71
defective /dɪˈfektɪv/ 71
defenceless /dɪˈfensləs/ 6
defend /dɪˈfend/ 6
defiance /dɪˈfaɪəns/ 70
defiant /dɪˈfaɪənt/ 70
deficit /ˈdefɪsɪt/ 48
deforestation /diːˌfɒrɪˈsteɪʃn/ 29
defraud /dɪˈfrɔːd/ 35
defrost /diːˈfrɒst/ 74
defy /dɪˈfaɪ/ 70
degree of /dɪˈgriː əv/ 45

VOWELS: æ cat | ɑː father | e ten | ɜː bird | ə about | ɪ sit | iː see | i many | ɒ got | ɔː saw | ʌ up | ʊ put | uː too | u actual |
aɪ my | aʊ now | eɪ say | əʊ go | ɔɪ boy | ɪə near | eə hair | ʊə pure

dejected /dɪˈdʒektɪd/ 78
delegate sth to /ˈdelɪgeɪt ... tə/ 49
delicate /ˈdelɪkət/ 12
delude yourself /dɪˈluːd jɔːˌself/ 53
deluge /ˈdeljuːdʒ/ 49
dent N, V /dent/ 52, 54
dent sb's confidence /ˌdent ... ˈkɒnfɪdəns/ 54
dent sb's reputation /ˌdent ... repjuˈteɪʃn/ 54
dependent on /dɪˈpendənt ˌɒn/ 76
depict /dɪˈpɪkt/ 70
depopulated /diːˈpɒpjuleɪtɪd/ 74
deport /dɪˈpɔːt/ 32
deportation /diːpɔːˈteɪʃn/ 32
deposit account /dɪˈpɒzɪt əˌkaʊnt/ 48
depreciate /dɪˈpriːʃieɪt/ 74
deprivation /deprɪˈveɪʃn/ 18
deprived /dɪˈpraɪvd/ 18
depth /depθ/ 42
depth as in out of your depth 56
derogatory /dəˈrɒgətri/ 1
describe /dɪˈskraɪb/ 6
desert V /dɪˈzɜːt/ 43
deserve /dɪˈzɜːv/ 41
desire /dɪˈzaɪə(r)/ 32
desperate /ˈdespərət/ 15
desperately /ˈdespərətli/ 15
desperation /despəˈreɪʃn/ 15
despicable /dɪˈspɪkəbl/ 17
despise /dɪˈspaɪz/ 17
despondent /dɪˈspɒndənt/ 78
destabilize /diːˈsteɪbəlaɪz/ 74
detain /dɪˈteɪn/ 35
detect /dɪˈtekt/ 53
deter /dɪˈtɜː(r)/ 18, 36
deteriorate /dɪˈtɪəriəreɪt/ 53, 56
deterioration /dɪtɪəriəˈreɪʃn/ 53
determine /dɪˈtɜːmɪn/ 72
deterrent /dɪˈterənt/ 18, 36
detrimental effect /detrɪˌmentl ɪˈfekt/ 18, 52
devalued /diːˈvæljuːd/ 74
devastated /ˈdevəsteɪtɪd/ 15
deviate /ˈdiːvieɪt/ 36
deviation /diːviˈeɪʃn/ 36
device /dɪˈvaɪs/ 55
devise /dɪˈvaɪz/ 9
diagnose /ˈdaɪəgnəʊz/ 30
diagnosis /daɪəgˈnəʊsɪs/ 30
diagnostic /daɪəgˈnɒstɪk/ 30
diarrhoea /daɪəˈrɪə/ 13
die down /ˌdaɪ ˈdaʊn/ 4
die out /ˌdaɪ ˈaʊt/ 29
difference as in make a difference 52
different as in entirely different 4
differentiate /dɪfəˈrenʃieɪt/ 37
difficulty as in great difficulty 4
diffident /ˈdɪfɪdənt/ 14
dig /dɪg/ 24
dignified /ˈdɪgnɪfaɪd/ 17
dignity /ˈdɪgnəti/ 17
dilapidated /dɪˈlæpɪdeɪtɪd/ 55
din /dɪn/ 58
dire /ˈdaɪə(r)/ 22

direction as in head in the right/wrong direction 42
directly /dəˈrektli, dɪ-, daɪ-/ 79
disadvantaged /dɪsədˈvɑːntɪdʒd/ 74
disappear from sight /dɪsəˌpɪə frəm ˈsaɪt/ 11
disappear from view /dɪsəˌpɪə frəm ˈvjuː/ 11
disapproving /dɪsəˈpruːvɪŋ/ 1
discard /dɪsˈkɑːd/ 13
discharge sb /dɪsˈtʃɑːdʒ .../ 33
disclose /dɪsˈkləʊz/ 15
disclosure /dɪsˈkləʊʒə(r)/ 15
discomfort /dɪsˈkʌmfət/ 11
discourteous /dɪsˈkɜːtiəs/ 19
discreet /dɪˈskriːt/ 7
discreetly /dɪˈskriːtli/ 7
discriminate /dɪˈskrɪmɪneɪt/ 32
discrimination /dɪskrɪmɪˈneɪʃn/ 32
discursive /dɪsˈkɜːsɪv/ 69
discussion as in under discussion 77
disgrace /dɪsˈgreɪs/ 19
disgraceful /dɪsˈgreɪsfl/ 19
disgusting /dɪsˈgʌstɪŋ/ 12, 58
dislike as in take an instant dislike to 16
dislocate /ˈdɪsləkeɪt/ 13
dismantle /dɪsˈmæntl/ 63
disorder /dɪsˈɔːdə(r)/ 13
disorientated /dɪsˈɔːriənteɪtɪd/ 40
display N, V /dɪˈspleɪ/ 6
disposable /dɪˈspəʊzəbl/ 26, 28
dispose of sth /dɪˈspəʊz əv .../ 28
dispute N /dɪˈspjuːt/ 50
dispute as in settle a dispute 4, 50
disregard N /dɪsrɪˈgɑːd/ 76
disrepair as in fall into disrepair 55
disrespectful /dɪsrɪˈspektfl/ 19
disrupt /dɪsˈrʌpt/ 45
disruptive /dɪsˈrʌptɪv/ 45
dissolve /dɪˈzɒlv/ 13
dissuade sb from doing sth /dɪˈsweɪd ... frəm ˌduːɪŋ .../ 63
distant /ˈdɪstənt/ 14
distinction as in make a distinction 37
distinguish between /dɪˈstɪŋgwɪʃ bɪˌtwiːn/ 37
distinguished /dɪˈstɪŋgwɪʃt/ 78
distort /dɪˈstɔːt/ 53
distract sb from sth /dɪˈstrækt ... frəm .../ 25
distracted as in be distracted by sth 25
distribute /dɪˈstrɪbjuːt/ 42
distribution /dɪstrɪˈbjuːʃn/ 42
diverse /daɪˈvɜːs/ 21, 37
diversity /daɪˈvɜːsəti/ 37
divert /daɪˈvɜːt/ 29
dividend /ˈdɪvɪdənd/ 46
DIY (= do-it-yourself) /ˌdiː ˌaɪ ˈwaɪ/ 73
do N /duː/ 26, 58
do V /duː/ 2
do as in inclined to do sth 50
do a search /ˌduː ə ˈsɜːtʃ/ 31
do away with /ˌduː əˈweɪ ˌwɪð/ 63
do for /ˈduː ˌfɔː(r), fə(r)/ 2

do no such thing /ˌduː ˌnəʊ ˌsʌtʃ ˈθɪŋ/ 4
do sb a favour /ˌduː ... ə ˈfeɪvə(r)/ 5
do sth at the last minute /ˌduː ... ət ðə ˌlɑːst ˈmɪnɪt/ 57
do sth up /ˌduː ... ˈʌp/ 55
do the weeding /ˌduː ðə ˈwiːdɪŋ/ 24
do your fair share /ˌduː jɔː ˌfeə ˈʃeə(r)/ 18
doddery /ˈdɒdəri/ 7
dodgy /ˈdɒdʒi/ 58
domestic /dəˈmestɪk/ 37
dominant /ˈdɒmɪnənt/ 23
dominate /ˈdɒmɪneɪt/ 23
don't ask me /ˌdəʊnt ˌɑːsk ˈmiː/ 59
don't count your chickens /ˌdəʊnt ˌkaʊnt jə ˈtʃɪkɪnz/ 20
don't count your chickens before they're hatched /ˌdəʊnt ˌkaʊnt jə ˌtʃɪkɪnz bɪˌfɔː ˌðeə ˈhætʃt/ 20
don't hold your breath /ˌdəʊnt ˌhəʊld jə ˈbreθ/ 59
don't judge a book by its cover /ˌdəʊnt ˌdʒʌdʒ ə ˌbʊk ˌbaɪ ɪts ˈkʌvə(r)/ 14
don't you dare /ˌdəʊnt ju ˈdeə(r)/ 40
donor /ˈdəʊnə(r)/ 30
doors as in behind closed doors 39
dosage /ˈdəʊsɪdʒ/ 13
dose /dəʊs/ 13
down-to-earth /ˌdaʊn tu ˈɜːθ/ 14
downfall /ˈdaʊnfɔːl/ 70
downhill as in go downhill 56
download V /daʊnˈləʊd/ 31
downright /ˈdaʊnraɪt/ 19
downs as in ups and downs 16
downsize /daʊnˈsaɪz/ 80
downsizing /daʊnˈsaɪzɪŋ/ 80
downwards /ˈdaʊnwədz/ 19
draft as in the draft 37
drag /dræg/ 58
drag sth out /ˌdræg ... ˈaʊt/ 63
drain V /dreɪn/ 20
drastic /ˈdræstɪk/ 40
draw /drɔː/ 23
draw attention to /ˌdrɔː əˈtenʃn ˌtuː, tə/ 7
drawback /ˈdrɔːbæk/ 45
drawing pin /ˈdrɔːɪŋ ˌpɪn/ 3
drawn as in be drawn against 23
drawn as in be drawn to 14
dream /driːm/ 62
dream up /ˌdriːm ˈʌp/ 31
dress as in fancy dress 3
dried fruit /ˌdraɪd ˈfruːt/ 20
drive sb crazy /ˌdraɪv ... ˈkreɪzi/ 52
drive sb insane /ˌdraɪv ... ɪnˈseɪn/ 52
drive sb mad /ˌdraɪv ... ˈmæd/ 52
driving licence /ˈdraɪvɪŋ ˌlaɪsəns/ 3
driving seat /ˈdraɪvɪŋ ˌsiːt/ 42
drop in the ocean /ˌdrɒp ɪn ði ˈəʊʃn/ 39
drop out /ˌdrɒp ˈaʊt/ 3
dropout /ˈdrɒpaʊt/ 3
drown sth out /ˌdraʊn ... ˈaʊt/ 26
drowsiness /ˈdraʊzinəs/ 13
drowsy /ˈdraʊzi/ 13

CONSONANTS: b bad | d did | f fall | g get | h hat | j yes | k cat | l leg | m man | n now | p pen | r red | s see | t tea | v van | w wet | z zoo | ʃ shoe | ʒ vision | tʃ chain | dʒ jam | θ thin | ð this | ŋ sing

241

drug addict /ˈdrʌɡ ˌædɪkt/ 25
drug-trafficking /ˈdrʌɡ ˌtræfɪkɪŋ/ 35
drunk /drʌŋk/ 26
dry up /ˌdraɪ ˈʌp/ 47
dump sb /ˈdʌmp ˌ.../ 41
duplicate v /ˈdjuːplɪkeɪt/ 71
during /ˈdjʊərɪŋ/ 57
dust as in the dust settles 46
duty /ˈdjuːti/ 75
duty-free /ˌdjuːti ˈfriː/ 75
dying for sth to eat /ˌdaɪɪŋ fə ˌ... tu
ˈiːt/ 58

e- /iː/ 31
e-business /ˈiː ˌbɪznəs/ 31
e-learning /ˈiː ˌlɜːnɪŋ/ 31
earth as in What/Where on earth . . .
? 60
earn sb's respect /ˌɜːn ˌ... rɪˈspekt/ 16
ease v /iːz/ 11
easier said than done /ˌiːziə ˌsed ðən
ˈdʌn/ 66
easy as in take it easy 21
easy-going /ˌiːzi ˈɡəʊɪŋ/ 58
eat as in dying for sth to eat 58
eat your words /ˌiːt jɔː ˈwɜːdz/ 20
eco- /ˈiːkəʊ/ 28
eco-disaster /ˌiːkəʊ dɪzˈɑːstə(r)/ 28
eco-friendly /ˌiːkəʊ ˈfrendli/ 28
eco-home /ˌiːkəʊ ˈhəʊm/ 28
ecology /iˈkɒlədʒi/ 28
economic boom /iːkəˌnɒmɪk
ˈbuːm/ 47
economic migrant /iːkəˌnɒmɪk
ˈmaɪɡrənt/ 32
economic slump /iːkəˌnɒmɪk
ˈslʌmp/ 47
economical with the
truth /iːkəˌnɒmɪkl ˌwɪð ðə ˈtruːθ/ 53
economize /ɪˈkɒnəmaɪz/ 48, 75
ecstatic /ɪkˈstætɪk/ 15
effect /ɪˈfekt/ 13, 18, 22, 52
effort /ˈefət/ 4
egg sb on /ˌeɡ ˌ... ˈɒn/ 52
elapse /ɪˈlæps/ 57
elated /ɪˈleɪtɪd/ 15
electrify /ɪˈlektrɪfaɪ/ 75
eligible /ˈelɪdʒəbl/ 34
eliminate /ɪˈlɪmɪneɪt/ 11, 23
elimination /ɪlɪmɪˈneɪʃn/ 11
embark on /ɪmˈbɑːk ˌɒn/ 76
embellish /ɪmˈbelɪʃ/ 53
embodiment /ɪmˈbɒdimənt/ 70
embody /ɪmˈbɒdi/ 70
emerge /ɪˈmɜːdʒ/ 39
emergence /ɪˈmɜːdʒəns/ 39
emigrant /ˈemɪɡrənt/ 32
emigrate /ˈemɪɡreɪt/ 32
emigration /emɪˈɡreɪʃn/ 32
eminent /ˈemɪnənt/ 78
emission /ɪˈmɪʃn/ 28
emit /ɪˈmɪt/ 28
emotion /ɪˈməʊʃn/ 6
emotive /ɪˈməʊtɪv/ 6
empirical /ɪmˈpɪrɪkl/ 71
empiricism /ɪmˈpɪrɪsɪzəm/ 71

employment agency /ɪmˈplɔɪmənt
ˌeɪdʒənsi/ 34
encl. (= enclosed) 73
enclosed /ɪnˈkləʊzd/ 13
encompass /ɪnˈkʌmpəs/ 37
encounter /ɪnˈkaʊntə(r)/ 45
encourage /ɪnˈkʌrɪdʒ/ 45
encroach /ɪnˈkrəʊtʃ/ 29, 45
end as in the end justifies the
means 66
end result /ˌend rɪˈzʌlt/ 52
endangered /ɪnˈdeɪndʒəd/ 29
endangered species /ɪnˌdeɪndʒəd
ˈspiːʃiːz/ 29
endow sb/sth with /ɪnˈdaʊ ˌ... wɪð
ˌ.../ 70
energetically /enəˈdʒetɪkli/ 12
energy-saving /ˈenədʒi ˌseɪvɪŋ/ 28
enforce /ɪnˈfɔːs/ 27
enforcement /ɪnˈfɔːsmənt/ 27
enhance /ɪnˈhɑːns/ 7
enlist /ɪnˈlɪst/ 37
enlisted /ɪnˈlɪstɪd/ 37
enough as in strangely/oddly/curiously
enough 79
enquire as in I am writing to enquire
whether 67
enrich /ɪnˈrɪtʃ/ 24
enrol /ɪnˈrəʊl/ 33
ensuing /ɪnˈsjuːɪŋ/ 40
ensure /ɪnˈʃʊə(r)/ 34
enter /ˈentə(r)/ 31
enterprise (= ability to think of new
ideas) /ˈentəpraɪz/ 45
enterprise (= project) /ˈentəpraɪz/ 28
entice /ɪnˈtaɪs/ 35, 46
entirely /ɪnˈtaɪəli/ 4
entirely different /ɪnˌtaɪəli ˈdɪfrənt/ 4
entirely responsible /ɪnˌtaɪəli
rɪˈspɒnsəbl/ 4
entitled as in be entitled to 44
entitlement /ɪnˈtaɪtlmənt/ 44
environmentally-friendly
/ɪnvaɪrənˌmentəli ˈfrendli/ 28
equal /ˈiːkwəl/ 42
equal as in all things being equal 60
equality /iˈkwɒləti/ 42
equalize /ˈiːkwəlaɪz/ 75
equally /ˈiːkwəli/ 42, 79
equities /ˈekwətiz/ 47
era /ˈɪərə/ 30, 57
eradicate /ɪˈrædɪkeɪt/ 30
error as in trial and error 61
escape as in (have a) narrow
escape 4
essentially /ɪˈsenʃəli/ 79
establish /ɪˈstæblɪʃ/ 72
ETA (= estimated time of arrival) /ˌiː
ˌtiː ˈeɪ/ 73
ethnic group /ˌeθnɪk ˈɡruːp/ 32
ethnic minority /ˌeθnɪk maɪˈnɒrəti/ 32
etiquette /ˈetɪket/ 19
euphemism /ˈjuːfəmɪzəm/ 80
euphoric /juːˈfɒrɪk/ 15
evaluate /ɪˈvæljueɪt/ 69
evaluation /ɪvælju'eɪʃn/ 69
even so /ˌiːvn ˈsəʊ/ 64

event /ɪˈvent/ 6
eventful /ɪˈventfl/ 6
events as in sequence of events 52
every bit as /ˈevri ˌbɪt əz/ 60
evidently /ˈevɪdəntli/ 79
evil /ˈiːvl/ 78
evolution /iːvəˈluːʃn/ 27
evolve /ɪˈvɒlv/ 27
exacerbate /ɪɡˈzæsəbeɪt/ 54
exact /ɪɡˈzækt/ 1
exaggerate /ɪɡˈzædʒəreɪt/ 7
exaggeration /ɪɡzædʒəˈreɪʃn/ 7
example as in perfect example 4
example as in set an example 18, 50
exceed /ɪkˈsiːd/ 8, 13
exceed sb's expectations /ɪkˌsiːd ˌ...
ˌekspekˈteɪʃəns/ 13
excel /ɪkˈsel/ 6
excellent /ˈeksələnt/ 6
exception as in take exception 19
exceptional /ɪkˈsepʃənl/ 78
excerpt /ˈeksɜːpt/ 76
excess /ɪkˈses/ 8
excess as in in excess of 13
excessive /ɪkˈsesɪv/ 8
exchange as in in exchange for 77
exclusive N, ADJ /ɪkˈskluːsɪv/ 41
exclusively /ɪkˈskluːsɪvli/ 36
excruciating /ɪkˈskruːʃieɪtɪŋ/ 40
exemplary /ɪɡˈzempləri/ 19
exemplify /ɪɡˈzemplɪfaɪ/ 69, 75
exhausted /ɪɡˈzɔːstɪd/ 78
exhaustive /ɪɡˈzɔːstɪv/ 78
expect /ɪkˈspekt/ 18
expectations as in exceed sb's
expectations 13
expenses /ɪkˈspensɪz/ 44
expire /ɪkˈspaɪə(r)/ 13
expiry date /ɪkˈspaɪəri ˌdeɪt/ 13
explain /ɪkˈspleɪn/ 6
exploit v /ɪkˈsplɔɪt/ 35
exploitation /eksplɔɪˈteɪʃn/ 35
explore /ɪkˈsplɔː(r)/ 69
expose /ɪkˈspəʊz/ 70
extend /ɪkˈstend/ 57
extensive damage /ɪkˌstensɪv
ˈdæmɪdʒ/ 4
extent /ɪkˈstent/ 45, 64
exterior N, ADJ /ɪkˈstɪəriə(r)/ 37
external /ɪkˈstɜːnl/ 37
extinct /ɪkˈstɪŋkt/ 29
extinction /ɪkˈstɪŋkʃn/ 29
extinguish the fire /ɪkˌstɪŋgwɪʃ ðə
ˈfaɪə(r)/ 4
extra /ˈekstrə/ 45
extract N /ˈekstrækt/ 76
extraordinarily /ɪkˈstrɔːdnrəli/ 22
extravagant /ɪkˈstrævəɡənt/ 48
extreme /ɪkˈstriːm/ 42
extremist /ɪkˈstriːmɪst/ 42
eye v /aɪ/ 11
eye as in have an eye for sth 25
eye as in have your eye on sth 25
eye contact /ˈaɪ ˌkɒntækt/ 8
eye strain /ˈaɪ ˌstreɪn/ 11
eyesight /ˈaɪsaɪt/ 11
eyesore /ˈaɪsɔː(r)/ 4

fabulous /ˈfæbjələs/ 22
face V /feɪs/ 54
face as in familiar face   4
face as in lose face   60
face as in to sb's face   16
face the prospect of /ˈfeɪs ðə ˌprɒspekt əv/ 4
face the prospect that /ˈfeɪs ðə ˌprɒspekt ðət/ 4
face up to /ˈfeɪs ˌʌp tə/ 54
facet /ˈfæsɪt/ 71
facilitate /fəˈsɪlɪteɪt/ 27
fact as in as a matter of fact   64
fail as in without fail   77
fail to do sth /ˈfeɪl tə ˌduː ˌ.../ 51
faint ADJ /feɪnt/ 12
fair share as in do your fair share   18
faith /feɪθ/ 32
fall into decay /ˌfɔːl ˌɪntə dɪˈkeɪ/ 55
fall into disrepair /ˌfɔːl ˌɪntə ˌdɪsrɪˈpeə(r)/ 55
falsehood /ˈfɔːlshʊd/ 53
fame /feɪm/ 41
familiar face /fəˌmɪliə ˈfeɪs/ 4
familiarize /fəˈmɪliəraɪz/ 75
famous last words /ˌfeɪməs ˌlɑːst ˈwɜːdz/ 66
fancy (= be attracted to) /ˈfænsi/ 8
fancy (= want to do) /ˈfænsi/ 26
fancy dress /ˌfænsi ˈdres/ 3
fao (= for the attention of) /ˌef ˌeɪ ˈəʊ/ 73
far as in as far as sth is concerned   79
far as in so far, so good   66
far-reaching /ˌfɑː ˈriːtʃɪŋ/ 42
fastidious /fəˈstɪdiəs/ 33
fate /feɪt/ 70
faulty /ˈfɔːlti/ 71
favour N /ˈfeɪvə(r)/ 5
favour V /ˈfeɪvə(r)/ 42
favour as in be in favour of   42
feather /ˈfeðə(r)/ 62
feature /ˈfiːtʃə(r)/ 7
fed up with /ˌfed ˈʌp ˌwɪð/ 61
feeble /ˈfiːbl/ 22
feelings as in suppress your feelings   15
fellow ADJ /ˈfeləʊ/ 41
fennel /ˈfenl/ 20
fertile /ˈfɜːtaɪl/ 24
fertility /fəˈtɪləti/ 24
fib /fɪb/ 53
fiddle with /ˈfɪdl ˌwɪð/ 8
fierce criticism /ˌfɪəs ˈkrɪtɪsɪzəm/ 4
fight a losing battle /ˌfaɪt ə ˌluːzɪŋ ˈbætl/ 60
figurative /ˈfɪɡərətɪv/ 1
figuratively /ˈfɪɡərətɪvli/ 1
final /ˈfaɪnl/ 6
final outcome /ˌfaɪnl ˈaʊtkʌm/ 52
final resort /ˌfaɪnl rɪˈzɔːt/ 60
finalize /ˈfaɪnəlaɪz/ 6, 75
financially /faɪˈnænʃəli, fə-/ 79
findings /ˈfaɪndɪŋz/ 41
fingernails /ˈfɪŋɡəneɪlz/ 8
fingertips /ˈfɪŋɡətɪps/ 12
fire /ˈfaɪə(r)/ 4

fire as in come under fire   39
firearm /ˈfaɪərɑːm/ 35
firing as in in the firing line   39
firmly /ˈfɜːmli/ 12
first and foremost /ˌfɜːst ən ˈfɔːməʊst/ 61
first come, first served /ˌfɜːst ˌkʌm ˌfɜːst ˈsɜːvd/ 66
fish out of water /ˌfɪʃ ˌaʊt əv ˈwɔːtə(r)/ 20
fishy /ˈfɪʃi/ 12, 20
fist /fɪst/ 8
fit in /ˌfɪt ˈɪn/ 45
flak /flæk/ 58
flames /fleɪmz/ 4
flattering /ˈflætərɪŋ/ 7
flee /fliː/ 32
flirt V /flɜːt/ 8
flood V /flʌd/ 39
flop N, V /flɒp/ 56
flourishing /ˈflʌrɪʃɪŋ/ 21
flower /ˈflaʊə(r)/ 24
focused /ˈfəʊkəst/ 25
folded arms /ˌfəʊldɪd ˈɑːmz/ 8
follow /ˈfɒləʊ/ 6
follow in sb's footsteps /ˌfɒləʊ ɪn ˌ... ˈfʊtsteps/ 17
following (= further to) /ˈfɒləʊɪŋ/ 67
following (= group of supporters) /ˈfɒləʊɪŋ/ 6
food miles /ˈfuːd ˌmaɪlz/ 28
food processor /ˈfuːd ˌprəʊsesə(r)/ 20
foolproof /ˈfuːlpruːf/ 75
foot as in not put a foot wrong   56
footings /ˈfʊtɪŋz/ 72
footprint as in carbon footprint   28
footsteps as in follow in sb's footsteps   17
4 (= for)   73
for some reason /fə ˌsʌm ˈriːzn/ 60
for the time being /fə ðə ˌtaɪm ˈbiːɪŋ/ 57
force as in air force   37
forced labour /ˌfɔːst ˈleɪbə(r)/ 35
4 (= fore)   73
foregone conclusion /ˌfɔːɡɒn kənˈkluːʒn/ 59
forest fire /ˌfɒrɪst ˈfaɪə(r)/ 4
forever /fərˈevə(r)/ 79
forge V /fɔːdʒ/ 35
forgery /ˈfɔːdʒəri/ 35
forgive /fəˈɡɪv/ 6
form /fɔːm/ 23
formal /ˈfɔːml/ 69
format N /ˈfɔːmæt/ 31
former ADJ /ˈfɔːmə(r)/ 46
former N /ˈfɔːmə(r)/ 37
formerly /ˈfɔːməli/ 55
foremost as in first and foremost   61
foster /ˈfɒstə(r)/ 45
foul play /ˌfaʊl ˈpleɪ/ 39
foundations /faʊnˈdeɪʃnz/ 42
fragrance /ˈfreɪɡrəns/ 12
fragrant /ˈfreɪɡrənt/ 12
frail /freɪl/ 7
frailty /ˈfreɪlti/ 7
frankly /ˈfræŋkli/ 79

fraud /frɔːd/ 35
freckles /ˈfreklz/ 7
-free /friː/ 75
free of charge /ˌfriː əv ˈtʃɑːdʒ/ 33
-friendly /ˈfrendli/ 28
friendly fire /ˌfrendli ˈfaɪə(r)/ 80
friendly takeover /ˌfrendli ˈteɪkəʊvə(r)/ 46
from time to time /frəm ˌtaɪm tə ˈtaɪm/ 73
frown on/upon /ˈfraʊn ˌɒn, əˌpɒn/ 19
fruit machine /ˈfruːt məˌʃiːn/ 3
fruity /ˈfruːti/ 12
fryer as in deep fat fryer   20
fuel V /ˈfjuːəl/ 46
fulfil your potential /fʊlˌfɪl jɔː pəˈtenʃəl/ 56
fulfilling /fʊlˈfɪlɪŋ/ 45
fully inclusive /ˌfʊli ɪnˈkluːsɪv/ 6
fund /fʌnd/ 48
fundamental /ˌfʌndəˈmentl/ 37
funding /ˈfʌndɪŋ/ 37
funds /fʌndz/ 29
furnish /ˈfɜːnɪʃ/ 6
furnished /ˈfɜːnɪʃt/ 6
furniture /ˈfɜːnɪtʃə(r)/ 6
further /ˈfɜːðə(r)/ 45
further to /ˈfɜːðə tə/ 67
fuss /fʌs/ 18
fyi (= for your information)   73

gadget /ˈɡædʒɪt/ 25
gain N /ɡeɪn/ 47
gain access to /ˌɡeɪn ˈækses ˌtuː, tə/ 33
gain control of /ˌɡeɪn kənˈtrəʊl əv/ 76
gain sb's respect /ˌɡeɪn ˌ... rɪˈspekt/ 16
gale-force winds /ˌɡeɪl ˌfɔːs ˈwɪndz/ 4
gallop N, V /ˈɡæləp/ 9
gang /ɡæŋ/ 35
gap /ɡæp/ 57
garlic crusher /ˈɡɑːlɪk ˌkrʌʃə(r)/ 20
gatecrasher /ˈɡeɪtkræʃə(r)/ 26
gaze N, V /ɡeɪz/ 11
gem /dʒem/ 38
gene /dʒiːn/ 29
gene pool /ˈdʒiːn ˌpuːl/ 29
generalization as in make generalizations about   8
generalize /ˈdʒenrəlaɪz/ 8, 75
generate /ˈdʒenəreɪt/ 52
genetic /dʒəˈnetɪk/ 71
genetics /dʒəˈnetɪks/ 71
gently /ˈdʒentli/ 12
genuine (= real) /ˈdʒenjuɪn/ 55
genuine (= sincere) /ˈdʒenjuɪn/ 67
gesture /ˈdʒestʃə(r)/ 8
get a scoop /ˌɡet ə ˈskuːp/ 41
get acclimatized /ˌɡet əˈklaɪmətaɪzd/ 32
get accustomed /ˌɡet əˈkʌstəmd/ 32
get away from it all /ˌɡet əˈweɪ frəm ɪt ˈɔːl/ 21
get by /ˌɡet ˈbaɪ/ 63
get carried away /ˌɡet ˌkærid əˈweɪ/ 26
get hold of /ˌɡet ˈhəʊld əv/ 33

get nowhere /ˌget 'nəʊweə(r)/ 59
get out of hand /ˌget ˌaʊt əv 'hænd/ 49
get out of sth /ˌget 'aʊt əv ˌ.../ 2
get sb down /ˌget ... 'daʊn/ 54
get sb to do sth /ˌget ... tə 'duː ˌ.../ 2
get somewhere /'get ˌsʌmweə(r)/ 59
get sth across /ˌget ... ə'krɒs/ 63
get the hang of /ˌget ðə 'hæŋ əv/ 32
get there /ˌget 'ðeə(r)/ 59
get through /ˌget 'θruː/ 23
get to grips with /ˌget tə 'grɪps ˌwɪð/ 54
get-together /'get təˌgeðə(r)/ 26, 58
get up sb's nose /ˌget ʌp ˌ... 'nəʊz/ 14
get used to /ˌget 'juːst ˌtuː, tə/ 32
getting on (a bit) /ˌgetɪŋ 'ɒn (ə ˌbɪt)/ 80
getting on for as in be getting on for 7
ghost story /'gəʊst ˌstɔːri/ 22
giant /'dʒaɪənt/ 77
giggle /'gɪgl/ 51
ginger (= colour of hair) /'dʒɪndʒə(r)/ 7
ginger (= spice) /'dʒɪndʒə(r)/ 20
girder /'gɜːdə(r)/ 72
give birth /ˌgɪv 'bɜːθ/ 41
give in /ˌgɪv 'ɪn/ 18
give or take /ˌgɪv ɔː 'teɪk/ 65
give sb a say /ˌgɪv ... ə 'seɪ/ 34
give sth a go /ˌgɪv ... ə 'gəʊ/ 14
give sth a try /ˌgɪv ... ə 'traɪ/ 14
give sth away (= disclose sth) /ˌgɪv ... ə'weɪ/ 15
give sth away (= lose a game, etc.) /ˌgɪv ... ə'weɪ/ 23
glare N, V /gleə(r)/ 11
glimpse N, V /glɪmps/ 11
gloss over sth /ˌglɒs 'əʊvə ˌ.../ 53
go as in give sth a go / have a go 14
go as in have a go at sb 17
go as in make a go of sth 56
go-ahead /'gəʊ əˌhed/ 38
go back /ˌgəʊ 'bæk/ 27
go bankrupt /ˌgəʊ 'bæŋkrʌpt/ 46
go by /ˌgəʊ 'baɪ/ 57
go down that road /ˌgəʊ ˌdaʊn ˌðæt 'rəʊd/ 46
go down with /ˌgəʊ 'daʊn ˌwɪð/ 63
go downhill /ˌgəʊ daʊn'hɪl/ 56
go for a hike /ˌgəʊ fər ə 'haɪk/ 9
go for a stroll /ˌgəʊ fər ə 'strəʊl/ 9
go for a wander /ˌgəʊ fər ə 'wɒndə(r)/ 21
go from strength to strength /ˌgəʊ frəm ˌstreŋθ tə 'streŋθ/ 56
go in one ear and out of the other /ˌgəʊ ˌɪn ˌwʌn ˌɪər ən ˌaʊt əv ði 'ʌðə(r)/ 59
go mad /ˌgəʊ 'mæd/ 15
go off /ˌgəʊ 'ɒf/ 12
go on and on /ˌgəʊ ˌɒn ən 'ɒn/ 18
go on at /ˌgəʊ 'ɒn ət/ 63
go out /ˌgəʊ 'aʊt/ 4
go pear-shaped /ˌgəʊ 'peə ˌʃeɪpt/ 20

go red /ˌgəʊ 'red/ 8
go to pieces /ˌgəʊ tə 'piːsɪz/ 23
go under /ˌgəʊ 'ʌndə(r)/ 46
go up in flames /ˌgəʊ ˌʌp ɪn 'fleɪmz/ 4
goad V /gəʊd/ 52
goal as in common goal 45
goalposts as in move the goalposts 39
gobsmacked /'gɒbsmækt/ 15
gold /gəʊld/ 62
gonna /'gɒnə, 'gənə/ 2
good as in it's no good + ing 59
good as in so far, so good 66
good as in too good to be true 60
good as new /ˌgʊd əz 'njuː/ 55
good company /ˌgʊd 'kʌmpəni/ 26
good laugh /ˌgʊd 'lɑːf/ 58
good run /ˌgʊd 'rʌn/ 23
google sb/sth /'guːgl ˌ.../ 31
gorgeous /'gɔːdʒəs/ 7
gossip N, V /'gɒsɪp/ 17
government funding /ˌgʌvnmənt 'fʌndɪŋ/ 37
gradual decline /ˌgrædʒuəl dɪ'klaɪn/ 29
grant /grɑːnt/ 34
grate V /greɪt/ 20
grater /'greɪtə(r)/ 20
gr8 (= great) 73
great chance /ˌgreɪt 'tʃɑːns/ 23
great difficulty /ˌgreɪt 'dɪfɪkəlti/ 4
great honour /ˌgreɪt 'ɒnə(r)/ 4
green /griːn/ 28
grim /grɪm/ 43
gripping /'grɪpɪŋ/ 22
groundbreaking /'graʊndbreɪkɪŋ/ 28
grounds /graʊndz/ 35
group therapy /ˌgruːp 'θerəpi/ 36
growing /'grəʊɪŋ/ 54
growing concern /ˌgrəʊɪŋ kən'sɜːn/ 4
growl /graʊl/ 10
grudge N /grʌdʒ/ 76
gruelling /'gruːəlɪŋ/ 40
gtg (= got to go / I've got to go) 73
guarantee N, V /ˌgærən'tiː/ 45
guard N, V /gɑːd/ 37
guarded /'gɑːdɪd/ 15
guerrilla warfare /gəˌrɪlə 'wɔːfeə(r)/ 37
guess what! /ˌges 'wɒt/ 60
guidelines /'gaɪdlaɪnz/ 7
gutted /'gʌtɪd/ 15
guy /gaɪ/ 58

habitat /'hæbɪtæt/ 29
hack into /'hæk ˌɪntuː, ˌɪntə/ 31
half-truth /'hɑːf ˌtruːθ/ 53
halt V /hɔːlt/ 50
hammer sb /'hæmə(r)/ 58
hand (= have a nice day) 73
hand as in be out of hand 49
hand sth over /ˌhænd ... 'əʊvə(r)/ 51
handle /'hændl/ 6
handling /'hændlɪŋ/ 6
handover /'hændəʊvə(r)/ 51
hands as in safe pair of hands 42

hang as in get the hang of 32
happen to /'hæpən tə/ 60
happen to as in if anything happens to sb 80
happy as in not entirely happy 4
happy-go-lucky /ˌhæpi ˌgəʊ 'lʌki/ 14
hard-hit /ˌhɑːd 'hɪt/ 49
hard of hearing /ˌhɑːd əv 'hɪərɪŋ/ 80
hard-wearing /ˌhɑːd 'weərɪŋ/ 3
hate as in pet hate 51
have a go /ˌhæv ə 'gəʊ/ 14
have a go at sb /ˌhæv ə ˌgəʊ ət '.../ 17
have a narrow escape /ˌhæv ə ˌnærəʊ ɪ'skeɪp/ 4
have a say in sth /ˌhæv ə 'seɪ ɪn ˌ.../ 34
have access to /ˌhæv 'ækses ˌtuː, tə/ 33
have an eye for sth /ˌhæv ən 'aɪ fə ˌ.../ 25
have control over /ˌhæv kən'trəʊl ˌəʊvə(r)/ 76
have no desire to do sth /ˌhæv 'nəʊ dɪˌzaɪə tə ˌduː ˌ.../ 32
have sb/sth in mind /ˌhæv ... ɪn 'maɪnd/ 59
have second thoughts /ˌhæv ˌsekənd 'θɔːts/ 2
have your cake and eat it /ˌhæv jɔː ˌkeɪk ən 'iːt ˌɪt/ 20
have your eye on sth /ˌhæv jɔːr 'aɪ ɒn ˌ.../ 25
hay fever /'heɪ ˌfiːvə(r)/ 13
hazard as in occupational hazard 36
haze /heɪz/ 11
hazy /'heɪzi/ 11
head V /hed/ 42
head as in bury your head in the sand 50
head as in off the top of my head 59
head as in two heads are better than one 66
head for /'hed ˌfɔː(r), fə(r)/ 25
head in the right/wrong direction /ˌhed ɪn ðə ˌraɪt, ˌrɒŋ də'rekʃn, dɪ-, daɪ-/ 42
head towards /'hed təˌwɔːdz/ 25
headache as in splitting headache 13
headquarters /hed'kwɔːtəz/ 73
healthcare /'helθkeə(r)/ 44
healthy /'helθi/ 47
hearing as in hard of hearing 80
hearing from you as in I look forward to hearing from you 67
heart /hɑːt/ 6
heart as in not have the heart to do sth 15
heart as in wear your heart on your sleeve 15
heart as in sb's heart is not in sth 15
heartbroken /'hɑːtbrəʊkən/ 15
heartless /'hɑːtləs/ 6
heat V /hiːt/ 42
heated debate /ˌhiːtɪd dɪ'beɪt/ 42
heated discussion /ˌhiːtɪd dɪ'skʌʃn/ 42
hectic /'hektɪk/ 51
hedge /hedʒ/ 24

heel /hi:l/ 13
heighten /'haɪtn/ 75
helicopter /'helɪkɒptə(r)/ 37
help yourself to sth /ˌhelp jə'self tə ˌ.../ 80
hence /hens/ 68
henceforth /hens'fɔ:θ/ 68
herb /hɜ:b/ 20
hereditary /hə'redɪtri/ 71
heredity /hə'redəti/ 71
hero /'hɪərəʊ/ 17
heroine /'herəʊɪn/ 17
hide /haɪd/ 7
high blood pressure /ˌhaɪ 'blʌd ˌpreʃə(r)/ 13
high-pitched /ˌhaɪ 'pɪtʃt/ 10
high priority /ˌhaɪ praɪ'ɒrəti/ 49
high profile /ˌhaɪ 'prəʊfaɪl/ 34
highlight /'haɪlaɪt/ 69
hike (= walk in the country) N, V /haɪk/ 9
hike (= sudden increase) /haɪk/ 47
hindsight as in with hindsight 57
hint of irony /ˌhɪnt əv 'aɪrəni/ 1
hips /hɪps/ 7
hit back at /ˌhɪt 'bæk ət/ 63
hit the roof /ˌhɪt ðə 'ru:f/ 15
hit as in severely hit 49
hitherto /hɪðə'tu:/ 68
hobby /'hɒbi/ 25
hold as in get hold of 33
hold sb responsible for /ˌhəʊld ˌ... rɪ'spɒnsəbl fə/ 4
hold sb/sth up /ˌhəʊld ˌ... 'ʌp/ 3
hold-up /'həʊld ˌʌp/ 3
home /həʊm/ 23
home as in broken home 18
honest as in to be honest 64, 79
honest as in to be perfectly honest 79
honour as in great honour 4
honour as in in honour of 77
hoot N, V /hu:t/ 10
hoots of derision /ˌhu:ts əv də'rɪʒn/ 10
horn /hɔ:n/ 29
horrified /'hɒrɪfaɪd/ 15
host /həʊst/ 26
hostess /'həʊstes/ 26
hostile /'hɒstaɪl/ 16
hostile takeover /ˌhɒstaɪl 'teɪkəʊvə(r)/ 46
hostility /hɒ'stɪləti/ 16, 32
house N /haʊs/ 6
housing /'haʊzɪŋ/ 6
how dare you /ˌhaʊ 'deə ju:/ 40
howl V /haʊl/ 10
howl in pain /ˌhaʊl ɪn 'peɪn/ 10
howl with laughter /ˌhaʊl wɪð 'lɑ:ftə(r)/ 10
HQ (= headquarters) /ˌeɪtʃ 'kju:/ 73
huge /hju:dʒ/ 37
hum /hʌm/ 51
human remains /ˌhju:mən rɪ'meɪnz/ 55
human-trafficking /'hju:mən ˌtræfɪkɪŋ/ 35

humble /'hʌmbl/ 17
humiliate /hju:'mɪlieɪt/ 53
humiliated /hju:'mɪlieɪtɪd/ 53
humiliated as in be humiliated 60
humiliation /hju:mɪli'eɪʃn/ 53
humility /hju:'mɪləti/ 17
hustle and bustle /ˌhʌsl ən 'bʌsl/ 61
hypocrisy /hɪ'pɒkrəsi/ 17
hypocrite /'hɪpəkrɪt/ 17
hypocritical /ˌhɪpə'krɪtɪkl/ 17
hypotheses /haɪ'pɒθəsi:z/ 71
hypothesis /haɪ'pɒθəsɪs/ 69, 71
hypothesize /haɪ'pɒθəsaɪz/ 69, 71
hypothetical /ˌhaɪpə'θetɪkl/ 71
hysterical /hɪ'sterɪkl/ 15

I agree /ˌaɪ ə'gri:/ 64
I am delighted to inform you that /ˌaɪ æm dɪ'laɪtɪd tu ɪnˌfɔ:m ju: ðət/ 67
I am writing in response to /ˌaɪ æm 'raɪtɪŋ ɪn rɪˌspɒns tə/ 67
I am writing to enquire whether /ˌaɪ æm 'raɪtɪŋ tu ɪnˌkwaɪə ˌweðə(r)/ 67
I am writing to inform you of my intention to /ˌaɪ æm 'raɪtɪŋ tu ɪnˌfɔ:m ju: əv maɪ ɪnˌtenʃn tə/ 67
I am writing to inform you that /ˌaɪ æm 'raɪtɪŋ tu ɪnˌfɔ:m ju: ðət/ 67
I could do with /ˌaɪ ˌkʊd 'du: wɪð/ 59
I have to admit /ˌaɪ 'hæftu ədˌmɪt/ 60
I haven't a clue /ˌaɪ ˌhævnt ə 'klu:/ 59
I haven't the faintest idea /ˌaɪ ˌhævnt ðə ˌfeɪntɪst aɪ'dɪə/ 59
I look forward to hearing from you /ˌaɪ 'lʊk ˌfɔ:wəd tə ˌhɪərɪŋ frəm ju:/ 67
I regret to inform you that /ˌaɪ rɪ'gret tu ɪnˌfɔ:m ju: ðət/ 67
I would be grateful if you could /ˌaɪ wʊd bi 'greɪtfl ɪf ju: kʊd/ 67
I would like to draw your attention to /ˌaɪ wʊd 'laɪk tə ˌdrɔ: jɔ:r əˌtenʃn tə/ 67
idea as in I haven't / not have the faintest idea 59
idealist /aɪ'di:əlɪst/ 17
idealistic /ˌaɪdi:ə'lɪstɪk/ 17
identify /aɪ'dentɪfaɪ/ 75
idiom /'ɪdiəm/ 59
idol /'aɪdl/ 17
idolize /'aɪdəlaɪz/ 17
if all else fails /ˌɪf ˌɔ:l ˌels 'feɪlz/ 60
if anything happens to sb /ˌɪf ˌeniθɪŋ 'hæpəns tə ˌ.../ 80
if you don't mind my/me asking /ˌɪf ju: ˌdəʊnt ˌmaɪnd ˌmaɪ, ˌmi 'ɑ:skɪŋ/ 60
-ify /ˌɪˌfaɪ/ 75
iirc (= if I remember/recall correctly) 73
ill- /ɪl/ 74
ill-advised /ˌɪl əd'vaɪzd/ 74
ill-informed /ˌɪl ɪn'fɔ:md/ 74
ill-prepared /ˌɪl prɪ'peəd/ 74
ill-treated /ˌɪl 'tri:tɪd/ 74
illusion as in create an illusion 7
illustrate /'ɪləstreɪt/ 69

illustrious /ɪ'lʌstriəs/ 78
imagine /ɪ'mædʒɪn/ 75
imho (= in my humble opinion) 73
imitate /'ɪmɪteɪt/ 24
imitation /ˌɪmɪ'teɪʃn/ 24
immaculate /ɪ'mækjələt/ 33
immigrant /'ɪmɪgrənt/ 32
immigration /ˌɪmɪ'greɪʃn/ 32
imminent /'ɪmɪnənt/ 46
immune system /ɪ'mju:n ˌsɪstəm/ 71
immunity /ɪ'mju:nəti/ 71
impact N /'ɪmpækt/ 18
impeccable /ɪm'pekəbl/ 19
impetuous /ɪm'petʃuəs/ 14
implausible /ɪm'plɔ:zəbl/ 78
implement V /'ɪmplɪment/ 27
implementation /ˌɪmplɪmen'teɪʃn/ 27
implication /ˌɪmplɪ'keɪʃn/ 8
imply /ɪm'plaɪ/ 8
impose /ɪm'pəʊz/ 27
imprison /ɪm'prɪzn/ 36
imprisonment /ɪm'prɪznmənt/ 36
impulse /'ɪmpʌls/ 25
impulse to do sth /ˌɪmpʌls tə 'du: ˌ.../ 25
impulsive /ɪm'pʌlsɪv/ 14
in any case /ˌɪn 'eni ˌkeɪs/ 64
in captivity /ˌɪn kæp'tɪvəti/ 29
in command /ˌɪn kə'mɑ:nd/ 37
in company /ˌɪn 'kʌmpəni/ 26
in conclusion /ˌɪn kən'klu:ʒn/ 68
in credit /ˌɪn 'kredɪt/ 48
in crisis /ˌɪn 'kraɪsɪs/ 36
in current use /ˌɪn ˌkʌrənt 'ju:s/ 1
in custody /ˌɪn 'kʌstədi/ 35
in danger /ˌɪn 'deɪndʒə(r)/ 29, 77
in decline /ˌɪn dɪ'klaɪn/ 29
in due course /ˌɪn ˌdju: 'kɔ:s/ 57
in excess of /ˌɪn ɪk'ses əv/ 13
in exchange for /ˌɪn ɪks'tʃeɪndʒ fə(r)/ 77
in good form /ˌɪn ˌgʊd 'fɔ:m/ 23
in great form /ˌɪn ˌgreɪt 'fɔ:m/ 23
in honour of /ˌɪn 'ɒnər əv/ 77
in memory of /ˌɪn 'meməri əv/ 77
in mint condition /ˌɪn ˌmɪnt kən'dɪʃn/ 55
in motion /ˌɪn 'məʊʃn/ 72
in office /ˌɪn 'ɒfɪs/ 77
in passing /ˌɪn 'pɑ:sɪŋ/ 77
in perfect condition /ˌɪn ˌpɜ:fɪkt kən'dɪʃn/ 55
in possession of /ˌɪn pə'zeʃn əv/ 77
in power /ˌɪn 'paʊə(r)/ 77
in regard to /ˌɪn rɪ'gɑ:d tə/ 68
in reply to /ˌɪn rɪ'plaɪ tə/ 67
in reserve /ˌɪn rɪ'zɜ:v/ 37
in retrospect /ˌɪn 'retrəspekt/ 57
in search of /ˌɪn 'sɜ:tʃ əv/ 25
in season /ˌɪn 'si:zn/ 28
in sb's way /ˌɪn ˌ... 'weɪ/ 56
in tears /ˌɪn 'tɪəz/ 15
in the centre /ˌɪn ðə 'sentə(r)/ 42
in the firing line /ˌɪn ðə 'faɪərɪŋ ˌlaɪn/ 39
in the nude /ˌɪn ðə 'nju:d/ 78

CONSONANTS: b **b**ad | d **d**id | f **f**all | g **g**et | h **h**at | j **y**es | k **c**at | l **l**eg | m **m**an | n **n**ow | p **p**en | r **r**ed | s **s**ee | t **t**ea | v **v**an | w **w**et | z **z**oo | ʃ **sh**oe | ʒ vi**s**ion | tʃ **ch**ain | dʒ **j**am | θ **th**in | ð **th**is | ŋ si**ng**

in the process of doing sth /ˌɪn ðə ˈprəʊses əv ˌduːɪŋ ˌ.../ 24
in the public eye /ˌɪn ðə ˌpʌblɪk ˈaɪ/ 41
in the region of /ˌɪn ðə ˈriːdʒən əv/ 65
in the way /ˌɪn ðə ˈweɪ/ 56
in the wild /ˌɪn ðə ˈwaɪld/ 29
in touch /ˌɪn ˈtʌtʃ/ 77
in transition /ˌɪn trænˈzɪʃn/ 27
in trouble /ˌɪn ˈtrʌbl/ 77
in turmoil /ˌɪn ˈtɜːmɔɪl/ 47
in view of /ˌɪn ˈvjuː əv/ 68
inc. (= included/including) 73
incentive /ɪnˈsentɪv/ 18
incident /ˈɪnsɪdənt/ 52
incidentally /ˌɪnsɪˈdentli/ 64
incl. (= inclusive) 73
inclination /ˌɪnklɪˈneɪʃn/ 50
inclined to do sth /ɪnˌklaɪnd tə ˈduː ˌ.../ 50
include /ɪnˈkluːd/ 6
inclusive as in fully inclusive 6
incoherent /ˌɪnkəʊˈhɪərənt/ 69
income /ˈɪnkʌm/ 48
incomprehensible /ˌɪnkɒmprɪˈhensəbl/ 78
inconceivable /ˌɪnkənˈsiːvəbl/ 78
inconsiderate /ˌɪnkənˈsɪdərət/ 14
incurable /ɪnˈkjʊərəbl/ 30
indescribable /ˌɪndɪˈskraɪbəbl/ 6
indicate /ˈɪndɪkeɪt/ 6
indication /ˌɪndɪˈkeɪʃn/ 6
indirectly /ˌɪndəˈrektli, ˌɪndaɪ-/ 79
indiscreet /ˌɪndɪˈskriːt/ 7
indulge in /ɪnˈdʌldʒ ˌɪn/ 25
industrial dispute /ɪnˌdʌstriəl dɪˈspjuːt/ 50
industrialize /ɪnˈdʌstriəlaɪz/ 75
ineligible /ɪnˈelɪdʒəbl/ 34
inevitable /ɪnˈevɪtəbl/ 16
inevitably /ɪnˈevɪtəbli/ 16
inexcusable /ˌɪnɪkˈskjuːzəbl/ 6
inexplicable /ˌɪnɪkˈsplɪkəbl/ 6
infamous /ˈɪnfəməs/ 78
infested /ɪnˈfestɪd/ 40
inflation-proof savings /ɪnˌfleɪʃn ˌpruːf ˈseɪvɪŋz/ 75
information as in should you require any further information 67
informed as in keep sb informed 33
inherent /ɪnˈherənt/ 70
initial /ɪˈnɪʃl/ 16
initially /ɪˈnɪʃəli/ 16
initiative /ɪˈnɪʃətɪv/ 45
inmate /ˈɪnmeɪt/ 36
innermost thoughts /ˌɪnəməʊst ˈθɔːts/ 15
innovative /ˈɪnəvətɪv/ 55
inoffensive /ˌɪnəˈfensɪv/ 19
insane /ɪnˈseɪn/ 70
insanity /ɪnˈsænəti/ 70
insert V /ɪnˈsɜːt/ 71
insertion /ɪnˈsɜːʃn/ 71
insight into /ˈɪnsaɪt ˌɪntu/ 45
insipid /ɪnˈsɪpɪd/ 12
insolence /ˈɪnsələns/ 19
insolent /ˈɪnsələnt/ 19
insoluble /ɪnˈsɒljəbl/ 54

inspection /ɪnˈspekʃn/ 71
inspector /ɪnˈspektə(r)/ 35
inspiration /ˌɪnspəˈreɪʃn/ 17
inspirational /ˌɪnspəˈreɪʃənl/ 17
inspire /ɪnˈspaɪə(r)/ 17
install /ɪnˈstɔːl/ 31
instant as in take an instant dislike to 16
instinct /ˈɪnstɪŋkt/ 15
instinctive /ɪnˈstɪŋktɪv/ 15
insult V /ɪnˈsʌlt/ 1
insulting /ɪnˈsʌltɪŋ/ 1
insurmountable /ˌɪnsəˈmaʊntəbl/ 54
integrate /ˈɪntɪgreɪt/ 32
integration /ˌɪntɪˈgreɪʃn/ 32
integrity /ɪnˈtegrəti/ 14
intelligible /ɪnˈtelɪdʒəbl/ 78
intense /ɪnˈtens/ 75
intensify /ɪnˈtensɪfaɪ/ 75
intent on/upon /ɪnˈtent ˌɒn, ə,pɒn/ 76
intention /ɪnˈtenʃn/ 67
inter- /ˈɪntə/ 74
interact /ˌɪntərˈækt/ 74
interaction /ˌɪntərˈækʃn/ 74
interchangeable /ˌɪntəˈtʃeɪndʒəbl/ 1
interdependent /ˌɪntədɪˈpendənt/ 74
interest-free /ˌɪntrəst ˈfriː/ 75
interfere /ˌɪntəˈfɪə(r)/ 50
interference /ˌɪntəˈfɪərəns/ 50
interior N, ADJ /ɪnˈtɪəriə(r)/ 37
interminable /ɪnˈtɜːmɪnəbl/ 49
internal /ɪnˈtɜːnl/ 37
internet café /ˈɪntənet ˌkæfeɪ/ 31
interpret /ɪnˈtɜːprɪt/ 1
interpretation /ɪnˌtɜːprɪˈteɪʃn/ 1
interrelated /ˌɪntərɪˈleɪtɪd/ 74
interrogate /ɪnˈterəgeɪt/ 53
interrogation /ɪnˌterəˈgeɪʃn/ 53
interrupt /ˌɪntəˈrʌpt/ 63
interval /ˈɪntəvl/ 57
intervene in sth /ˌɪntəˈviːn ɪn ˌ.../ 50
intervention /ˌɪntəˈvenʃn/ 50
into /ˈɪntuː, ˈɪntə/ 58
intrinsic /ɪnˈtrɪnzɪk/ 70
intrude into sth /ɪnˈtruːd ˌɪntə ˌ.../ 41
intrusion /ɪnˈtruːʒn/ 41
inundated /ˈɪnʌndeɪtɪd/ 49
invade /ɪnˈveɪd/ 30
invaluable /ɪnˈvæljuəbl/ 78
invariably /ɪnˈveəriəbli/ 79
invasion /ɪnˈveɪʒn/ 30
invasive /ɪnˈveɪsɪv/ 30
invest /ɪnˈvest/ 47
investigation as in under investigation 77
investor /ɪnˈvestə(r)/ 47
invisible /ɪnˈvɪzəbl/ 11
involvement /ɪnˈvɒlvmənt/ 76
IQ /ˌaɪ ˈkjuː/ 73
ironic /aɪˈrɒnɪk/ 1
irony /ˈaɪrəni/ 1
irreversible /ˌɪrɪˈvɜːsəbl/ 27
irritated /ˈɪrɪteɪtɪd/ 11
irritation /ˌɪrɪˈteɪʃn/ 11
isolated /ˈaɪsəleɪtɪd/ 21
issue a warrant /ˌɪʃuː ə ˈwɒrənt/ 35
it's about time /ˌɪts əˌbaʊt ˈtaɪm/ 57

it's been one of those days /ˌɪts bɪn ˌwʌn əv ˌðəʊz ˈdeɪz/ 59
it's high time /ˌɪts ˈhaɪ ˌtaɪm/ 57
it's more trouble than it's worth /ˌɪts ˌmɔː ˈtrʌbl ðən ˌɪts ˈwɜːθ/ 60
it's no good + ing /ˌɪts ˌnəʊ ˈgʊd/ 59
it's no use + ing /ˌɪts ˌnəʊ ˈjuːs/ 59
it's none of your business /ˌɪts ˌnʌn əv jɔː ˈbɪznɪs/ 73
it's not sb's day /ˌɪts nɒt ˌ... ˈdeɪ/ 59
it's true /ˌɪts ˈtruː/ 64
itch /ɪtʃ/ 13
itchy /ˈɪtʃi/ 13
itemize /ˈaɪtəmaɪz/ 75
-ize 75

jam N, V /dʒæm/ 51
jargon /ˈdʒɑːgən/ 31
jaw /dʒɔː/ 12
join in /ˌdʒɔɪn ˈɪn/ 26
joint /dʒɔɪnt/ 46
jointly /ˈdʒɔɪntli/ 46
jot sth down /ˌdʒɒt ˌ... ˈdaʊn/ 49
jubilant /ˈdʒuːbɪlənt/ 15
judge as in don't judge a book by its cover 14
juggle /ˈdʒʌgl/ 45
jump to conclusions /ˌdʒʌmp tə kənˈkluːʒnz/ 8
junior /ˈdʒuːniə(r)/ 33
justifiable /ˈdʒʌstɪfaɪəbl/ 36
justification /ˌdʒʌstɪfɪˈkeɪʃn/ 36, 69
justify /ˈdʒʌstɪfaɪ/ 36, 69

keep /kiːp/ 2
keep control of /ˌkiːp kənˈtrəʊl əv/ 76
keep sb going /ˌkiːp ˌ... ˈgəʊɪŋ/ 2
keep sb informed /ˌkiːp ˌ... ɪnˈfɔːmd/ 33
keep sth in perspective /ˌkiːp ˌ... ɪn pəˈspektɪv/ 54
keep still /ˌkiːp ˈstɪl/ 11
keep track of /ˌkiːp ˈtræk əv/ 48
keep your feet on the ground /ˌkiːp jɔː ˌfiːt ˌɒn ðə ˈgraʊnd/ 60
keep yourself occupied /ˌkiːp jɔːˌself ˈɒkjupaɪd/ 6
key as in the key to 7
keyhole surgery /ˌkiːhəʊl ˈsɜːdʒəri/ 33
kick up a fuss /ˌkɪk ˌʌp ə ˈfʌs/ 18
kidnap /ˈkɪdnæp/ 38
kidnapper /ˈkɪdnæpə(r)/ 38
kidnapping /ˈkɪdnæpɪŋ/ 38
kind of /ˈkaɪnd əv/ 65
kip /kɪp/ 58
kitchen scales /ˈkɪtʃɪn ˌskeɪlz/ 20
knock-on effect /ˌnɒkˌɒn ɪˈfekt/ 52
knock sb out of sth /ˌnɒk ˌ... ˈaʊt əv ˌ.../ 23
knockout /ˈnɒkaʊt/ 23

labour-saving /ˈleɪbə ˌseɪvɪŋ/ 28
ladle V /ˈleɪdl/ 20
laid-back /ˌleɪd ˈbæk/ 58
landfill /ˈlændfɪl/ 28
landfill site /ˈlændfɪl ˌsaɪt/ 28
lapse /læps/ 39

VOWELS: æ cat | ɑː father | e ten | ɜː bird | ə about | ɪ sit | iː see | i many | ɒ got | ɔː saw | ʌ up | ʊ put | uː too | u actual
aɪ my | aʊ now | eɪ say | əʊ go | ɔɪ boy | ɪə near | eə hair | ʊə pure

last chance /ˌlɑːst ˈtʃɑːns/ 23
last minute *as in* leave sth to/till the last minute 57
last-minute /ˌlɑːst ˈmɪnɪt/ 3
last resort /ˌlɑːst rɪˈzɔːt/ 60
last thing *as in* be the last thing on sb's mind 2
late *as in* better late than never 66
l8r (= later) 73
latter N /ˈlætə(r)/ 37
laugh N /lɑːf/ 58
law and order /ˌlɔːr ən ˈɔːdə(r)/ 61
lawnmower /ˈlɔːnməʊə(r)/ 24
lay down rules /ˌleɪ ˌdaʊn ˈruːlz/ 18
lay out /ˌleɪ ˈaʊt/ 3
lay siege to /ˌleɪ ˈsiːdʒ tə/ 43
lay sth on /ˌleɪ ˌ... ˈɒn/ 26
lay the foundations /ˌleɪ ðə faʊnˈdeɪʃnz/ 42
laze around /ˌleɪz əˈraʊnd/ 21
lead the charge /ˌliːd ðe ˈtʃɑːdʒ/ 9
leaf /liːf/ 24
leaf *as in* turn over a new leaf 36
leaflet /ˈliːflət/ 13
league /liːg/ 23
leak N /liːk/ 39
leak sth to sb /ˈliːk ˌ... tə ˌ.../ 39
lean towards /ˈliːn təˌwɔːdz/ 8
leap to conclusions /ˌliːp tə kənˈkluːʒnz/ 8
lease N /liːs/ 67
least *as in* at the very least 77
leave *as in* maternity/paternity leave 44
leave sth to sb /ˈliːv ˌ... tə ˌ.../ 2
leave sth to/till the last minute /ˌliːv ˌ... tə, tɪl ðə ˌlɑːst ˈmɪnɪt/ 57
leave sth with sb /ˈliːv ˌ... wɪð ˌ.../ 2
left-wing /ˌleft ˈwɪŋ/ 42
legal battle /ˈliːgl ˌbætl/ 39
legalize /ˈliːgəlaɪz/ 75
leisure pursuits /ˈleʒə pəˌsjuːts/ 25
lemon squeezer /ˈlemən ˌskwiːzə(r)/ 20
lemony /ˈleməni/ 12
lengthen /ˈleŋθən/ 7
lentils /ˈlentlz/ 20
let-down /ˈlet ˌdaʊn/ 3
let sb down /ˌlet ˌ... ˈdaʊn/ 3, 23, 56
let sb go /ˌlet ˌ... ˈgəʊ/ 80
let sleeping dogs lie /ˌlet ˌsliːpɪŋ ˌdɒgz ˈlaɪ/ 66
let your hair down /ˌlet jɔː ˈheə ˌdaʊn/ 60
lethal weapon /ˌliːθl ˈwepən/ 37
lethargic /ləˈθɑːdʒɪk/ 13
lethargy /ˈleθədʒi/ 13
level playing field /ˌlevl ˈpleɪɪŋ ˌfiːld/ 39
level with /ˈlevl ˌwɪð/ 53
Liberal /ˈlɪbərəl/ 42
liberalism /ˈlɪbərəlɪzəm/ 42
life expectancy /ˈlaɪf ɪkˌspektənsi/ 3
life-threatening /ˈlaɪf ˌθretnɪŋ/ 18
light a fire /ˌlaɪt ə ˈfaɪə(r)/ 4
lightly /ˈlaɪtli/ 12

lightning never strikes twice /ˌlaɪtnɪŋ ˌnevə ˌstraɪks ˈtwaɪs/ 66
lightning never strikes twice in the same place /ˌlaɪtnɪŋ ˌnevə ˌstraɪks ˌtwaɪs ɪn ðə ˌseɪm ˈpleɪs/ 66
like chalk and cheese /ˌlaɪk ˌtʃɔːk ən ˈtʃiːz/ 20
like new /ˌlaɪk ˈnjuː/ 55
likelihood /ˈlaɪklihʊd/ 29
likely story /ˈlaɪkli ˌstɔːri/ 59
limit *as in* set a limit 50
limp N, V /lɪmp/ 9
link /lɪŋk/ 31
literal /ˈlɪtərəl/ 1
literary /ˈlɪtərəri/ 1
live and let live /ˌlɪv ən ˌlet ˈlɪv/ 66
live at peace with /ˌlɪv ət ˈpiːs wɪð/ 32
live in a world of your own /ˌlɪv ɪn ə ˌwɜːld əv ˌjɔːr ˈəʊn/ 60
live with /ˈlɪv ˌwɪð/ 76
liven sth up /ˌlaɪvn ˌ... ˈʌp/ 26
liven up /ˌlaɪvn ˈʌp/ 26
load N /ləʊd/ 72
loads of /ˈləʊdz əv/ 65
lock sb up /ˌlɒk ˌ... ˈʌp/ 36
locked in battle /ˌlɒkt ɪn ˈbætl/ 39
lodged in sth /ˈlɒdʒd ɪn ˌ.../ 40
log /lɒg/ 62
log in/out /ˌlɒg ˈɪn, ˈaʊt/ 31
log on/off /ˌlɒg ˈɒn, ˈɒf/ 31
logic /ˈlɒdʒɪk/ 79
logical /ˈlɒdʒɪkl/ 79
logically /ˈlɒdʒɪkli/ 79
lol (= laughing out loud) 73
lol (= lots of love) 73
loner /ˈləʊnə(r)/ 26
long and hard /ˌlɒŋ ən ˈhɑːd/ 61
long-lived /ˌlɒŋ ˈlɪvd/ 71
long-sighted /ˌlɒŋ ˈsaɪtɪd/ 11
long-term /ˌlɒŋ ˈtɜːm/ 13
long weekend /ˌlɒŋ wiːkˈend/ 3
loo /luː/ 58
look down on sb /ˌlʊk ˈdaʊn ɒn ˌ.../ 17
look forward *as in* I look forward to hearing from you 67
look out for /ˌlʊk ˈaʊt ˌfɔː(r), fə(r)/ 8
look up /ˌlʊk ˈʌp/ 16
look up to sb /ˌlʊk ˈʌp tə ˌ.../ 17
looking back /ˌlʊkɪŋ ˈbæk/ 57
loosen /ˈluːsn/ 7
loosen up /ˌluːsn ˈʌp/ 9
lose control of /ˌluːz kənˈtrəʊl əv/ 76
lose face /ˌluːz ˈfeɪs/ 60
lose track of /ˌluːz ˈtræk əv/ 48
lose your appetite /ˌluːz jɔː ˈæpətaɪt/ 12
lose your temper /ˌluːz jɔː ˈtempə(r)/ 15
loss /lɒs/ 47
lousy /ˈlaʊzi/ 58
love (= darling) /lʌv/ 58
love is blind /ˌlʌv ɪz ˈblaɪnd/ 66
low blood pressure /ˌləʊ ˈblʌd ˌpreʃə(r)/ 13
low-pitched /ˌləʊ ˈpɪtʃt/ 10
low priority /ˌləʊ praɪˈɒrəti/ 49

lower class /ˌləʊə ˈklɑːs/ 19
luck *as in* no such luck 59
luck *as in* stroke of luck 56
lucrative /ˈluːkrətɪv/ 45
lunch break /ˈlʌntʃ ˌbreɪk/ 57
lure V /lʊə(r), ljʊə(r)/ 46
lying down *as in* not take sth lying down 46

mad *as in* go mad 15
magistrate /ˈmædʒɪstreɪt/ 35
magnet /ˈmægnət/ 75
magnetic /mægˈnetɪk/ 75
main concern /ˌmeɪn kənˈsɜːn/ 4
maintain the status quo /meɪnˌteɪn ðə ˌsteɪtəs ˈkwəʊ/ 42
major /ˈmeɪdʒə(r)/ 54
major change /ˌmeɪdʒə ˈtʃeɪndʒ/ 27
make *as in* What do you make of …? 14
make a bid for /ˌmeɪk ə ˈbɪd ˌfɔː(r), fə(r)/ 46
make a comeback /ˌmeɪk ə ˈkʌmbæk/ 56
make a commitment /ˌmeɪk ə kəˈmɪtmənt/ 6
make a confession /ˌmeɪk ə kənˈfeʃn/ 6
make a dash /ˌmeɪk ə ˈdæʃ/ 9
make a difference /ˌmeɪk ə ˈdɪfrəns/ 52
make a distinction /ˌmeɪk ə dɪˈstɪŋkʃn/ 37
make a fuss about /ˌmeɪk ə ˈfʌs əˌbaʊt/ 18
make a go of sth /ˌmeɪk ə ˈgəʊ əv ˌ.../ 56
make a meal of sth /ˌmeɪk ə ˈmiːl əv ˌ.../ 20
make a mess /ˌmeɪk ə ˈmes/ 18
make a rapid recovery /ˌmeɪk ə ˌræpɪd rɪˈkʌvəri/ 40
make a sacrifice /ˌmeɪk ə ˈsækrɪfaɪs/ 16
make a speedy recovery /ˌmeɪk ə ˌspiːdi rɪˈkʌvəri/ 40
make cutbacks /ˌmeɪk ˈkʌtbæks/ 48
make fun of /ˌmeɪk ˈfʌn əv/ 1
make generalizations about /ˌmeɪk ˌdʒenrəlaɪˈzeɪʃnz əˌbaʊt/ 8
make it /ˈmeɪk ˌɪt/ 56
make it clear /ˌmeɪk ɪt ˈklɪə(r)/ 4
make it sth /ˈmeɪk ɪt ˌ.../ 2
make it up with /ˌmeɪk ɪt ˈʌp ˌwɪð/ 63
make light of /ˌmeɪk ˈlaɪt əv/ 54
make out (= claim) /ˌmeɪk ˈaʊt/ 63
make sb feel welcome /ˌmeɪk ˌ... ˌfiːl ˈwelkʌm/ 26
make sb/sth out (= see/hear with difficulty) /ˌmeɪk ˌ... ˈaʊt/ 11
make that sth /ˈmeɪk ðæt ˌ.../ 2
make things difficult /ˌmeɪk ˌθɪŋz ˈdɪfɪkəlt/ 16
make up (= comprise) /ˌmeɪk ˈʌp/ 37
make up for /ˌmeɪk ˈʌp fə(r)/ 63
make your mouth water /ˌmeɪk jɔː ˈmaʊθ ˌwɔːtə(r)/ 12

CONSONANTS: b **b**ad | d **d**id | f **f**all | g **g**et | h **h**at | j **y**es | k **c**at | l **l**eg | m **m**an | n **n**ow | p **p**en | r **r**ed | s **s**ee | t **t**ea | v **v**an | w **w**et | z **z**oo | ʃ **sh**oe | ʒ vi**s**ion | tʃ **ch**ain | dʒ **j**am | θ **th**in | ð **th**is | ŋ si**ng**

malice /'mælɪs/ 17
malicious /mə'lɪʃəs/ 17
malnourished /mæl'nʌrɪʃt/ 74
manifesto /mænɪ'festəʊ/ 34
manners /'mænəz/ 19
march N, V /mɑ:tʃ/ 9
massage N, V /'mæsɑ:dʒ/ 12
maternity leave /mə'tɜ:nəti ˌli:v/ 44
maternity unit /mə'tɜ:nəti ju:nɪt/ 71
matter as in as a matter of fact 64
maximize /'mæksɪmaɪz/ 28
mayor /'meə(r)/ 34
mayoress /meə'res/ 34
meadow /'medəʊ/ 24
meal as in make a meal of sth 20
means /mi:nz/ 42
means as in by means of 77
means as in the end justifies the
    means 66
measure /'meʒə(r)/ 39
medicine as in complementary
    medicine 33
medieval /medi'i:vl/ 55
mediocre /mi:di'əʊkə(r)/ 22
meet the needs of /ˌmi:t ðə 'ni:dz
    əv/ 72
memory as in in memory of 79
mentally /'mentəli/ 79
merciful /'mɜ:sɪfl/ 70
merciless /'mɜ:sɪləs/ 70
mercy /'mɜ:si/ 70
merely /'mɪəli/ 37
merger /'mɜ:dʒə(r)/ 46
merit as in on merit 77
mess /mes/ 18
messy /'mesi/ 18
metaphor /'metəfə(r)/ 39
meticulous /mə'tɪkjələs/ 33
microscope /'maɪkrəskəʊp/ 42
Middle Ages /ˌmɪdl 'eɪdʒɪz/ 55
middle class /ˌmɪdl 'klɑ:s/ 19
migrant as in economic migrant 32
migration /maɪ'greɪʃn/ 32
military ADJ /'mɪlətri/ 37
military operation /ˌmɪlətri
    ɒpə'reɪʃn/ 37
military service /ˌmɪlətri 'sɜ:vɪs/ 37
mind as in be the last thing on sb's
    mind 2
mind as in bear sth in mind 8
mind as in bored out of your
    mind 22
mind as in have sb/sth in mind 59
mind as in my mind goes a complete
    blank 59
mind as in set sb's mind at rest 54
mind like a sieve /ˌmaɪnd ˌlaɪk ə
    'sɪv/ 62
mind you /ˌmaɪnd 'ju:/ 64
mind your own business /ˌmaɪnd jɔ:r
    ˌəʊn 'bɪznəs/ 73
minds as in be in two minds about 2
minimize /'mɪnɪmaɪz/ 28
minister /'mɪnɪstə(r)/ 38
minor /'maɪnə(r)/ 54
minority as in ethnic minority 32
minute as in at the last minute 57

mint as in in mint condition 55
minute as in the minute 25
mis- /mɪs/ 74
miscalculate /ˌmɪs'kælkjəleɪt/ 74
miscast /mɪs'kɑ:st/ 22
misconceived /ˌmɪskən'si:vd/ 74
misconception /ˌmɪskən'sepʃn/ 74
misdiagnose /ˌmɪs'daɪəgnəʊz/ 74
misfire /ˌmɪs'faɪə(r)/ 74
mishandle /ˌmɪs'hændl/ 74
misinform /ˌmɪsɪn'fɔ:m/ 74
misinterpret /ˌmɪsɪn'tɜ:prɪt/ 8
misinterpretation /ˌmɪsɪntɜ:prɪ'teɪʃn/ 8
misjudge /ˌmɪs'dʒʌdʒ/ 74
mislay /ˌmɪs'leɪ/ 74
mislead /ˌmɪs'li:d/ 14
misleading /ˌmɪs'li:dɪŋ/ 14
mismanage /ˌmɪs'mænɪdʒ/ 74
misplace /ˌmɪs'pleɪs/ 74
misprint N /'mɪsprɪnt/ 74
miss out on /ˌmɪs 'aʊt ɒn/ 63
missile /'mɪsaɪl/ 37
mistake N, V /mɪ'steɪk/ 6
mistreat /mɪs'tri:t/ 74
mix V /mɪks/ 20
mix-up /'mɪks ʌp/ 33
moan V /məʊn/ 58
moaning /'məʊnɪŋ/ 58
mobilize /'məʊbəlaɪz/ 37
mock /mɒk/ 1
model as in role model 18
moderate ADJ /'mɒdərət/ 42
modernize /'mɒdənaɪz/ 75
moist /mɔɪst/ 11
molecular /mə'lekjələ(r)/ 71
molecule /'mɒlɪkju:l/ 71
moment as in at a moment's
    notice 77
moment as in the moment 25
money talks /ˌmʌni 'tɔ:ks/ 66
morale /mə'rɑ:l/ 45
more as in the more the merrier 66
mortality rate /mɔ:'tæləti ˌreɪt/ 30
motion /'məʊʃn/ 72
motive /'məʊtɪv/ 52
motive as in ulterior motive 2
motto /'mɒtəʊ/ 66
mount V /maʊnt/ 46
mount up /ˌmaʊnt 'ʌp/ 48
mouse /maʊs/ 62
mouth ulcer /'maʊθ ˌʌlsə(r)/ 13
mouth-watering /'maʊθ ˌwɔ:tərɪŋ/ 12
move the goalposts /ˌmu:v ðə
    'gəʊlpəʊsts/ 39
mow the lawn /ˌməʊ ðə 'lɔ:n/ 24
msg (= message) 73
mud /mʌd/ 24
muddle /'mʌdl/ 33
muddy /'mʌdi/ 24
muscle /'mʌsl/ 13
musty /'mʌsti/ 12
mutate /mju:'teɪt/ 71
mutation /mju:'teɪʃn/ 71
mutual /'mju:tʃuəl/ 45
mutual as in by mutual consent 36
my mind goes a complete blank /ˌmaɪ
    ˌmaɪnd ˌgəʊz ə kəm,pli:t 'blæŋk/ 59

my mind goes blank /ˌmaɪ ˌmaɪnd
    ˌgəʊz 'blæŋk/ 59
myob (= mind your own
    business) 73

n (= and) 73
n (= in) 73
nag /næg/ 18
nail-biting /'neɪl ˌbaɪtɪŋ/ 22
nail polish /'neɪl ˌpɒlɪʃ/ 3
naive /naɪ'i:v/ 14
naivety /naɪ'i:vəti/ 14
naked /'neɪkɪd/ 78
namely /'neɪmli/ 53
narrative /'nærətɪv/ 69
narrator /nə'reɪtə(r)/ 69
narrow escape /ˌnærəʊ ɪ'skeɪp/ 4
narrow-minded /ˌnærəʊ 'maɪndɪd/ 3
nasty /'nɑ:sti/ 13
nationalization /ˌnæʃnəlaɪ'zeɪʃn/ 50
nationalize /'næʃnəlaɪz/ 75
nationwide /ˌneɪʃn'waɪd/ 34
native /'neɪtɪv/ 32
natural habitat /ˌnætʃrəl 'hæbɪtæt/ 29
naturally /'nætʃrəli/ 79
nature /'neɪtʃə(r)/ 18, 24
nature reserve /'neɪtʃə rɪˌzɜ:v/ 29
nauseating /'nɔ:zieɪtɪŋ/ 12
navy /'neɪvi/ 37
NB /ˌen 'bi:/ 73
needless to say /'ni:dləs tə ˌseɪ/ 53
needs as in meet the needs of 72
neglect N, V /nɪ'glekt/ 51
neglect to do sth /nɪ'glekt tə ˌdu:
    ˌ.../ 51
negligence /'neglɪdʒəns/ 33
negligent /'neglɪdʒənt/ 33, 78
negligible /'neglɪdʒəbl/ 78
nerve /nɜ:v/ 13
nest N, V /nest/ 24
network N /'netwɜ:k/ 34
neutral /'nju:trəl/ 23
never-ending /ˌnevər 'endɪŋ/ 3, 49
nevertheless /ˌnevəðə'les/ 64
new as in like new 55
new era /ˌnju: 'ɪərə/ 57
newlyweds /'nju:lɪwedz/ 41
news as in no news is good news 66
next of kin /ˌnekst əv 'kɪn/ 3
nick sth /'nɪk ˌ.../ 58
no chance /'nəʊ ˌtʃɑ:ns/ 59
no doubt /'nəʊ ˌdaʊt/ 26
no matter what /ˌnəʊ ˌmætə 'wɒt/ 49
no matter when /ˌnəʊ ˌmætə
    'wen/ 49
no news is good news /ˌnəʊ ˌnju:z ɪz
    ˌgʊd ˌnju:z/ 66
no reason /'nəʊ ˌri:zn/ 52
no regard for /'nəʊ rɪˌgɑ:d fə(r)/ 76
no such luck /ˌnəʊ ˌsʌtʃ 'lʌk/ 59
no way /ˌnəʊ 'weɪ/ 59
no wonder /ˌnəʊ 'wʌndə(r)/ 60
noise /nɔɪz/ 4
none as in second to none 33
nose as in get up sb's nose 14
nose as in poke/stick your nose in
    sth 51

VOWELS: æ cat | ɑ: father | e ten | ɜ: bird | ə about | ɪ sit | i: see | i many | ɒ got | ɔ: saw | ʌ up | ʊ put | u: too | u actual |
aɪ my | aʊ now | eɪ say | əʊ go | ɔɪ boy | ɪə near | eə hair | ʊə pure

nosey /ˈnəʊzi/ 58
nostalgia /nɒˈstældʒə/ 32
nostalgic /nɒˈstældʒɪk/ 32
nosy /ˈnəʊzi/ 58
not entirely happy /ˌnɒt ɪnˌtaɪəli ˈhæpi/ 4
not entirely satisfied /ˌnɒt ɪnˌtaɪəli ˈsætɪsfaɪd/ 4
not entirely sure /ˌnɒt ɪnˌtaɪəli ˈʃʊə(r)/ 4
not exactly bright /ˌnɒt ɪgˌzæktli ˈbraɪt/ 80
not have the faintest idea /ˌnɒt ˌhæv ðə ˌfeɪntɪst aɪˈdɪə/ 59
not have the heart to do sth /ˌnɒt ˌhæv ðə ˈhɑːt tə ˌduː ˌ.../ 15
not necessarily /ˌnɒt nesəˈserəli/ 8
not put a foot wrong /ˌnɒt ˌpʊt ə ˌfʊt ˈrɒŋ/ 56
not take sth lying down /ˌnɒt ˌteɪk ˌ... ˌlaɪŋ ˈdaʊn/ 46
nothing is too much trouble /ˌnʌθɪŋ ɪz ˌtuː ˌmʌtʃ ˈtrʌbl/ 33
notice v /ˈnəʊtɪs/ 6
notice as in at short notice   77
notice as in take notice of   33
noticeable /ˈnəʊtɪsəbl/ 6
notorious /nəʊˈtɔːriəs/ 78
notwithstanding /nɒtwɪθˈstændɪŋ/ 68
now and again /ˌnaʊ ən əˈgen/ 57
nowhere as in get nowhere   59
nuclear capability /ˌnjuːkliə keɪpəˈbɪləti/ 37
nuclear reactor /ˌnjuːkliə riˈæktə(r)/ 37
nuclear weapon /ˌnjuːkliə ˈwepən/ 37
nude /njuːd/ 78
nursery rhyme /ˈnɜːsəri ˌraɪm/ 3
nurture N, V /ˈnɜːtʃə(r)/ 18
nut /nʌt/ 20
nutcase /ˈnʌtkeɪs/ 20
nutty /ˈnʌti/ 12

objective /əbˈdʒektɪv/ 71
objectivity /ɒbdʒekˈtɪvəti/ 71
observant /əbˈzɜːvənt/ 8
observation /ɒbzəˈveɪʃn/ 8
observe /əbˈzɜːv/ 8
obstacle /ˈɒbstəkl/ 56
obstinacy /ˈɒbstɪnəsi/ 8
obstinate /ˈɒbstɪnət/ 8
obvious /ˈɒbviəs/ 27
obviously /ˈɒbviəsli/ 79
occupant /ˈɒkjəpənt/ 72
occupational hazard /ɒkjuˌpeɪʃənl ˈhæzəd/ 36
occupied /ˈɒkjupaɪd/ 6
occupy /ˈɒkjupaɪ/ 6
occur /əˈkɜː(r)/ 54
ocean as in drop in the ocean   39
-odd /ɒd/ 65
oddly enough /ˌɒdli ɪˈnʌf/ 79
odds as in against all (the) odds   40
odour /ˈəʊdə(r)/ 12
of course /əv ˈkɔːs/ 79
off as in be off   25
off as in go off   12

off form /ˌɒf ˈfɔːm/ 23
off-putting /ˌɒf ˈpʊtɪŋ/ 3
off the beaten track /ˌɒf ðə ˌbiːtn ˈtræk/ 21
off the top of my head /ˌɒf ðə ˌtɒp əv ˌmaɪ ˈhed/ 59
offence as in take offence   4, 19
offensive /əˈfensɪv/ 19
office as in in office   77
officially /əˈfɪʃəli/ 79
old-fashioned /ˌəʊld ˈfæʃnd/ 1
on and on as in go on and on   18
on at as in go on at   63
on balance /ˌɒn ˈbæləns/ 77
on behalf of sb /ˌɒn bɪˈhɑːf əv ˌ.../ 34
on fire /ˌɒn ˈfaɪə(r)/ 4
on hold /ˌɒn ˈhəʊld/ 77
on merit /ˌɒn ˈmerɪt/ 77
on principle /ˌɒn ˈprɪnsəpl/ 17
on reflection /ˌɒn rɪˈflekʃn/ 77
on sb's behalf /ˌɒn ˌ... bɪˈhɑːf/ 34
on standby /ˌɒn ˈstændbaɪ/ 28
on the brink of /ˌɒn ðə ˈbrɪŋk əv/ 38
on the cards /ˌɒn ðə ˈkɑːdz/ 46
on the contrary /ˌɒn ðə ˈkɒntrəri/ 77
on the edge of your seat /ˌɒn ði ˌedʒ əv ˌjɔː ˈsiːt/ 22
on the left /ˌɒn ðə ˈleft/ 42
on the right /ˌɒn ðə ˈraɪt/ 42
on the rocks /ˌɒn ðə ˈrɒks/ 41
on the surface /ˌɒn ðə ˈsɜːfɪs/ 14
on the verge of sth /ˌɒn ðə ˈvɜːdʒ əv ˌ.../ 23, 24
on the whole /ˌɒn ðə ˈhəʊl/ 64
once as in at once   77
once bitten, twice shy /ˌwʌns ˌbɪtn ˌtwaɪs ˈʃaɪ/ 66
one thing leads to another /ˌwʌn ˌθɪŋ ˌliːdz tu əˈnʌðə(r)/ 52
one time as in at one time   57
ongoing /ˈɒnɡəʊɪŋ/ 27
only just /ˈəʊnli ˌdʒʌst/ 11
opaque /əʊˈpeɪk/ 1
open-minded /ˌəʊpən ˈmaɪndɪd/ 3
operation /ɒpəˈreɪʃn/ 37
opinion as in second opinion   33
opinion poll /əˈpɪnjən ˌpəʊl/ 39
opposed to /əˈpəʊzd tə/ 42
opposition /ɒpəˈzɪʃn/ 42
or so /ˌɔː ˈsəʊ/ 65
or something /ˌɔː ˈsʌmθɪŋ/ 65
or something along those lines /ˌɔː ˈsʌmθɪŋ əˌlɒŋ ˌðəʊz ˌlaɪnz/ 65
or something like that /ˌɔː ˈsʌmθɪŋ ˌlaɪk ˌðæt/ 65
or something of that sort /ˌɔː ˈsʌmθɪŋ əv ˌðæt ˌsɔːt/ 65
or something on those lines /ˌɔː ˈsʌmθɪŋ ˌɒn ˌðəʊz ˌlaɪnz/ 65
or thereabouts /ˌɔː ˈðeərəbaʊts/ 65
ordeal /ɔːˈdiːl/ 38
organ /ˈɔːɡən/ 30
organized crime /ˌɔːɡənaɪzd ˈkraɪm/ 35
origin /ˈɒrɪdʒɪn/ 6
originate /əˈrɪdʒɪneɪt/ 6
oust /aʊst/ 38

out- /aʊt/ 25
out of date /ˌaʊt əv ˈdeɪt/ 55
out of hand /ˌaʊt əv ˈhænd/ 49
out of hours /ˌaʊt əv ˈaʊəz/ 33
out of luck /ˌaʊt əv ˈlʌk/ 77
out of respect /ˌaʊt əv rɪˈspekt/ 77
out of season /ˌaʊt əv ˈsiːzn/ 28
out of sight /ˌaʊt əv ˈsaɪt/ 77
out of sight, out of mind /ˌaʊt əv ˌsaɪt ˌaʊt əv ˈmaɪnd/ 66
out of touch /ˌaʊt əv ˈtʌtʃ/ 77
out of your depth /ˌaʊt əv ˌjɔː ˈdepθ/ 56
outbreak /ˈaʊtbreɪk/ 3
outcome /ˈaʊtkʌm/ 52
outcome as in final outcome   52
outdoor pursuits /ˌaʊtdɔː pəˈsjuːts/ 25
outgoings /ˈaʊtɡəʊɪŋz/ 48
outlay /ˈaʊtleɪ/ 3
outline N, V /ˈaʊtlaɪn/ 69
outlive /aʊtˈlɪv/ 25
outlook /ˈaʊtlʊk/ 47
outnumber /aʊtˈnʌmbə(r)/ 25
outside chance /ˌaʊtsaɪd ˈtʃɑːns/ 23
outspend /aʊtˈspend/ 25
outstanding /aʊtˈstændɪŋ/ 78
outweigh /aʊtˈweɪ/ 25
ovenproof /ˈʌvnpruːf/ 75
over- 74
over the moon /ˌəʊvə ðə ˈmuːn/ 15
over time /ˌəʊvə ˈtaɪm/ 57
overbook /əʊvəˈbʊk/ 74
overcome /əʊvəˈkʌm/ 54, 56
overdose /ˈəʊvədəʊs/ 74
overdraft /ˈəʊvədrɑːft/ 48
overdrawn as in be overdrawn   48
overemphasize /əʊvərˈemfəsaɪz/ 74
overload v /əʊvəˈləʊd/ 74
overrated /əʊvəˈreɪtɪd/ 74
overreact /əʊvəriˈækt/ 52
overwhelm /əʊvəˈwelm/ 43
overwhelmed /əʊvəˈwelmd/ 49
owe sb a favour /ˌəʊ ˌ... ə ˈfeɪvə(r)/ 5
owl /aʊl/ 10
own company /ˌəʊn ˈkʌmpəni/ 26
own up /ˌəʊn ˈʌp/ 63
ox /ɒks/ 62

pacify /ˈpæsɪfaɪ/ 75
package /ˈpækɪdʒ/ 44
packaging /ˈpækɪdʒɪŋ/ 55
pain /peɪn/ 58
pain in the neck /ˌpeɪn ɪn ðə ˈnek/ 58
panel /ˈpænl/ 72
panic-stricken /ˈpænɪk ˌstrɪkən/ 3
papaya /pəˈpaɪə/ 20
paper as in wrapping paper   1
paper clip /ˈpeɪpə ˌklɪp/ 3
paper jam /ˈpeɪpə ˌdʒæm/ 51
parachute /ˈpærəʃuːt/ 37
partially sighted /ˌpɑːʃəli ˈsaɪtɪd/ 11
party as in centre party   42
pass /pɑːs/ 57
pass away /ˌpɑːs əˈweɪ/ 80
pass on /ˌpɑːs ˈɒn/ 80
pass the buck /ˌpɑːs ðə ˈbʌk/ 50
passer-by /ˌpɑːsə ˈbaɪ/ 3

CONSONANTS: b **bad** | d **did** | f **fall** | g **get** | h **hat** | j **yes** | k **cat** | l **leg** | m **man** | n **now** | p **pen** | r **red** | s **see** | t **tea** | v **van** | w **wet** | z **zoo** | ʃ **shoe** | ʒ **vision** | tʃ **chain** | dʒ **jam** | θ **thin** | ð **this** | ŋ **sing**

passing *as in* in passing   77
passion /ˈpæʃn/ 14
passion fruit /ˈpæʃn ˌfruːt/ 20
passionate /ˈpæʃənət/ 14
password /ˈpɑːswɜːd/ 31
past *as in* be past it   56
pastime /ˈpɑːstaɪm/ 25
pat V /pæt/ 12
paternity leave /pəˈtɜːnəti ˌliːv/ 44
paunch /pɔːntʃ/ 7
pay attention /ˌpeɪ əˈtenʃn/ 7
pay dispute /ˈpeɪ dɪˌspjuːt/ 50
pay sb a compliment /ˌpeɪ ˌ... ə ˈkɒmplɪmənt/ 16
PC (= police constable) /ˌpiː ˈsiː/ 35
PC (= politically correct) /ˌpiː ˈsiː/ 73
peacekeeping /ˈpiːskiːpɪŋ/ 37
peacekeeping force /ˈpiːskiːpɪŋ ˌfɔːs/ 37
pear-shaped *as in* go pear-shaped   20
peel V /piːl/ 20
peeler /ˈpiːlə(r)/ 20
peer pressure /ˌpɪə ˈpreʃə(r)/ 18
pejorative /pəˈdʒɒrətɪv/ 1
pencil sth in /ˌpensl ˌ... ˈɪn/ 40
pension /ˈpenʃn/ 44
pent-up /ˌpent ˈʌp/ 15
peppery /ˈpepəri/ 12
per /pɜː(r)/ 48
perceive /pəˈsiːv/ 19
perennial /pəˈreniəl/ 54
perfect example /pɜːfɪkt ɪɡˈzɑːmpl/ 4
performance-related /pəˈfɔːməns rɪˌleɪtɪd/ 44
perks /pɜːks/ 44
perplexed /pəˈplekst/ 78
persist /pəˈsɪst/ 13
persistent /pəˈsɪstənt/ 13
personality /pɜːsəˈnæləti/ 41
personalize /ˈpɜːsənəlaɪz/ 75
personally /ˈpɜːsənəli/ 79
perspective *as in* keep sth in perspective   54
perspiration /pɜːspəˈreɪʃn/ 8
perspire /pəˈspaɪə(r)/ 8
persuade sb to do sth /pəˌsweɪd ˌ... tə ˈduː ˌ.../ 63
pertinent /ˈpɜːtɪnənt/ 67
pet hate /ˌpet ˈheɪt/ 51
phase /feɪz/ 1, 57
phenomena /fəˈnɒmɪnə/ 71
phenomenal /fəˈnɒmɪnl/ 31
phenomenally /fəˈnɒmɪnəli/ 22, 31
phenomenon /fəˈnɒmɪnən/ 71
phoney N, ADJ /ˈfəʊni/ 53
photocopier /ˈfəʊtəʊkɒpiə(r)/ 51
physically /ˈfɪzɪkli/ 79
pick and choose /ˌpɪk ən ˈtʃuːz/ 61
pick sb/sth up /ˌpɪk ˌ... ˈʌp/ 63
pick up /ˌpɪk ˈʌp/ 63
pieces *as in* go to pieces   23
pieces *as in* take sth to pieces   63
pile up /ˌpaɪl ˈʌp/ 51
pin *as in* drawing pin   3
pinch (with fingers) /pɪntʃ/ 12
pinch (= steal) /ˈpɪntʃ/ 58
pitiful /ˈpɪtɪfl/ 70

placate /pləˈkeɪt/ 75
plague /pleɪɡ/ 49
plain /pleɪn/ 67
plant N, V /plɑːnt/ 24
plastic surgery /ˌplæstɪk ˈsɜːdʒəri/ 33
plausible /ˈplɔːzəbl/ 78
play a part /ˌpleɪ ə ˈpɑːt/ 18
plea /pliː/ 38
please accept my sincere condolences /ˌpliːz əkˌsept maɪ sɪnˌsɪə kənˈdəʊlənsɪz/ 67
please do not hesitate to contact me /ˌpliːz ˌduː nɒt ˈhezɪteɪt tə ˌkɒntækt ˈmiː/ 67
please find enclosed /ˈpliːz ˌfaɪnd ɪnˌkləʊzd/ 67
pls (= please)   73
plummet /ˈplʌmɪt/ 30, 47
plunge /plʌndʒ/ 47
poacher /ˈpəʊtʃə(r)/ 29
poaching /ˈpəʊtʃɪŋ/ 29
point /pɔɪnt/ 6
point *as in* breaking point   43
point *as in* there's no point in + ing   59
point *as in* to the point   67
pointless /ˈpɔɪntləs/ 6
poke fun at /ˌpəʊk ˈfʌn ət/ 1
poke your nose in sth /ˌpəʊk jɔː ˈnəʊz ˌɪntə ˌ.../ 51
police V /pəˈliːs/ 34
police chief /pəˈliːs ˌtʃiːf/ 38
police constable /pəˈliːs ˌkʌnstəbl/ 35
police force /pəˈliːs ˌfɔːs/ 35
police officer /pəˈliːs ˌɒfɪsə(r)/ 35
policing /pəˈliːsɪŋ/ 34
political asylum /pəˌlɪtɪkl əˈsaɪləm/ 32
politically correct /pəˌlɪtɪkli kəˈrekt/ 73
poll /pəʊl/ 39
pomegranate /ˈpɒmɪɡrænɪt/ 20
pool V /puːl/ 45
poor taste *as in* be in poor taste   19
pop in /ˌpɒp ˈɪn/ 26
pop over /ˌpɒp ˈəʊvə(r)/ 26
pop round /ˌpɒp ˈraʊnd/ 26
popularize /ˈpɒpjələraɪz/ 75
populated /ˈpɒpjəleɪtɪd/ 74
portray /pɔːˈtreɪ/ 70
portrayal /pɔːˈtreɪəl/ 70
pose a threat to /ˌpəʊz ə ˈθret tə/ 29
posh /pɒʃ/ 58
position /pəˈzɪʃn/ 69
possession *as in* in possession of   77
post /pəʊst/ 62
posthumously /ˈpɒstjəməsli/ 53
pot *as in* the pot calling the kettle black   66
potential /pəˈtenʃl/ 56
pour sth out /ˌpɔː ˌ... ˈaʊt/ 15
poverty /ˈpɒvəti/ 29
practically /ˈpræktɪkli/ 79
practice *as in* put sth into practice   27
practice makes perfect /ˌpræktɪs ˌmeɪks ˈpɜːfekt/ 66
prbly (= probably)   73
precedent /ˈpresɪdənt/ 50

precise /prɪˈsaɪs/ 1
precisely /prɪˈsaɪsli/ 79
precision /prɪˈsɪʒn/ 1
predominantly /prɪˈdɒmɪnəntli/ 79
prejudice against /ˈpredʒudɪs əˌɡenst/ 32
prejudiced /ˈpredʒudɪst/ 32
present V /prɪˈzent/ 69
presentation /preznˈteɪʃn/ 69
preservation /prezəˈveɪʃn/ 55
preserve /prɪˈzɜːv/ 55
press-up /ˈpres ˌʌp/ 9
pressure *as in* under pressure   23, 47
presumably /prɪˈzjuːməbli/ 79
pretentious /prɪˈtenʃəs/ 14
prevention is better than cure /prɪˌvenʃn ɪz ˌbetə ðən ˈkjʊə(r)/ 66
previously /ˈpriːviəsli/ 55
price tag /ˈpraɪs ˌtæɡ/ 25
primarily /praɪˈmerəli/ 79
principal concern /ˈprɪnsəpl kənˌsɜːn/ 4
principles /ˈprɪnsəplz/ 17
prior to /ˈpraɪə tə/ 68
prioritize /praɪˈɒrətaɪz/ 49
priority /praɪˈɒrəti/ 49
privacy /ˈprɪvəsi/ 41
privatization /praɪvətaɪˈzeɪʃn/ 50
privatize /ˈpraɪvətaɪz/ 50, 75
proactive /prəʊˈæktɪv/ 50
probability /prɒbəˈbɪləti/ 29
probe N, V /prəʊb/ 50
problem *as in* tackle a problem   50
procedure /prəˈsiːdʒə(r)/ 30, 71
proceeds /ˈprəʊsiːdz/ 35
process *as in* in the process of doing sth   24
procrastinate /prəʊˈkræstɪneɪt/ 50
procrastination /prəʊkræstɪˈneɪʃn/ 50
productive /prəˈdʌktɪv/ 49
profile *as in* high profile   34
prolly (= probably)   73
prolong /prəˈlɒŋ/ 57, 63
promote /prəˈməʊt/ 34, 45
promoted *as in* be promoted   23
promotion (= movement up to a higher league) /prəˈməʊʃn/ 23
promotion (= support) /prəˈməʊʃn/ 34
prompt ADJ /prɒmpt/ 49
prompt V /prɒmpt/ 52
promptly /ˈprɒmptli/ 49
prone to /ˈprəʊn tə/ 30
pronounced limp /prəˌnaʊnst ˈlɪmp/ 9
-proof /pruːf/ 75
proportion /prəˈpɔːʃn/ 36
propose /prəˈpəʊz/ 5
pros and cons /ˌprəʊz ən ˈkɒnz/ 45
prospect *as in* face the prospect of   4
prosperity /prɒˈsperəti/ 70
prosperous /ˈprɒspərəs/ 70
protagonist /prəˈtæɡənɪst/ 70
protest *as in* storm of protest   39
provision /prəˈvɪʒn/ 44
provocation /prɒvəˈkeɪʃn/ 52
provoke /prəˈvəʊk/ 52
prudence /ˈpruːdns/ 50

VOWELS: æ cat | ɑː father | e ten | ɜː bird | ə about | ɪ sit | iː see | i many | ɒ got | ɔː saw | ʌ up | ʊ put | uː too | u actual |
aɪ my | aʊ now | eɪ say | əʊ go | ɔɪ boy | ɪə near | eə hair | ʊə pure

prudent /'pru:dnt/ 50
prune V /pru:n/ 24
pry into /praɪ ˌɪntə/ 41
PS /ˌpi: 'es/ 73
PTO (= please turn over) /ˌpi: ti: 'əʊ/ 73
public eye as in in the public eye 41
pull a muscle /ˌpʊl ə 'mʌsl/ 13
pull the strings /ˌpʊl ðə 'strɪŋz/ 42
pull your weight /ˌpʊl jɔ: 'weɪt/ 18
pulse /pʌls/ 20
pun /pʌn/ 40
puncture N, V /'pʌŋktʃə(r)/ 40
pungent /'pʌndʒənt/ 12
punishing /'pʌnɪʃɪŋ/ 40
punishment as in capital punishment 36
pure /pjʊə(r)/ 75
purely /'pjʊəli/ 79
purely by chance /ˌpjʊəli ˌbaɪ 'tʃɑ:ns/ 79
purify /'pjʊərɪfaɪ/ 75
pursue /pə'sju:/ 27
pursuit /pə'sju:t/ 25
push V /pʊʃ/ 2
push and shove /ˌpʊʃ ən 'ʃʌv/ 61
pushy /'pʊʃi/ 14
put /pʊt/ 2
put a strain on /ˌpʊt ə 'streɪn ˌɒn/ 16
put out as in be put out 19
put out a fire /ˌpʊt ˌaʊt ə 'faɪə(r)/ 4
put sb at ease /ˌpʊt ˌ... ət 'i:z/ 33
put sb at their ease /ˌpʊt ˌ... ət ðeər 'i:z/ 33
put sth down /ˌpʊt ˌ... 'daʊn/ 80
put sth into (a bank account) /ˌpʊt ˌ... 'ɪntə/ 48
put sth into practice /ˌpʊt ˌ... ɪntə 'præktɪs/ 27
put sth into words /ˌpʊt ˌ... ɪntə 'wɜ:dz/ 2
put sth right /ˌpʊt ˌ... 'raɪt/ 51
put sth to sleep /ˌpʊt ˌ... tə 'sli:p/ 80
put your feet up /ˌpʊt jɔ: 'fi:t ˌʌp/ 24
put your foot in it /ˌpʊt jɔ: 'fʊt ɪn ˌɪt/ 19
puzzle V /'pʌzl/ 53
puzzled /'pʌzld/ 53, 78

qualification /ˌkwɒlɪfɪ'keɪʃn/ 23
qualify /'kwɒlɪfaɪ/ 23
quantify /'kwɒntɪfaɪ/ 75
quick-witted /ˌkwɪk 'wɪtɪd/ 14
quid /kwɪd/ 58
quote V /kwəʊt/ 39

r (= are) 73
racket /'rækɪt/ 58
radical /'rædɪkl/ 42
radical change /ˌrædɪkl 'tʃeɪndʒ/ 27
radish /'rædɪʃ/ 20
rage as in road rage 52
rain as in torrential rain 4
raise /reɪz/ 54, 63
raise funds /ˌreɪz 'fʌndz/ 29
raisins /'reɪznz/ 20
rake N /reɪk/ 62

rally (= support sb) /'ræli/ 41
rally (= increase in value) /'ræli/ 47
ramshackle /'ræmʃækl/ 55
random /'rændəm/ 43
rank /ræŋk/ 35
ransom /'rænsəm/ 38
rash ADJ /ræʃ/ 14
rash N /ræʃ/ 13
rat-infested /'ræt ɪnˌfestɪd/ 40
rate N /reɪt/ 30
rate V /reɪt/ 31
rate as in at any rate 64
rattle N, V /'rætl/ 10
re- 74
reach /ri:tʃ/ 4
reactionary /ri'ækʃənri/ 42
realistic /ˌri:ə'lɪstɪk/ 79
realistically /ˌri:ə'lɪstɪkli/ 79
realize your potential /ˌri:əlaɪz jɔ: pə'tenʃəl/ 56
reappraise /ˌri:ə'preɪz/ 74
reason as in for some reason 60
reason as in no reason 52
reason as in within reason 14
reassess /ˌri:ə'ses/ 74
reassure /ˌri:ə'ʃʊə(r)/ 54
rebel N /'rebl/ 17
rebel V /rɪ'bel/ 17
rebellious /rɪ'beljəs/ 17
recall V /rɪ'kɔ:l/ 73
recharge your batteries /ri:ˌtʃɑ:dʒ jɔ: 'bæt(ə)riz/ 21
rechargeable battery /ri:ˌtʃɑ:dʒəbl 'bæt(ə)ri/ 28
recognition /ˌrekəg'nɪʃn/ 6
recognize /'rekəgnaɪz/ 6
recollect /ˌrekə'lekt/ 73
recollection /ˌrekə'lekʃn/ 73
reconciled as in be reconciled with 63
reconciled to /'rekənsaɪld tə/ 76
reconditioned /ˌri:kən'dɪʃnd/ 55
reconstruct /ˌri:kən'strʌkt/ 74
record as in set a record /'rekɔ:d/ 50
recover /rɪ'kʌvə(r)/ 47
recovery as in make a rapid/speedy recovery 40
recuperate /rɪ'ku:pəreɪt/ 33
recuperation /rɪku:pə'reɪʃn/ 33
recur /rɪ'kɜ:(r)/ 9
recurrent /rɪ'kʌrənt/ 9
recycle /ˌri:'saɪkl/ 28
recycling /ˌri:'saɪklɪŋ/ 28
red as in be in the red 48
referral /rɪ'fɜ:rəl/ 33
referred as in be referred to sb 33
reflect /rɪ'flekt/ 5
reflection as in on reflection 77
reform N, V /rɪ'fɔ:m/ 27
refreshing change /rɪˌfreʃɪŋ 'tʃeɪndʒ/ 27
refuel /ˌri:'fju:əl/ 74
refuge as in seek/take refuge 32
refugee /ˌrefju'dʒi:/ 32
regain your senses /rɪˌgeɪn jɔ: 'sensɪz/ 40
regard sb/sth as /rɪ'gɑ:d ˌ... əz/ 19, 36

regarding /rɪ'gɑ:dɪŋ/ 67, 68
regardless of /rɪ'gɑ:dləs əv/ 54
region as in in the region of 65
register N /'redʒɪstə(r)/ 69
register V /'redʒɪstə(r)/ 33
registered user /ˌredʒɪstəd 'ju:zə(r)/ 31
regulations as in rules and regulations 61
rehab /'ri:hæb/ 41
rehabilitate /ˌri:ə'bɪlɪteɪt/ 36
rehabilitation /ri:əbɪlɪ'teɪʃn/ 36
reinforced /ˌri:ɪn'fɔ:st/ 72
reinvent /ˌri:ɪn'vent/ 74
reject V /rɪ'dʒekt/ 46
rejection /rɪ'dʒekʃn/ 46
relatively /'relətɪvli/ 79
relax /rɪ'læks/ 21
release V /rɪ'li:s/ 12
relegated as in be relegated 23
relegation /relɪ'geɪʃn/ 23
relentless /rɪ'lentləs/ 9
religious faith /rɪˌlɪdʒəs 'feɪθ/ 32
relocation /ri:ləʊ'keɪʃn/ 44
reluctance /rɪ'lʌktəns/ 16
reluctant /rɪ'lʌktənt/ 16
remaining /rɪ'meɪnɪŋ/ 40
remains /rɪ'meɪnz/ 55
remand V /rɪ'mɑ:nd/ 35
remanded in custody /rɪˌmɑ:ndɪd ɪn 'kʌstədi/ 35
remark /rɪ'mɑ:k/ 19
remarkable /rɪ'mɑ:kəbl/ 21
remarkably /rɪ'mɑ:kəbli/ 21
remedy N /'remədi/ 76
reminiscent of /remɪ'nɪsnt əv/ 76
remote /rɪ'məʊt/ 21
renovate /'renəveɪt/ 55
reoffend /ˌri:ə'fend/ 36
reoffender /ˌri:ə'fendə(r)/ 36
repel /rɪ'pel/ 71
repercussions /ri:pə'kʌʃnz/ 52
replicate /'replɪkeɪt/ 71
reply as in in reply to 67
represent /reprɪ'zent/ 70
representative of /reprɪ'zentətɪv əv/ 76
reproduce /ˌri:prə'dju:s/ 55
reproduction /ˌri:prə'dʌkʃn/ 55
reputable /'repjətəbl/ 6
reputation /repju'teɪʃn/ 6
resent /rɪ'zent/ 16
resentment /rɪ'zentmənt/ 16
reserve /rɪ'zɜ:v/ 29
reserve as in in reserve / the reserve 37
resident N /'rezɪdənt/ 34, 72
resigned to /rɪ'zaɪnd tə/ 76
resilience /rɪ'zɪliəns/ 70
resilient /rɪ'zɪliənt/ 70
resist /rɪ'zɪst/ 27, 72
resistance /rɪ'zɪstəns/ 27
resistant to /rɪ'zɪstənt tə/ 76
resolution /rezə'lu:ʃn/ 50
resolve /rɪ'zɒlv/ 50
resort as in last/final resort 60
resounding /rɪ'zaʊndɪŋ/ 56
respect N, V /rɪ'spekt/ 16

CONSONANTS: b **bad** | d **did** | f **fall** | g **get** | h **hat** | j **yes** | k **cat** | l **leg** | m **man** | n **now** | p **pen** | r **red** | s **see** | t **tea** | v **van** |
w **wet** | z **zoo** | ʃ **shoe** | ʒ **vision** | tʃ **chain** | dʒ **jam** | θ **thin** | ð **this** | ŋ **sing**

respectful /rɪ'spektfl/ 19
response *as in* I am writing in
  response to 67
responsible /rɪ'spɒnsəbl/ 4
rest *as in* the rest 23
restoration /restə'reɪʃn/ 21, 27
restore /rɪ'stɔ:(r)/ 21, 27
restrict /rɪ'strɪkt/ 30
restriction /rɪ'strɪkʃn/ 30, 72, 76
resume /rɪ'z(j)u:m/ 30
resumption /rɪ'zʌmpʃn/ 30
retain /rɪ'teɪn/ 21
retaliate /rɪ'tælieɪt/ 52, 63
retaliation /rɪtæli'eɪʃn/ 52
retell /ri:'tel/ 74
retention /rɪ'tenʃn/ 21
retribution /retrɪ'bju:ʃn/ 36
retrospect *as in* in retrospect 57
reveal /rɪ'vi:l/ 15
revelation /revə'leɪʃn/ 15
revenge /rɪ'venʤ/ 36
reversal /rɪ'vɜ:sl/ 27
reverse v /rɪ'vɜ:s/ 27
reversible /rɪ'vɜ:səbl/ 27
revert back to /rɪ'vɜ:t ,bæk tə/ 27
revert to /rɪ'vɜ:t tə/ 27
revolting /rɪ'vɒltɪŋ/ 12
rewarding /rɪ'wɔ:dɪŋ/ 45
rewrite v /ri:'raɪt/ 74
rhino /'raɪnəʊ/ 29
riddle /'rɪdl/ 38
ride *as in* bumpy ride 47
right away /,raɪt ə'weɪ/ 77
right-wing /,raɪt 'wɪŋ/ 42
rigorous /'rɪgərəs/ 49, 72
rip-off /'rɪp ,ɒf/ 58
rip sb off /,rɪp ,... 'ɒf/ 58
road *as in* go down that road 46
road rage /'rəʊd ,reɪʤ/ 52
roar N, V /rɔ:(r)/ 10
roar with laughter /rɔ:(r) wɪð
  'lɑ:ftə(r)/ 10
rock v /rɒk/ 41, 42
rock the boat /,rɒk ðə 'bəʊt/ 42
rocks *as in* on the rocks 41
rocket v /'rɒkɪt/ 30, 41
role model /'rəʊl ,mɒdl/ 18
roof *as in* hit the roof 15
roots /ru:ts/ 24
round /raʊnd/ 23
round about /'raʊnd ə,baʊt/ 65
RSVP /,ɑ:r ,es ,vi: 'pi:/ 73
rubbish /'rʌbɪʃ/ 22
rubble /'rʌbl/ 43
ruins /'ru:ɪnz/ 55
rule sth out /,ru:l ,... 'aʊt/ 38
rules and regulations /,ru:lz ən
  regju'leɪʃnz/ 61
rumble N, V /'rʌmbl/ 10
rumour /'ru:mə(r)/ 41
run /rʌn/ 31
run *as in* bad/good run 23
run-down /,rʌn 'daʊn/ 55
runner-up /,rʌnər 'ʌp/ 23
runners-up /,rʌnəz 'ʌp/ 23
rushed off your feet /,rʌʃt ,ɒf ,jɔ:
  'fi:t/ 33

rustle N, V /'rʌsl/ 10
ruthless /'ru:θləs/ 14
ruthlessly /'ru:θləsli/ 49

s/t (= something) 73
sacrifice V, N /'sækrɪfaɪs/ 16
sae (= stamped addressed
  envelope) /,es ,eɪ 'i:/ 73
safe /seɪf/ 42
safe *as in* better safe than sorry 66
safe and sound /,seɪf ən 'saʊnd/ 61
safe pair of hands /,seɪf ,peər əv
  'hændz/ 42
sage /seɪʤ/ 20
saliva /sə'laɪvə/ 12
salty /'sɔ:lti/ 12
same *as in* all the same 64
sample /'sɑ:mpl/ 67
sand *as in* bury your head in the sand
sane /seɪn/ 70
sarcasm /'sɑ:kæzəm/ 1
sarcastic /sɑ:'kæstɪk/ 1
satisfied *as in* not entirely satisfied 4
savings account /'seɪvɪŋz ə,kaʊnt/ 48
say N /seɪ/ 34
saying *as in* as I was saying 64
sb's bark is worse than their bite /,...
  ,bɑ:k ɪz ,wɜ:s ðən ðeə 'baɪt/ 10
sb's heart is not in sth /,... ,hɑ:t ɪz ,nɒt
  'ɪn ,.../ 15
scales *as in* kitchen scales 20
scalp /skælp/ 13
scandal /'skændl/ 41
scanner /'skænə(r)/ 30
scarce /skeəs/ 43
scarcity /'skeəsəti/ 43
scare sb out of their wits /,skeə ,...
  ,aʊt əv ,ðeə 'wɪts/ 22
scathing /'skeɪðɪŋ/ 39
scatter /'skætə(r)/ 24
scenery /'si:nəri/ 24
scenes *as in* behind the scenes 39
sceptical about sth /'skeptɪkl ə,baʊt
  ,.../ 14
scepticism /'skeptɪsɪzəm/ 14
schedule N /'ʃedju:l/ 49
scheme N /ski:m/ 38, 44
scoop /sku:p/ 41
scrape through /,skreɪp 'θru:/ 56
scratch v /skrætʃ/ 13
screech N, V /skri:tʃ/ 10
scroll v /skrəʊl/ 31
scroll bar /'skrəʊl ,bɑ:(r)/ 31
scrutinize /'skru:tənaɪz/ 71
scrutiny /'skru:təni/ 71
seal v /si:l/ 73
search *as in* do a search 31
search *as in* in search of 25
season *as in* in / out of season 28
seat *as in* on the edge of your
  seat 22
second-hand /,sekənd 'hænd/ 55
second opinion /,sekənd ə'pɪnjən/ 33
second to none /,sekənd tə 'nʌn/ 33
secret *as in* the secret of your
  success 56
seed /si:d/ 24

seek refuge /,si:k 'refju:ʤ/ 32
segregate /'segrɪgeɪt/ 36
segregation /segrɪ'geɪʃn/ 36
self- /self/ 36
self-assessment /,self ə'sesmənt/ 36
self-catering /,self 'keɪtərɪŋ/ 36
self-contained /,self kən'teɪnd/ 36
self-esteem /,self ɪ'sti:m/ 54
self-explanatory /,self ɪk'splænətri/ 1
sell like hot cakes /,sel ,laɪk 'hɒt
  ,keɪks/ 62
senate /'senət/ 38
senator /'senətə/ 38
send sb/sth flying /,send ,... 'flaɪɪŋ/ 2
senior /'si:niə(r)/ 33
sensational /sen'seɪʃənl/ 22
sense /sens/ 1
senses *as in* regain your senses 40
sentimental /sentɪ'mentl/ 22
sequence of events /,si:kwəns əv
  ɪ'vents/ 52
sergeant /'sɑ:ʤənt/ 35
serve /sɜ:v/ 37
set N /set/ 22
set v /set/ 50
set a budget /,set ə 'bʌʤɪt/ 34
set a date /,set ə 'deɪt/ 50
set a limit /,set ə 'lɪmɪt/ 50
set a precedent /,set ə 'presɪdənt/ 50
set a record /,set ə 'rekɔ:d/ 50
set a standard /,set ə 'stændəd/ 50
set an example /,set ən ɪg'zɑ:mpl/ 18,
  50
set fire to /,set 'faɪə tə/ 4
set phrase /,set 'freɪz/ 59
set sb/sth back /,set ,... 'bæk/ 3
set sb's mind at rest /,set ,... 'maɪnd ət
  ,rest/ 54
set sth aside /,set ,... ə'saɪd/ 49
set sth off /,set ,... 'ɒf/ 46
setback /'setbæk/ 3, 54
settle a dispute /,setl ə dɪ'spju:t/ 4, 50
settle an argument /,setl ən
  'ɑ:gjumənt/ 4
settle down /,setl 'daʊn/ 16
severe /sɪ'vɪə(r)/ 6
severely hit /sɪ,vɪəli 'hɪt/ 49
severity /sɪ'verəti/ 6
shake sth off /,ʃeɪk ,... 'ɒf/ 63
shake sth up /,ʃeɪk ,... 'ʌp/ 3
shake-up /'ʃeɪk ,ʌp/ 3
shallow /'ʃæləʊ/ 22
share *as in* do your fair share 18
shareholder /'ʃeəhəʊldə(r)/ 46
shark-infested /'ʃɑ:k ɪn,festɪd/ 40
shed /ʃed/ 24
sheer desperation /,ʃɪə
  despə'reɪʃn/ 15
sheet /ʃi:t/ 62
shell N, V /ʃel/ 43
shelter v /'ʃeltə(r)/ 40
shock *as in* culture shock 32
shop around /,ʃɒp ə'raʊnd/ 25
shop till you drop /ʃɒp ,tɪl ,ju:
  'drɒp/ 25
shopaholic /ʃɒpə'hɒlɪk/ 25
short cut /,ʃɔ:t 'kʌt/ 3

VOWELS: æ cat | ɑ: father | e ten | ɜ: bird | ə about | ɪ sit | i: see | i many | ɒ got | ɔ: saw | ʌ up | ʊ put | u: too | u actual |
aɪ my | aʊ now | eɪ say | əʊ go | ɔɪ boy | ɪə near | eə hair | ʊə pure

short-lived /ˌʃɔːt ˈlɪvd/ 71
short-sighted /ˌʃɔːt ˈsaɪtɪd/ 11
short-term /ˌʃɔːt ˈtɜːm/ 13
shortage /ˈʃɔːtɪdʒ/ 48
shortfall /ˈʃɔːtfɔːl/ 48
shortly /ˈʃɔːtli/ 57
should you require any further
    information /ˌʃʊd ju: rɪ ˌkwaɪər ˌeni
    ˌfɜːðər ɪnfəˈmeɪʃn/ 67
shove /ʃʌv/ 61
show sth off /ˌʃəʊ ˌ... ˈɒf/ 7
show up /ˌʃəʊ ˈʌp/ 63
shrewd /ʃruːd/ 14
shy /ʃaɪ/ 14
sick and tired of /ˈsɪk ən ˌtaɪəd əv/ 61
side effect /ˈsaɪd ɪˌfekt/ 13
sideways /ˈsaɪdweɪz/ 73
siege /siːdʒ/ 43
sieve N, V /sɪv/ 20, 62
sight /saɪt/ 11
simplification /ˌsɪmplɪfɪˈkeɪʃn/ 6
simplify /ˈsɪmplɪfaɪ/ 6, 75
simply (= just) /ˈsɪmpli/ 79
simply (= purely) /ˈsɪmpli/ 79
sincere /sɪnˈsɪə(r)/ 67
single-minded /ˌsɪŋgl ˈmaɪndɪd/ 3
single sb/sth out /ˌsɪŋgl ˌ... ˈaʊt/ 41
sink in /ˌsɪŋk ˈɪn/ 63
sink or swim /ˌsɪŋk ɔː ˈswɪm/ 42
sit on the fence /ˌsɪt ˌɒn ðə ˈfens/ 69
sit still /ˌsɪt ˈstɪl/ 11
site N /saɪt/ 24
slam V /slæm/ 10
slang /slæŋ/ 1
slash V /slæʃ/ 47
sleep as in put sth to sleep 80
sleep like a log /ˌsliːp ˌlaɪk ə ˈlɒg/ 62
slice V /slaɪs/ 20
slide /slaɪd/ 12
slight accent /ˌslaɪt ˈæksənt/ 4
slope N, V /sləʊp/ 24
slot machine /ˈslɒt məˌʃiːn/ 3
sluggish /ˈslʌgɪʃ/ 9
sluggishness /ˈslʌgɪʃnəs/ 9
slump N, V /slʌmp/ 47
small world /ˌsmɔːl ˈwɜːld/ 66
smiley /ˈsmaɪli/ 73
smuggle /ˈsmʌgl/ 35
smuggling /ˈsmʌglɪŋ/ 35
snap sth up /ˌsnæp ˌ... ˈʌp/ 47
snarl V /snɑːl/ 10
sniff /snɪf/ 51
sniper /ˈsnaɪpə(r)/ 43
snob /snɒb/ 17
so far, so good /ˌsəʊ ˌfɑː ˌsəʊ ˈgʊd/ 66
soak sth up /ˌsəʊk ˌ... ˈʌp/ 21
soar /sɔː(r)/ 47
sociable /ˈsəʊʃəbl/ 26
social /ˈsəʊʃl/ 79
socialism /ˈsəʊʃəlɪzəm/ 42
socialist /ˈsəʊʃəlɪst/ 42
socialize /ˈsəʊʃəlaɪz/ 26, 75
socially /ˈsəʊʃəli/ 79
software /ˈsɒftweə(r)/ 31
soil /sɔɪl/ 24
solely /ˈsəʊli/ 45
solicitor /səˈlɪsɪtə(r)/ 35

solidify /səˈlɪdɪfaɪ/ 75
soluble /ˈsɒljəbl/ 13
solution /səˈluːʃn/ 76
somehow /ˈsʌmhaʊ/ 65
somehow or other /ˈsʌmhaʊ ɔːr
    ˌʌðə(r)/ 65
something /ˈsʌmθɪŋ/ 65
something along those lines /ˈsʌmθɪŋ
    əˌlɒŋ ˌðəʊz ˌlaɪnz/ 65
something to do with /ˈsʌmθɪŋ tə ˌduː
    wɪð/ 65
somewhat /ˈsʌmwɒt/ 79
somewhere as in get somewhere 59
somewhere in the region of /ˈsʌmweər
    ˌɪn ðə ˌriːdʒn əv/ 65
soon /suːn/ 57
sooner or later /ˈsuːnər ɔː ˌleɪtə(r)/ 61
sorry to keep you waiting /ˈsɒri tə
    ˌkiːp juː ˌweɪtɪŋ/ 59
sort as in or something of that sort 65
sort of /ˈsɔːt əv/ 65
sort sth out /ˌsɔːt ˌ...ˈaʊt/ 50
sought after /ˈsɔːt ˌɑːftə(r)/ 29
soul /səʊl/ 11
sound as in safe and sound 61
sound effects /ˈsaʊnd ɪˌfekts/ 22
soundproof /ˈsaʊndpruːf/ 75
sour /ˈsaʊə(r)/ 12
sour grapes /ˌsaʊə ˈgreɪps/ 20
source N /sɔːs/ 39
spade /speɪd/ 24
spam /spæm/ 31
spamming /ˈspæmɪŋ/ 31
spare part /ˌspeə ˈpɑːt/ 3
spark V /spɑːk/ 39, 52
speaking /ˈspiːkɪŋ/ 79
special effort /ˌspeʃl ˈefət/ 4
specialize /ˈspeʃəlaɪz/ 75
species /ˈspiːʃiːz/ 29
spectacular /spekˈtækjələ(r)/ 11
speed limit /ˈspiːd ˌlɪmɪt/ 13
spell /spel/ 57
spell sth out /ˌspel ˌ... ˈaʊt/ 67
spice /spaɪs/ 20
spin N, V /spɪn/ 42
spin doctor /ˈspɪn ˌdɒktə(r)/ 42
spin-off /ˈspɪn ɒf/ 52
spine-tingling /ˈspaɪn ˌtɪŋglɪŋ/ 22
spirit /ˈspɪrɪt/ 1
spite /spaɪt/ 17
spiteful /ˈspaɪtfl/ 17
spk (= speak) 73
splash N, V /splæʃ/ 10
splitting headache /ˌsplɪtɪŋ ˈhedeɪk/ 13
spokesman /ˈspəʊksmən/ 34
spokesperson /ˈspəʊkspɜːsn/ 34
spokeswoman /ˈspəʊkswʊmən/ 34
spontaneity /ˌspɒntəˈneɪəti/ 14
spontaneous /spɒnˈteɪniəs/ 14
spot V /spɒt/ 11
spotless /ˈspɒtləs/ 33
spotlessly clean /ˌspɒtləsli ˈkliːn/ 33
sprain V /spreɪn/ 13
spread /spred/ 4
spread gossip /ˌspred ˈgɒsɪp/ 17
spree /spriː/ 25
sprint V /sprɪnt/ 9

sprouts as in bean sprouts 20
squander /ˈskwɒndə(r)/ 8
squash /skwɒʃ/ 20
squeak V /skwiːk/ 10
squeaky /ˈskwiːki/ 10
squeeze V /skwiːz/ 12, 20
squelch V /skweltʃ/ 10
sry (= sorry) 73
stables /ˈsteɪblz/ 55
stacks of /ˈstæks əv/ 65
stage /steɪdʒ/ 1, 57
stagger V /ˈstægə(r)/ 9
stake as in at stake 50
stance /stɑːns/ 69
stand-offish /ˌstænd ˈɒfɪʃ/ 14
stand still /ˌstænd ˈstɪl/ 11
stand up for /ˌstænd ˈʌp ˌfɔː(r),
    fə(r)/ 34
stand up to /ˌstænd ˈʌp ˌtuː, tə/ 72
standard as in set a standard 50
standardize /ˈstændədaɪz/ 75
standby as in on standby 28
starving /ˈstɑːvɪŋ/ 58
state V /steɪt/ 1
stated dose /ˌsteɪtɪd ˈdəʊs/ 13
status quo /ˌsteɪtəs ˈkwəʊ/ 42
stay put /ˌsteɪ ˈpʊt/ 40
stay still /ˌsteɪ ˈstɪl/ 11
steadily /ˈstedɪli/ 12
steady decline /ˌstedi dɪˈklaɪn/ 29
steam V /stiːm/ 20
steamer /ˈstiːmə(r)/ 20
stem N /stem/ 24
stem from /ˈstem frəm/ 76
stench /stentʃ/ 12
step aside /ˌstep əˈsaɪd/ 46
step down /ˌstep ˈdaʊn/ 46
step sth up /ˌstep ˌ... ˈʌp/ 50
stereotype /ˈsteriətaɪp/ 32
stereotypical /ˌsteriəˈtɪpɪkl/ 32
stethoscope /ˈsteθəskəʊp/ 30
stew V /stjuː/ 20
stick N /stɪk/ 58
stick at /ˈstɪk ət/ 63
stick out /ˌstɪk ˈaʊt/ 7
stick to sth /ˈstɪk tə ˌ.../ 49
stick up for /ˌstɪk ˈʌp ˌfɔː(r), fə(r)/ 16,
    34
stick your nose in sth /ˌstɪk jɔː ˈnəʊz
    ɪn ˌ.../ 51
stiff /stɪf/ 9
stiff as in bored stiff 22
stiffness /ˈstɪfnəs/ 9
stifle /ˈstaɪfl/ 45
still (= mind you) /stɪl/ 64
still (= without moving) /stɪl/ 11
still as in better still 28
stimulate /ˈstɪmjuleɪt/ 12
stingy /ˈstɪndʒi/ 58
stir-fry /ˈstɜː ˌfraɪ/ 20
stomach upset /ˈstʌmək ˌʌpset/ 13
storm of protest /ˌstɔːm əv
    ˈprəʊtest/ 39
story /ˈstɔːri/ 69
straightaway /ˌstreɪtəˈweɪ/ 77
straighten /ˈstreɪtn/ 7
straightforward /streɪtˈfɔːwəd/ 67

CONSONANTS: b bad | d did | f fall | g get | h hat | j yes | k cat | l leg | m man | n now | p pen | r red | s see | t tea | v van |
w wet | z zoo | ʃ shoe | ʒ vision | tʃ chain | dʒ jam | θ thin | ð this | ŋ sing

253

strain *as in* eye strain 11
strain *as in* put a strain on   16
strangely enough /ˈstreɪndʒli ɪˌnʌf/ 79
strategic /strəˈtiːdʒɪk/ 34
strategy /ˈstrætədʒi/ 34
stray /streɪ/ 40
stream /striːm/ 49
strength *as in* go from strength to
   strength 56
strengthen /ˈstreŋθn/ 7, 47
strenuous /ˈstrenjuəs/ 9
stressed out /ˌstrest ˈaʊt/ 49
stretching /ˈstretʃɪŋ/ 9
strictly /ˈstrɪktli/ 79
stride *as in* take sth in your stride   54
strike sb as /ˈstraɪk ˌ... əz/ 14
stringent /ˈstrɪndʒənt/ 72
strings *as in* pull the strings   42
stripe /straɪp/ 7
stroke V /strəʊk/ 8, 12
stroke of luck /ˌstrəʊk əv ˈlʌk/ 56
stroke of sth /ˈstrəʊk əv ˌ.../ 56
stroll N, V /strəʊl/ 9
strong accent /ˌstrɒŋ ˈæksənt/ 4
strong criticism /ˌstrɒŋ ˈkrɪtɪsɪzəm/ 4
stubborn /ˈstʌbən/ 8
stubbornness /ˈstʌbənnəs/ 8
stuff /stʌf/ 65
stunned /stʌnd/ 15
stunning /ˈstʌnɪŋ/ 21
style /staɪl/ 69
stylistic /staɪˈlɪstɪk/ 69
subject matter /ˈsʌbdʒekt ˌmætə(r)/ 67
subject to /ˈsʌbdʒekt tə/ 76
subjective /səbˈdʒektɪv/ 71
subservient to /səbˈsɜːviənt tə/ 76
subsidize /ˈsʌbsədaɪz/ 48
subsidized /ˈsʌbsədaɪzd/ 44
subsidy /ˈsʌbsədi/ 48
substitute N /ˈsʌbstɪtjuːt/ 76
subtle /ˈsʌtl/ 12, 27
subtract sth from /səbˈtrækt ˌ...
   frəm/ 48
success *as in* the secret of your
   success 56
suffer abuse /ˌsʌfə əˈbjuːs/ 6
sultanas /sʌlˈtɑːnəz/ 20
sum N /sʌm/ 48
sum sth up /sʌm ˌ... ˈʌp/ 69
summarize /ˈsʌməraɪz/ 69
summary /ˈsʌməri/ 4, 69
superficial /suːpəˈfɪʃl/ 22
superfluous /suːˈpɜːfluəs/ 67
supple /ˈsʌpl/ 9
support /səˈpɔːt/ 46
suppress your feelings /səˌpres ˈjɔː
   ˈfiːlɪŋz/ 15
sure *as in* not entirely sure 4
surface *as in* on the surface 14
surge N, V /sɜːdʒ/ 47
surgery *as in* cosmetic/keyhole/plastic
   surgery 33
surplus /ˈsɜːpləs/ 48
survey N /ˈsɜːveɪ/ 41
survival rate /səˈvaɪvl ˌreɪt/ 30s
sustain /səˈsteɪn/ 53
sustainability /səˌsteɪnəˈbɪləti/ 28

sustainable /səˈsteɪnəbl/ 28
swamp /swɒmp/ 40
swamped /swɒmpt/ 49
swampland /ˈswɒmplænd/ 40
sway /sweɪ/ 72
sweat N, V /swet/ 8
sweeping change /ˌswiːpɪŋ ˈtʃeɪndʒ/ 27
sweet /swiːt/ 2
switch to /ˈswɪtʃ tə/ 28
symbolize /ˈsɪmbəlaɪz/ 75
synonym /ˈsɪnənɪm/ 1
synonymous /sɪˈnɒnɪməs/ 1
synopsis /sɪˈnɒpsɪs/ 70

ta /tɑː/ 58
tabloid /ˈtæblɔɪd/ 41
tackle /ˈtækl/ 54
tackle a problem /ˌtækl ə ˈprɒbləm/ 50
tag *as in* price tag 25
tail back /ˌteɪl ˈbæk/ 3
tailback /ˈteɪlbæk/ 3
take a chance on sth /ˌteɪk ə ˈtʃɑːns ɒn
   ˌ.../ 40
take a heavy toll on /ˌteɪk ə ˌhevi ˈtɒl
   ɒn ˌ.../ 29
take action /ˌteɪk ˈækʃn/ 40
take an instant dislike to /ˌteɪk ən
   ˌɪnstənt dɪsˈlaɪk tə/ 16
take exception to /ˌteɪk ɪkˈsepʃn tə/ 19
take in /ˌteɪk ˈɪn/ 5
take it easy /ˌteɪk ˌɪt ˈiːzi/ 21
take no notice of /ˌteɪk ˌnəʊ ˈnəʊtɪs
   əv/ 33
take notice of /ˌteɪk ˈnəʊtɪs əv/ 33
take offence /ˌteɪk əˈfens/ 4, 19
take refuge /ˌteɪk ˈrefjuːdʒ/ 32
take revenge /ˌteɪk rɪˈvendʒ/ 36
take sb in /ˌteɪk ˌ... ˈɪn/ 63
take sb/sth seriously /ˌteɪk ˌ...
   ˈsɪəriəsli/ 34, 54
take sth apart /ˌteɪk ˌ... əˈpɑːt/ 63
take sth away from /ˌteɪk ˌ... əˈweɪ
   frəm/ 48
take sth in your stride /ˌteɪk ˌ... ɪn ˌjɔː
   ˈstraɪd/ 54
take sth out (of a bank account) /ˌteɪk
   ˌ... ˈaʊt/ 48
take sth to pieces /ˌteɪk ˌ... tə
   ˈpiːsɪz/ 63
take the blame /ˌteɪk ðə ˈbleɪm/ 4
take to /ˈteɪk tə/ 14
takeover /ˈteɪkəʊvə(r)/ 46
talk sb into / out of doing sth /ˌtɔːk ˌ...
   ˌɪntə, ˌaʊt əv ˈduːɪŋ ˌ.../ 63
talk sth up /ˌtɔːk ˌ... ˈʌp/ 53
tank /tæŋk/ 37
taste *as in* be in bad/poor taste 19
tasteful /ˈteɪstfl/ 78
tasteless /ˈteɪstləs/ 78
tasty /ˈteɪsti/ 78
tax-free /ˌtæks ˈfriː/ 75
team spirit /ˌtiːm ˈspɪrɪt/ 45
tear (from the eye) /tɪə(r)/ 11
tears *as in* bored to tears 22
tears *as in* burst into tears 4
tears *as in* in tears / close to tears 15
technical /ˈteknɪkl/ 79

technically /ˈteknɪkli/ 79
technique /tekˈniːk/ 79
tedious /ˈtiːdiəs/ 22
tell *as in* to tell you the truth 64
temper *as in* lose your temper   15
tension /ˈtenʃn/ 12
terminate /ˈtɜːmɪneɪt/ 67
territorial /terəˈtɔːriəl/ 29
territory /ˈterətri/ 29
thank you for /ˈθæŋk ˌjuː fə/ 67
the best of both worlds /ðə ˌbest əv
   ˈbəʊθ ˌwɜːldz/ 60
the best thing /ðə ˈbest ˌθɪŋ/ 59
the bubble will burst /ðə ˌbʌbl ˌwɪl
   ˈbɜːst/ 47
the draft /ðə ˈdrɑːft/ 37
the dust settles /ðə ˌdʌst ˈsetlz/ 46
the end justifies the means /ði ˌend
   ˌdʒʌstɪfaɪz ðə ˈmiːnz/ 66
the faintest idea /ðə ˌfeɪntɪst aɪˈdɪə/ 59
the go-ahead /ðə ˌgəʊ əˌhed/ 38
the key to /ðə ˈkiː tə/ 7
the military /ðə ˈmɪlətri/ 37
the minute /ðə ˈmɪnɪt/ 25
the moment /ðə ˈməʊmənt/ 25
the more the merrier /ðə ˌmɔː ðə
   ˈmeriə(r)/ 66
the pot calling the kettle black /ðə
   ˌpɒt ˌkɔːlɪŋ ðə ˌketl ˈblæk/ 66
the reserve /ðə rɪˈzɜːv/ 37
the rest /ðə ˈrest/ 23
the secret of /ðə ˈsiːkrət əv/ 7
the secret of your success /ðə ˌsiːkrət
   əv ˌjɔː səkˈses/ 56
the thing is /ðə ˈθɪŋ ˌɪz/ 60
the tide is turning /ðə ˌtaɪd ɪz
   ˈtɜːnɪŋ/ 39
the way things are /ðə ˌweɪ ˌθɪŋz
   ˈɑː(r)/ 39
theoretically /θɪəˈretɪkli/ 79
theory /ˈθɪəri/ 71
therapeutic /θerəˈpjuːtɪk/ 36
therapy /ˈθerəpi/ 36
there's no point in + ing /ˌðeərz ˈnəʊ
   ˌpɔɪnt ɪn/ 59
thereabouts /ˌðeərəˈbaʊts/ 65
thick /θɪk/ 2
thick-skinned /ˌθɪk ˈskɪnd/ 3
thing *as in* be the last thing on sb's
   mind 2
thing *as in* the thing is   60
things /θɪŋz/ 16
think sth up /ˌθɪŋk ˌ... ˈʌp/ 9
think up /ˌθɪŋk ˈʌp/ 31
thorough /ˈθʌrə/ 72
thoughtful /ˈθɔːtfl/ 14
thrash V /θræʃ/ 58
threat *as in* pose a threat to 29
threat *as in* under threat 29
threatened with /ˈθretnd ˌwɪð/ 29
thrifty /ˈθrɪfti/ 48
thriving /ˈθraɪvɪŋ/ 21
throughout /θruːˈaʊt/ 57
thus /ðʌs/ 68
thx (= thanks) /73
tide *as in* the tide is turning   39
tied up *as in* be tied up 2

VOWELS: æ cat | ɑː father | e ten | ɜː bird | ə about | ɪ sit | iː see | i many | ɒ got | ɔː saw | ʌ up | ʊ put | uː too | u actual |
aɪ my | aʊ now | eɪ say | əʊ go | ɔɪ boy | ɪə near | eə hair | ʊə pure

tight /taɪt/ 58
tight corner /ˌtaɪt ˈkɔːnə(r)/ 39
tight-fisted /ˌtaɪt ˈfɪstɪd/ 58
tighten /ˈtaɪtn/ 7
tighten your belt /ˌtaɪtn jɔː ˈbelt/ 46
till /tɪl/ 25
time /taɪm/ 57
time as in as time went by 16
time-consuming /ˈtaɪm kənˌsjuːmɪŋ/ 26
time flies /ˌtaɪm ˈflaɪz/ 57
times as in behind the times 57
tip N /tɪp/ 40
tip the balance /ˌtɪp ðə ˈbæləns/ 46
tiptoe V /ˈtɪptəʊ/ 9
tired as in sick and tired of 61
TLC (= tender loving care) /ˌtiː ˌel ˈsiː/ 73
tnx (= thanks) 73
2 (= to) 73
to a degree /ˌtu ə dɪˈgriː/ 45
to a large extent /ˌtu ə ˈlɑːdʒ ɪkˌstent/ 64
to an extent /ˌtu ən ɪkˈstent/ 45
to be honest /ˌtə bi ˈɒnɪst/ 64, 79
to be perfectly honest /ˌtə bi ˈpɜːfɪktli ˌɒnɪst/ 79
to sb's face /ˌtə ... ˈfeɪs/ 16
to tell you the truth /ˌtə ˌtel juː ðə ˈtruːθ/ 64
to the point /ˌtə ðə ˈpɔɪnt/ 67
2day (= today) 73
toll as in take a heavy toll on 29
2moro (= tomorrow) 73
2nite (= tonight) 73
tone /təʊn/ 67
tongue-tied /ˈtʌŋ ˌtaɪd/ 3
tons of /ˈtʌnz əv/ 65
2 (= too) 73
too good to be true /ˌtuː ˌgʊd tə bi ˈtruː/ 60
top as in be on top 23
top priority /ˌtɒp praɪˈɒrəti/ 49
torrential rain /təˌrenʃl ˈreɪn/ 4
total chaos /ˌtəʊtl ˈkeɪɒs/ 4
touch as in in / out of touch 77
tough /tʌf/ 16
tower /ˈtaʊə(r)/ 55
toxic /ˈtɒksɪk/ 28
trace V /treɪs/ 55
trace of irony /ˌtreɪs əv ˈaɪrəni/ 1
track as in off the beaten track 21
traditional /trəˈdɪʃənl/ 79
traditionally /trəˈdɪʃənəli/ 79
trafficking /ˈtræfɪkɪŋ/ 35
train of thought /ˌtreɪn əv ˈθɔːt/ 49
trait /treɪt/ 14
transaction /trænˈzækʃn/ 48
transform /trænsˈfɔːm/ 27
transformation /ˌtrænsfəˈmeɪʃn/ 27
transition /trænˈzɪʃn/ 27
transparent /trænsˈpærənt/ 1
transplant N /ˈtrænsplɑːnt/ 30
transplant V /trænsˈplɑːnt/ 30
travel agency /ˈtrævl ˌeɪdʒənsi/ 34
travel expenses /ˈtrævl ɪkˌspensɪz/ 44

travelling expenses /ˈtrævlɪŋ ɪkˌspensɪz/ 44
trek N, V /trek/ 21
trial as in clinical trial 33
trial and error /ˌtraɪəl ən ˈerə(r)/ 61
tricky /ˈtrɪki/ 56
trigger V /ˈtrɪgə(r)/ 47
trivial /ˈtrɪviəl/ 54
tropical /ˈtrɒpɪkl/ 20
trouble as in in trouble 77
trouble as in it's more trouble than it's worth 60
trouble as in nothing is too much trouble 33
trouble-free /ˌtrʌbl ˈfriː/ 75
true as in it's true 64
true as in too good to be true 60
truly /ˈtruːli/ 79
trustworthy /ˈtrʌstwɜːði/ 14
truth as in economical with the truth 53
truth as in to tell you the truth 64
ttyl (= talk to you later) 73
tumble dryer /ˌtʌmbl ˈdraɪə(r)/ 28
turbulence /ˈtɜːbjələns/ 47
turbulent /ˈtɜːbjələnt/ 47
turmoil /ˈtɜːmɔɪl/ 47
turn as in the tide is turning 39
turn out (= attend an event) /ˌtɜːn ˈaʊt/ 3
turn out badly /ˌtɜːn ˌaʊt ˈbædli/ 56
turn out well /ˌtɜːn ˌaʊt ˈwel/ 56
turn over a new leaf /ˌtɜːn ˌəʊvər ə ˌnjuː ˈliːf/ 36
turn sth down /ˌtɜːn ... ˈdaʊn/ 46
turn up /ˌtɜːn ˈʌp/ 63
turnout /ˈtɜːnaʊt/ 3
twist N (in a plot) /twɪst/ 22
twist V (twist your ankle) /twɪst/ 13
two heads are better than one /ˌtuː ˌhedz ə ˌbetə ðən ˈwʌn/ 66
two wrongs don't make a right /ˌtuː ˌrɒŋz ˌdəʊnt ˌmeɪk ə ˈraɪt/ 66

u (= you) 73
ulterior motive /ʌlˌtɪəriə ˈməʊtɪv/ 2
ultimately /ˈʌltɪmətli/ 79
ultra- /ˈʌltrə/ 55
ultra-cautious /ˌʌltrə ˈkɔːʃəs/ 55
ultra-modern /ˌʌltrə ˈmɒdn/ 55
un- /ʌn/ 74
unanimous /juːˈnænɪməs/ 22
unanimously /juːˈnænɪməsli/ 22
unappealing /ˌʌnəˈpiːlɪŋ/ 18
unappetizing /ʌnˈæpɪtaɪzɪŋ/ 12
unarmed combat /ˌʌnɑːmd ˈkɒmbæt/ 37
unbeaten /ʌnˈbiːtn/ 23
unbiased /ʌnˈbaɪəst/ 71
uncomfortable /ʌnˈkʌmftəbl/ 15
unconvincing /ˌʌnkənˈvɪnsɪŋ/ 22, 78
uncooked /ʌnˈkʊkt/ 74
under /ˈʌndə(r)/ 77
under- /ˈʌndə(r)/ 74
under attack /ˌʌndər əˈtæk/ 77
under construction /ˌʌndə kənˈstrʌkʃn/ 77

under control /ˌʌndə kənˈtrəʊl/ 49
under discussion /ˌʌndə dɪˈskʌʃn/ 77
under investigation /ˌʌndər ɪnvestɪˈgeɪʃn/ 77
under pressure /ˌʌndə ˈpreʃə(r)/ 23, 47
under the microscope /ˌʌndə ðə ˈmaɪkrəskəʊp/ 42
under the weather /ˌʌndə ðə ˈweðə(r)/ 59
under threat /ˌʌndə ˈθret/ 29
undercooked /ˌʌndəˈkʊkt/ 74
underdeveloped /ˌʌndədɪˈveləpt/ 74
underemployed /ˌʌndərɪmˈplɔɪd/ 74
underfed /ˌʌndəˈfed/ 74
undergo /ˌʌndəˈgəʊ/ 21
underlying /ˌʌndəˈlaɪɪŋ/ 47
undermine /ˌʌndəˈmaɪn/ 45
undernourished /ˌʌndəˈnʌrɪʃt/ 74
underpaid /ˌʌndəˈpeɪd/ 74
underpin /ˌʌndəˈpɪn/ 47
underprivileged /ˌʌndəˈprɪvəlɪdʒd/ 74
underrated /ˌʌndəˈreɪtɪd/ 74
undersold /ˌʌndəˈsəʊld/ 74
undeveloped /ˌʌndɪˈveləpt/ 74
uneasy /ʌnˈiːzi/ 15
unemployed /ˌʌnɪmˈplɔɪd/ 74
uneventful /ˌʌnɪˈventfl/ 6
unflattering /ʌnˈflætərɪŋ/ 7
unforgivable /ˌʌnfəˈgɪvəbl/ 6
unfurnished /ʌnˈfɜːnɪʃt/ 6
unintelligible /ˌʌnɪnˈtelɪdʒəbl/ 78
unique /juˈniːk/ 21
unit /ˈjuːnɪt/ 71
unlike /ʌnˈlaɪk/ 70
unmitigated /ʌnˈmɪtɪgeɪtɪd/ 56
unofficially /ˌʌnəˈfɪʃəli/ 79
unpaid /ʌnˈpeɪd/ 74
unpalatable /ʌnˈpælətəbl/ 53
unproductive /ˌʌnprəˈdʌktɪv/ 49
unsold /ʌnˈsəʊld/ 74
unspoilt /ʌnˈspɔɪlt/ 21
unstuck as in come unstuck 56
unwilling /ʌnˈwɪlɪŋ/ 16
unwind /ʌnˈwaɪnd/ 21
up against it /ˌʌp əˈgenst ˌɪt/ 56
up to date /ˌʌp tə ˈdeɪt/ 55
upload /ʌpˈləʊd/ 31
upper class /ˌʌpə ˈklɑːs/ 19
uprooted as in be uprooted 32
ups and downs /ˌʌps ən ˈdaʊnz/ 16
upset stomach /ʌpˌset ˈstʌmək/ 13
upwards /ˈʌpwədz/ 19
urge (sb to do) sth /ˈɜːdʒ (ˌ... tə ˌduː) ˌ.../ 38
urgent /ˈɜːdʒənt/ 54
use as in it's no use + ing 59
user as in registered user 31
user-friendly /ˌjuːzə ˈfrendli/ 28
username /ˈjuːzəneɪm/ 31
usual /ˈjuːʒuəl/ 19
utter /ˈʌtə(r)/ 22
utter chaos /ˌʌtə ˈkeɪɒs/ 4

vaccinate /ˈvæksɪneɪt/ 30
vaccination /ˌvæksɪˈneɪʃn/ 30

CONSONANTS: b **b**ad | d **d**id | f **f**all | g **g**et | h **h**at | j **y**es | k **c**at | l **l**eg | m **m**an | n **n**ow | p **p**en | r **r**ed | s **s**ee | t **t**ea | v **v**an | w **w**et | z **z**oo | ʃ **sh**oe | ʒ vi**s**ion | tʃ **ch**ain | dʒ **j**am | θ **th**in | ð **th**is | ŋ si**ng**

vaccine /ˈvæksiːn/ 30
value V /ˈvæljuː/ 45
valueless /ˈvæljuːləs/ 78
values /ˈvæljuːz/ 17
vandalism /ˈvændəlɪzəm/ 75
vandalize /ˈvændəlaɪz/ 75
vanish into thin air /ˌvænɪʃ ˌɪntə ˌθɪn ˈeə(r)/ 11
vast /vɑːst/ 37
venture /ˈventʃə(r)/ 28
venue /ˈvenjuː/ 23
verge as in on the verge of sth 23, 24
verification /ˌverɪfɪˈkeɪʃn/ 71
verify /ˈverɪfaɪ/ 71
vertical /ˈvɜːtɪkl/ 72
vertical load /ˌvɜːtɪkl ˈləʊd/ 72
vibrant /ˈvaɪbrənt/ 21
vice /vaɪs/ 14
victorious /vɪkˈtɔːriəs/ 23
victory /ˈvɪktəri/ 23
video clip /ˈvɪdiəʊ ˌklɪp/ 31
videoblog /ˈvɪdiəʊblɒg/ 31
view V /vjuː/ 19
view as in in view of 68
vigorously /ˈvɪgərəsli/ 12
vile /vaɪl/ 58
virtual /ˈvɜːtʃuəl/ 31
virtually /ˈvɜːtʃuəli/ 1, 79
virtue /ˈvɜːtʃuː/ 14
virtuous /ˈvɜːtʃuəs/ 14
virus /ˈvaɪrəs/ 31
visible /ˈvɪzəbl/ 11
vision /ˈvɪʒn/ 11
visualize /ˈvɪʒuəlaɪz/ 75
visually impaired /ˌvɪʒuəli ɪmˈpeəd/ 80
volatile /ˈvɒlətaɪl/ 47
volatility /vɒləˈtɪləti/ 47
voluntary /ˈvɒləntri/ 34
voluntary sector /ˈvɒləntri ˌsektə(r)/ 34
volunteer /vɒlənˈtɪə(r)/ 34
vow N /vaʊ/ 38
vow to do sth /ˈvaʊ tə ˌduː .../ 38
vulgar /ˈvʌlgə(r)/ 17
vulnerable /ˈvʌlnərəbl/ 15

w/ (= with) 73
w/o (= without) 73
waiting as in sorry to keep you waiting 59
wander /ˈwɒndə(r)/ 21
wander as in go for a wander 21
war zone /ˈwɔː ˌzəʊn/ 43
warfare /ˈwɔːfeə(r)/ 37
warily /ˈweərəli/ 11
warm up (= become interesting) /ˌwɔːm ˈʌp/ 26
warm up (= do physical exercises) /ˌwɔːm ˈʌp/ 9
warm welcome /ˌwɔːm ˈwelkʌm/ 26
warrant /ˈwɒrənt/ 35
water V /ˈwɔːtə(r)/ 12
water as in fish out of water 20
water-saving /ˈwɔːtə ˌseɪvɪŋ/ 28
waterproof /ˈwɔːtəpruːf/ 75
way ADV /weɪ/ 56
way as in by the way 64

way as in in sb's/the way 56
way as in no way 59
way as in the way things are 16
weaken /ˈwiːkən/ 7, 47
weapon /ˈwepən/ 37
wear off /ˌweər ˈɒf/ 63
wear your heart on your sleeve /ˌweə jɔː ˌhɑːt ɒn jɔː ˈsliːv/ 15
weather as in under the weather 59
web browser /ˈweb ˌbraʊzə(r)/ 31
weeding as in do the weeding 24
weeds /wiːdz/ 24
weekend as in long weekend 3
weight as in pull your weight 18
weird /wɪəd/ 78
welcome N, ADJ /ˈwelkəm/ 26
welcome change /ˌwelkəm ˈtʃeɪndʒ/ 27
What a cheek! /ˌwɒt ə ˈtʃiːk/ 19, 58
What a disgrace! /ˌwɒt ə dɪsˈgreɪs/ 19
What a nerve! /ˌwɒt ə ˈnɜːv/ 58
What can you expect? /ˌwɒt kən ˌjuː ɪkˈspekt/ 18
What do you expect? /ˌwɒt də ˌjuː ɪkˈspekt/ 18
What do you make of ...? /ˌwɒt də ˌjuː ˈmeɪk əv/ 14
What on earth . . . ? /ˈwɒt ɒn ˌɜːθ/ 60
whatever /wɒtˈevə(r)/ 49
wheelchair as in be confined to a wheelchair 30
whenever /wenˈevə(r)/ 49
Where on earth . . . ? /ˈweər ɒn ˌɜːθ/ 60
wherever /weərˈevə(r)/ 49
whisk N /wɪsk/ 20
white lie /ˌwaɪt ˈlaɪ/ 53
wholesale change /ˌhəʊlseɪl ˈtʃeɪndʒ/ 27
wicked /ˈwɪkɪd/ 78
widespread criticism /ˌwaɪdspred ˈkrɪtɪsɪzəm/ 4
widespread damage /ˌwaɪdspred ˈdæmɪdʒ/ 4
wild as in in the wild 29
wildlife /ˈwaɪldlaɪf/ 24
wildlife reserve /ˈwaɪldlaɪf rɪˌzɜːv/ 29
win sb's respect /ˌwɪn ... rɪˈspekt/ 16
wind sth up /ˌwaɪnd ... ˈʌp/ 46
winds as in gale-force winds 4
wink V /wɪŋk/ 73
wipe sb/sth out /ˌwaɪp ... ˈaʊt/ 29, 30
wipe sth off sth /ˌwaɪp ... ˈɒf .../ 47
wire as in barbed wire 3
wisdom /ˈwɪzdəm/ 50
wise /waɪz/ 50
with hindsight /ˌwɪð ˈhaɪndsaɪt/ 57
with reference to /ˌwɪð ˈrefrəns tə/ 67
with regard to /ˌwɪð rɪˈgɑːd tə/ 68
withdraw /wɪðˈdrɔː/ 48
within reason /wɪˌðɪn ˈriːzn/ 14
without fail /wɪˈðaʊt ˈfeɪl/ 77
withstand /wɪðˈstænd/ 72
wknd (= weekend) 73
wok /wɒk/ 20
wolf /wʊlf/ 10
wooden /ˈwʊdn/ 22

woody /ˈwʊdi/ 12
words as in eat your words 20
words as in famous last words 66
words as in put sth into words 2
work like a dream /ˌwɜːk ˌlaɪk ə ˈdriːm/ 62
work out /ˌwɜːk ˈaʊt/ 9
work sth out /ˌwɜːk ... ˈaʊt/ 48
workaholic /wɜːkəˈhɒlɪk/ 25
working class /ˌwɜːkɪŋ ˈklɑːs/ 19
workout /ˈwɜːkaʊt/ 9
world as in be in a world of your own 60
worlds as in the best of both worlds 60
worldwide /ˈwɜːldwaɪd/ 34
worn out /ˌwɔːn ˈaʊt/ 3, 78
worship V /ˈwɜːʃɪp/ 17
worthless /ˈwɜːθləs/ 6, 78
worthwhile /wɜːθˈwaɪl/ 6
worthy /ˈwɜːði/ 6
wrapping paper /ˈræpɪŋ ˌpeɪpə(r)/ 1
wreck V /rek/ 38
wrinkles /ˈrɪŋkəls/ 7
wriggle out of /ˌrɪgl ˈaʊt əv/ 46
write-off /ˈraɪt ˌɒf/ 3
write sth off /ˌraɪt ... ˈɒf/ 3
wrongs as in two wrongs don't make a right 66

x (= kiss) 73
xlnt (= excellent) 73

yield N /jiːld/ 47
you bet /ju ˈbet/ 59
you can never tell /ju kən ˌnevə ˈtel/ 66
you can say that again /ju kən ˌseɪ ˈðæt əˌgen/ 59
you can't be serious /ju ˈkɑːnt bi ˌsɪəriəs/ 59
you never know /ju ˌnevə ˈnəʊ/ 60
your best bet /jɔː ˌbest ˈbet/ 59
your guess is as good as mine /ˈjɔː ˌges ɪz əz ˌgʊd əz ˈmaɪn/ 59
your own boss /jɔːr ˌəʊn ˈbɒs/ 45
your own company /jɔːr ˌəʊn ˈkʌmpəni/ 26
you're joking /jɔː ˈdʒəʊkɪŋ/ 59
you're kidding /jɔː ˈkɪdɪŋ/ 59
you're not gonna believe this /jɔːr ˌnɒt ˌgɒnə bəˈliːv ˌðɪs ˌgɒnə/ 2
you're only young once /jɔːr ˌəʊnli ˌjʌŋ ˈwʌns/ 66
you've got nothing to lose /juːv ˌgɒt ˌnʌθɪŋ tə ˈluːz/ 59
yr (= your) 73
yr (= you're) 73

zone /zəʊn/ 43

VOWELS: æ cat | ɑː father | e ten | ɜː bird | ə about | ɪ sit | iː see | i many | ɒ got | ɔː saw | ʌ up | ʊ put | uː too | u actual |
aɪ my | aʊ now | eɪ say | əʊ go | ɔɪ boy | ɪə near | eə hair | ʊə pure